Born of Conviction

Form of Consecration

BORN OF CONVICTION

White Methodists and Mississippi's Closed Society

JOSEPH T. REIFF

OXFORD
UNIVERSITY PRESS

OXFORD
UNIVERSITY PRESS

Oxford University Press is a department of the University of
Oxford. It furthers the University's objective of excellence in research,
scholarship, and education by publishing worldwide.
Oxford is a registered trade mark of Oxford University Press
in the UK and in certain other countries.

Published in the United States of America by
Oxford University Press
198 Madison Avenue, New York, NY 10016, United States of America

Cover photograph © Flip Schulke

New Revised Standard Version Bible, copyright 1989, Division
of Christian Education of the National Council of the Churches of Christ
in the United States of America. Used by permission. All rights reserved.

Library of Congress Cataloging-in-Publication Data
Reiff, Joseph T.
Born of conviction : white Methodists and Mississippi's closed society / Joseph T. Reiff.
pages cm
Includes bibliographical references and index.
ISBN 978–0–19–024681–5 (cloth : alk. paper)
1. Methodist Church—Mississippi—History. 2. Race relations—Religious aspects—
Methodist Church. 3. Mississippi—Church history.
4. Gulfport (Miss.)—History. I. Title.
BX8248.M7R45 2016
287'.676209046—dc23
2015007682

5 7 9 8 6 4
Printed in the United States of America
on acid-free paper

To my parents,
Lee H. Reiff and Geraldine Long Reiff,
whose words and example taught me to give
true respect to all persons,
in Mississippi and throughout the world;

and to my wife,
Betty Clark Reiff,
whose tenacious love and support have sustained me in our
partnership in marriage, parenting, ministry, and life in and
beyond Mississippi

*Then Jesus said to them, "Prophets are not without honor,
except in their hometown, and among their own kin, and
in their own house."*

—MARK 6:4, NRSV

Contents

PART IV: *Memory and Legacy*

Born of Conviction *Cast of Characters*

The twenty-eight signers in signature order, church served in 1962–3, and left or stayed?

*Jerry Furr, associate pastor at Galloway Memorial, Jackson; left Mississippi in 1963

*Maxie D. Dunnam, pastor at Trinity, Gulfport; left Mississippi in 1964

*Jim L. Waits, pastor at Epworth, Biloxi; left Mississippi in 1965/1967 **M**

*O. Gerald Trigg, pastor at Caswell Springs, Jackson County; left Mississippi in 1964 **M**

James B. Nicholson, pastor at Byram; left Mississippi in 1963

Buford A. Dickinson, pastor at Decatur; left Mississippi in 1964

James S. Conner, pastor at Brandon; stayed **M**

J. W. Holston, pastor at Carthage; left Mississippi in 1963 **M**

James P. Rush, pastor at Philadelphia Circuit, Neshoba County; left Mississippi in 1963 **M**

Edward W. McRae, pastor at Oakland Heights, Meridian; left Mississippi in 1963

Joseph C. Way, pastor at Soule's Chapel, Lauderdale County; left Mississippi in 1964 **M

***Wallace E. Roberts, pastor at Vimville, Lauderdale County; left Mississippi in 1963 **M**

Summer Walters, associate pastor at Jefferson Street, Natchez; left Mississippi in 1963 **M**

Bill Lampton, pastor at Pisgah, Pike County; left Mississippi in 1963 **M**

Marvin Moody, pastor at Oak Grove, Lamar County; left Mississippi in 1963/1964

Keith Tonkel, pastor at Guinn Memorial, Gulfport; stayed **M**

John Ed Thomas, associate pastor at First, Gulfport; stayed **M**

Inman Moore Jr., pastor at Leggett Memorial, Biloxi; left Mississippi in 1963 **M**

Denson Napier, pastor at Richton; stayed

Rod Entrekin, pastor at Wesson; stayed **M**

Harold Ryker, pastor at Beauvoir, Biloxi; stayed

N. A. Dickson, pastor at First, Columbia; stayed **M**

Ned Kellar, pastor at Sandersville; left Mississippi in 1963

Powell Hall, pastor at Scooba; left Mississippi in 1971

Elton Brown, pastor at Lovely Lane, Natchez; stayed **M**

****Bufkin Oliver, pastor at Ellisville; left Mississippi in 1963 **M**

Jack Troutman, pastor at Big Point, Jackson County; left Mississippi in 1964

Wilton Carter, pastor at Lake; left Mississippi in 1963

   *Creators of the statement   **M** = Millsaps College graduate
   **Never transferred out of Conference; returned to Mississippi in 1987
   ***Went to seminary in 1963; transferred to North Mississippi Conference upon return to Mississippi in 1966
   ****Returned to North Mississippi Conference in 1967

Other important characters

Marvin A. Franklin, bishop of white Mississippi and North Mississippi Conferences, 1948–64

Edward J. Pendergrass Jr., bishop of white Mississippi and North Mississippi Conferences, 1964–72

J. Willard Leggett Jr., Jackson District Superintendent, 1959–65; conference political leader and opponent of Born of Conviction **M**

Sam E. Ashmore, Editor, *Mississippi Methodist Advocate*, 1955–66; public supporter of Born of Conviction **M**

J. P. Stafford, Mississippi Conference Lay Leader, 1947–64; public supporter of Born of Conviction

W. B. Selah, senior pastor at Galloway Memorial, Jackson, 1945–63; public supporter of Born of Conviction

Roy C. Clark, senior pastor at Capitol Street, Jackson, 1953–63; supporter of Born of Conviction **M**

Abbreviations

BOP	Bishop's Office Papers, J. B. Cain Archives of Mississippi Methodism, Millsaps College
CME	Christian Methodist Episcopal Church (formerly Colored Methodist Episcopal)
COFO	Council of Federated Organizations
CORE	Congress of Racial Equality
DH	Mississippi Coast *Daily Herald*
DMC	*Discipline of The Methodist Church*, 1940–64
DUMC	*Discipline of The United Methodist Church, 1968–present*
GM	*General Minutes of The Methodist Church* or *The United Methodist Church*
JBCA	J. B. Cain Archives of Mississippi Methodism, Millsaps College
JCL	Jackson *Clarion-Ledger*
JDN	*Jackson Daily News*
JMC	*Journal of the Mississippi Conference, SEJ*, 1939–68
JPS	Jackson (Mississippi) Public Schools
JSCAC	*Journal of the Southern California-Arizona Conference*
MAMML	Mississippi Association of Methodist Ministers and Laymen
MCA	Millsaps College Archives
MCHR	Mississippi Council on Human Relations
MCJ	*Mississippi Conference Journal, SEJ*, 1969–present
MDAH	Mississippi Department of Archives and History
MEC	Methodist Episcopal Church
MECS	Methodist Episcopal Church, South
MEJ	*McComb Enterprise-Journal*
MFDP	Mississippi Freedom Democratic Party
MMA	*Mississippi Methodist Advocate*

MS	*Meridian Star*
MSM	Methodist Student Movement
MSSC Records	Records of the Mississippi State Sovereignty Commission
MSUSCD	Special Collections Department, Mitchell Memorial Library, Mississippi State University
MUMM	Mississippi United Methodist Ministry
NAACP	National Association for the Advancement of Colored People
NCC	National Council of Churches
NYT	*New York Times*
PMPC	Pascagoula/Moss Point (Mississippi) *Chronicle*
PP	Private Papers
PTLA	Pitts Theology Library Archives, Emory University
SEJ	Southeastern Jurisdiction, The Methodist Church and UMC (all-white from 1939 to 1968)
SMU	Southern Methodist University
SNCC	Student Non-violent Coordinating Committee
SSN	*Southern School News*, a monthly publication of the Southern Education Reporting Service, 1954–65
UMC	United Methodist Church
UMDASC	Department of Archives and Special Collections, J. D. Williams Library, University of Mississippi
USMMLA	McCain Library and Archives, University of Southern Mississippi

Introduction

At the Church Steps

> Confronted with the grave crises precipitated by racial
> discord within our state in recent months, and the
> genuine dilemma facing persons of Christian con-
> science, we are compelled to voice publicly our con-
> victions. Indeed, as Christian ministers and as native
> Mississippians, sharing the anguish of all our people,
> we have a particular obligation to speak.
>
> —"BORN OF CONVICTION" STATEMENT, *MMA*,
> January 2, 1963

IN HIS APRIL 1963 "Letter from Birmingham Jail," addressed to eight
white clergy leaders, Dr. Martin Luther King Jr. confessed major disap-
pointments in the white moderate, whom he had come to see as a greater
"stumbling block" to the black freedom struggle than the White Citizens'
Council or the Ku Klux Klan, and in "the white church and its leadership,"
whom he had hoped "would be among our strongest allies" and "would
serve as the channel through which our just grievances could reach the
power structure." White moderates and church leaders had earned the
criticism, though King noted some exceptions. One he could have mentioned occurred three months earlier in Mississippi, when twenty-eight
white Methodist ministers, frustrated with the silence of their own annual
conference leaders, issued a public manifesto in support of race relations change. Signed by white moderate and liberal pastors, the "Born of

Conviction" statement illustrates the difficulties suffered, lessons learned, and rewards gained by mainstream Mississippians who dared to question the segregated, white supremacist status quo.[1]

"Born of Conviction," written in October 1962 and published in the *Mississippi Methodist Advocate* on January 2, 1963, responded to the turmoil surrounding the September 30, 1962, riot at Ole Miss when James Meredith finally arrived to enroll as the school's first known African American student. The statement called for freedom of the pulpit, reminded readers of the Methodist *Discipline*'s claim that the teachings of Jesus "[permit] no discrimination because of race, color, or creed," expressed support for the public schools and opposition to any attempt to close them when desegregation came, and affirmed the signers's opposition to Communism. On January 3, every Mississippi daily paper reported on it. Though a few lay and clergy persons affirmed it publicly, the overwhelming majority expressed shock, outrage, and in some cases, bewilderment.[2]

Most of the signers experienced ostracism, persecution, threats, and some violence. Their conference leaders provided little support, and some of the Twenty-Eight, as they were quickly dubbed, received reprimands from church superiors. The few Mississippi Methodists who defended the statement after its publication also suffered repercussions. The signers also received messages of gratitude, mostly private. Though they appreciated the encouragement, they needed more public affirmation; just as Dr. King expressed frustration at the silence of white moderates, so also the public reticence of all but a few Born of Conviction supporters represented a moral failure and contributed to the exodus of many of the signers. Within eighteen months of the statement's release, seventeen signers had left the Mississippi Conference. Two others departed shortly thereafter, and the twentieth left Mississippi in 1971. Eight of the signers remained in the Mississippi Conference for the rest of their careers, and three others eventually returned to the state—two in the mid-1960s.

In 1963, University of Mississippi historian James W. Silver labeled Mississippi the "Closed Society." Its "all-pervading doctrine" of white supremacy demanded adherence to the "true faith" and the appearance of a "united front." True commitment "[required] that nonconformists and dissenters from the code be silenced, or, in a crisis, driven from the community. Violence and the threat of violence . . . confirmed and enforced the image of unanimity." With white Mississippi's very identity threatened in the early 1960s by the civil rights movement, "no forthright challenge of the society [was] tolerated for long and . . . repercussions [were] quick and sure." Silver used the response to Born of Conviction as a prime example and reported that the Closed Society "battered the outspoken young preachers upon the anvil of public opinion." The Closed Society seemed monolithic, and its view of the world captivated most white Mississippians, including many Methodists. Born of Conviction signers articulated the "genuine dilemma facing persons of Christian conscience" in early 1963, even though they knew that no dilemma existed for the majority of whites, who could only imagine segregation now, tomorrow, and forever. In response to Dr. King's frustration at the general failure of the white church, its leaders, and the moderates within it to support the movement, the Born of Conviction story offers an explanation, though not a justification, for that failure.[3]

In the midst of the public commotion, private response told a more complicated tale: the statement struck a nerve with whites who did perceive a dilemma and struggled with the guilt they felt at the multiple injustices of the system, even though they could not articulate it well and felt powerless to act. The Twenty-Eight spoke to and for them "as Christian ministers and as native Mississippians, sharing the anguish of all our people." In some congregations, the controversy pushed church members to talk about race relations on a deeper level. White Methodists could more easily dismiss the witness of civil rights activists, whom they saw as radicals and outsiders, than they could ignore what their preacher said about race.[4]

Historians have given much attention to the role of religion in the civil rights era on all sides, from the Beloved Community inclusivity of the movement to the segregationist concern for racial purity. Dr. King characterized the white church as mostly silent in response to the evils of the segregated system, and Samuel S. Hill's 1966 classic, *Southern Churches in Crisis*, supported King's criticism. Yet, in his 2004 work, *A Stone of Hope*, David Chappell argues the religious perspective of civil rights leaders triumphed because "white churches were unwilling to make sacrifices to preserve segregation" and splintered into "hopeless disarray and confusion over racial matters." In his view, the white church's lack of support for the movement matters less than its failure to back the movement's opponents and rally to the segregationist cause.[5]

Not surprisingly, this claim has evoked dissent. Jane Dailey finds evidence of a "titanic struggle waged by participants on both sides of the conflict to harness the immense power of the divine to their cause." Peter Slade demonstrates how members of Jackson, Mississippi's First Presbyterian Church employed "a consistent and effective ecclesial strategy for maintaining the Southern white hegemony running unbroken from the debate on slavery through to school desegregation." Carolyn Dupont asserts that in Mississippi, not only did white Protestants "fail to fight *for* black equality, they often labored mightily *against* it."[6]

Each of these characterizations of mainstream white religious response to the civil rights movement—that whites sat on the sidelines, or significantly failed to support segregation, or indeed actively resisted race relations change—captures a part of the whole truth, and the Born of Conviction story provides ample evidence for all three and adds an example of white mainstream support for the civil rights movement represented by the statement. The Twenty-Eight broke the deafening silence of white Mississippi Conference Methodists in the months following the Ole Miss crisis and offered a theological alternative to white supremacy. Their manifesto fell far short of the prophetic pronouncements of Dr. King, but their white Mississippi Methodist clergy colleague and Jackson Movement leader, Ed King, understood and appreciated the significance of their effort. He called it "the strongest, most carefully thought out statement by any group of white Mississippians up to that time about the racial problems of the state."[7]

Responses to Born of Conviction ranged all the way from scattered violence, numerous threats (mostly anonymous), and the doctrinaire pronouncements of the segregationist group Mississippi Association of Methodist Ministers and Laymen (MAMML) to a few public and many more private expressions of support. On the local level, church members who rejected their offending pastors exemplify white Christians struggling mightily to maintain segregation, but some segregationist members, who considered new perspectives as the result of their pastor's witness or disagreed but still supported their pastor, illustrate Chappell's claim that whites failed to rally for the cause.

This array of viewpoints illustrates the complex role of religious faith and practice in the civil rights era, and thus this book adds to recent literature attending to nonmovement perspectives in the civil rights years in the Deep South. As Dailey states, religion was important for all parties involved in the struggle. No recent work illustrates that better than Charles Marsh's *God's Long Summer*, which describes and interprets the faith of Mississippi movement leaders Fannie Lou Hamer, Cleveland Sellers, and Ed King, as well as two segregationists: Jackson First Baptist Church pastor Douglas Hudgins and Ku Klux Klan leader Sam Bowers. Marsh omits a profile of the faith of white folks like the Born of Conviction signers and the significant minority of white Mississippi Methodists who supported them, and the present volume offers a complex portrait of the faith of many such persons—primarily the Twenty-Eight, but also others—all of whom sought to live out their Christian convictions in a difficult time. In some ways they were heroes, but they were also flawed human beings who finally refused to go along with the white Mississippi status quo or wanted to protest but struggled with their fears and remained silent.[8]

Focus on the religious faith of white Mississippi Methodists necessitates attention to Christian theological concerns. Aside from the practical meaning of the command to love one's neighbor, the central issue was ecclesiological—the purpose of the church and its relationship to the world. Because the Twenty-Eight objected to the white Mississippi Conference's apparent complicity with the Closed Society ethic, they offered an alternative witness. Among the many critical responses to their statement came the claim that they had abandoned the central purpose of Methodism: winning souls to Christ. White Southern Protestants, Sam Hill explains, insisted "Christian congregations have neither example nor instruction impelling them to forsake their soul-winning duties in the interest . . . of Christianizing the social order. Absorption in efforts of this kind only serves to dilute the authentic Christian responsibility." Southern Presbyterians elevated this dualism between temporal and spiritual matters to a doctrine, the "spirituality of the church," and Joel Alvis, Peter Slade, and Carolyn Dupont have each shown how important it became as support for the segregated white supremacist system in Mississippi. Born of Conviction rejected this dualism and asserted that if the church said nothing in response to the Ole Miss riot and the larger climate of massive resistance, then it participated fully in the evils of the segregated system. Signer Elton Brown insisted to his Natchez parishioners in 1963 that the church could not avoid involvement in social and political issues, because "everything that touches human society at any point has a religious significance."[9]

Historian Wayne Flynt claims that in the white church in those years, "lay people charted the course on race relations." The Born of Conviction controversy explores the classic problem of the locus of authority for interpreting Christian tradition in light of life in the world. The Twenty-Eight exercised their mandate as clergy to apply the "expressed witness of our Church" in an explosive social crisis. A dramatic contest resulted, with many lay and some fellow clergy voices expressing strident opposition and invoking a different practical theological understanding colored by their failure to distinguish the Christian faith from undying maintenance of the "Southern way of life" and the orthodoxy of the Closed Society.[10]

The conflict also aggravated deep denominational tensions between white Southern Methodism and the more liberal national church, as well as a generational struggle between a traditional paternalistic understanding of clergy leadership in an annual conference and the new perspectives on social justice garnered from seminary education by the mostly younger ministers who signed Born of Conviction. This thoroughly Methodist story examines how representatives of a white religious institution, the Mississippi Conference of The Methodist Church, dealt with a cataclysmic social, ecclesial, and fundamentally human crisis in the early 1960s and struggled to make sense of their vocation to witness to the Gospel of Christ in that historical moment.[11]

Though several other clergy groups issued public statements on race relations in the South during those years, most were ecumenical and included more signatures. Some individual Southern ministers took a stand on the race issue in their churches in the 1950s or 1960s and often suffered as a result, but this is the story of twenty-eight ministers of one denomination and one judicatory unit within that church who took a stand together in Mississippi, generally considered the most recalcitrant Southern state, during the time when its resistance peaked. Responses to individual signers and the effects that signing had on their subsequent careers varied and illustrated the range of white Methodist engagement with the social upheaval caused by the Mississippi civil rights movement in 1962 and beyond.[12]

The Twenty-Eight suffered consequences for their stand, and more than two-thirds of them either felt forced to leave Mississippi or chose to do so. The history of white Southern dissent in the century or so after the Civil War contains many examples of persons who challenged the racial status quo, experienced varying levels of persecution, and left their homes, most often to reside outside the South. The Born of Conviction story not only provides a case study on the white Methodist Church's response to the civil rights movement in Mississippi, but it also explores a larger institutional and regional drama. From the mid-1950s through the early 1970s, scores of pastors transferred out of the Mississippi Conference, including nineteen of the Twenty-Eight. The race issue played a major role in those departures, but it must also be understood in light of the conference's internal politics.

Most interpreters have cited Born of Conviction as a prime example of the "they spoke out and were forced out of Mississippi" narrative to show the state's characteristic rejection of the "nonconformists and dissenters" who earned James Silver's sympathy. Viewed through this lens alone, it is a hero story focused exclusively on the statement and the majority of signers who departed. As the record shows, however, many who left chose to leave; only a few were truly forced. In addition, as the widow of a signer who left declares, the "real heroes [are] the ones who stayed," and this claim invites emphasis on a different part of the plot.[13]

This story involves more than thirty major characters, several minor characters, and thirty-nine white Methodist congregations served by the signers in twenty-three South Mississippi communities, along with other churches that responded publicly or privately to the statement. Because interviews with signers and many others done forty or more years after these events took place provide a major (though by no means the only) source for this story, the book occasionally makes use of remembered dialogue. Though well aware of the vagaries of human memory, I have chosen to use such dialogue because the ways participants remember these events play an important role in interpretation of the story.

The narrative introduces the signers across nine chapters and reveals both the longer and the more immediate historical contexts for the statement, the influences on those who signed, and their reasons for signing. The January 1963 controversy merits telling both as a media event on a statewide and national scale and as a series of local church and community events across South Mississippi where the Twenty-Eight served as pastors. The third section of the book critiques the "spoke out, forced out" narrative in detail by examining what became of the signers and how they continued their social witness in subsequent ministry. The final section evaluates the importance of the Born of Conviction statement and considers the experiential and interpretive divide between the signers who left the state and those who stayed, followed by a discussion of the legacy of Born of Conviction in the lives of signers, their descendants, and the current generation of Mississippi Conference ministers; in a contemporary social controversy in the United Methodist Church; and in Mississippi race relations, including the ministry of United Methodism in the state.

Martin Luther King criticized the eight white clergymen whom he addressed in the Birmingham letter because they urged blacks to adopt a gradualist strategy: be patient, do not support demonstrations in the streets, and "unite locally in working peacefully for a better Birmingham."

His classic response argued for civil disobedience and "constructive, non-violent tension which is necessary for growth." The situation in early 1960s Mississippi called for something much more radical than gradualism; as King reminded his readers, "justice too long delayed is justice denied." The courageous work of hundreds of "local people" in the civil rights movement in the state, joined by outsiders like Bob Moses and the 1964 Freedom Summer workers, proved indispensable to the black freedom struggle. The Born of Conviction statement played a crucial role in the white community in early 1963 because it created a significant crack in the Closed Society's united front, and those who signed truly did the right thing.[14]

However, statements alone do not suffice; they must be lived out in continued action in subsequent years. Extensive race relations change accomplished through direct action, legislation, and court decisions must be implemented over time in local communities. Gradualism had an appropriate place as a secondary strategy, after adequate recognition of the injustices of the system and the unavoidable push toward revolutionary change. The work of the eight Born of Conviction signers who stayed, along with many other leaders, black and white, played a profound role in transforming churches and communities toward a new Mississippi. Those efforts did not achieve complete success but deserve recognition nonetheless.

Dr. King also spoke for the civil rights movement when he considered white churches in the Deep South: "What kind of people worship here? Who is their God? Where were their voices when the lips of Governor Barnett dripped with words of interposition and nullification?" He wanted the white church to support the black freedom struggle or at least consent to participate in meaningful dialogue about it. Yet the church usually refused to do either.[15]

On Sunday morning, October 20, 1963, I sat with my mother and brother in our 1954 Chevrolet, parked at the curb on Jackson, Mississippi's West Capitol Street, and watched as some visitors approached the entrance of our church, Capitol Street Methodist. Male ushers and a Jackson policeman at the church steps blocked the group of three women—two black and one white—and two white Methodist clergymen from Chicago, whose presence represented the claim that ongoing segregation was an issue involving the whole church and could not be considered simply a local Mississippi matter. After some conversation we could not hear, the policeman arrested the visitors, who had sought to engage the church guards in dialogue toward a new understanding of Christian race relations.[16]

Those church visitors stood in the wide gap between mainstream whites and the civil rights movement and invited the church members guarding the steps to join them, but the guards refused. The episode, one of many at the steps of this and other Jackson congregations between 1963 and 1966, represents the dominant civil rights era historical narrative of the barriers to change zealously guarded by white Mississippi Christians. The signers of the 1963 Born of Conviction statement, frustrated at the failure of conference leaders to take the first steps, seized the moment in early 1963 and sought to bridge that gap. They believed that "as Christian ministers and as native Mississippians," they had "a particular obligation to speak," to join the conversation and address the intersection of the black freedom struggle with the faith of white Methodist Christians in Mississippi. Their effort created numerous "theaters of complex theological drama," that shed light on the past, present, and future struggle toward racial reconciliation and justice in church and society. This book tells their story and the story of the white Methodist church in Mississippi, a diverse institution that both resisted race relations change and fostered the ministers who took a bold step to end that resistance.[17]

Born of Conviction

PART I

Prelude to a Crisis

I

Methodism and Mississippi

> *[The] Annual Conference from the first has been
> the minister's church.*
>
> —NOLAN B. HARMON, *The Organization of The Methodist
> Church*, 1953

> *Also, an annual conference is a dramatic public focus-
> ing of the highest thought and deepest conscience
> of Methodism.*
>
> —ROY C. DELAMOTTE, 1955

BORN OF CONVICTION is a Mississippi story and a Methodist story, and the narratives intertwine. Mississippi, which National Association for the Advancement of Colored People (NAACP) national leader Roy Wilkins called "absolutely at the bottom of the list" because of its "inhuman-ity, murder, brutality, and racial hatred," powerfully influenced white Mississippi Conference Methodism. In that world, several perennial American Methodist issues colored the Christian witness of Mississippi Conference clergy and laity: regionalism, tradition in tension with new ideas, emphasis on individual sin at the expense of a larger social/systemic awareness, and the white Methodist struggle to understand and confront racism. As the 1950s faded into the 1960s, the conference's response to the race issue became increasingly naïve and irrelevant.[1]

*American Methodism in the South:
Race and Regionalism*

Founded in eighteenth-century England, John Wesley's Methodist Movement sought to "spread scriptural holiness over the land," and Wesley emphasized both personal and social holiness in the Christian life. The latter entailed a communal focus in which individuals supported and held each other accountable in class meetings for their growth in faith and Christian witness in the world. Methodists established societies in the American colonies in the late 1760s, and the Methodist Episcopal Church (MEC) came to life officially in 1784.[2]

From the beginning, American Methodists struggled with the issue of race and the place of blacks in the church. Wesley's opposition to slavery led to initial prohibitions against Methodist slave ownership in the new nation, but the principle proved difficult to enforce in practice, especially because Methodism took hold so successfully in the southern states. The Methodist combination of "heart religion" and an inclusive gospel attracted white and black alike. Yet even as Methodists reached out to blacks, both slave and free, the growing church exhibited a thoroughgoing ambivalence regarding adherence to antislavery beliefs and full inclusion in worship. A double standard developed that accommodated to the culture of the slave states while it upheld the slavery prohibition in the North. The tensions—between antislavery and racism, between inclusion and exclusion—resulted in gradual changes in Methodist race relations, including

the softening of Methodist critiques of slavery, the exclusion of African Americans from leadership roles in the church, the close monitoring (where possible) of black religious gatherings, the denominational prescriptions of more acceptable forms of religious expression, and the gradual separation of blacks and whites, first within interracial churches and then into separate congregations.[3]

As the nation pushed at the limits of the frontier, so did American Methodism. In 1799 Tobias Gibson founded a MEC congregation at Washington, near Natchez in the Mississippi Territory, and he soon established a circuit extending north to Vicksburg. The Methodist presence grew along with the territory's settlement; the Mississippi Annual Conference held its first session in 1813, four years before Mississippi statehood.[4]

Methodists did not escape the growing conflicts over slavery before the Civil War, and their inevitable division resulted from the clash between the abolitionist fervor in the North and the hardening insistence on honoring regional cultural norms and law in the South. When Bishop James Andrew, residing in Georgia, became a slaveholder due to his wife's inheriting slaves, northern delegates to the 1844 General Conference insisted he must free his slaves in order to continue in the episcopal office. Southerners resisted, pointing to Georgia law that prohibited manumission of slaves; they also claimed the General Conference had no authority to make such a demand. By the end of the debate they had split into northern (MEC) and southern (Methodist Episcopal Church, South—MECS) bodies.[5]

After the Civil War, the division in American Methodism remained. The MEC created a segregated structure with separate African American annual conferences, and it also extended its mission work into former Confederate territory to invite freed slaves to become Methodist. In Mississippi, this resulted in the creation of a mission conference in 1865 that became the black MEC Mississippi Conference in 1869. The MECS had grown sufficiently in the state to warrant a new white North Mississippi Annual Conference in 1870, while the same division occurred in the black MEC conference in 1891 with the first session of the Upper Mississippi Annual Conference. Thus at the turn of the twentieth century, there were four Methodist Episcopal judicatory bodies in the state—two white MECS and two black MEC annual conferences. By that time the MEC and the MECS had established a fraternal relationship and begun conversations about unification into one Methodist denomination. These discussions included the smaller Methodist Protestant Church, which had split from the MEC in 1830. The talks stretched across decades before they achieved the goal.[6]

The more serious conflicts plaguing ecclesial bodies burrow into church institutional frameworks for generations, and the two main issues at stake in the 1844 split—race relations and the tension between connectional allegiance to the General (national) Church and regional cultural concerns—remained central in the negotiations toward reunion. In 1918 the MECS insisted the proposed new church should be white, with MEC blacks completely separated into an independent body joined with the three existing African American Methodist churches—African Methodist Episcopal (AME), AME Zion, and Colored Methodist Episcopal (CME). The Southern church eventually accepted a plan dividing the reunited church into five geographical jurisdictions plus the Central Jurisdiction for the black annual conferences. This represented a concession from the Southern church: they agreed to join a denomination with African American members. However, the new jurisdictional structure allowed Southern whites to elect their own bishops and remain segregated from blacks in the new

Methodist Church except at the General Church level, where clergy and lay delegates represented the Central Jurisdiction annual conferences at General Conference and on General boards and agencies.[7]

By 1938 the Plan of Union had gained approval by all bodies involved, including the Methodist Protestants, but a minority of MEC members (black and white) opposed it because of the segregated structure, and a smaller minority of MECS members voted against it because of their historic mistrust of the MEC and a desire to remain in a white-only church. After the 1939 Uniting Conference, the first General Conference of the new Methodist Church met in 1940. Membership in the denomination exceeded 7.7 million, including more than 350,000 African American members. Though they were less than 5 percent of the total, the Methodist Church numbered more black members than all other mainline white Protestant denominations combined.[8]

Without the jurisdictional structure, the MECS would not have approved the Plan of Union. "Segregation was the price of unification," many claimed. The resulting formalized regionalism proved an additional price, and the establishment of the Central Jurisdiction made Methodist segregation more institutionally formal. The approval of the Plan of Union represented a victory for institutional concerns (the desire for unification) over justice concerns (arguments against the segregated structure). Though the majority of black members (clergy and lay) had opposed the plan, they remained a part of the new church because they believed the future of American race relations would not be served well by an exclusively white denomination. In addition, the Central Jurisdiction gave them opportunities for self-determination (e.g., electing their own bishops) and for a demonstration of their abilities as full participants in the life of the unified church. Ultimately, in Central Jurisdiction leader James S. Thomas's words, they "maintained a stubborn belief that the racial diversity of the church was important and that the Central Jurisdiction, though a high price for the union of the church, would not live forever."[9]

However, most Southern white Methodists understood the Plan of Union to imply an unwritten agreement that there would be no changes for a time, and conservatives viewed the Central Jurisdiction as permanent. The arrangement preserved segregation in the church and in the minds of members of the white Mississippi Conference and North Mississippi Conference; its ministers and churches exhibited scant awareness of and had little if any contact with their Central Jurisdiction Mississippi Conference and Upper Mississippi Conference counterparts (Figure 1.1).[10]

FIGURE I.I Map of Mississippi, showing dividing line between the white North Mississippi and Mississippi Annual Conferences and between the Central Jurisdiction (black) Upper Mississippi and Mississippi Annual Conferences, 1962–3. Map by Edward H. Davis.

The Mississippi Annual Conference,
Southeastern Jurisdiction

Twenty years before the creation of the Born of Conviction statement, the Mississippi Annual Conference of the Southeastern Jurisdiction of the new Methodist Church met in November 1942 at Crawford Street

Church in Vicksburg. Two weeks earlier in the same town, the *other* Mississippi Conference held its 1942 meeting. The ministers and lay-persons attending the prior meeting came from churches in the same South Mississippi communities as the white conference's churches, but as African Americans they belonged to a separate annual conference in the Central Jurisdiction.[11]

The 1940 Methodist *Discipline* (the church's law book) defines the annual conference as "the basic body in the church." It has functioned in American Methodism as a mediating structure between the General Church and local churches and as the central link of the Methodist "con-nection," the ties binding all Methodists together across the entire orga-nizational structure and the responsibilities they share from the local level to national and global levels. Annual conferences are divided into geographic districts, each led by a district superintendent chosen by the bishop; the district superintendents comprise the bishop's cabinet. The white Mississippi Conference, covering the southern half of the state, had six districts then: Meridian, Jackson, and Vicksburg, with Hattiesburg and Brookhaven to the south and Seashore on the Gulf Coast.[12]

The bishop and cabinet appoint a pastor to serve each local church. Many smaller Mississippi Conference churches share a pastor with one or more neighboring congregations, forming a pastoral charge. Churches do not hire or fire pastors; appointments are reviewed annually by the bishop and the cabinet in consultation with churches and pastors and formal-ized at the annual conference session. Ministers serve the same church or charge for a period of years until they move to another appointment or depart by another route (retirement, leave of absence, transfer to another annual conference, etc.). Appointments can change mid-year in unusual circumstances.[13]

In early American Methodism, annual conference meetings consisted mainly of ministers; by the 1930s, the official membership of annual con-ference sessions had become half clergy and half laity. Ministers saw the conference first as a body of Methodist clergy—a sacred community of men called to preach and committed to church service. This understand-ing of "conference" developed from John Wesley's conferences: gather-ings of preachers to confer about theological, missional, organizational, and practical issues and to set the pastoral appointments for the coming year.[14]

Thus an integral part of any annual conference is the "traveling preach-ers" who enter the ministry by fulfilling qualifications specified by the

Discipline. In the 1940s, a minister seeking ordination graduated from college and either earned a seminary degree or pursued the denomination's four-year Course of Study while serving as an approved supply pastor. Through successful completion of either route, ministers eventually qualified for elder's orders and full membership in the conference, subject to a vote by ministerial members. An appointment is guaranteed to full members, who promise to "go where [they] are sent."[15]

Annual conferences develop their own culture, especially among the clergy members, because as Mississippi native Nolan Harmon, a MECS and Methodist preacher eventually elected a bishop, wrote, the conference is the "minister's church," a fellowship of deep significance that "becomes increasingly dear to him with the passage of time, and as the different conferences develop their own special ways of thought, and those inconsequential but characteristic ways of doing things, which speak of a corporate individuality, the members themselves seem to partake of the same characteristics which enwrap all." American Methodist historian Russell Richey characterizes annual conferences as centrally meaningful, not only for their political organization but also for the way they structure time and space for American Methodists. Like any community with deep emotional bonds, this sense of kinship in Methodist annual conferences has fostered a perennial mixture of feelings, ranging from shared celebration and genuine love to bitter conflict.[16]

In the 1940s white Mississippi Conference, the traditions of the MECS still remained strong among clergy, including training for the ministry through the Course of Study instead of attending a seminary and honoring one's "father in the ministry," the pastor most responsible for one's decision to become a preacher or the clergy leader to whom one looked first for guidance and example in the conference. This traditional conservative worldview also assumed segregation in the church structure as a given and valued the Southern white regional perspective to the point of provincialism.[17]

John Willard Leggett Jr. best represented that ongoing conservative leadership tradition. Born in the Copiah County community of Allen in 1907, he graduated from Copiah-Lincoln Junior College and Millsaps College and then joined the Mississippi Conference on trial in 1930. He received additional training through the MECS's Course of Study program and began serving as a pastor in 1931. He claimed Tom Prewitt, a minister eight years his senior, and his uncle, J. T. Leggett, the recognized conference leader in the 1920s, as his fathers in the ministry. Willard Leggett married Louise Finch in 1933. By 1942, he was pastor at First Methodist in Laurel.[18]

A moderate perspective also developed in the conference, which honored the MECS's past but valued seminary education and expressed less suspicion of non-Southern ideas. Moderates also accepted and assumed the segregated denominational structure but did not necessarily see it as permanent. Brunner M. Hunt, pastor at Main Street Church in Hattiesburg in the mid-1940s, and William Bryan Selah, pastor at Galloway Memorial Church in Jackson beginning in 1945, exemplified this view. Hunt was born in 1900 in Georgia and moved to Mississippi at age twelve, while Selah, born in 1896, grew up in Missouri. Hunt graduated from Emory University's Candler School of Theology and Selah from Yale Divinity School.[19]

Four Future Born of Conviction Signers

Four of the eventual signers of Born of Conviction had initiated the process toward ministerial membership in the conference by the fall of 1942. Like Leggett, all of them graduated from Millsaps College, but unlike their senior colleague, they earned seminary degrees. Seminary education for Mississippi Conference ministers had not yet become the norm, but the percentage of seminary-trained pastors had begun to grow and increased steadily after World War II. All four of these men gravitated to the conference's moderate faction.

Howard Bufkin Oliver was born in 1917 near the Mississippi Gulf Coast. The seventh child of his family, his mother steered him toward a call to the ordained ministry. He graduated from Jones County Junior College in Ellisville and went to Millsaps from 1940 to 1942, where he met and married Elizabeth Robinson. Bufkin Oliver served his first pastorate at Sharon in Madison County as a student, and he joined the Mississippi Conference on trial in 1942. In 1943 he enrolled in seminary at Drew University and served a church in Lebanon, New Jersey. When he returned to Mississippi in 1946, the conference appointed him to Scooba.[20]

Born in New Orleans in 1918, James Sydney Conner grew up in Hattiesburg and graduated from high school at sixteen. An accomplished pianist, he performed a rare sophomore recital at Millsaps College and earned a bachelor of arts in history at twenty. He worked in a Hattiesburg bank and decided in 1940 to enter the ministry. At Emory's Candler School of Theology, Conner developed an interest in philosophical theology, the field of L. E. Loemker, a professor for whom he worked as student assistant. In June 1943 he returned to Mississippi, served briefly at Tylertown, and was admitted on trial and sent to Scooba at the November 1943 annual conference.[21]

James William Holston, born in the small Stone County community of Bond in Southeast Mississippi in 1923, preached his first sermon at seventeen and became a student pastor at Mentorum in 1942 while a junior at Millsaps. His mother had wanted to be a missionary, but her father forbade it; two of her sons became Methodist ministers. During Holston's senior year he served as pastor at D'Lo and then went to Candler. He married Jacksonian Bennie Hunnicutt in 1945, and they returned from Atlanta in 1946 for him to serve at Clinton, just west of Jackson.[22]

Nathan Andrew Dickson, born in Hattiesburg in 1918, graduated from Jones County Junior College and went to Mississippi State to study entomology; he soon felt called to the ministry and transferred to Millsaps. There he met Mary Myers, and they married in 1941. By 1942, N. A. Dickson had been approved as a local preacher, and in March 1943 he was appointed student pastor at the Barlow Charge in Copiah County. Admitted on trial in 1944, he attended Candler from 1945 to 1948 and returned to Mississippi for an appointment at Pachuta.[23]

The Conference Leader

One MECS tradition that continued in the conference in the 1940s and beyond related to leadership and a sense of conference identity. Every four years, annual conference clergy and laity each elect delegates to the denomination's quadrennial General and Jurisdictional Conferences—the former is the worldwide legislative meeting and the only body that can speak officially for the denomination; the latter serves primarily to elect bishops. The minister elected first to General Conference is considered the conference leader, the one whom the majority of ministers see as their best representative. Chosen seventh of eight in 1943 by his clergy colleagues as a 1944 Jurisdictional Conference delegate, Willard Leggett (Figure 1.2) joined a delegation led on the laity side by Mississippi Governor Thomas Bailey. At the 1947 annual conference, Leggett, by then pastor of Jackson's Capitol Street Church, was elected on the first ballot to lead the 1948

FIGURE 1.2 J. Willard Leggett Jr. in 1971. Courtesy of the Mississippi United
Methodist Foundation, Inc.

General Conference delegation. This began Leggett's leadership and even
dominance of the conference, which lasted for decades.[24]

At the 1948 Southeastern Jurisdictional Conference, Mississippi
received a new bishop. Marvin Augustus Franklin (Figure 1.3) was born in
the northeast Georgia hills in 1894, licensed to preach at age sixteen, and
joined the North Georgia Annual Conference in 1913. He graduated Phi
Beta Kappa from the University of Georgia in 1915; he did not attend seminary. By the time of his election to bishop in 1948, he had served as pastor
of prestigious churches in Atlanta, Jacksonville, and Birmingham. Many
in the Mississippi Conference came to believe that Willard Leggett unduly
influenced Bishop Franklin, episcopal leader of the conference from 1948
to 1964. Southeastern Jurisdiction episcopal elections are fierce political
battles with behind-the-scenes vote trading, and 1948 was no exception.
A story made the rounds that Leggett supported the unsuccessful candidacy of John Branscomb of Florida. At a dinner of Mississippi delegates
for the newly elected and Mississippi-assigned Bishop Franklin, Leggett

FIGURE 1.3 Bishop Marvin A. Franklin. Courtesy of J. B. Cain Archives of Mississippi Methodism, Millsaps College.

reportedly welcomed Franklin to Mississippi and claimed he had worked hard to get the new bishop elected. Some cited this supposed sense of obligation Franklin felt to Leggett as evidence for Leggett's influence over him. True or not, the story became part of the lore surrounding Leggett's power in those years.[25]

In the MECS, nonresident bishops had presided over several annual conferences and left many of the details of running each conference to one or more trusted presiding elders (the previous name for district superintendents). In the post-1939 church, bishops lived within their episcopal territory; Franklin resided in Jackson and led two and eventually three white annual conferences that together formed his area: Mississippi, North Mississippi, and Memphis. In such an arrangement, bishops still depended on their district superintendents in each conference, due to the virtual impossibility to know every pastor and congregation well. For eleven of Franklin's years in Mississippi, Leggett served on the cabinet and made it his mission to know pastors and churches all over the conference.

Roy Clark, pastor of Capitol Street Church from 1953 to 1963 (and later elected a bishop), describes Franklin as more passive in the appointment process than other bishops of that era. Clark, a leader in the conference's moderate faction, remembers criticizing Leggett in a conversation with the bishop, and Franklin defended Leggett by saying that in cabinet appointment-making sessions, when the group had difficulty deciding how to match pastors with congregations, Leggett usually proposed the best solutions. Leggett had mastered the complex puzzle of Methodist appointment making.[26]

An annual conference is an arena of achievement for ministers, and most of them measure their success in terms of the churches they have served and how well they have done there. In the usual pattern, ministers serve a few years in an appointment and then move to a place with a higher salary. Ministers with more experience, ability, success, and the right political connections usually ascend to the top churches in the conference. This "appointment ladder" ideally encourages better pastoral leadership because ministers who wish to succeed in the system will work harder and perhaps become better pastors. It also introduces a strong element of competition, and some ministers learn to work the system to their advantage. Thus itinerant ministers who have promised to go where sent and share communal bonds with their colleagues sometimes view those whose climb up the ladder is faster than their own with envy and even bitterness.

In this system, the persons who make pastoral appointments exercise a great deal of power. During the 1950s and 1960s, Willard Leggett was the power broker of the Mississippi Conference, the de facto "Bishop of Mississippi." In any annual conference there is influence to be wielded in the making of pastoral appointments and many other aspects of conference business. In response to a request to describe the culture of the conference in those years, virtually all of the Twenty-Eight and other Mississippi Conference ministers from that era interviewed for this study promptly mentioned conference politics and the power of Leggett and his group. One minister summed it up: "The conference was small enough so that it could easily enough be dominated by a strong personality, and that's exactly what happened."[27]

This created a conflict in the conference between the more conservative traditionalists and the moderates. General Conference elections in the Mississippi Conference became battlegrounds with high stakes. In 1951, Leggett was again elected first by clergy, with moderate Brunner

Hunt second and Leggett ally Tom Prewitt third. Moderate W. B. Selah won a spot on the Jurisdictional Conference delegation, joined by another moderate and two ministers identified with Leggett.[28]

In 1955, a group of moderates determined to unseat the nascent Leggett power bloc organized and recruited votes for their alternate slate with talk of a new day in the conference and a larger vision than Leggett represented. They wrested the top two clergy delegate slots from Leggett hands, with Hunt, then pastor of Central Church in Meridian, elected on the first ballot and Selah, still at Jackson Galloway, on the second. Leggett was chosen on the third ballot, and the selection of Prewitt completed the delegation. This setback may have surprised Leggett, but his troops organized better for the 1959 election, when Leggett returned to the top spot, and the other three clergy General Conference delegate slots went to persons clearly associated with him. At least half of the Jurisdictional Conference delegates elected that year were also Leggett men.[29]

During annual conference meetings when elections were held, the Leggett forces exercised extreme discipline, with a slate of candidates and a cadre of ministerial sergeants who made sure their troops stayed on or near the conference floor, always ready to vote as soon as the previous ballot was reported. With the exception of the 1955 election, no opposition attempt could match the Leggett group's structure and commitment. In 1959, after the moderate group met in Jackson at the King Edward Hotel, Leggett informants reported by phone to their leader with a list of attendees.[30]

Leggett's remarkable organization can be documented through oral histories, election results, and my own experience in later years, but his opponents also claimed that the conference leader and his group manipulated people. J. W. Leggett mastered not only Methodist appointment making but also the skills of power politics. Even perennial opponents recognized him as a leader of great ability, and one said that if Leggett had been a lawyer, he could have been governor of Mississippi. Art O'Neil Jr., a new minister in the conference in the late 1950s, considered Leggett his friend in those years and remembered how Leggett endeared himself to many conference preachers through assistance in their financial difficulties and with personal visits and genuine expressions of care, especially in times of trouble.[31]

This generous, paternalistic style of leadership and relationship fostered intense loyalty and obligation to Leggett among many conference ministers. Sometimes Leggett or his lieutenants tried to gain new supporters with claims of responsibility for a good pastoral appointment to supposed beneficiaries. The usual pattern involved Leggett devotees cultivating younger ministers and promising them career success and other benefits in exchange for support of the Leggett faction. This was part of the Methodist tradition of close relations between older and younger ministers, and the paternalism of Leggett and his group was not unusual. However, Leggett opponent Roy Clark summed up his criticism in a 1965 interview: "When you move into a highly charged political situation and a man deliberately sees this as the means whereby he will ingratiate people, ... where it becomes a technique, then ... it becomes more ... 'corrupt' than it is normally, in the sense that this [takes advantage of] a natural selfishness, a natural desire to have myself protected and cared for."[32]

Some ministers claimed in those years, either through personal experience or knowledge of the fate of other pastors, that "If you didn't go along, you didn't get along." In other words, failure to support Leggett could result in punitive consequences—poor pastoral appointments, efforts to discredit opponents, and occasional attempts to push ministers out of the conference. Such pressure came in a variety of ways, including conversations with Leggett or persuasive visits by Leggett supporters to ministers who needed to be brought in line. The report to Leggett on the 1959 opposition meeting illustrates the usual political desire to know the plans of one's opponents, but the spying activity intimidated opposition ministers with fear of appointment punishments and other reprisals because they dared to challenge the Leggett group's dominance. This atmosphere led Art O'Neil to transfer out of the conference in 1960 at twenty-seven years of age. Though Leggett, O'Neil's district superintendent at the time, never asked him for any favors, the young minister saw men coming out of annual conference sessions in tears because of perceived punishments from the Leggett forces. O'Neil's nonpolitical father, a minister in the conference, had friends in both political groups; the younger O'Neil felt pressured from both directions to join a side. When an opportunity came to transfer to the North Georgia Conference, O'Neil took it, partly because of Mississippi Conference politics.[33]

O'Neil's story exemplifies a larger narrative of Mississippi Conference Methodism in those years, as well as the perennial Methodist clash of tradition and new ideas. The postwar boom meant growth, with total church membership increasing about 6 percent in the 1950s and many new ministers joining the conference, more than half of them seminary graduates. By 1960, however, an increasing number of seminary-trained ministers were leaving the conference, and eventually two-thirds of those who signed Born of Conviction in 1963 would join them. The political control of the conference by the Leggett faction played a central role in this exodus, and the combination of the race issue and the cultural climate of massive resistance in Mississippi added to the problem.[34]

White Methodists and the Closing of Mississippi Society

Two other familiar Southern Methodist themes—race and regionalism—continued to influence the white Mississippi Conference in the postwar era, along with the perennial Southern Protestant tendency to emphasize individual sin over social sin. "Southern Evangelicals," historian David Harrell argues, "have been more individualistic, less confident in social reform," and "southern religion has been more given to sectarianism in the twentieth century." The approach to and avoidance of the race issue by white Methodists in South Mississippi in those years, as well as their insistence that the rest of the nation, including Methodist churches in other regions, should leave them alone to work out relations with blacks on a voluntary basis, illustrate his claims well. Mississippi Conference leaders also consistently expressed more concern for the preservation and success of the institutional church than any real desire for justice in race relations.[35]

After the 1939 reunification, American Methodists proceeded slowly on the issue of race. The 1944 General Conference instituted a Commission to Consider the Relations of All Races in The Methodist Church and named future Mississippi Bishop Marvin Franklin, still an Alabama local church pastor, as a Southeastern Jurisdiction representative. The twenty-five member group took no radical action but urged the 1948 General Conference to support "increased interracial meetings, an end to restrictive housing covenants, equal justice, voting rights, strengthened minority ministry, and establishment of a permanent office on race relations within the church bureaucracy." At his Birmingham church, Franklin preached at least two sermons during the war that showed awareness of and willingness to name systemic evil resulting from racism and economic oppression. His main target was Nazi Germany, and he spoke in general terms of brotherhood and implied the validity of separate but equal treatment of the races. But he also noted the injustice of a system in which "eight million share-croppers have a family income of less than $250 a year" and asserted that "no race, or class, or people must be exploited." He also celebrated American freedom of speech: "We may say what none will agree with but we may say it without fear of punishment."[36]

Franklin's election to the episcopacy and assignment to Mississippi in 1948 muted his witness. The Mississippi bishop's office proved a more closely examined platform than the pulpit at Birmingham's Highlands Methodist Church. Soon after he arrived in Mississippi, Franklin called publicly for more equitable dealings with African Americans in three spheres: schools (which still should be separate, but needed to be "greatly improved"), better housing to allow the African American "an increasing opportunity to make his contribution as a citizen," and a general call for white leaders to work toward "good feeling, better understanding, and finer cooperation" with blacks in order to "live together and work out their common problems." The statement typified the Southern white moderate gradualist view on race in those years: a cautious and benevolent paternalism that called for fair treatment of blacks yet still assumed segregation as a given, both in society and the church. Any change should be slow and deliberate, not revolutionary and not through civil disobedience or sit-in demonstrations.[37]

For more traditional Southerners, even a little change in race relations over time seemed too fast. The Methodist Church's slow but steady warming to such concerns alienated many church members in the Deep South. The 1948 General Conference added to the *Discipline* a statement on "The Christian Church and Race" that declared *"without equivocation"* that racial discrimination was both "unchristian" and "evil" and reminded Methodists that the 1944 General Conference resolution establishing the commission on which Franklin had served declared, " 'We look to the ultimate elimination of racial discrimination within The Methodist Church.' " By 1956, the statement in the *Discipline* said, "The teaching of our Lord is that all men are brothers. The Master permits no discrimination because of race, color, or national origin."[38]

So, white Mississippi Conference Methodists felt a mild push from the General Church on the issue of race. At home, pressure intensified from white culture in the state to remain faithful to the segregated, white supremacist worldview as the result of the US Supreme Court's 1954 *Brown* decision and the gradual "closing" of Mississippi society. Historian Charles Eagles argues that by 1955 the founding of the White Citizens' Councils and the first massive resistance legislation virtually ended tolerance for dissent in the state. Although some whites seemed resigned at first to eventual school desegregation after *Brown*, virtually no leaders emerged to show the way toward peaceful and gradual change. Author Walter Lord asserts that in 1954 the church in Mississippi said nothing in response to *Brown*, but in August 1954, the Episcopal Diocese of Mississippi's Department of Christian Social Relations published in the diocesan paper a fairly strong statement in support of the Court's decision, written by Duncan Gray Jr., a priest and son of the diocesan bishop. The statement drew severe criticism in the state from Episcopalians and non-Episcopalians.[39]

The silence from state and national political leaders and from most of the church created a "vacuum" into which "roared a cyclone—an ardent band of white supremacists whose sense of purpose was matched only by their skill." The massive resistance they launched destroyed any chance for peaceful acceptance of desegregation. Duncan Gray Jr., witnessed this change in the Mississippi Delta town of Cleveland when shortly after *Brown*, the local school board chairman acknowledged privately to Gray that the schools would be integrated in a few years. Within a few months the board chairman had joined the public chorus of whites insisting integration would and should *never* come.[40]

Credit for the transformation belongs mainly to the Citizens' Councils, a movement founded in July 1954 which within a year claimed sixty thousand members in 253 chapters spread across the state. Labels such as "bigotry with a kind of Rotarian respectability" and the "uptown Klan" capture the success, power, and tactics of this organization. In towns and counties across Mississippi, the council's repressive methods included publishing the names of blacks who signed NAACP school desegregation petitions, which resulted in lost jobs for those employed by whites and lost business for black businessmen who had white clientele. This "economic war of attrition" successfully squelched desegregation and voting registration attempts by blacks until the 1960s, and any white dissent to this massive resistance drew swift punishment.[41]

No published comment on the May 1954 *Brown* decision came from Bishop Franklin or the *Mississippi Methodist Advocate* editor until the December 1 issue included a story on the Methodist Council of Bishops' resolution supporting *Brown* and calling on Methodists to do so. Bishop Franklin said, "No one in the Southeast is crusading for the resolution or what it calls for," and the Southeastern Jurisdiction bishops had "earnestly requested that the Council of Bishops make no statement on the Supreme

Court decision." In an editorial, *Advocate* editor Clinton T. Howell said, "Our white people must pay heed to the Negro's appeal for safety and justice. Negroes should understand that real progress will come only by gradual evolution, not by revolution." Just before Christmas another editorial revealed that some white Mississippi Methodist local church Official Boards had circulated a resolution reading "Whereas the *Mississippi Methodist Advocate* praises the Supreme Court decision and approves of integration. . . ." A shocked Howell responded, "This editor has published no editorial statement concerning the Supreme Court decision."[42]

Mississippi legislators jumped on the resistance bandwagon with a constitutional amendment allowing them to close public schools if integration occurred and to fund white private schools; voters ratified the amendment in December 1954 by more than a two to one margin. Another 1954 constitutional amendment approved by the state's mostly white voters gave county officials broad powers to prevent black voter registration. Eventually the legislature passed a "breach of the peace" statute to facilitate punishment of civil disobedience and an interposition resolution that denied the validity of *Brown*.[43]

In early 1955, more than two hundred Mississippi Methodists formed an organization called Mississippi Association of Methodist Ministers and Laymen (MAMML) to work for "the preservation of present racial customs and the continuance of separate churches, conferences, and jurisdictions for the white membership and the Negro membership." Following the example of a similar group founded in Alabama a few months earlier, MAMML vigorously opposed "efforts being made and means being used to promote a policy of full racial integration within the Methodist Church." Some observers labeled MAMML the Methodist version of the Citizens' Council.[44]

Yet some Methodists still offered mild dissent. In April 1955, the white Mississippi Conference Women's Society of Christian Service (WSCS) meeting in Jackson, with representatives from churches across South Mississippi, heard a speech by Dan Whitsett, a Methodist minister from Sylacauga, Alabama, in which he criticized the Citizens' Councils and spoke in favor of integration. The women voted 129 to 62 to uphold their previous endorsement of the Charter of Racial Policies of the Women's Division of the denomination's Board of Mission. The charter concerned location of Women's Division national meetings in places where blacks would have equal access to all facilities, and it said, "Where law prohibits or custom prevents the immediate achievement of these objectives, workers and local boards are charged with the responsibility of creating a public opinion which may result in changing such laws and customs." The policy did not apply to Mississippi WSCS meetings, and an officer of the all-white Mississippi group emphasized that the charter "represents goals and ideals toward which we will work. . . . It does not represent church laws to be enforced, but a policy which individual members can consider." Sam Barefield, Director of the Wesley Foundation at Mississippi Southern College, reported in a national Methodist youth publication that Bishop Franklin had "wondered out loud whether or not the ladies had to take such a stand *just now*."[45]

However, ministers in the conference knew better than to speak against the tide. Any doubts regarding the wisdom of this caution ceased after another 1955 race relations controversy. Roy Delamotte, a Moss Point native, Millsaps graduate, and close friend of future Born of Conviction signer James Conner, had completed a PhD in comparative religion at Yale and returned to Mississippi to take a pastoral appointment that year. He had been gone for more than a decade and intended to keep silent on the race issue for at least a year in order to establish relationships with church people. However, at the June 1955 annual conference session, he grew increasingly disillusioned with the group's intention "to just ignore the whole segregation problem ... what is perhaps the sternest moral challenge the Southern churches have faced in their entire history." Ministers he had known in school seemed resigned to this, even though segregation in the denomination disturbed them. Delamotte found it inexcusable that clergy and laity of the conference remained silent about the injustices suffered by blacks in Mississippi, and he said, "I felt that someone *must* speak."[46]

When a resolution to the 1956 General Conference that called for continuation of the present segregated jurisdictional system came up for action on the conference floor, Delamotte asked for a protest vote against it. A debate ensued, and only a couple of people voted with him. Then Henry Bullock, a Mississippian serving as Editor of Church School Publications for the denomination, proposed a resolution "confessing our sense of guilt in the area of race." Moderate clergy leaders Brunner Hunt and W. B. Selah, both elected as General Conference delegates that year, spoke against Delamotte's and Bullock's motions. Hunt claimed the resolution protested by Delamotte did not refer to race and "pertained only to the jurisdictional system," and Selah argued, "Bullock's resolution sounds beautiful. It means nothing. When all this tumult is over we've still got to give the Negro and every other man equality and fairness." Bullock's motion also failed to pass, with the vote about two to one against.[47]

Then the lay delegate from the church where Delamotte was slated to serve informed the district superintendent they would not accept their new pastor. That night, after extensive cabinet deliberations, the superintendent informed Delamotte that no church in the conference would take him. A few days later, he transferred to the Holston Conference. His sin was twofold: he had questioned the status quo on race relations and challenged the conference leadership. As another conference minister remembered it decades later, Delamotte "spoke his voice on the Conference floor, and you weren't supposed to do that." To Delamotte, "an annual conference is a dramatic public focusing of the highest thought and deepest conscience of Methodism." The church's purpose includes speaking out against social and systemic injustice, even when such prophetic proclamation challenges the prevalent societal ethic.[48]

The controversy made front-page news in the Jackson papers, and conference leaders viewed it as an embarrassment. Delamotte had betrayed his brothers in the "minister's church" and had harmed the conference's image in Mississippi society. To them the church functioned primarily as a preserver of tradition and a proclaimer of individual salvation. Earlier that year, future Born of Conviction signer Elton Brown, serving at Chunky in the Meridian District, participated in meetings of the opposition group intent on electing the General Conference delegate slate opposed to the Leggett faction. When Willard Leggett, then the Meridian district superintendent, learned he had attended, Leggett reportedly said, "Elton Brown better not have been at that meeting!" Leggett came to Brown's church for the Quarterly Conference and preached a sermon entitled "The Weevil in the Boll," which told of a Delta farmer who planted cotton, certain he would reap a wonderful harvest, but boll weevils attacked and destroyed the crop. Brown heard it as a warning to him: if you go against the accepted culture of the conference and challenge the acknowledged clergy leader, you threaten the highly prized unity of that body and jeopardize its evangelistic and institutional harvest.[49]

To Delamotte, race relations and the injustice inherent in the segregated, white supremacist system represented a moral crisis that must be addressed directly by the church. Yet white Mississippi Conference Methodists denied this urgency and failed to address the systemic evil, even in the face of vicious violence and murder in the state, such as the August 1955 killing of Emmett Till and the sham trial acquitting his executioners. In the 1950s, temperance and the evils of alcohol received much more official attention from the conference than race relations, both in print and through the use of resources. The *Advocate* regularly ran antialcohol cartoons or articles, reflecting a traditional denominational emphasis, but by the 1950s the national Methodist Church had begun to focus more on race relations, labor relations, and peace/world order. Temperance and alcohol education were deemed important enough by the Mississippi Conference to appoint a full-time executive secretary of the Mississippi Church Council on Alcohol Education; future Born of Conviction signer James Conner held the post from 1954 to 1961.[50]

The conference wanted to protect its standing in white Mississippi, but it took little to upset the state's guardians of racial purity. In 1956, the new *Advocate* editor, moderate North Mississippi Conference minister Sam Ashmore, sought to inject some common sense into the massive resistance hysteria by saying, "The problem of integration is small compared with what might happen if we in the south fail to maintain a free public school system. To deny public schooling to the poor and under-privileged at a time when Russia is outstripping us in the race for trained minds seems downright stupid, to say nothing of being un-Christian and undemocratic." He added, "We must question the wisdom of men who preach Hitler's doctrine of racial superiority. We have no right to deny people the right of full citizenship nor stand in the way of their democratic rights." In response, *Jackson Daily News* editor Frederick Sullens attacked Ashmore as "among those spineless and unthinking members of the clergy who think segregation is 'in violation of the Christian spirit'" and asserted that "in the South we do preach the doctrine of racial superiority and intend to keep on doing so. Any white man who does not feel he belongs to a superior race does not deserve to be called a white man." He also sounded the segregationist apocalyptic note: "You are either for us or you are against us. There is no middle ground, no place for neutrals, and certainly no place for persons who advocate abject surrender."[51]

Moderates in the Mississippi Conference subscribed to a gradualist view of race, and thus they supported the passage of Amendment IX to the Constitution of The Methodist Church. Approved by the 1956 General Conference and then ratified by annual conferences the following year, the amendment created a procedure for a Central Jurisdiction Conference to join its appropriate geographic jurisdiction if all bodies involved approved. Although this made desegregation possible, Southeastern Jurisdiction Conferences soon embraced it because of its voluntaristic regional option feature, which meant integration with black conferences would not be forced on them. The Mississippi Conference overwhelmingly approved Amendment IX in 1957. The *Jackson Daily News* headlined the story "State Methodist Group Opens Its Doors to Negro Churches," and a few lay delegates opposed approval. Brunner Hunt supported Methodist connectionalism when he told the conference, "The Methodist Church is not a provincial church. We belong to a worldwide church, and men of reason cannot listen to extremists on either side." However, he also assured them, "The Southern tradition of local self-government is written in the constitution when this amendment is approved."[52]

The Mississippi Conference Committee on Social and Economic Relations cautioned in its 1959 report that the problem of race relations "must be settled by each section of the country to its own satisfaction, and each section should have that privilege." If the majority of all races in a region desire integration, then so be it, but "where the majority of the members of all races desire separation of the races, they should be accorded the privilege of remaining separate, provided no race is discriminated against by being deprived of equal opportunities." The committee also expressed concern that Methodist church school literature and youth publications presented a one-sided, prointegration view.[53]

Any hopes for slow, voluntary, gradual progress toward better race relations entertained by conference moderates were dashed by two opposing events. The Citizens' Council helped elect Ross Barnett governor in late 1959, and the group gained even more power, thanks in part to state funds from the State Sovereignty Commission, established by the legislature in 1956 to ensure that the segregated system would remain intact. The commission sponsored elaborate spying and vigilance against any chinks in the white supremacist system's armor, and thus Mississippi partially resembled a totalitarian police state. On the other side, the civil rights movement in Mississippi picked up a new head of steam in the early 1960s and fervently opposed gradualism, because "justice too long delayed is justice denied."[54]

The biggest race relations controversy the Mississippi Conference faced prior to Born of Conviction came in early 1960 with the introduction of the state legislature's Church Property Bill. Should the denomination change its social policy or attempt to integrate its churches, the measure allowed a local congregation to withdraw from its parent church and maintain ownership of its property. The primary target of the bill was the Methodist Church, because its historic trust clause stipulated that if a congregation chose to leave the denomination, its property reverted to the annual conference. The bill's sponsors believed white Mississippi Methodists would put their allegiance to the state and segregation ahead of their ties to Methodist law, support creation of a legal weapon to trump the trust clause, and thus resist the liberalizing, integrating tendencies of the General Church.[55]

However, although a few North Mississippi congregations, mostly in the Delta, and one Mississippi Conference church, Raymond, proclaimed their support for the bill, several Mississippi Methodist groups on conference and district levels registered public opposition to it. A number of local churches also publicly expressed their disagreement, including Wesson, Mendenhall, and Biloxi's Leggett Memorial, led at the time by future Born of Conviction signers Rod Entrekin, James Holston, and Inman Moore Jr. Various pieces in the *Mississippi Methodist Advocate* opposed the bill, including the text of a February 7 sermon by Roy Clark, pastor of Jackson's Capitol Street Church.[56]

Most notably, this was one of the rare occasions in his sixteen years as bishop in Mississippi that Marvin Franklin responded directly, publicly, and with all the force of his appropriate authority to a controversial issue, because of the threat to the institutional church. In a front page *Advocate* column on February 3, Franklin called the bill **"a dangerous proposal"** that would **"promote disunity and division at a time when all Mississippians should stand united to build a greater state."** He claimed the bill "on the surface . . . may appeal to some but it has within it the seed of death" because it would result in state control of the church. Franklin's opposition brought attacks, including a letter in the *Clarion-Ledger* that particularly bothered him: "Bishop Franklin is so confused in the teachings of God's Holy Word that he has chosen the teachings of Communism instead of sticking to the Word of God."[57]

At a February 29 public hearing on the bill, Baptist, Catholic, Episcopalian, and Methodist voices opposed it, including W. B. Selah, who argued that if integration ever came to a local Methodist church, it would only be by the will of the congregation. He claimed, "No bishop will ever appoint a Negro pastor to a white church in Mississippi. It could not happen." Among the legislators who spoke against the bill were Methodists Joe Wroten, son of a North Mississippi Conference preacher, and Stone Barefield, brother of Mississippi Southern Wesley Foundation Director Sam Barefield. One Methodist layman spoke in support of the bill. Stanny Sanders of Greenwood told the joint committee that "if Mississippi churches are willing to accept integration, you don't need this bill, but, if they are not, then the act is a necessity." Sanders asserted, "You cannot expect [state Methodist leaders] to oppose integration when their own church and literature teach that segregation is un-Christian."[58]

After the legislation passed and Governor Barnett signed it, Sanders chided the *Advocate*'s Sam Ashmore for the paper's fervent opposition to the legislation, and he sought Ashmore's views on the General Church's pronouncements on race. In a private letter to Sanders, Ashmore replied, "The Methodist Church does not believe in *forced* integration any more than it believes in *forced* segregation." He added, "The church is opposed to discrimination against any human being, and with that we go along."[59]

MAMML fully supported the Church Property Bill. John C. Satterfield, past president of the American Bar Association, prominent Mississippi Conference layman from Yazoo City, advisor to Governor Ross Barnett, and charter member of MAMML, wrote a conciliatory statement published in the *Advocate* after the bill's passage. He called Mississippi Methodists to "join hands to support our great church and the cause of Christ," because conference leaders and members "stand solidly for the Southern way of life which has permitted Methodists of both races to work for the best interests of the church for many years in their own conferences, organizations and churches." He closed with these words:

> I feel that all we lack is an understanding of the facts by our brethren in other areas of the country and a realization by them that the maintenance of the integrity of the two great races in our churches, our schools and our homes is not only consistent with the principles of Jesus Christ but also permits the rendition of service within each race to a far greater degree than would integration.[60]

Satterfield, MAMML members, and many other white Mississippi Methodists believed the increasingly bold pronouncements on race relations by Methodists on the national level were simply wrong, and that all sensible Mississippi Methodists agreed. In an attempt to explain why so many Mississippi Methodist ministers opposed the Church Property Bill, a *Clarion-Ledger* columnist reported, "Some said ... that the many preachers and near preachers who offered evidence against the bill obviously spoke as they were directed by the rules of the higherups." Surely, the reasoning went, if these ministers were allowed to think and speak for themselves, they would agree fully with Satterfield's vision.[61]

By early 1960, Bufkin Oliver, James Conner, James Holston, and N. A. Dickson had all spent more than a decade as full-time pastors in the Mississippi Conference. Conner married Betty Langdon in 1949, and the four ministers' families had fifteen children among them. Thirteen of the other future Born of Conviction signers served as full-time pastors in the conference by then—four of them in their first year out of seminary. Seven others still attended seminary at that point, while three were finishing college and serving churches as student pastors, and one worked as a Boy Scout executive in Texas. Although the vast majority of white Mississippi Methodists either agreed with John Satterfield's perspective on the church and race or struggled with the issue in ambivalent silence, nonetheless the formative experiences of the eventual Twenty-Eight led them to think and speak for themselves and offer an alternative to maintenance of "racial integrity" in Mississippi.

2

The Road to Born of Conviction: Sources of Dissent

THE GUARDIANS OF racial integrity in post-*Brown* Mississippi saw control of not only public speech but also *thought* as crucial for the survival of the Closed Society. In 1964, James Silver said that people in Mississippi "no longer [have] freedom of choice in the realm of ideas because [their] ideas must first be harmonized with the orthodoxy." Segregation and its maintenance trumped other concerns. Joseph Wroten, Methodist layman and one of the few state legislators willing to vote against massive resistance legislation, lamented in the early 1960s that "Mississippi is going down the road to thought control." The Mississippi State Sovereignty Commission relished its role as "thought control watchdog." Whites found it exceedingly difficult to speak out publicly against the status quo.[1]

Yet even in the most repressive societies, the ability to think for oneself is still possible. The seeds for the public dissent expressed in Born of Conviction and the rising generation's new vision of the church took root years earlier in the signers' experiences in their families, churches, college and seminary education, and work as Mississippi Conference pastors. Four young ministers in the Mississippi Conference—Jerry Furr, Maxie Dunnam, Jerry Trigg, and Jim Waits—conceived the idea of a public statement in response to the massive resistance activities by white Mississippians that culminated in the Ole Miss riot. All four were born in the 1930s and came of age in a Mississippi that took segregation and the inequality of the races—both *de jure* and *de facto*—for granted. A Presbyterian clergy contemporary, William McAtee, who grew up in Brookhaven, put it this way: "In high school, my experience with race was one of benign denial shrouded in a cloak of silence." And yet, each of the four who wrote the Born of Conviction statement in the fall of 1962, along with others who signed it with them, became aware of the injustice of Jim Crow Mississippi as they grew up and had begun to desire change in both church and society.[2]

Family and Church

Maxie Dunnam, the youngest of five children, was born in Neshoba County in 1934; the family soon moved one hundred miles south to settle near Richton. Dunnam's parents had little education and struggled during the Depression to make ends meet. His father labored in the timber industry until World War II, when he became a welder in the Mobile and Pascagoula shipyards. As a young child, Dunnam learned human relations by observing his father. Murdock "Mutt" Dunnam worked with a black man named Rube Whitney. The two men depended on each other: the more productive their work, the better for both their families. An unspoken but clear expectation existed in the Dunnam family: they would treat Whitney with respect.[3]

The family did not attend church regularly in Dunnam's early years. When he professed faith in Christ just before his thirteenth birthday at the small country Baptist church near their home east of town, his father joined him, and both were baptized by immersion. During his high school years, Maxie Dunnam participated in youth activities at the Methodist Church in Richton, and the pastor, David McKeithen, often loaned him books. McKeithen and his wife Margaret opened their parsonage home to Dunnam and his friends and became increasingly important to him. He joined the Richton Methodist Church and soon spoke with McKeithen about his sense of calling to the ordained ministry. Two things drew him to Methodism—open communion, where anyone was welcome to participate (his Baptist church had a members-only closed communion), and an educated clergy. Dunnam appreciated McKeithen's intellectual and theological depth, and he met other well-educated Methodist ministers at Hattiesburg District youth meetings.[4]

The birth of Oscar Gerald Trigg came in 1934 in rural Clarke County, Mississippi. His father came from a well-to-do farming family in adjoining Wayne County. When Jerry Trigg turned seven, the family moved to the Clarke County seat of Quitman. In high school, Trigg served as captain of the football team, vice president of the student body, and president of the band. His mother, a schoolteacher, went to work for the Clarke

County Department of Public Welfare when they moved to Quitman and became director, a position she held for more than twenty years. Trigg's father worked as a traveling salesman and eventually represented a national insurance company. In his high school and college years, Jerry Trigg argued with his father about the use of courtesy titles for blacks. The elder Trigg took the accepted view that one did not address black men and women as "Mr." and "Mrs.," but the son disagreed. Trigg often accompanied his mother on home visits for her Welfare Department casework, and he noticed that she treated black and white families with the same respect.[5]

The family attended Quitman Methodist Church, and in Jerry Trigg's teen years, the pastor was Bill McLelland, an energetic man whose charismatic leadership attracted many of the town's teens. McLelland's people skills and intellectual depth impressed Trigg the most. For example, at the start of each day, McLelland read Greek and Hebrew. Though he had excelled as a seminary student at Drew University and his professors strongly encouraged him to stay in academics, he dedicated his life to the local pastorate in the Mississippi Conference.[6]

Jerry Trigg became involved in church youth events beyond Quitman and served as an officer of the Meridian District and conference-wide youth organizations. These leadership activities, along with powerful experiences at his home church, including a service led by guest minister Lavelle Woodrick, led Trigg to commit himself to the ordained ministry.[7]

Jim Waits, born in 1935 in Ellisville, took his place as the youngest of three sons. His father worked for the Masonite Corporation in Laurel but soon moved the family to Hattiesburg and took a job as a salesman for a wholesale hardware company. Jim Waits's parents had typical white Southern views about race and religion, yet they encouraged him to develop an open mind and did not restrict his activities as severely as most middle-class white parents in 1940s and 1950s Mississippi.[8]

The Waits family joined Main Street Methodist Church in downtown Hattiesburg, and Waits remembers the Sunday School teachers as "consistently non-ideological and broadly inclusive." In his teen years the church's youth activities and the examples of two of the church's ministers—senior pastor John W. Moore and associate A. Eugene Dyess—strongly shaped his convictions and sense of vocation. In 1953 during his junior year in high school, the black Central Jurisdiction St. Paul Methodist Church, situated five blocks north of Main Street Church, sponsored a youth activities week and invited the youth from Main Street. Due to encouragement by Gene Dyess, Waits and some other Main Street young people attended the event.[9]

At St. Paul on that Saturday night, the black preacher leading the service invited anyone who felt called to full-time Christian service to come to the altar. Jim Waits had seriously considered a vocation to ordained ministry and decided the time had come to make it public, so he responded. Word of his declaration spread quickly through Main Street Church the next day. Waits was the first member of the congregation to pursue ordination since future Born of Conviction signer James Conner more than a decade earlier, and the church celebrated the news. However, some vocal members grumbled that Waits had done so at a black church and that Gene Dyess had encouraged church youth to go to the event. As Waits remembers it, Moore supported Dyess's action at a church board meeting, and in response to continued complaints of Waits's declaration at St. Paul, Moore retorted, "Now, brethren, it appears to me if that had happened in Hell it would have been good news!"[10]

Born in 1930, Jerry Furr spent his childhood in the Battlefield Park neighborhood, a mile southwest of downtown Jackson. His father was a plumber, and his mother worked at an overall factory. With his mother and older brother, Furr occasionally attended Grace Methodist Church on their block, but they were not active members. As a child, Jerry Furr occasionally walked the railroad tracks with a black friend, but when they arrived at the Buck Theater on West Capitol Street, Furr could sit on the main floor to watch the movie, while his friend had to go to the balcony. The young Furr also frequented the Boys Club in South Jackson, and one of the staff members there hinted at the need for changes in race relations.[11]

In 1942 the family moved to Pascagoula, where Furr's father worked as a plumber and pipefitter at the Ingalls Shipyard. Thanks to vastly increased production to support the war effort, Pascagoula became a boomtown, and Furr found it an exciting place to be. He learned to play pool from his father; the protégé gambled, often won, and became known as a pool shark. At Pascagoula High, he courted Marlene Byrd, a couple of years his junior. Her father, a juvenile officer, knew Furr by reputation and tried at first to discourage the relationship.[12]

After graduation from high school in 1947, Furr went to Mississippi Southern College in Hattiesburg, in spite of his father's advice to get a job as a plumber or another trade because he had already been to school too long. Because Marlene Byrd remained in high school, Furr came home to visit on weekends and attended church with her at Pascagoula First Methodist. The minister was Harland Hilbun, a fire and brimstone preacher and dynamic pastor who actively recruited young men for the Methodist ministry. Furr envisioned a career with the YMCA or Boys Club, but Hilbun pushed him toward the ministry. When Furr and Marlene Byrd married in 1950, he served as student pastor on the East Columbia charge at a salary of $1,400 a year.[13]

All the Born of Conviction signers were nurtured in Mississippi Conference churches and received inspiration and guidance from pastors and laypeople in their congregations and the conference. James Nicholson credited Methodist layman and educator R. Lanier Hunt, brother of conference moderate pastor Brunner Hunt, as the source of his awakening in race relations. In 1941 Hunt spoke at Copiah-Lincoln Junior College where Nicholson attended high school and invited the students to imagine what it would be like if they were Negroes. What would they not be able to do that they took for granted in their lives? This gentle prodding pricked the conscience of seventeen-year-old preacher's kid Nicholson, and for the rest of his life he saw Hunt as a hero.[14]

As he came of age in Jackson, Powell S. Hall Jr. read constantly and developed a reputation as a brain. Hall's Capitol Street Methodist Church friends nicknamed him Bunky after a 1930s comic strip character known for his astounding vocabulary. Hall especially loved stories of Christian martyrs and Hebrew prophets. As a teen in the 1940s, he read a book by E. Stanley Jones that discussed the story of Peter and Cornelius in Acts 10 and Peter's proclamation, "I truly understand that God shows no partiality, but in every nation anyone who fears him and does what is right is acceptable to him." A light went on for Bunky Hall; he became convinced that the Mississippi system of segregation and white supremacy was basically unchristian.[15]

Rod Entrekin grew up in Meridian's Central Methodist Church, where he joined at age ten and made a commitment to the ordained ministry during the summer after he graduated from high school in 1945. To earn money for college, he worked at a laundry for the next year. In the summer of 1946, he went on a youth trip to Lake Junaluska Assembly, a Methodist retreat center in Western North Carolina, and attended a class on Christian brotherhood. Upon his return home, Entrekin spoke at Central's Wednesday evening prayer meeting. He shared some ideas from the class and discussed both the global need for people to work for peace and the local need to "work for 'brotherhood' among all people." A few weeks later, Entrekin learned from the church's education director that a church member had directed the pastor to tell him never to make such remarks again. The pastor, W. A. Tyson, did not mention it to Entrekin.[16]

During the initial furor over the *Brown* decision, at age seventeen James Rush felt called to the ministry, primarily due to his sense of the injustice of race relations in Mississippi. His father had a job helping farmers secure federal loan assistance. In addition to the elder Rush's regular office hours, borrowers of both races often came to the Rush home near the town of Lake on Saturdays. The family received any visitors in their living room, regardless of race, and Mr. and Mrs. Rush taught their sons not to address blacks by their first names, as was the custom, but with courtesy titles as they would white adults. James Rush grew up in Lake Methodist Church and came to believe that the Christian faith had something to say in response to racial injustice.[17]

Mississippi Southern College, Methodist Student Movement, and Millsaps College

In 1951 Maxie Dunnam became the first member of his family to go to college. He attended Mississippi Southern, a state school in Hattiesburg, and eventually served as a student pastor on the McLain Charge in Perry County. At Southern, Sam Barefield (Figure 2.1), an open-minded and socially aware Methodist clergyman, directed the Wesley Foundation, the campus ministry organization for Methodists. The combination of programs that pushed students to raise questions about the segregated Mississippi culture and occasional trips to national student conferences opened Dunnam to the world beyond white Mississippi. Ten of the eventual Born of Conviction signers graduated from Mississippi Southern, and several viewed Barefield as an important mentor.[18]

Their number included Ed McRae, another of Harland Hilbun's ministerial recruits from Pascagoula First Methodist. McRae went to Southern in 1951 because Hilbun insisted there was no true religion at Millsaps College, the Methodist school in Jackson. Barefield's influence drew McRae toward more liberal views. McRae met Millsaps philosophy major Martina Riley at a summer Methodist student conference at Lake Junaluska, North Carolina. She became state president of the Methodist Student Movement (MSM), an organization of Methodist college students in which he participated as well. Attendance at MSM meetings outside the

FIGURE 2.1 Sam Barefield in the 1950s. Courtesy of Beth, Steven, and Irl Barefield.

state exposed them to several nationally renowned theologians; one event involved students from eighty nations and included debates on apartheid in South Africa and segregation in the U.S. South.[19]

The Mississippi MSM worked unsuccessfully against passage of the December 1954 state constitutional amendment to allow closure of public schools should integration be forced upon them. The group also adopted a constitution in 1954 that recognized all Mississippi Methodist students, regardless of race, as members of the organization. They sought to hold an interracial Mississippi MSM meeting, but could not find a location. The next year at Lake Junaluska, the MSM groups representing annual conferences throughout the South passed a resolution, introduced by Mississippian Paul Cotten (another of Barefield's students), that called for the abolition of the Central Jurisdiction, the separate Methodist Church structure for black churches. Ed McRae and Martina Riley participated in these MSM actions and attended integrated MSM meetings at Lake Junaluska with some Central Jurisdiction college students. Blacks were not allowed to swim in the Junaluska pool, however, and the group held long intense debates on whether they would return to Lake Junaluska for future meetings. Ultimately they sent resolutions to the Junaluska Board of Trustees and boycotted the pool.[20]

Although Jerry Furr also attended Southern, his full awakening came elsewhere. In June 1951, he moved to the Puckett-Johns charge in Rankin County with a parsonage nicer than any house in which he had ever lived. Furr did not return to Southern that fall, because he and his wife now lived seventy miles from Hattiesburg. For a while he focused solely on his pastoral work, but that changed when Marion Smith, a Mississippi Conference minister serving his final year as president of Millsaps College, paid him a visit at Puckett. Furr remembers that Smith said, "You think Puckett is the center of the universe, but it's not. Let's get you up to Millsaps to finish your degree." Southern had opened a new window for Furr, and Millsaps furthered that process.[21]

Millsaps College, founded in Jackson by the Mississippi and North Mississippi Conferences of the MECS in 1890, became a common destination for young white Mississippi men preparing for the Methodist ministry. It also developed a climate allowing students to consider the injustices of the rigid line between the races. As early as 1935, four Millsaps students visited the campus of Tougaloo College, an African American school on the northern edge of Jackson, for a YMCA meeting. McComb native and World War II veteran George Maddox enrolled at Millsaps in 1946 and found a small group of professors, such as Marguerite Goodman (English), Vernon Wharton (History and Sociology), and James Ferguson (History), who sought through their classes or extracurricular activities to offer ideas different from the segregated life and white supremacist views of Mississippi.[22]

Also in 1946, Rod Entrekin, one of sixteen of the Twenty-Eight who graduated from Millsaps, enrolled as a preministerial student there. He joined the interracial Intercollegiate Council, started in the 1930s by Tougaloo Chaplain William A. Bender, Millsaps professor Henry Bullock, and others. About fifteen Millsaps students attended meetings at African American schools in the area such as Tougaloo, Jackson College, Campbell College, Christian Missionary Institute at Edwards, and Alcorn A & M. During Entrekin's tenure as council chair in his junior and senior years, Bender still provided the main leadership for the organization. The group had always met on the campuses of the black schools until 1949, when Entrekin got permission from President Marion Smith to host a meeting at Millsaps. The event caused no controversy. On another occasion, Entrekin presided over a Methodist student meeting at Millsaps at which a field director from Rust College, a black Methodist school in Holly Springs, Mississippi, addressed the group. After the guest left, two students challenged Entrekin because he had addressed the black man as "Mister," but others present silenced the critics.[23]

The more open environment at Millsaps made a huge impact on all the signers who attended there, including Jerry Furr, who only stayed a semester or two in 1951–2 and then finished at Southern, and Wilton Carter, who was there for the 1956–7 academic year. Carter's Millsaps experience caused much theological reflection and a new direction in his spiritual journey. He had come from a conservative background in rural Jackson County on the Gulf Coast, and his courses in philosophy and religion disturbed him, especially those taught by N. Bond Fleming, a philosopher and Methodist minister from Georgia who had earned a PhD at Boston University. At first Carter prayed for Fleming, convinced the professor was wrong to push students toward critical thought about life, ideas, and faith, but eventually Carter decided that much of his own conservative theology did not connect with real life.[24]

Jerry Trigg and Jim Waits both attended Millsaps and became friends. Trigg was a junior when Waits arrived as a freshman in the fall of 1954. Like Trigg, Waits had served as an officer of the Mississippi Conference Methodist Youth Fellowship. During his college years he became vice president of the National Methodist Youth Conference and experienced with gratitude that group's racial inclusiveness. At one national youth conference outside the South, Waits roomed with a black student, and he met Andrew Young at another national event.[25]

Along with his national Methodist youth activities, Waits found time to be involved in student government and served as president of the Millsaps Student Senate in his senior year, 1957–8. At the formal opening of the new Student Union building in the fall of 1957, in a speech on "What Millsaps Means to the Student," he said he and his fellow students were exposed to new ideas and dared to think for themselves. Millsaps meant "freedom ... a reality demanding certain responsibility" and "seeking truth—the truth that sets men free."[26]

In the wake of Mississippi massive resistance after the *Brown* decision, that sense of freedom came under attack during a controversy at Millsaps in March 1958 over two sessions of an "Interdenominational Discussion Groups" event. Planned by the Millsaps Christian Council, the program included six separate discussion series on a range of topics scheduled for four consecutive Mondays during the month. On Monday, March 3, Dr. Ernst Borinski, a German immigrant and sociologist at Tougaloo, spoke on "The Christian and Race Relations." The audience of sixteen included John Wright, who reported with alarm that Borinski "made bold advocacy of racial integration" and said "racial segregation violates Christian premises." Borinski's critic's father was Ellis Wright, a member of Galloway Methodist Church and president of the Jackson Citizens' Council, the group central to the fight against race relations change in Mississippi.[27]

That same week, George Maddox, now a Millsaps sociology professor, moderated a discussion of race relations at a Social Science Forum, an interracial event at Tougaloo put on periodically by Borinski. Thirty Millsaps students attended, and a news story quoted one who said there were "no basic differences" between the races, while another noted that Millsaps "probably has more in common with Tougaloo than the other white colleges of the state." A Tougaloo student added, "I thought the average Mississippian was impregnable, that you couldn't get an idea through to him. At least, I found out that we can communicate."[28]

Jim Waits, one of five future Born of Conviction signers at Millsaps then, published an article on the controversy in *Concern*, a national Methodist magazine. The students learned how fervently the guardians of the Closed Society desired that every institution and individual adhere to the true faith. The impending March 10 appearance of Glenn E. Smiley, Methodist minister and national field secretary for the Fellowship of Reconciliation, at the discussion series added to the furor; the press called him a "second integrationist." Millsaps canceled Smiley's appearance; President H. Ellis Finger blamed it on misleading press coverage.[29]

The Citizens' Council's Ellis Wright expressed shock at these events and publicly asked Finger to clarify the college's position on segregation. He reminded Finger that the council and "patriotic public officials are engaged in a life and death struggle for our very existence against an enemy with whom there is no compromise. It is intolerable for Millsaps College . . . to be in the apparent position of undermining everything we are fighting for."[30]

President Finger, a graduate of Millsaps and Yale Divinity School and a highly respected North Mississippi Conference minister, sought to minimize damage to the institution and still maintain its integrity. His public statement in response to the controversy epitomizes the Mississippi moderate perspective in the late 1950s. Finger called the invitations to Borinski and Smiley "exceedingly regrettable" and promised that his administration "will urge all committees inviting guest speakers to exercise care and caution in the selection of appropriate personnel." He also revealed that John Satterfield, a Millsaps alumnus and prominent Mississippi Conference layman, would present the segregationist view at another session of the race relations series.[31]

Finger (Figure 2.2) closed with four premises in direct response to Wright: the right of students to hear different points of view, the claim that Millsaps did not aim to indoctrinate its students, a reminder of the importance of freedom of speech, and finally,

> Every thoughtful person needs carefully to consider that if freedom is attacked at one college, it will eventually be attacked at all educational institutions. Moreover, every pulpit, every newspaper, every individual could be pressured. Differences of opinion are to be welcomed. The only alternative is dreaded thought control. Millsaps College joins with the entire Christian Church, of which it is an

FIGURE 2.2 Jim Waits, Lee Reiff (author's father, Millsaps Religion professor from 1960–4, 1965–92), Bishop Roy C. Clark (pastor of Jackson's Capitol Street Church, 1953–63), Bishop H. Ellis Finger (President of Millsaps, 1952–64), and George Maddox (Millsaps Sociology professor in late 1950s) in 2000. Courtesy of Lynn Clark.

integral part, in pledging to its constituents its devotion to preserving a climate where freedom may prosper and where intimidation, fear and bondage are doomed.

Two weeks later, the Millsaps Board of Trustees, chaired by Bishop Marvin A. Franklin, issued a statement of confidence in President Finger and the faculty, asserted the College's purpose "is not to tell people what to think but to teach them how to think," and added, "Neither segregation nor integration is an issue at Millsaps College. Segregation has always been, and is now, the policy of Millsaps College. There is no thought, purpose, or intention on the part of those in charge of its affairs to change this policy."[32]

These responses did not satisfy the Citizens' Council, which viewed Finger's argument for academic freedom as a "thick smoke screen." Wright wrote Finger demanding that he fire George Maddox (Figure 2.2); Finger refused. However, Maddox, concerned that his ongoing activities might harm the college and tired of the many threatening phone calls he had received, left for a postdoctoral fellowship at Duke in 1959.[33]

Jerry Trigg, finishing his second year at Vanderbilt Divinity School, wrote to Ellis Wright during the controversy: "The young people now receiving high school and college education had better be prepared to do a great deal more than quote pious platitudes and rattle off snappy phrases in favor of their 'way of life.'" The Millsaps Student Senate, led by Jim Waits (Figure 2.2), insisted that "the current issue before us is not race, but rather whether the subject of race—or any other subject—may be explored honestly and without bias." The ado fomented by the Citizens' Council and the college's response to it had challenged the students' "right to inquire into such matters and the right of others to furnish us with this information. . . . We regard this as a violation of our freedom of inquiry and expression."[34]

Finger's mail ran two to one in his support over the next few weeks. The positive responses congratulated him for putting the Citizens' Council in its place and echoed the academic freedom argument; the negative letters bemoaned the "alien ideas with which the students . . . are being indoctrinated" and promised never to support Millsaps again. Two writers—one a Mississippi Conference pastor, the other a retired Methodist deaconess—took Finger to task because he called the invitations to Borinski and Smiley "exceedingly regrettable." Clara Mae Sells, the deaconess, commented, "It is true that you are in a difficult position, but it is also true that the South needs firm and forward-looking Christian leadership."[35]

Seminary

All but one of the Born of Conviction signers went to seminary—nineteen to Emory's Candler School of Theology, two each to Southern Methodist University's (SMU) Perkins School of Theology, Vanderbilt, and Yale Divinity School, and one each to Drew and Duke—while 63 percent of all the ministers ordained elder in the conference from 1956 to 1963 received seminary training. The Conference Board of Ministerial Training and Qualifications actively encouraged seminary education by the 1950s, but a strong suspicion of such training still existed in the conference among many laity and some clergy leaders. When future signer Jack Troutman graduated from Mississippi Southern in 1956, he planned to attend Candler and thought he had a student appointment lined up in North Georgia. When it fell through, his district superintendent, Van Landrum, encouraged him to forego seminary; he could be ordained through the Course of Study route taken by most of Landrum's generation. If Troutman would stay at Stringer, where he had served while in college, Landrum promised to take care of him with a better appointment soon. When Wilton Carter graduated from Southern in 1959, he had served a student appointment in Covington County for two years. Members of his churches encouraged him to stay on and cautioned that seminary would ruin him.[36]

Troutman and Carter refused to give up on seminary education. A young businessman in Bay Springs, a town near Stringer, offered to pay Troutman's Emory tuition and a small monthly stipend. Troutman gratefully accepted the gift, moved his family to Atlanta, and worked part-time as a barber during his years at Candler. Carter, now married to Dolores Cumbest, stayed in Covington County an additional year but then also went to Candler in 1960. In January 1961, when Hamilton Holmes and Charlayne Hunter were admitted by court order as the first black students at the University of Georgia and white students rioted in protest, seminarian Carter watched news coverage on television. This experience opened his eyes to the reality and injustice of the segregation he had simply accepted as a youngster in Mississippi.[37]

When Jerry Furr finished his college degree at Mississippi Southern in 1953, his mentor Harland Hilbun worried that his time at Millsaps had been a bad influence and encouraged him to go to Asbury Seminary in Kentucky. Furr took the advice and spent one quarter there, but he found Asbury too theologically conservative. He transferred to Candler in January of 1954, and his world opened further. Maxie Dunnam arrived at Candler in 1955 and soon met Jerry Morris, whom he married in 1957. In Atlanta he connected with two mentors who continued what Sam Barefield had started. Claude Thompson, a Candler professor who belonged to the NAACP, and Dow Kirkpatrick, pastor of St. Mark's Methodist in Atlanta, both influenced Dunnam through public advocacy of equality and a new day in race relations.[38]

Upon graduation from Millsaps in 1956, Jerry Trigg had also planned to attend Candler until the dean at Vanderbilt Divinity School invited him to visit the Nashville campus. The last-minute recruiting worked; Trigg went to Vanderbilt and spent three years in the rich academic and ministerial environment. In 1957 he married Rose Cunningham, his college debate partner and daughter of W. J. Cunningham, a prominent North Mississippi Conference minister.[39]

At Millsaps College, future Born of Conviction signer Joe Way began to think more deeply about the race issue in Mississippi. Then in seminary at Vanderbilt in the late 1950s, he had black classmates and friends and closely observed the Nashville sit-in movement in early 1960. His fellow student James Lawson was expelled from the Divinity School in March as a result of his public statements encouraging students he had trained to continue their sit-ins in violation of the law. Over half the Divinity School faculty resigned when the university's chancellor, Harvie Branscomb, denied readmission to Lawson. Way did not participate in the sit-in campaign, but he graduated that spring convinced of the injustice of segregation.[40]

When Jim Waits graduated from Millsaps in 1958, he chose to attend Yale Divinity School, despite the concern expressed by his parents and some Mississippi ministers that he should go to a good southern school like Emory. Millsaps faculty mentors, along with Yale alumni President Finger and Roy C. Clark (Figure 2.2), pastor of Jackson's Capitol Street Methodist Church, supported his decision. During his years in New Haven, the teaching and writings of two professors, Christian ethicists H. Richard Niebuhr and James Gustafson, inspired him to formulate a clearer understanding of the Christian mandate to seek equality for all and to oppose the unjust system of white supremacy.[41]

Pastoral Experience

Born in 1937, future Born of Conviction signer Ned Kellar grew up in Picayune and became a Methodist in high school when he dated the daughter of the preacher at First Methodist Church. He attended Mississippi Southern in the late 1950s and found an important mentor in Denson Napier, Sam Barefield's successor at the Wesley Foundation and also an eventual member of the Twenty-Eight. Kellar served as a student pastor and met his future wife, Dorothy Dickinson, in one of his churches. Her minister brother, Buford Dickinson, also a member of the Twenty-Eight, co-officiated with Napier at their wedding. When he graduated, the Kellars moved to Atlanta for his seminary training at Candler. When he finished in 1962, his appointment to Sandersville keenly disappointed him. He had often driven through the town and had vowed to quit the ministry if appointed there. He knew how conservative the people of Jones County were, and he could not imagine why the conference would send him to that pastoral charge:

> Didn't the bishop know that I had been active in a group while at Emory that plotted and planned to do something positive about the race issue in Mississippi? Those evenings when I sat around with other students and talked about making a change in the state would be wasted if I was sent to Sandersville. I knew these people would never appreciate my ministry because I was one of those liberals on the race issue.

In spite of his misgivings, as a Methodist preacher, Kellar went where he was sent.[42]

The world of a theological seminary differs greatly from the world of the local parish. Some professors spoke of the need for racial justice, and fellowships formed among students who believed in and wanted to work for a new day in race relations. Though Candler would not enroll its first black student until 1965, Mississippi ministerial candidates who attended Duke, Perkins, Vanderbilt, and Yale had a few black classmates. New graduates returning to Mississippi in the years after the *Brown* decision crossed a distinct boundary from a world that hoped for a new day in race relations to the world of rigid segregation; severe political, economic, and social oppression; and increasing resistance to change. Even vague visions of race relations change had become increasingly forbidden.[43]

Some future Born of Conviction signers decided to apply the alternative views they had learned from their family, church, college, and seminary experiences in their pastoral appointments in the early 1960s, though they risked disapproval and even rejection from their congregations as civil rights activity in Mississippi increased. When Ed McRae graduated from Mississippi Southern in 1955, he went to seminary at Candler, and two years later he married Martina Riley when she graduated from Millsaps. After he finished Candler in 1958, they spent a year abroad at the University of Edinburgh. In 1959 the McRaes returned to Mississippi for his appointment to Hickory in Newton County. The new pastor knew enough not to be direct about his views on race relations, but he often preached about brotherhood. The McRaes became close friends with one couple and shared their real feelings about race with them. Their friends listened but also talked with others about the pastoral couple's views. This led to the congregation asking for McRae to move after a year.[44]

Powell Hall believed he was moved from an appointment because of his sermonic response to racist violence nearby. J. Horace Germany, a white Church of God minister with Mississippi roots, had founded Bay Ridge Christian College on his own land in southern Neshoba County for black students wishing to obtain a college education in preparation for ministry. In August 1960, a group of white residents, including Germany's cousin, launched an organized effort to close the college, which had six black male students and had started construction of a building. On August 26, a crowd of men ambushed Germany, beat him severely, and threatened him with more violence. Soon after, he moved the college to Texas.[45]

Several months after Germany's beating, Hall preached an antilynching sermon on his four-church charge at Lake; one of the churches was at Conehatta, twenty miles from the site of Germany's college. Hall could not believe the local authorities would tolerate such vicious behavior and finally decided to address it in a sermon. He said that when we put up with people doing something so terribly wrong it brings a judgment on us: "Whenever a group feels there is no truth but its truth, no order but its order, then they feel that an attack on [that truth] is an attack on God. This is unconscious idolatry." The sermon led some members to request that he move, and the district superintendent obliged them in 1962. Hall later believed he was right to make this stand but speculated he could have been less blunt in how he said it.[46]

On rare occasions, future signers spoke out against injustice and managed to avoid the punishment of a move. On April 24, 1960, a group of black men, women, and children led by Dr. Gilbert Mason attempted to use the whites-only beach in Biloxi. A white mob met and assaulted them with iron pipes, chains, and baseball bats while police officers watched. This brought a response from R. Inman Moore Jr. (Figure 2.3), pastor of Leggett Memorial Methodist Church right on the beach in Biloxi. Moore, who served as a pharmacist's mate in the Navy in the South Pacific during World War II and then returned to graduate from Millsaps College in 1947, had been out of seminary since 1949 and now served his third pastoral appointment. He had supported equal rights for blacks in his heart and had preached occasional sermons on brotherhood, but he did not take a stand on the issue until the violence on the beach near his church.[47]

The following Sunday, Moore's sermon condemned the beatings and explored the problem of race relations. He listed various injustices endured by blacks in Mississippi and called for a reasoned approach to the issue. He argued it was wrong to deny the vote to blacks and that the idea of white supremacy needed to be dispelled, among other reasons

FIGURE 2.3 Inman Moore in the pulpit at Leggett Memorial, early 1960s. Courtesy of Inman Moore.

because it was "the kind of stuff Hitler fed on." Rather than blame civil rights activity on Communism, Moore insisted that Christianity should be blamed, because Christians had told downtrodden peoples all over the world that " 'you are the sons and daughters of God.' " Such a claim means "God loves his black children just as much as he does his white children." He attacked the supposed biblical arguments for inequality and separation of the races and asked,

> Have I read the Bible wrong here? Someone says the Bible tells of the black man being cursed by God. No, it does not say that. It does say that Noah cursed his son Ham who is considered to be the father of the African Negro. But Noah's curse is vastly different from God's curse. Every day human beings curse other human beings. But not the God revealed by Jesus Christ. "I am come," Jesus said, "that all men might have life and that they might have it more abundantly."

Moore remained at the church another three years, but the chairman of the Official Board, a man Moore respected greatly, never spoke to him again after the sermon.[48]

The four creators of the Born of Conviction statement—Dunnam, Trigg, and Waits, and Furr—also faced the mounting tensions of early 1960s Mississippi as pastors. In 1958, Maxie and Jerry Dunnam moved to his first full-time church appointment, Gautier in Jackson County on the Mississippi Gulf Coast. A year later, he started a new congregation in Gulfport, soon known as Trinity Methodist. In Gulfport Dunnam (Figure 2.4) became friends with Henry C. Clay Jr., pastor of St. Mark's Methodist, a black congregation of the Central Jurisdiction Mississippi Conference. White and black Methodist pastors in most Mississippi communities normally had little contact with each other then, but both men readily crossed that line.[49]

In 1961, Clay's church hosted an event featuring some white missionaries to South Africa, and Dunnam and a few other whites attended. When the program ended, city police cars sat outside because word had leaked of an integrated meeting at the church. Dunnam went home, but at midnight Clay called to say the police chief insisted that Clay provide names of all the whites who had attended. Dunnam told Clay he could release his name. A few days later a city official cautioned Dunnam of the dangers of attending meetings with "Communists."[50]

FIGURE 2.4 Maxie Dunnam in early 1960s. Courtesy of Maxie and Jerry Dunnam.

When he graduated from Vanderbilt in 1959, Jerry and Rose Trigg moved to Caswell Springs Methodist Church in Jackson County on the Gulf Coast. He had not imagined himself in such a rural area, but the vibrant community responded to his energetic leadership. The church built a new sanctuary in 1960, and members tolerated Trigg's fairly bold approach to race relations issues. He posted a comparative photo essay on a bulletin board at the church that clearly showed the inferior facilities of the county's black schools; he labeled the display "Our County's Separate but Equal Schools." In 1961, Trigg issued a public statement charging that the segregationist MAMML regularly made "consistently cowardly attacks on almost everything Methodist . . . all under the cloak of anonymity" and asked MAMML to reveal the names of its members, especially any ministerial members. MAMML refused.[51]

Upon graduation from Yale in 1961, Jim Waits returned to Mississippi and employed his youth ministry experience as Conference Director of Youth Work for a year. Stationed in the Methodist Building in downtown Jackson across the street from the state capitol building, he had a front row seat from which to observe the ongoing Freedom Rides and the continuing development of the Jackson civil rights movement, led by Medgar Evers and Tougaloo students and some faculty. Just prior to his return from Connecticut, nine Tougaloo students entered the white Jackson Public Library, three blocks from the Methodist Building, on March 27 and refused to leave when asked, which resulted in their arrest by Jackson police. The library sit-in ignited the Mississippi movement; two weeks later, the NAACP launched "Operation Mississippi," an organized campaign to desegregate public facilities.[52]

In 1956 Jerry Furr graduated from seminary and took an appointment at the Seashore Methodist Campground on Biloxi Beach as the first pastor of a new church, Leggett Memorial, named for J. T. Leggett, uncle of the conference's clergy leader, Willard Leggett. When Furr arrived, Sunday services took place in an open air tabernacle; as instructed, he proceeded to tear it down and build a church. An Ocean Springs architect designed the sanctuary Furr wanted, an A-frame structure with an all-glass front looking out on the Mississippi Sound, and it opened in early 1958. Furr sought to create a different kind of church, and the proximity of Keesler Air Force Base aided him in the effort. Church members from the military meant more diversity in geographic background. In the three years he served there, the church grew to more than two hundred members. The Furrs became close friends with the Dunnams while in Biloxi, and when Furr left Leggett Memorial in June 1959, he remained in touch with Dunnam.[53]

Furr moved from Biloxi to Wesson, forty miles south of Jackson in Copiah County, but he only stayed a few months. Early in the fall of 1959, he received a phone call from Dr. William Bryan Selah, senior pastor at Galloway Memorial Methodist in downtown Jackson, the largest church in Mississippi Methodism. Selah wanted him to come to Galloway as his associate pastor. Furr thanked Selah but expressed skepticism, because he had just moved to Wesson. He remembers that Selah, a close friend of Bishop Franklin, replied, "Oh, I'll have Marvin take care of that." The bishop, whose office was across a narrow parking lot from Selah's, took care of it, and the Furrs moved to Jackson in October 1959.[54]

Furr found Selah to be an inspiring pastoral mentor who delegated significant responsibility to his associate, and Furr viewed the senior pastor as smart, aware, and liberal. On occasion, Selah invited Furr to join him for an afternoon of fishing, and they took off for Galloway member C. R.

Ridgway's cabin near Star, twenty miles southeast of Jackson. As Selah stood on the small pier, he smoked Roi-Tan cigars and expertly fished for bass. All the while he talked to Furr about changes he wanted to see in Mississippi—changes that would have to come slowly, pushed a little at a time. In Furr's view, Selah "walked a delicate, fine line in a very troubled time."[55]

In the spring of 1961, the bus trips of the Freedom Riders through the Deep South made national headlines. The state of Mississippi struck a deal with the Kennedy administration: the Freedom Riders would not be subjected to the violence they had experienced in Alabama, but when they arrived in Jackson, they would be arrested. On June 12, 1961, Galloway's Official Board discussed how the church should respond if any Freedom Riders sought to attend its worship services. Hugh Smith introduced the following resolution: "that the greeters or ushers of the church are hereby instructed to decline to admit any person or persons, white or colored, who, in the judgment of the greeters or ushers, seek admission for the purpose of creating an incident, resulting in a breach of the peace."[56]

Selah spoke against the proposal and urged the board to plan to seat such visitors and treat them as they would treat any other church visitor. He read them a proposed "Statement to the Freedom Riders" to use in worship if and when such groups came to Galloway. If ushers seated Freedom Riders, then Selah could tell them, "If you came to embarrass us by flouting an old custom, you have not succeeded. If you hoped to be turned away so that you could use the incident for propaganda purposes, you have failed." Selah's proposed statement continued,

> It is not sinful for white people to prefer to worship with white people or for colored people to prefer to worship with colored people. The sin comes when a church seeks to put up a color bar before the Cross of Christ. As Christians we cannot say to anybody, "You cannot come into the house of God." To discriminate against a man because of the color of his skin is contrary to the will of God.

He concluded his argument to the board with the claim that no body in the Methodist Church, from the General Conference down to the Official Board of the local church, "can put up a color bar in the church. That matter is determined by the nature of Christianity. The house of God is a place of prayer for all people—black and white." Galloway members almost universally loved and respected Selah, but his strong statement opposing the closed door resolution failed to prevent its passage. Four board members, including John R. Wright of the Citizens' Council, spoke in favor of the resolution, while only Robert Ezelle spoke against, and it passed by a vote of 102 to 31, with seventeen abstentions.[57]

The rabid insistence on maintenance of segregation at all costs in Mississippi effectively stymied public response by most whites in the years after *Brown*. It took the absurd machinations of the white power structure in 1962 to push some whites finally to speak out against the madness and offer mild support to the state's civil rights movement.

3

Mississippi 1962

THE TIGHT CONTROL of race relations by the white power structure in Mississippi began to fall apart in 1962. James Meredith's successful entry into Ole Miss provides the most obvious evidence for this claim, and the desperate attempt to prevent his admission, both by state officials and the mob that gathered on the campus, shocked the world and moderate white Mississippians. The dominant white response in the state to the Ole Miss riot focused the blame on outsiders—the Kennedys, the federal government, the marshals on the campus—as well as Meredith. However, after years of virtual silence, a few white moderates and liberals in the church finally spoke to counter the madness of massive resistance. To the disappointment of some white Mississippi Conference ministers, most of this response came from the northern part of the state, not from any Methodist leaders in their conference.

That frustrating silence can be blamed on a number of factors, including the continuing fear of those leaders to rock the boat and thus focus part of the segregationist hostility on Mississippi Methodism, along with the segregationist views of a large number of white Methodists in the state. A less obvious yet also important factor was the political control of the conference by Willard Leggett. The developing black freedom struggle on the state and local community levels together with the political drama on the white Mississippi Conference scene both affected white Methodist pastors who struggled to discern their calling in such a troubled situation. This motley sequence of 1962 events sheds light on the intertwined societal pathology of white Mississippi, the emerging campaign of the state's civil rights movement, and the ongoing struggles of Mississippi Conference Methodists. Out of this volatile mix came the Born of Conviction statement.

The Meredith Case and the Developing Mississippi Movement

The dogged determination of the black Air Force veteran James Meredith to enter Ole Miss caused the most conflict in 1962. Eight years after the *Brown* decision, Mississippi remained one of three Southern states with completely segregated schools. Kosciusko native Meredith began his quest for admission to the University of Mississippi in early 1961; he knew that along with his personal courage, he would need the legal support of the NAACP in order to succeed. The NAACP took the case, thanks mainly to the efforts of Mississippi Field Secretary Medgar Evers. The university denied Meredith admission in February 1961 as soon as he revealed his race, and the case bounced around in the courts for the next eighteen months. Highlights included the December 1961 District Court opinion that Meredith was not denied admission on racial grounds and the flurry of rulings, counterrulings, legislative and gubernatorial actions, and secret negotiations between Governor Barnett and the Kennedy administration. The litigation proceeded through the summer into early fall, and a riot ensued after Meredith's arrival at Ole Miss on September 30, 1962.[1]

The Mississippi State Sovereignty Commission and the Citizens' Council combined to tighten Mississippi repression in the early 1960s; organized Ku Klux Klan activity began in 1963. To that list one must add the press. Some Mississippi newspaper editors spoke against the segregationist tide, most notably in Lexington (Hazel Brannon Smith), Petal (P. D. East), Greenville (Hodding Carter II and III), Pascagoula (Ira Harkey), Tupelo (George McLean), and Jackson and McComb (Oliver Emmerich). But the main Jackson papers, the Hederman family–owned *Clarion-Ledger* and *Jackson Daily News*, wielded the most influence in the state by far. For a few years in the 1950s and early 1960s, a Jackson businessman published a more moderate daily competitor, the *State Times*, but it folded by 1962. Backed up by segregationist dailies in Meridian, Hattiesburg, and other cities, along with the harangues of small-town weekly editors like Mary Cain in Summit, the two Jackson dailies offered a regular dose of segregationist propaganda that strongly reinforced the Closed Society orthodoxy. In Adam Nossiter's words, the Hederman papers were "the mirror of white Jackson's never-never land."[2]

This phrase was also used to describe Mississippi in 1962. During the legal battle surrounding Meredith's application, on January 12 Judge John Minor Wisdom commented in an opinion for the Fifth Circuit Court of

Appeals that the case "was tried below and argued here in the eerie atmosphere of never-never land." The image implies a fantasy world where most white Mississippians saw everything through the lens of one reality: the paramount necessity to maintain segregation of the races, even if it entailed the claim that segregation had nothing to do with the rejection of Meredith's application. As Student Non-Violent Coordinating Committee (SNCC) civil rights leader and African American New Yorker Bob Moses said, "When you're not in Mississippi, it's not real and when you're there the rest of the world isn't real."[3]

The ongoing drama of the Meredith case made headlines through the year, but the local community organizing efforts of the civil rights movement in the state picked up steam as well, mostly under the media radar. SNCC activity, supported by local NAACP chapters and some Congress of Racial Equality (CORE) workers, had begun in the Southwest Mississippi counties of Pike, Amite, and Walthall in the summer of 1961. The lessons learned there by movement leaders led to better planning and the formation in early 1962 of the Council of Federated Organizations (COFO) in an attempt to ensure that all the national civil rights groups present in the state worked together. By early summer, community organizing continued in Jackson and launched in the Delta and other areas of the state.[4]

The Stained Glass Jungle

The white Mississippi Conference showed little awareness of the gathering storm on the civil rights front in those days. It continued to avoid the race issue and the clear injustices of the state's system of white supremacy. At its June 1962 session in Biloxi, those gathered received the report of the conference's Board of Social Concerns. Three of the document's ten items related to the "liquor problem within our state," while three others nibbled at the edges of the race issue: one celebrated the annual conference offering in support of the state's black Methodist school, Rust College; another reported a meeting of some white Methodist clergy and laity with a few Methodist legislators "for informal discussion of key problems within our state"; and the final item noted "widely differing opinions among the people of our state on matters of grave public concern" and affirmed "the privilege of every individual to hold and express his viewpoints without prejudice against him." The last sentence expressed the board's disapproval of legislative appropriation of state tax funds "to any organization to be used for the promotion of partisan viewpoints," a reference to the funneling of money to the Citizens' Council.[5]

That report revealed scant awareness of the political, social, and economic realities faced then on a daily basis by African Americans in Mississippi. The political attention of most pastors in the conference in June 1962 centered on their own organization, due to the publication that month of Gregory Wilson's *The Stained Glass Jungle*, a novel about a Methodist annual conference controlled by a political boss, one of its district superintendents. Most conference ministers knew the pseud-onymous author's real identity: Roy Delamotte, the minister who caused public controversy over the ongoing segregated Methodist Church struc-ture at the 1955 Mississippi Conference meeting, left that same month to work as a pastor in East Tennessee, and now served as a professor at Paine College, a historically African American school in Georgia related to the CME Church. They also believed the novel was about the Mississippi Conference and that the Reverend Dr. Frederick John Worthington, the political boss in the novel's fictional annual conference, was modeled on Willard Leggett, now the Jackson district superintendent.[6]

Some ministers accused Leggett, the real Mississippi Conference clergy leader and power broker, of an abuse of power, though one minister qualified that accusation years later with the contention that such claims may have been true, or they may been mythological. The publication of Delamotte's novel contributed significantly to the Leggett legend. In the late 1950s while he worked on the book, Delamotte asked Betty Conner, the wife of future Born of Conviction signer James Conner and Leggett's secre-tary at Jackson's Capitol Street Church before her 1949 wedding, to describe her former boss. Delamotte insisted he was not writing about Leggett or Mississippi and wanted to be sure the villain of his book did not resemble the Mississippi leader. Yet just after its publication in 1962, James Conner heard a Mississippi pastor insist that the book depicted their conference.[7]

The novel examines the conflict between ministerial service and vocation, on the one hand, and ambition, on the other. The competi-tive element in the Methodist system that can push ministers to great lengths to succeed on the appointment ladder, along with the potential for manipulation and abuse by those in power, are the primary sources for Roy Delamotte's "stained glass jungle" metaphor. Delamotte under-stood the political realities of his fictional annual conference to be rep-resentative of many actual annual conferences, not just Mississippi, and distinguished Methodist clergy readers across the country recognized the general truths about Methodism in the book, including the politics. A Florida Conference minister wrote, "I have known men who fit the description of all the characters. There were scenes which were so real that I wondered indeed if they were not from our conference. If they were not, then I am more sure than ever that the story portrays vividly the general situation."[8]

Delamotte admitted to his editor that he drew some material for the book from his knowledge of the Mississippi Conference. He avoided locating the novel in the South to prevent readers from identifying the story's villain with Leggett and had no desire to attack him. However, the book's authorship was a poorly kept secret, and literary creations, once released, are fair interpretive game, no matter the author's intentions. One of Leggett's lieutenants, asked to review the book prior to its publication, also believed the book depicted the Mississippi Conference and Leggett.[9]

Willard Leggett believed he always sought to do what was best for the church and conference as an institution. A year before his death, Leggett said, "I joined the conference in 1930 and was appointed to the Clinton Methodist Church with J. T. Leggett as my presiding elder. From 1930 to 1990 there has not been an hour in my life that I have been free from the burden and responsibility of a church or some agency of the Methodist Church." His whole life was the church; he had no significant outside interests. A Mississippi minister close to Leggett and his family offered this interpretation:

> I think Willard Leggett saw himself as someone defending the church that he loved, defending the church to whom he'd given his life, understood in those terms . . . warm pastoral care for everyone who shared that. You get out of your place and try to do something to the church that he saw as hurting it, [then] some real viciousness could come out of that.

Delamotte presents his novel's political boss, F. J. Worthington, in a similar light. In a climactic scene, the main character tells Worthington, "I have fought your views and methods, but at no time have I questioned the sincerity of your claim to be seeking only the ultimate best interests of the church." In the early 1960s, Leggett viewed any attempt by Mississippi Conference clergy to challenge the segregated status quo in the state as harmful to the church.[10]

By the time the Fifth Circuit Court of Appeals' June 1962 ruling ordered Meredith's admission, the eventual Twenty-Eight were all stationed in the churches where they would take their stand with the Born of Conviction statement in January 1963. They were spread around the Mississippi Conference's six districts, with eight in Seashore, seven in Meridian, five in Hattiesburg, four in Jackson, and two each in Brookhaven and Vicksburg. Seventeen of them had already served in their current church for at least a year, while eleven moved to a new appointment in June 1962. Six had just returned to Mississippi from seminary.

Rejecting the Red Scare: The Trigg-Lowman Debate

On Monday evening, July 30, 1962, as the legal case heading toward the inevitable admission of James Meredith to Ole Miss continued in the news, a different but related conflict drew media attention. Jerry Trigg (Figure 3.1) debated Myers G. Lowman, Executive Secretary of Circuit Riders, Inc., in the Crown Room of Jackson's King Edward Hotel before an audience of three hundred people. The confrontation focused on

FIGURE 3.1 Jerry Trigg in 1960. Courtesy of Jerry and Rose Trigg.

Lowman's claim of "widespread Communist infiltration of Methodist Churches." He had dared any Mississippi Methodist minister to debate him on the subject, and when no one else rose to the challenge, Trigg accepted. A Millsaps classmate later described Trigg as "in his element with the debate team at Millsaps. [I] heard him once comment that he would debate anyone, anywhere, at any time." He and his debate partner and future wife, Rose Cunningham, had excelled on both regional and national levels in 1956. To prepare for the 1962 debate, Trigg obtained a tape of Lowman's standard speech and formulated responses to each of its arguments.[11]

Formed by a group of Methodists in 1951 in response to controversies surrounding the Methodist Federation for Social Action, the Cincinnati-based Circuit Riders sought "to oppose socialism and communism in our (Methodist) Church." Eventually it became only a vehicle for Executive Secretary Lowman's anti-Communist activities: speaking, writing, and compiling "lists of names and the affiliations these persons are alleged to have with the Communist or pro-Communist organizations." Lowman called himself an "internationally recognized anti-communist," but a 1960 Methodist General Conference report commented, "We regret that any Methodist contribute either money or leadership to such organizations as Circuit Riders, Inc. which utilize 'guilt by association' and 'fellow-traveler' approaches as they stir up unjustified suspicion and develop unfounded fears."[12]

In the early 1960s, Lowman, a Methodist layman and business executive, found work in Mississippi as a speaker sponsored by the State Sovereignty Commission as part of its ongoing mission to connect the state's civil rights movement with Communism. In early 1961, the Sovereignty Commission paid Lowman almost $4,000 for two speaking tours in Mississippi, on the theme "Subversion Challenges Sovereignty." While he usually found appreciative audiences, he met with criticism when he spoke at Ole Miss on the night of February 20 and Professor James Silver and some students challenged his views. The next evening in Starkville, North Mississippi Conference minister R. Glenn Miller gave an invocation unsympathetic to Lowman's cause prior to Lowman's speech. In June 1962, the North Mississippi Conference passed a resolution defending the Methodist Church against Lowman's accusations.[13]

At the July 1962 debate between Lowman and Trigg, the audience was equally divided between supporters for each man. Several carloads of members from Trigg's church on the Gulf Coast drove the 170 miles

to support their pastor, while members of the unofficial Methodist segregationist group MAMML turned out for Lowman, whom they saw as
supportive of the racial status quo. Lowman had reiterated his offer to pay
a $500 reward to anyone who could disprove his claim of the Communist
infiltration of Methodism, and as the evening progressed, whenever
Trigg thought he had the upper hand, he told Lowman he could make the
check to Caswell Springs Methodist Church. Trigg quoted from a letter
he received from FBI Director J. Edgar Hoover: "This is not the time for
name calling or publicity-seeking charges designed to confuse, divide and
weaken. The clergy of America need the full support of patriotic citizens
in our common struggle against the enemy," and then asked whether it
made more sense to heed Hoover or Lowman. Although the *Mississippi
Methodist Advocate* agreed with other reporters that the debate did not
change the minds of the people who attended, it also said that Trigg
"pointed out that innuendoes, half-truths and the sowing of seeds of suspicion against the Church and her leaders were aiding the Communist
conspiracy rather than hindering it."[14]

After the debate ended, two MAMML members confronted Trigg and
warned that even though he had enjoyed himself that evening, he might
experience difficulty when it came time to move to another church in
the conference. In the weeks after the debate, MAMML ran articles in
its newsletter attacking Trigg, including Lowman's claims that Trigg and
others refused to acknowledge the obvious Communist infiltration in the
Methodist Church. Although Trigg and Lowman did not discuss race in
the debate, MAMML and other defenders of segregation saw Lowman as
their champion because they equated advocacy of desegregation and racial
justice with Communism.[15]

The Riot at Ole Miss

With the beginning of the fall semester in September 1962, James
Meredith's journey toward registration as an Ole Miss student neared
its end, accompanied by further desperate resistance by state officials and the mass hysteria that resulted in violence on the campus.
Although many share the blame for the Ole Miss debacle, Governor
Ross Barnett has gone down in history as a singular failure in the crisis and "the ultimate caricature of the racist demagogues of the massive resistance period." On September 13, in response to yet another
federal court order for the state to enroll Meredith, Barnett vowed "no

school will be integrated in Mississippi while I am your governor" and insisted that state officials must be "prepared to suffer imprisonment for this righteous cause." He had almost complete support; only a small minority of whites, including two legislators—Joe Wroten, a Methodist layman from Greenville, and Karl Wiesenburg of Pascagoula—spoke against what Wiesenburg called "an orgy of rebellion against constituted authority and the federal government." An ecumenical group of eight white ministers in Oxford bucked the tide of support for Barnett; on September 16, they called for a peaceful resolution to the Ole Miss crisis. One of them, Duncan Gray Jr., rector of St. Peter's Episcopal Church, also encouraged his congregation to "do everything in our power as Christians to insure the peaceful and orderly admission of James Meredith to the University."[16]

Although Mississippi Conference Methodists kept silent in the public arena, some pastors encountered the anger of their parishioners that month. On a Sunday morning before worship, the chairman of the Sandersville Methodist Church's Official Board asked pastor and future Born of Conviction signer Ned Kellar what he thought should be done about James Meredith's persistent attempts to attend Ole Miss. Kellar responded that Meredith should be admitted, and this evoked anger and disbelief from his interrogator. Kellar remembers responding, "I think the United States Government will place him in Ole Miss. Maybe we ought to accept that and go on with life." The man replied, "Preacher, you better remember where you are."[17]

On September 25, 1962, a new act unfolded in the Mississippi Conference political drama. At the Brookhaven District Pastors' meeting in McComb, District Superintendent Norman U. Boone read a statement condemning the political pressures on pastors in anticipation of the 1963 Annual Conference elections for clergy delegates to the 1964 General and Jurisdictional Conferences. Boone spoke out "because some have already taken it upon themselves . . . to come into this District to ascertain how the pastors plan to vote in the coming election in the Annual Conference." As a veteran of the political battles of the conference over the past dozen years, Boone expressed anger in response to the suggestions made by these political operatives that votes for the right slate of delegates would ensure preferential treatment in the appointment process and failure to vote this way would result in punishment. While the existence of Leggett group political activity was old news, discussion in a public forum was unusual, and later that fall, the ministers in the district voted to pay for

Boone's statement to be duplicated and distributed to all ministers in the conference.[18]

Also on September 25, Meredith arrived at the State College Board office in the Woolfolk State Office Building in Jackson in one of several attempts to register. Governor Barnett stopped Meredith, Chief US Marshal James McShane, and Justice Department representative John Doar in the hall outside the office and refused to let them enter. It was another episode in Barnett's political theatrics, captured by television cameras. Barnett claimed, "My conscience is clear." The next day, Meredith attempted to register on the Ole Miss campus, and Lieutenant Governor Paul B. Johnson, aided by state troopers, stopped him.[19]

That weekend, the Ole Miss football team played Kentucky in Jackson on Saturday night, September 29, and Governor Barnett made a brief, defiant speech on the field at halftime. Gerald Blessey, then a junior at Ole Miss who became a state legislator and mayor of Biloxi, later remembered the reaction to the speech:

> I looked back at the crowd and I saw anger in the faces of the people right next to me, and it sort of flashed through my mind that those Rebel flags looked like swastikas. . . . [These] were just ordinary school kids who were being whipped into a fever pitch of emotion by their own leaders . . . it was just like the Nazis had done.[20]

By late afternoon Sunday, September 30, 1962, word had spread that James Meredith was on his way to the University of Mississippi. Meredith secretly settled in his dorm under heavy guard. Three hundred federal marshals surrounded the Lyceum Building at the center of campus, and a large crowd of students and assorted other persons from around the state and beyond gathered. The situation in front of the Lyceum gradually worsened until about eight o'clock that evening, when the marshals, who had endured verbal taunts, spit, and thrown bricks, bottles, rocks, iron pipes, and Molotov cocktails, fired tear gas canisters into the crowd, which numbered 1,500 to 2,000 people and later grew as large as 3,000. An already chaotic scene disintegrated, and when the tear gas and smoke cleared the next morning, federal troops occupied the school and the town of Oxford. Casualties numbered two people dead and hundreds injured, including 160 marshals, twenty-eight of them wounded by gunfire. On Monday morning, October 1, James Meredith officially registered as a student and attended his first class.[21]

Like many Mississippi pastors, Ned Kellar lived in a town where some residents considered going to Oxford in response to the call from General Edwin Walker and others to stop Meredith and defend white Mississippi's honor against the encroaching federal government. On Sunday night, September 30 at the Sandersville parsonage, the Kellars stayed up late viewing news coverage of the riot and went to bed deeply disturbed. Ed McRae, pastor of Oakland Heights Methodist Church in Meridian, also stayed up to watch. He remembers that when the local station signed off for the night by playing the "Star Spangled Banner," he stood and sang along with tears in his eyes and thought, "I'm an American first; this is my country. I cannot agree with what's happening up there at Ole Miss and where the leaders of this state are taking us." The governor, legislators, and others with legal authority had brazenly defied the federal government and the US court system. Jerry Furr, associate pastor at Jackson's Galloway Church, knew John Satterfield, MAMML member, prominent attorney, and advisor to Governor Barnett. On Monday morning, October 1, Furr sent Satterfield a telegram asking him to "please—immediately urge the Governors [sic] personal appeal state-wide for obedience to the law. Urge peaceful compliance to constituted authorities."[22]

Who Is to Blame? Responses to the Ole Miss Riot

In a reflection on the riot written two years later, author Walker Percy observed, "When Meredith finally did walk the paths at Ole Miss, his fellow students cursed and reviled him. But they also wept with genuine grief. It was as if he had been quartered in their living room." The Mississippi State Junior Chamber of Commerce released a pamphlet that claimed Meredith's admission to Ole Miss resulted from a flagrant federal disregard for both the law and due judicial process. In this view, the "brutality" of the federal marshals caused the riot, although accounts of the night's events from the hundreds of reporters present offered a much different story. James Silver's *Mississippi: The Closed Society* and his numerous letters to the editor challenged the veracity of this party line, summed up by former Congressman Frank Smith as a "massive campaign . . . to convince Mississippians that they were the innocent victims of a subversive attack by brutal tyrants in Washington, intent upon destroying Mississippi because it was the last bulwark of constitutional government." Many white Mississippians expressed their hatred for the Kennedys with such vitriol that at the news of the president's assassination in November 1963, white school children in numerous places across the state cheered and celebrated his death.[23]

An ecumenical group of Oxford clergy responded to the Ole Miss riot by issuing a call for repentance "for our collective and individual guilt in the formation of the atmosphere which produced the strife at the University of Mississippi." Less than a week later, the North Mississippi Conference District Superintendents published a statement "whole-heartedly endors[ing]" it. Written while Bishop Franklin was out of the country, their statement affirmed freedom of the pulpit and expressed confidence in their ministers and support of them "in the preaching of the whole Gospel in the Spirit of Christ." The Mississippi Conference Cabinet and Bishop Franklin remained silent on the matter. The North Mississippi endorsement did not appear in the secular press and caused little controversy, but it drew a typical "Mississippi standard version" response from a Jackson layman, who failed to see why North Mississippi Methodists needed to repent and added,

> Could it be that the Methodist people should repent because we object to having Negroes attend our churches ... and because we don't want them to enroll in the University and our public schools and intermarry with our young people and thus mongrelize the race? It would seem to me that the repentance should be on the part of the Federal Government that has laid aside the constitution and run rough-shod over our Governor and our State. ...[24]

A few weeks later, Mississippi Baptists read an impassioned response from Antonina Canzoneri, a Mississippi missionary in Nigeria: "You send us out here to preach that Christ died for all men. Then you make a travesty of our message by refusing to associate with some of them just because of the color of their skin." Canzoneri's mother, Governor Barnett's first cousin, responded in the Jackson press, "Antonina doesn't understand that Ross is doing the best he can. She's been over there and doesn't know all about the situation here." Yet the missionary understood the cost of her letter: "... I am wounding some of the dearest people in the world, but Jesus says, 'He that loves father or mother more than Me is not worthy of Me.'" Turning the usual accusations of Communist influence on the civil rights movement on their head, she closed by saying, "The Communists do not need to work against the preaching of the gospel [in

Africa] by Americans; you are doing it quite adequately. Wake up! Look at what is happening in the world! Be courageous; act like Christians!" White Mississippi Methodists read a similar letter from one of their missionaries, Dot Hubbard, a Millsaps graduate working as a teacher in South Korea, though her statement took a more subtle and hopeful tone.[25]

North Mississippi Conference minister Sam Ashmore, editor of *The Mississippi Methodist Advocate*, a weekly newspaper serving both white Mississippi annual conferences, was sixty-eight in October 1962. As a pastor he had excelled at leading various North Mississippi congregations out of debt, and although he had no journalistic experience, his appointment as *Advocate* editor in 1955 came because the paper had financial troubles. He had not been known as a prophetic minister, but events in the ensuing years led him to speak with uncommon boldness. His wife, Ann Lewis Ashmore, served as an uncredited assistant over the eleven years he edited the *Advocate*, and she likely wrote or collaborated on many editorials (Figure 3.2).[26]

In an editorial published October 10, Ashmore said the blame for the riot belonged to all white Mississippi Methodists. "Yes, the church is partly

FIGURE 3.2 Sam and Ann Lewis Ashmore, 1960s. Courtesy of Harjes family.

responsible for what happened at Ole Miss," Ashmore concluded, because Methodists failed to speak out and allowed "the voice of moderation and goodwill" to be "completely ignored." Now the white Mississippi Methodist Church had to choose "whether she loses her life for Christ's sake and finds it in this hour of crisis or whether she really loses her life in pious platitudes and innocuous activity in a day which demands courageous witness."[27]

On October 2, a group of more than one hundred business and professional leaders met at the King Edward Hotel in Jackson and issued a statement asking all public officials "to advocate forthrightly and immediately the maintenance of law and order." But criticisms of the Oxford riot and the climate of massive resistance represented a faint hum compared to the roar of the white Mississippi party line, and some white Methodist pastors in South Mississippi were bitterly disappointed in the lack of public comment from Bishop Franklin and their district superintendents. Born of Conviction signer James Conner later explained, "We did not feel fit to make such a statement (or to suffer its consequences!). But we have not had the leadership on the state level . . . to give us a clear sense of direction and purpose for these times."[28]

Maxie Dunnam and Jerry Trigg detested this silence, and in October 1962 they experienced the conference leadership's timidity and desire not to stir things up after the Ole Miss riot in another way. In early January 1962, Dunnam and Trigg had spent a week in Florida at a Christian ashram led by E. Stanley Jones, a world-renowned Methodist missionary and evangelist who spent decades in India. Jones's radical commitment to the Christian faith and the vision of an inclusive Kingdom of God led to his falsely being called a Communist. His accusers were also offended at his insistence on racial inclusivity at his Christian ashrams. Adapted from the Hindu ashram, the events eschewed the artificial lines of race and class and offered those present an experience of intimate fellowship where they could consider the claims of Jesus for their lives. Dunnam and Trigg had a transformative experience at the Florida event.[29]

In consultation with Trigg and others, Dunnam decided to invite Jones to Mississippi for a week-long Christian ashram. He discussed the idea with Bishop Marvin Franklin in late summer, and Franklin approved. The race issue did not come up in the conversation. Jones committed to a date. However, while Franklin was in Asia on a tour of Methodist missionary sites in October of 1962, the Conference Youth Camp Committee turned down the request to hold the event at Camp Wesley Pines, a new conference facility in Gallman, due to an understanding when rights to the land had been secured "that we would not promote integrated meetings in the camp until such time as the Mississippi Conference became an integrated church." They did not wish to "bring pressure" on the rest of the conference by allowing an integrated meeting at the camp, and they believed such a move was "too explosive" at a time of "tense" conditions in the state just after the Ole Miss riot. Dunnam responded by moving the planned event to Gulfside, the Central Jurisdiction assembly ground in Waveland on the Gulf Coast, but eventually he and Jones cancelled the event.[30]

Freedom of the Pulpit?

The dilemma for white Mississippi ministers in these days centered on the words they might speak as religious leaders. Some were staunch segregationists, while more pastors believed they should keep silent. Some wanted to provide prophetic leadership in their local churches in this time of crisis but agonized over the risks involved. In Ned Kellar's words, "Wasn't the pulpit a place where divisive issues were addressed? Didn't I have the responsibility to say something about all the anger and hatred that seemed to permeate the lives and souls of this community?" Kellar and others understood that they could speak and risk the anger of their parishioners or worse, or they could remain silent, appear to support the status quo, and struggle with the resulting pain in their own souls. Maxie Dunnam saw no choice in the matter. In a column written that fall for the Gulf Coast's *Daily Herald*, he warned, "In a day when we should be taking a stand on crucial issues, we dare not piddle with the insignificant. We dare not dabble with the unimportant and fail in the tremendous task to which we are called."[31]

Several white Methodist pastors in the Mississippi Conference sought to respond to the Ole Miss crisis from their pulpits. Some, like Rod Entrekin at Wesson, still exercised caution in their preaching and chose to broach the subject of race relations in indirect ways. After his 1953 graduation from seminary at Emory University, Entrekin became a full-time pastor in the Mississippi Conference, and in the fall of 1962, he had been at Wesson three years. In a sermon titled "The Disturbing Christ," he noted that "to be disturbed by Christ may well be a very good thing." He linked this idea to the current situation:

> Today . . . the Methodist Church . . . is under fire for speaking out on
> the social issues of importance to our day. *The Mississippi Methodist*
> *Advocate* was recently criticized for its commentary on the Ole

Miss Crisis. The true followers of Christ are always "disturbers" in keeping with his tradition. Our point is that Christ is the social conscience of our time just as He has always been accepted as the personal conscience of man. It is a painful thing to be disturbed, but the pain may well be a blessing, and it is surely a necessary thing.

Church members, some connected with Copiah-Lincoln Junior College, responded positively, though Entrekin believed this was because of the sermon's lack of specificity.[32]

Some Mississippi Conference pastors felt free to speak more directly to their congregations. After working for a year in the conference office, Jim Waits became pastor of Epworth Church in Biloxi. On an October 1962 Sunday, Waits's sermon, "The Question of Sovereignty," compared the state sovereignty trumpeted by Ross Barnett and the State Sovereignty Commission with the sovereignty of God. He criticized the Sovereignty Commission's tactics of spying on citizens and compared it to practices in the Soviet Union. The insistence on such human sovereignty "is nothing less than insistence on our own way—the evil self-centeredness which is the very essence of sin." Waits added, "In the conflicting issues we face here in the South, the Church has the opportunity to come to genuine self-understanding: to affirm that our love for each other goes deeper than the disagreements we may have on any issue." The current climate did not allow this:

How many times have you heard of preachers who were removed because they spoke their convictions on the race question? Are our convictions so insecure that they cannot even tolerate the expression of an opposing point of view? Have we come to the point in the Christian Church that our love and concern for another member is contingent on whether he agrees with us?

The sermon did not provoke noticeable controversy in Waits's church, and it was published in the *Advocate* that month.[33]

At Caswell Springs in neighboring Jackson County, Jerry Trigg preached a sermon series on the Lord's Prayer, and on September 30 he planned to focus on "And lead us not into temptation, but deliver us from evil." With the Meredith case coming to a head that day, Trigg awoke in the wee hours of the morning and rewrote his sermon. He preached about the rise of a "segregationist party" whose leader surrounded himself with state police and declared that only whites were acceptable. Those who claimed "the inferior races" had rights, he called Communists. The leader called for unity and insisted that his people could be a superior nation and need not conform to the rest of the world. By this point, the members of Trigg's congregation were convinced he was speaking of Mississippi Governor Ross Barnett, and a few of the two hundred in attendance walked out of the service. Then Trigg said, "So Adolph Hitler came to power in 1933." He concluded the sermon by warning that Mississippi Christians could soon be facing the same issues that faced German Christians in the past and pushed his congregation to consider where they stood in their current situation. As he left the sanctuary, he remembers a member told him, "Preacher, you were kind of tough on us today."[34]

Although the sermon did not cause serious problems for Trigg in the congregation, it did draw the attention of others in the community. One night during the next week, a cross was burned on the lawn between the church and the parsonage. The Triggs were not aware of the cross while it burned and only discovered it the next day when they found their two-and-a-half-year-old son holding a small charred piece of the cross on his shoulder and marching back and forth in the yard.[35]

Other Methodist ministers who sought to speak about the Ole Miss crisis encountered more hostility from church members. Bill Lampton grew up in Columbia, where his father owned a department store. He attended McCallie School in Chattanooga and graduated from Millsaps College in 1956. After seminary at Emory, he spent two years at Stringer in Jasper County and moved in 1961 to Pisgah in Pike County, northwest of McComb. White resistance activity increased in the area that year due to the efforts of SNCC and some local blacks to organize voter registration drives, sit-ins, and demonstrations in Pike and Amite counties.[36]

At Pisgah Church two weeks after the 1962 riot, Lampton preached on the Prodigal Son story in Luke. All human beings, he said, are kin, because God is the Father of all. Christians are called to be inclusive and embrace "our enemies, those who have wronged us, those unlike us, those whom we cannot understand." Lampton then applied this principle to comments about James Meredith by the notorious editor of the local *Summit Sun*: "This past week, Mary Cain referred to our most famous Mississippian at the University with the expression, 'his worthless hide.' Well, that may sell newspapers in Summit, Mississippi, but you can't match it with the Gospel of Jesus Christ!" Angry church members asked how they might cut Lampton's salary and oust him as their pastor. They warned him not to speak on the race issue again because of negative response in the community and the danger to his own professional future.[37]

Up the road in Byram, a rural community on the Pearl River just south of Jackson, James Nicholson had just been appointed to the Methodist Church in June 1962. His father was also a pastor in the Mississippi Conference. Born in 1923, Nicholson served in the Merchant Marines during World War II. While home on a leave, he heard his father preach a sermon on Jonah, and Nicholson felt a call to the ministry. After his discharge from the service, he married Alice Walker and served student pastorates while in college at Mississippi Southern. Upon graduation, Nicholson and his family moved to Dallas, where he began his seminary training at SMU's Perkins School of Theology. Given the young family's financial needs, Nicholson dropped out of seminary and went to work for the Boy Scouts, and in 1958 they moved to Beaumont, Texas, where he served as a Field Scout Executive for the next four years. When he made the decision to return to the pastorate in Mississippi in 1962, he had not quite finished his seminary degree.[38]

Nicholson had been gone from Mississippi for ten years, and when he returned, he soon faced a crisis. The Ole Miss riot and the reaction of most white Mississippians to it greatly disturbed Nicholson, and he wondered what the church might say in response. He hoped in vain that Bishop Franklin would say something, even if only to show he understood this anguish. Nicholson looked to large church pastors in Jackson, such as Galloway's W. B. Selah, to speak, but they also remained silent. He later described what pushed him to action: "I began to realize, why was I looking for the church to say something? Why did Bishop Franklin have to say it? Why did Dr. Selah have to say it? For the whole thing was bearing down on me. *What in Sam Hill were you ordained for?*"[39]

Nicholson (Figure 3.3) responded to this revelation with an October 21 sermon at Byram titled "Real Issues for These Times." He joined the Oxford ministers who had called for individual and collective repentance for Ole Miss, and proclaimed, "We have let prejudice shut out the Gospel and in many areas of our lives have turned to the gods of segregation and white supremacy to sustain us." He insisted schools should be kept open when desegregation came and asserted the education of children "is certainly more important than the doctrine of segregation. If the time ever comes when I must choose whether my children go to school with

FIGURE 3.3 James Nicholson, 1960s. Courtesy of James Nicholson family.

Negroes or else have no school at all, my children will go to school with Negroes."[40]

The next day the church's Official Board met without his knowledge and voted to demand his immediate dismissal. Nicholson reported that Willard Leggett, the district superintendent, told the church that the sermon was ill timed and promised that the pastor would not speak on race again. Nicholson completely disagreed with Leggett and had not promised to keep silent. He was permitted to stay at the church, but most of the one hundred members subsequently boycotted worship. Nicholson's wife and three children constituted the majority of the congregation on most Sundays.[41]

Each of these Mississippi Conference ministers understood the importance of their local congregational preaching in response to Ole Miss and the climate of massive resistance, but they believed a more public witness was also necessary. The next step was the Born of Conviction statement.

PART II

Born of Conviction: Call and Response

4

A Time to Speak

. . . a time to keep silence, and a time to speak . . .
—ECCLESIASTES 3:7B (NRSV)

THOUGH ALL FOUR creators of the Born of Conviction statement share the credit for its inception, the idea came from Jerry Furr, W. B. Selah's associate pastor at Jackson's Galloway Memorial. The Ole Miss riot pushed Furr to a crucial insight:

> Everything I learned at Millsaps and Emory was that the church said there's something wrong when people treat folks of other races badly. That stuck, and then Selah put meat and bones on that idea. . . . I thought we ought to try to do something . . . make a declaration. We had freedom riders from other places, but they were always dismissed because "they didn't know anything about Mississippi. They're not from here; they don't understand us."

So he concluded, "Some of us who are Mississippians ought to say something—people who were born in Mississippi and couldn't be dismissed as outsiders."[1]

Furr visited the Coast and met Maxie Dunnam, Jerry Trigg, and Jim Waits for lunch; they agreed it was time for action. They joined other Southern clergy groups in that era who sought to connect the Christian faith to the social upheaval resulting from civil rights movement efforts across the region. Like other clergy statements, Born of Conviction was offered as a public witness in response to a specific situation, and the quartet found a number of Mississippi Conference clergy colleagues willing to join them.

Public Statements and Action by Southern White Clergy in the Civil Rights Era

As the black freedom struggle and white resistance to it both intensified in the late 1950s and early 1960s, thoughtful church leaders found them difficult to ignore, and some responded by offering collective public witness. Many ministers were familiar with one precedent for such action: the 1934 Barmen Declaration by the Confessing Church movement in Germany. Barmen opposed the Nazi regime in its early days by asserting the Lordship of Christ in a situation where Hitler had become lauded as the Savior of Germany. The Confessing Church has been celebrated for its courage and prescience in offering timely dissent to the growing madness of Nazi rule.[2]

United Methodist Bishop Kenneth Carder, who presided over the Mississippi Conference from 2000 to 2004 and made racial reconciliation a focus of his episcopal leadership there, believes many ministers who served Southern churches in the 1950s and 1960s have asked themselves in retrospect, "Did I do what I should have done?" Evaluations of the response of Southern clergy in those years have produced a range of views. Some critics condemn the white church and its clergy leaders for inactivity and silence or for timid, ineffective attempts at witness. Others point to examples of the white church's active resistance to change. During those years, segregationists saw liberal clergy as failing to live up to their calling as guardians of the white South. One of the most often cited treatments of religion's role during this era claims that conservative white churches and their pastors did not rally sufficiently to support the status quo—they especially failed at articulating a clear theological defense of segregation.[3]

Between 1953 and 1963, some groups of Southern ministers in eleven states spoke—and in a few cases, acted—in attempts to argue for change, comment on a particular issue, or represent the church and the voice of reason in a potentially explosive situation. A full analysis of their efforts involves a number of factors, including their geographical location, the characteristics of the group joining together to speak, and the words they used. In most cases, it proved easier for ministers in the upper South to offer public comment on race relations than for those in the Deep South. Participants in most clergy proclamations were all white, resided in the same city, and represented a range of Protestant denominations, though some notable exceptions included other Christian clergy and Jewish rabbis. Often, prominent ministers joined in, and a few statements were endorsed by bishops. Infrequently, clergy from one denominational judicatory area banded together to make a declaration. Notably, a few proclamations involved participation by black ministers.[4]

Some statements were mainly practical and called for obedience to the law, freedom of speech, and peaceful and civil consideration of proposed change. Sometimes they criticized the massive resistance posturing of state officials, while a few declarations offered deeper theological reflection on race relations and linked specific scriptural or doctrinal claims to implications for the current crisis. Some pronouncements remained fairly general, even platitudinous, in their comments, while others focused on a specific issue or action with varying degrees of acuity. Some were thoroughly moderate, while a few flirted with ideas considered radical in the time and context in which they were put forth. Some included words that are now viewed as racist.

Those who make public proclamations expect a response, and all these offerings elicited varying degrees of approval, both public and private. In many cases, they also drew at least some public opposition and private harassment, threats, and occasional violence. Implications for a minister's career resulting from participation in a statement depended on a number of elements, including where the minister served (Upper South or Deep South? Urban or rural?), the current race relations climate where he lived, and the network of support that sustained him and other participants in that particular public effort.

The most important evaluative question centers on the good accomplished by these attempts at Christian witness. Clergy statements can be characterized as mere words, not nearly as significant as the actions of civil rights workers (including some clergy) who put their lives on the line to work for change and were obviously much more committed to the cause of civil rights and justice in race relations. Occasionally, a nonmovement clergyman took action that exhibited more solidarity with the movement. Yet some of the most dramatic memories of the civil rights era cluster around words: King's Birmingham letter and "I Have a Dream" speech, or Fannie Lou Hamer's testimony before the Credentials Committee at the 1964 Democratic Convention. The witness of the civil rights movement emerged from deep thought, careful planning, and expert strategy.[5]

Witness includes both word and action, and the two often overlap. The relationship can be conceived as a continuum, with words alone, virtually unsupported by any real action (thus "empty words") residing at one end. On the other extreme is ill-considered or reckless action emerging without benefit of careful thought and articulation. For a clergy statement to be judged effective there must be evidence that what it said had real power—some combination of the right words spoken at the right time along with a response that proves what was said hit a nerve. A combination of affirmation (public and private), intense negative reaction, and some evidence of long-term good results may prove the validity of a statement and qualify it as a form of meaningful action as well.

The most frequent impetus for Southern clergy statements in this era was the 1954 *Brown* decision and subsequent school desegregation struggles. In March, as the nation anticipated the Supreme Court ruling, the ministerial association in Gainesville urged Georgia citizens to uphold the public schools regardless of what the Court said; the ministers expressed faith in both constitutional government and the importance of public education. After the decision came in May, the three most prominent Protestant denominations in the South each endorsed it. At its 1954 General Assembly meeting, the Presbyterian Church in the United States commended the decision and urged its members to support its implementation. More importantly, the group passed "A Statement to Southern Christians" condemning segregation. The Southern Baptist Convention affirmed *Brown* at its 1954 meeting; the Virginia and North Carolina state conventions soon ratified that action. The Methodist Church's General Conference did not meet in 1954, but the denomination's Council of Bishops expressed its approval of *Brown* at its November meeting, in spite of pleas from the Southeastern Jurisdiction's bishops that the council take no action. The jurisdictional group, led by Bishop Clare Purcell of the North Alabama Conference, reiterated its opposition upon returning home from the meeting, and Mississippi's Bishop Franklin expressed this to the Jackson papers.[6]

In Mississippi, one predominantly white church body responded favorably to *Brown*. In August 1954, the Episcopal Diocese issued an extensive statement, written by Duncan Gray Jr., rector of the church in Cleveland, Mississippi. Approved by a small diocesan committee that included lay membership and one black member, the essay offered biblical, philosophical, and legal arguments in support of the Court's decision and asserted that such response was not merely political, but more importantly for Christians, moral and religious. Unlike most church statements of this era, this one claimed that an implication for Episcopalians was that their worship services should be open to all persons. Gray sent a copy of the statement in booklet form to state legislators with a cover letter inviting their response. Though he received negative feedback, the White Citizens' Council had not yet organized enough to mount the kind of coercion and retaliation for which it soon became known. National Episcopal Church leaders were so impressed with Gray's statement that they used it as a source for their General Convention's response to *Brown*.[7]

In North Carolina, numerous groups took actions declaring a new day in race relations. In 1954, the North Carolina Annual Conference of the Methodist Church passed a resolution in favor of *Brown* with only a few dissenting votes. In early 1955, the Raleigh ministerial association proclaimed that its occasional ecumenical worship services would be open to all, and Chapel Hill ministers established the Inter-Racial Fellowship for the Schools. In Greensboro, white and black ministers voted to merge their organizations by the fall of 1955, and in early 1956, the North Carolina Council of Churches urged its member bodies to accept the Supreme Court's decision fully and work toward an integrated public school system.[8]

Leaders and participants in the black freedom struggle did not limit their focus to school desegregation. During the 1955–6 bus boycott in Montgomery, Alabama, G. Stanley Frazer, pastor of St. James Methodist, actively opposed the boycott, while Ray E. Whatley at St. Mark's Methodist openly endorsed it in January 1956 and had to move to a new church after his annual conference met in May. The rest of the white Montgomery Methodist pastors remained silent on the issue. Robert Graetz, white pastor of a black American Lutheran Church congregation, became directly involved in the boycott.[9]

In Clinton, Tennessee, after hostile whites attacked blacks involved in desegregating the high school, Paul Turner, pastor of the one thousand member First Baptist Church, responded by encouraging his church to support law and order and then escorting the black students back to school on December 4, 1956. Afterward, twelve white men assaulted him. His congregation did not censure him; he remained there another two years. The interracial ministerial association in nearby Knoxville publicly supported the Clinton school desegregation and sent a resolution supporting the *Brown* decision to the governor. There were consequences for at least one minister: James Wilder, association president and pastor of Magnolia Avenue Methodist Church, received harassing telephone calls, and someone repeatedly dumped garbage on his lawn.[10]

As 1957 began, two interracial groups in Nashville—the clergy alliance and the Community Relations Conference—issued statements

urging the state legislature not to pass laws designed to resist desegregation. At the end of January, fifty-nine members of the interracial
Richmond Ministerial Association published a "Statement of Conviction"
calling the massive resistance laws passed a few months earlier by the
Virginia General Assembly "neither democratic nor Christian." The
Times-Dispatch, one of the daily papers that printed the manifesto, polled
more than four hundred Richmond area clergy and found that half agreed
with the association's statement, while 13 percent opposed it and 37 percent refused to comment. That summer, a collection of essays billed as a
moderate approach to race relations appeared in South Carolina. Called
South Carolinians Speak, the book, compiled by five white ministers (three
Episcopalians, a Presbyterian, and a Methodist) and including an introduction by the ministers and essays by twelve white laypersons, provoked
angry responses from many whites, including South Carolina's governor,
even though some of the essays were fairly traditional and even racist.
Claudia Thomas Saunders's offering, which suggested that school integration could be accomplished gradually, a grade at a time, resulted in the
bombing of her Gaffney home.[11]

The fall 1957 crisis in Little Rock, Arkansas, when nine black students
attempted to integrate Central High School, were stopped by the Arkansas
National Guard acting on orders from Governor Orval Faubus, and then
finally succeeded in attending the school after President Eisenhower
intervened, drew response from many clergy. Fifteen ministers issued
a statement protesting Faubus's action; a clergy group of comparable
size praised Faubus. The critics were joined by twenty-seven North
Arkansas Conference Methodist ministers, including Jonesboro District
Superintendent E. J. Holifield, who received some threatening letters as a
result. A few days later, an ecumenical and interracial group of thirty-five
pastors from a total of fourteen cities in the state followed with a "statement of convictions" that did not mention Faubus or other leaders but
stressed that "all are equal in God's sight" and invoked a Christian unity
"which transcends all racial, cultural and denominational differences." In
response to a Little Rock citywide prayer service organized by signers of
this statement and other clergy, a group of segregationist ministers held
an antiintegration prayer meeting attended by more than six hundred
people.[12]

Two months later, white ministers in Atlanta released a manifesto calling for protection of freedom of speech, obedience to the law, and preservation of the public school system at a time when the state of Georgia

considered closing schools to prevent desegregation. The statement also condemned "hatred and scorn for those of another race, or for those who hold a position different from our own" and insisted that lines of communication between black and white leaders be maintained. The eighty signers included the Episcopal bishop; twenty were Methodist, including L. Bevel Jones, who later reported that his church members were not surprised at his stand because of the content of his preaching. He received angry letters and phone calls from the community at large; another signer received a death threat. A few weeks later, thirty-three Columbus, Georgia, ministers, including thirteen Methodists and two rabbis, signed the same statement, and Atlanta Methodist pastor Dow Kirkpatrick observed that the Columbus group "did a far more impressive thing" than the Atlanta signers, because the much smaller city was more typical of the Deep South's resistant atmosphere. In 1958, a sequel to the Manifesto appeared, this time signed by 312 Atlanta area ministers and rabbis. Georgia's US Senator Richard Russell led a political attack on them, but Kirkpatrick claimed that church members of the signers did not condemn their pastors.[13]

In 1958, thirty-seven black ministers in the Mobile area petitioned the Mobile City Commission to desegregate the city buses there. An ecumenical group of thirty-one white ministers, including seventeen Methodists, publicly supported the petition. The white Methodist signers included Mobile District Superintendent Andrew Turnipseed, along with the pastors of six of Mobile's nine largest Methodist churches. The endorsement drew negative reaction: the burning of crosses on some church or parsonage lawns, attempts by laypeople to remove ministers from churches, and the withholding of funds in some congregations. A segregationist group of Mobile District laypeople launched a campaign to have Turnipseed replaced as superintendent. Bishop Bachman Hodge reappointed him to the Mobile District in late May 1958 but insisted that he leave the Alabama-West Florida Conference the next year. In 1959, Turnipseed transferred to the New York Conference.[14]

In Dallas, more than three hundred Protestant ministers declared "enforced segregation" to be "morally and spiritually wrong." The April 1958 proclamation, written by a small interracial group of ministers, included signers from thirteen denominations. Only white ministers signed, and the black co-authors concurred in this decision. The statement was presented to the public by a committee including the Methodist Bishop William C. Martin, the area's Episcopal bishop, the pastor of First

Presbyterian Church, and Foy Valentine, an official of the Texas Baptist Convention. A few months earlier, 173 ministers in Houston took a similar stand.[15]

In Virginia in June 1958, a group of twenty-eight Arlington ministers opposed the use of church buildings for private schools, and the Virginia Conference of the Methodist Church echoed this stand. The state's Baptist General Association refused to back Governor J. Lindsey Almond when he closed schools in some counties and the city of Norfolk to avoid desegregation in 1958. Sixty-six members of the interracial Protestant Norfolk Ministers Association called for the immediate reopening of schools there. The ecumenical Front Royal Ministerial Association issued a statement urging that the public schools be kept open, and forty-eight ministers of Falls Church and Fairfax County, Virginia, said, "Enforced segregation not only defies the basic law of the land but, more importantly, contradicts that very Gospel which we are called to preach." In 1959, 125 ministers and rabbis in Miami defended public schools and condemned "hatred and scorn for those of another race."[16]

In December 1958, *Pulpit Digest* published a survey of ministers in seventeen Southern states and found that almost four out of five supported compliance with *Brown*. Predictably, rates of approval were higher in the upper South, while positive responses ranged around 50 percent in states like Mississippi. Aside from possible issues with survey methods, it is important to note that what ministers said in an anonymous survey likely differed from what they were willing to express in public statements or in their congregations, especially in the Deep South.[17]

In New Orleans in 1960, St. Mark's Methodist Church pastor L. A. Foreman and his wife were one of only a few white families whose children kept attending William Frantz Elementary with the school's first black student, Ruby Bridges. On a daily basis, they faced groups of screaming white women demonstrating against the integration. In May 1961 in the state capital of Baton Rouge, fifty-three members of the East Baton Rouge Parish Ministerial Association signed "An Affirmation of Basic Religious Principles," which ran as an ad in the *Morning Advocate*. Offered as a response to "the continuing tensions in our community," it listed five biblical teachings and six affirmations. It culminated in three "Therefore" statements, including "Discrimination on account of race or religion is a violation of the divine law of Love." The statement led to the integration of the Ministerial Association. Signers came from seven Protestant denominations—half Southern Baptist or Methodist. Although a majority of the signers reported congregational support for their stand a month later, a layman's group organized to oppose them, and several newspaper letters to the editor also expressed disapproval. Virtually all of the Baptist signers were harassed for their participation, and all eventually left Baton Rouge. Charles McCullin, founding pastor at Brookstown Baptist Church, remained for seven years but endured continual opposition from a significant minority of church members.[18]

John Winn, pastor of St. Paul's Methodist, had recently agreed to become president of the ministerial association if they were willing to be more than a social group, and the statement grew out of that new commitment. Although Winn experienced some difficulties in his church due to his activism on the race issue during his eight-year tenure there, his signature on this affirmation caused little problem. The endorsement of the statement by D. W. Poole, the Baton Rouge District Superintendent, played a significant role in assuring that none of the ten other Methodists who signed had much difficulty in their churches.[19]

In the world of Catholicism in the US South, the North Carolina bishop made news in 1953 with a proclamation that there would be no segregation of races in churches in the Diocese of Raleigh, and he soon integrated the diocesan hospitals and schools. His colleague Archbishop Joseph Francis Rummel caused an uproar in the Diocese of New Orleans beginning in 1956 when he declared segregation "morally wrong and sinful." Although Rummel asserted as early as 1959 that diocesan schools would soon be integrated, segregationists mounted enough resistance to prevent it until 1962. Priests in the Baton Rouge area separately endorsed the 1961 Protestant "Affirmation of Basic Religious Principles."[20]

Birmingham proved particularly recalcitrant in response to movement efforts, and white church people participated in that resistance. North Alabama Methodists had formed a segregationist Association of Methodist Ministers and Laymen in 1955, but it went defunct. In March 1959, a new effort began at Highlands Methodist Church in Birmingham, with 1,800 people attending the first meeting of the Alabama Methodist Laymen's Union. Though the group sought to prevent change in the denomination's segregated structure (the Central Jurisdiction), the response exemplified the strength of white Methodist segregationist sentiment. Eugene "Bull" Connor, the infamous Birmingham Commissioner of Public Safety, was a Methodist.[21]

However, the climactic year of 1963 began with a different Alabama white church witness. In response to Governor George Wallace's defiant

"Segregation now, segregation tomorrow, segregation forever!" proclamation at his January 14 inauguration, a group of eleven clergy leaders
(Protestant, Catholic, Greek Orthodox, and Jewish), including the state's
two white Methodist bishops, published "An Appeal for Law and Order
and Common Sense." They urged peaceful compliance with any legal
desegregation orders and decried the attitude of rebellion exemplified by
the governor's speech. Though they received praise from some significant
voices, including Alabama's *Methodist Christian Advocate*, segregationist
objections proliferated. This January statement is not well-known, but
eight of those who signed it also responded to the April 1963 unrest in
Birmingham with the Good Friday Statement, counseling patience and
criticizing civil rights movement tactics. This second declaration is the
best-known Southern white clergy statement from the civil rights era,
because Martin Luther King Jr. replied directly to it in his "Letter from
Birmingham Jail."[22]

Many of these clergy statements from 1953–63 can be faulted for their
timidity and endorsement of gradualism. The most trenchant analysis of
these faults came in 1971 from Benjamin E. Mays, longtime president of
Morehouse College and a mentor of Dr. King. Mays criticized the signers
of the two Atlanta manifestos for their caution and for waiting more than
three years after the *Brown* decision to speak: they "certainly did not lead
in a program to abolish segregation in the public schools. Indeed, it can
hardly be said that they even followed." He condemned the 1957 statement's expression of opposition to intermarriage and "amalgamation of
the races" by pointing to the obvious irony of the sexual abuse of black
women by white men for centuries. He accused the signers of feeling
"compelled to say such things to please the white public" and suggested
that a segregationist could have signed the first statement. He dismissed
the 1958 statement as "a plea for gradualism" that called not for integration but for keeping law and order. He concluded with another example of
irony: the 1958 statement claimed that action to desegregate the schools
would come "only with the help of God," because human beings alone
could not accomplish it. In Mays's view, "It is indeed strange that when
man does evil, he has the will, but when he faces a moral crisis and needs
to do what is right, he calls on God to give him the strength to do it."[23]

However, on the fiftieth anniversary of the 1957 Manifesto, African
American United Methodist minister Joseph Lowery, former president
of the Southern Christian Leadership Conference, praised the statement
and its signers. He called it "a breath of fresh air" and considered it bold

for that time and situation. Today, he said, it sounds "mild and extremely cautious," but then "we welcomed it for we needed leadership from the church." Signer Bevel Jones, now a retired United Methodist bishop, sees the effort simply as Christian ministers trying to be faithful and true to their calling.[24]

Indeed, the evaluation of these efforts by mostly white clergy to contribute significantly to the conversation on civil rights in the 1950s and 1960s is a complex undertaking. Lowery's point about context is crucial, but there are problems with the statements. Sociologists Ernest Campbell and Thomas Pettigrew criticized Little Rock ministers for making "*no* systematic attempts . . . to appeal to the conscience of the community" and for mainly appealing for law and order rather than offering a Christian defense of the need for desegregation. White ministers spoke from a position of privilege and power, and though they meant well, they were constrained by knowledge of the perspectives of their parishioners, especially in the Deep South. Thus they often offered gradualist arguments; for instance, the 1958 Dallas statement condemned "enforced segregation," but editors of the *Dallas Morning News* also condemned "enforced integration." The key word for many moderates then was "voluntarism." They believed if Southerners were left alone, they would voluntarily work things out in race relations over time, and this was much better than "forcing" change. This oft-cited opinion combined with general calls to love one another led Yale theologian Julian Hartt to offer this comment in his 1958 critique of the Dallas statement:

> The trouble comes when the Christian tries to translate that supreme imperative of Christian morality into concrete attitudes toward social problems and into legislative policy and program. With what sorrow and penitence we must all remember here how easy it is for us to love our brothers as long as they are content to endure injustice for our sake, and how prone we are to feel a rising surge of irritation against them when they make a bold strike against injustice for their own sake.

As Reinhold Niebuhr correctly understood already in the 1930s, "the white race in America will not admit the Negro to equal rights if it is not forced to do so."[25]

Moderate and liberal white Southern clergy were caught between movement leaders and ardent segregationists. They also felt responsible for the institutional church, which had seen significant membership and financial growth in the postwar boom, so their concern for justice was tempered by caution and diplomacy. Their efforts to speak publicly about the turmoil of those days often represented a diluted "minimal consensus," as Hartt noted concerning the Dallas offering, and sometimes ministers signed a statement in spite of dissatisfaction with the communal effort. The declarations described here were mostly practical (calling for law and order, protection of free speech, and preservation of the public schools) and only nominally theological (the 1954 Mississippi Episcopalian statement and the Baton Rouge affirmation included the most thorough theological arguments). Yet even the relatively bland pronouncements written with colleagues could produce difficulties for each of them when they returned to their local congregations. Although Hartt thoroughly critiqued the Dallas statement, he conceded it was at least a beginning in a situation "where it could have been mortally easy to do nothing."[26]

Information on local church and community response to these group statements is sketchy at best; the more complete and often dramatic stories come not from the signers of group statements but from individual ministers in Deep South Protestant churches who took stands and often were expelled, or of rabbis around the South, including Mississippi leaders Perry Nussbaum in Jackson and Charles Mantinband in Hattiesburg. In Mississippi, after the 1954 statement by the Episcopal Diocese, there were no attempts by denominational or ecumenical groups of Mississippi ministers to say anything publicly until the crisis at Ole Miss in the fall of 1962, when a few ministers in Oxford called for Christians to keep peace and act in a manner consistent with the teachings of their faith and then called for repentance after the riot.[27]

"Born of the Deep Conviction of Our Souls . . ."

On Monday, October 15, 1962—a warm day with a high in the eighties and no rain—four young white Methodist ministers traveled to Perry County in Southeast Mississippi. A few miles south of Richton, they turned off Mississippi Highway 15 and drove east on the isolated Hintonville Road. Just across a wooden bridge over Thompson Creek, they turned right onto a narrow, winding track. They proceeded through two gates; as the tips of low-hanging tree limbs almost brushed their cars, the pastors drove two hundred yards to a fishing cabin, invisible from the road and aptly named

Hidden Haven. Maxie and Jerry Dunnam had recently purchased the property with a couple in their Gulfport church; though he had grown up near Richton, Dunnam knew nothing of the hideaway until he attended spiritual life retreats there in his college years.[28]

The group—Maxie Dunnam, Jerry Furr, Jerry Trigg, and Jim Waits—brought their Bibles and a copy of the 1960 *Book of Discipline*, the Methodist Church's official book of doctrine and polity. They had a specific mission in mind for their overnight retreat: to write a statement in response to the current social crisis epitomized by the violence two weeks earlier at the University of Mississippi on the night before James Meredith finally succeeded in registering as the first known African American student there. They had hoped Mississippi Conference leaders would speak out in response to the situation, but their bishop and others remained silent. It was time for someone to say publicly that not all white Mississippi Conference Methodists wished to be included in what historian James Silver would soon call the Closed Society's "united front" against any change in Mississippi race relations.[29]

The plan to create such a statement implied confidence in words to communicate and convince, or at least to witness to the truth as the four pastors understood it. They intended to compose a theological proclamation as an alternative to the dominant white Mississippi rhetoric. After a time of prayer, they discussed what they wanted to say. Over the next day they talked and wrote; in the night they took turns sleeping while the others kept at it. They considered including words of condemnation of the most vocal segregationist groups and leaders, but ultimately they agreed to offer positive affirmations. At times they agonized over single words or phrases.[30]

They settled on a manifesto of three paragraphs totaling 565 words (for full text, see Appendix 1). It began, "Confronted with the grave crises precipitated by racial discord within our state in recent months, and the genuine dilemma facing persons of Christian conscience, we are compelled to voice publicly our convictions. Indeed, as Christian ministers and as native Mississippians, sharing the anguish of all our people, we have a particular obligation to speak." The ministers addressed all who resisted change in the state, but more importantly, they spoke to those who were deeply troubled by this climate of massive resistance and by recent events but who felt powerless to do or say anything in response. The four men and those who joined them in signing the statement spoke "only for ourselves" but believed they gave voice to the views of many in the church who did not feel free to speak. Benjamin Mays criticized the Atlanta ministers for similar language and saw it as indicative of their fear, but it was not that simple for the Twenty-Eight. They could not pretend to speak for the conference as a whole or for many in their congregations, but they also understood their effort as offering a dissenting minority report.[31]

The heart of the statement began with the words "Born of the deep conviction of our souls as to what is morally right, we have been driven to seek the foundations of such convictions in the expressed witness of our Church." Convinced that Mississippi's leaders and too many members of white Mississippi Conference Methodist churches subscribed to a view of the world that denied some central claims of the Christian faith, the authors insisted that the church's historic teachings—both the words of Jesus and the traditions of Methodism—must guide the thought and action of Methodists in this crisis. This "expressed witness" led them to craft four affirmations pertinent to the current situation.

The first dealt with ownership of the church: "The Church is the instrument of God's purpose. . . . It is ours only as stewards under His Lordship." It should not be used simply as a tool to fortify the Closed Society, where many ministers felt severely restricted in what they could say in churches because of widespread resistance to *any* questions raised about the white supremacist orthodoxy and the legal, economic, and social system that severely restricted all aspects of the lives of blacks. The fervent opposition to change in Mississippi had intensified a climate in which fear ruled, but in order to carry out the purposes of God, the Church required "an atmosphere for responsible belief and free expression." To offer effective and true Christian leadership in this time, ministers needed the freedom to speak a word from the Lord, even if it challenged the status quo, and church members should both desire and support this freedom in their churches. Several previous clergy statements called for freedom of speech or freedom of the pulpit, but here the writers offered an ecclesiological foundation to support it: the church does not belong to the dominant culture but to God.

The next affirmation cited "the official position of The Methodist Church on race" as found in the 1960 *Discipline*. Quoted passages included "Our Lord Jesus Christ teaches that all men are brothers. He permits no discrimination because of race, color, or creed," and "God is Father of all people and races; . . . all men are brothers." Here the statement also cited a scripture passage, Galatians 3:26, invoked by the *Discipline* in support of these declarations: "In Christ Jesus you are all sons of God, through faith." Identity as a Methodist Christian trumped allegiance to white Mississippi, and because their proclamation would come from

Methodist ministers alone, they could offer this denomination-specific argument.[32]

Like many earlier clergy statements around the South, Born of Conviction also expressed support for public schools and opposition to their closing when inevitable desegregation came: "The Methodist Church is officially committed to the system of public school education and we concur. We are unalterably opposed to the closing of public schools on any level or to the diversion of tax funds to the support of private or sectarian schools." Some schools in Arkansas and Virginia had been closed in the late 1950s as a response to desegregation decrees, and the Mississippi legislature had already paved the way for such action in the Magnolia State with a constitutional amendment, approved by the overwhelmingly white electorate in late 1954.[33]

The final affirmation—not found in earlier statements—declared "an unflinching opposition to Communism," prefaced with the reminder that "In these conflicting times, the issues of race and Communism are frequently confused." In the present climate, anyone who dissented was routinely labeled a Communist. The Cold War gave the segregated system's guardians a language to demonize anyone who threatened the world view they frantically embraced. Born of Conviction quoted a 1961 Methodist Council of Bishops statement insisting that commitment to Jesus meant embracing his defense of "the underprivileged, oppressed, and forsaken" and remembering that he "challenges the status quo, calling for repentance and change wherever the behavior of men falls short of the standards of Jesus Christ."[34]

The paragraph containing these four affirmations concluded with a simple statement: "We believe that this is our task and calling as Christian ministers." They anticipated some objections to their public pronouncement on these matters, and so they asserted that the ministry and witness of the Christian Church included speaking a prophetic word against social injustice, especially when many in the church not only ignored that injustice but also believed the current state of affairs represented the appropriate order in the world. Many segregationist Christians argued then that the church had no business dealing in worldly, political affairs; its purpose was purely "spiritual." Yet Born of Conviction's claim that the duty and vocation of ministers entailed applying the church's "expressed witness" to a situation of turmoil in their society, coupled with the theological argument in the first affirmation regarding ownership of the church and freedom of the pulpit, rejected that dualism.[35]

The final paragraph of the manifesto, printed in all caps, argued that the foregoing words drew their authority from the Methodist Church's official position, "IN HARMONY WITH SCRIPTURE AND GOOD CHRISTIAN CONSCIENCE." As Wesleyan theologians, they understood their task to involve consideration of scripture, tradition (the official church position), reason, and experience (the last two both sources of Christian conscience). Having considered the current crisis using this method, they concluded that they had crafted a manifesto on which they could stand: "WE PUBLICLY DECLARE OURSELVES IN THESE MATTERS AND AGREE TO STAND TOGETHER IN SUPPORT OF THESE PRINCIPLES."

Interpreted from the perspective of the civil rights movement and with the hindsight gained since, the language of Born of Conviction seems mild. It did not call for integration in general or for the immediate desegregation of public schools or other facilities. Other than citing the general tenets of Christian brotherhood, the proscriptions against discrimination, and the Christian call to justice for the oppressed, the manifesto expressed no direct support for the aims of the civil rights movement, nor did it advocate civil disobedience or demonstrations to protest the refusal by the white power structure to change the system. On the Methodist denominational front, there was no demand for abolition of the segregated Central Jurisdiction.

In addition, like all of their white Southern clergy statement predecessors, the writers and eventual signers of this statement spoke from a position of white privilege and power, and what they were willing to say was limited by their caution and standing in that society. Mississippi movement leaders would likely not take much notice of their statement, and any potential backlash against it would pale in comparison to the persecution and danger experienced by the blacks and whites who fought for change on the movement's front lines.[36]

Nonetheless, when compared to all the clergy statements described in the preceding text, Born of Conviction stands out from most for at least two reasons, aside from the distinctive ecclesiological language already mentioned. Many of its predecessors called for "law and order," which could be read as not only condemning the violence of white resistance but also the civil disobedience of the movement (the Birmingham "Good Friday" statement said the latter most explicitly); Born of Conviction contained no such language. More importantly, given the critical element of the context in which these statements were issued, there was arguably no Southern clergy statement that came at a more crucial time than this one. The Little Rock declarations are comparable, given the intensity of the Central High crisis in 1957, but resistance in Arkansas never reached the sustained intensity or level of violence found in Mississippi, especially during the peak period of resistance in the Magnolia State from the fall of 1962 through the summer of 1964. As the writers of Born of Conviction believed, now that the dust had begun to settle from the Ole Miss riot, something more needed to be said, and January 1963 seemed a good time to do it. Their statement was far from perfect, but it was a beginning; these Mississippi pastors could no longer remain silent.[37]

In the last hours of the Hidden Haven retreat, the quartet constructed a list of potential signers and wondered what would happen when their words were read in Methodist churches in South Mississippi and beyond. They loaded their cars and drove out to Hintonville Road, crossed Thompson Creek, and left Perry County to return to their churches—Furr to Jackson, the others to the Gulf Coast—and to the reality of Mississippi in the fall of 1962. On that day, October 16, President Kennedy learned of Soviet missile bases in Cuba, and for the next thirteen days, the Cuban Missile Crisis unfolded. While that potential global catastrophe was resolved, work began to recruit additional signers for Born of Conviction.[38]

Signing Up

Jim Waits typed the statement at home in Biloxi in preparation for sharing it with potential signers. The time had come for some "courageous witness" in response to Sam Ashmore's "Who Is To Blame?" editorial. Thursday morning, November 1, 1962, the proclamation's four creators reconvened at Hidden Haven. They had mimeographed copies of the statement to distribute, and that afternoon a group of invited ministers met with them. The number is uncertain—perhaps fifteen or more; eventual signers Ned Kellar, Wilton Carter, Ed McRae, Bill Lampton, and Inman Moore were there, along with at least one who chose not to sign—Sam McRaney. Jim Waits had listed thirty-four potential signers on the back of a copy of the statement, and during the meeting, Maxie Dunnam noted by some of the names who had agreed to contact that person. Over the next few weeks, the four writers plus Inman Moore, Bill Lampton, Hubert Barlow, Ed McRae, and others contacted potential signers.[39]

Six weeks later on December 13, signers and potential signers gathered in Hattiesburg. They debated who else ought to be invited to enlist. Hubert Barlow, then serving at Magnolia, and his close friend Roy Eaton, pastor at Centerville, argued that all clergy in the conference should be given the chance to participate. They believed they could get as many as one hundred signatures. The statement would carry more weight if moderate leaders in the conference such as Roy Clark, John Moore, J. B. Cain, and Brunner Hunt (a district superintendent) endorsed it. The bishop would be forced to take it seriously, and many laypeople respected those leaders. Precedents for this approach abounded: the public statements in Little Rock, Mobile, and Baton Rouge all included a district superintendent and pastors of large churches among its Methodist signers. Born of Conviction's authors and some others at the meeting argued that larger church pastors should not be invited because they had more to lose. In addition, if the statement circulated more extensively now, it might never be published, given the political power of other conference leaders. Some also believed it was time for the younger generation to speak and offer a new direction for Mississippi Methodism.[40]

The latter view prevailed, and the meeting adjourned with the understanding that potential signers needed to commit by December 28 in time for the January 2 publication in the *Mississippi Methodist Advocate*. Barlow and Eaton, both of whom had agreed to sign by December 13, changed their minds about a week before publication, reiterating their arguments that the statement should be circulated more widely. They each felt remorse at their decision. Eaton explained, "I have been able to speak with some degree of freedom on the race issue. However, if my name appeared on the statement with the absence of almost all of the other preachers my laymen know, you can see that this would be a liability rather than a support." Barlow said, "I am concerned about being able to preach more than actually contained in the statement. I have been able to do this thus far and feel I can handle whatever I create personally, [whereas] a signed statement of only a small group may only confirm my 'people's opinions' about me." By the end of the Hattiesburg meeting only twenty had agreed to sign. Although Barlow withdrew, he followed through on his promise to contact Rod Entrekin.[41]

In addition to the four authors, Carter, Kellar, Lampton, McRae, and Moore all signed, along with Dunnam's best friend, Buford Dickinson. Others signed on from the Meridian District, including Powell Hall, Wallace Roberts, James Rush, and Joe Way. Because Dunnam, Trigg, Waits, and Moore all served in the Seashore District, four additional signers came from that area: Harold Ryker, John Ed Thomas, Keith Tonkel, and Jack Troutman. Bill Lampton successfully recruited his parents' pastor, N. A. Dickson of Columbia, and the other Hattiesburg District participants were Marvin Moody, Denson Napier, and Bufkin Oliver. Furr's fellow Jackson District ministers James Conner, James Holston, and James

Nicholson all signed. Rod Entrekin from the Brookhaven District and Elton Brown and Summer Walters from the Vicksburg District rounded out the Twenty-Eight. Most Southern clergy statements came from groups centered in one city and its surrounding area; the signers of Born of Conviction were spread across the roughly twenty-four thousand square miles of Mississippi's southern half (Figure 4.1).[42]

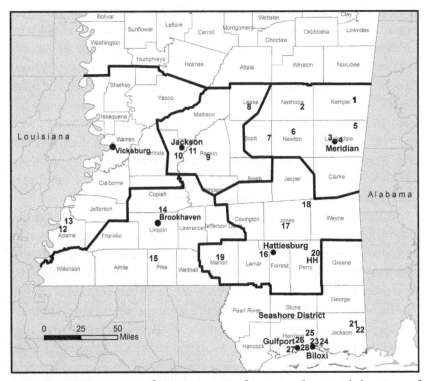

FIGURE 4.I District Map of Mississippi Conference, 1962–3, with locations of all signers. Map by Edward H. Davis. 1—Powell Hall, Scooba; 2—James Rush, Philadelphia Circuit; 3—Ed McRae, Oakland Heights, Meridian; 4—Wallace Roberts, Vimville; 5—Joe Way, Soule's Chapel; 6—Buford Dickinson, Decatur; 7—Wilton Carter, Lake; 8—James Holston, Carthage; 9—James Conner, Brandon; 10—James Nicholson, Byram; 11—Jerry Furr, Jackson Galloway, Associate; 12—Summer Walters, Natchez Jefferson Street, Associate; 13—Elton Brown, Natchez Lovely Lane; 14—Rod Entrekin, Wesson; 15—Bill Lampton, Pisgah; 16—Marvin Moody, Oak Grove; 17—Bufkin Oliver, Ellisville; 18—Ned Kellar, Sandersville; 19—N. A. Dickson, Columbia First; 20—Denson Napier, Richton; HH—Hidden Haven (Fishing Cabin where Born of Conviction was written); 21—Jerry Trigg, Caswell Springs; 22—Jack Troutman, Big Point; 23—Inman Moore, Biloxi Leggett Memorial; 24—Jim Waits, Biloxi Epworth; 25—Harold Ryker, Biloxi Beauvoir; 26—Maxie Dunnam, Gulfport Trinity; 27—Keith Tonkel, Gulfport Guinn Memorial; 28—John Ed Thomas, Gulfport First, Associate.

The ages of those who signed averaged thirty-two and ranged from twenty-five to fifty-six, but most were young: half under thirty and two-thirds under thirty-six. Five had at least ten years of full-time ministry experience, and another seven were veterans of at least five full-time years. The remaining sixteen had served less than five years—nine of those less than two years. Thus unlike the many statements that included prominent pastors, the largest congregation represented by its senior pastor in Born of Conviction was Columbia First (N. A. Dickson). The statement implied the signers were all Mississippi natives, but four were not born in the state, though all had lived there most of their lives. By January 1963 when the statement appeared, twenty-two of the signers were already fathers; ten of them had three or more children by that time, and all of the families combined numbered fifty-four children then, ranging in age from one month to eighteen years, with an additional child then *in utero* and born in March. The two oldest children were both in their first year at Millsaps College. Two signers had not yet married at that point. An additional twenty-two children were born to or adopted by the families of signers after March 1963; only one signer never had children.[43]

At least fifty-eight pastors were considered as candidates to sign the statement; their average age was also thirty-two. Two other ministers agreed to participate, but their names were not included. Signer Ed McRae told Rayford Woodrick about the statement in downtown Meridian on November 25. Woodrick, pastor at Andrew Chapel just north of Meridian, said he would be willing to sign, but that message never made it to those in charge of submitting the statement to the *Advocate*. Jerry Furr called his seminary friend Bill Lowry in Pearl just before Christmas and asked if he would be willing to sign. Lowry agreed, and Furr promised to get a copy to him and to get his official signature. The Lowry family went to Meridian for Christmas, and after they returned, Lowry heard from Furr that he had tried to reach him again and failed. The statement had already gone to press, so Lowry's name was omitted.[44]

Not all on the list of potential signers were contacted. Those who refused to sign gave various reasons, including fear they had not been at their churches long enough to weather the crisis that would surely come if their names were included, or lack of confidence in their own authority, or general unwillingness to offer such a public witness and a preference to work behind the scenes in their churches toward gradual change. Some said the statement did not say enough, but it is not clear they would have signed had the wording been stronger. One unnamed recruit reportedly

said, "It sounds innocuous enough," but he did not sign. Another poten-
tial participant, Eddie Starr, Roy Clark's associate pastor at Capitol Street
Church, declined because he was about to transfer to the Pacific Northwest
Annual Conference.[45]

Rose Trigg remembers that when her husband Jerry showed the statement to her, she said, "This is nothing. What do you expect to happen
out of this? It's just a statement of brotherhood. Everybody believes this."
Elton Brown, pastor at Lovely Lane Church in Natchez, thought it would
not cause controversy. Yet shortly after Ned Kellar returned home from
the November 1 meeting, he remembers attendee Sam McRaney stopping
by to see him and nervously asking if he had signed the statement. Kellar
had not yet committed to do so. McRaney said he would not sign and
warned, "Those who put their names to that statement will wish they had
their nickel back. . . . It's a statement advocating integration. . . . It will stir
up a hornet's nest." After McRaney left, Kellar told his wife there was no
cause for alarm. The next day he sent Maxie Dunnam not one, but two
post cards agreeing to sign.[46]

On December 27, Waits listed the twenty-three signers he knew had
committed at that point in the order their names eventually appeared in
the *Advocate*. According to one participant, the names were listed in the
order commitments were received. A flurry of five more officially signed
on by the deadline. The statement's creators had arranged with Sam
Ashmore to publish in the new year's first issue, and Ashmore inserted
a parenthetical note announcing that the statement came from "some of
the younger[,] . . . best trained and most promising ministers" of the conference and added, "We feel they express the conviction of the vast majority
of the clerical members of the conference." He also wrote an editorial on
"Freedom of the Pulpit" that ran in the same issue. One of its closing paragraphs said, "One may not agree with all the minister says, and yet, he
must respect his convictions. Could we say we have confidence in a minister of the gospel who did not preach his convictions, one who preached
only what the people wanted to hear? Give us a free pulpit or we shall soon
be without any freedom."[47]

Jim Waits sent advance copies of Born of Conviction to two North
Mississippi Conference ministers: Tupelo District Superintendent W. L.
Robinson and Bill Pennington, a pastor in Oxford and one of the ministers who issued the October Call for Repentance. Waits hoped "the statement, largely precipitated by the struggle of conscience so many of us
feel with regard to the race problem, may create a context for a clearer

witness in this area." He wanted ministers in North Mississippi to endorse it or issue a statement of their own. He also sent advance copies to the Associated Press and United Press International bureaus in Jackson, which ensured much wider publicity than the October 1962 Mississippi clergy statements.[48]

Some ministers refused to sign out of fear; others, like Summer Walters, associate pastor at Jefferson Street Church in Natchez, saw no cause for worry. While in Jackson visiting family just after Christmas 1962, Walters met Jerry Furr at his Galloway office. Furr showed Walters the statement, and Walters agreed to sign. He considered the statement to be relatively insignificant, because it stated ideas already in the *Discipline*, and he did not even keep a copy. Walters walked across the parking lot to the conference headquarters building to see Bill McLelland, Conference Director of Evangelism (and Jerry Trigg's pastor/mentor over a decade earlier), on some business. Years later, Walters remembered that during the meeting, McLelland mentioned a rumor about a statement being circulated that was so radical, it would "'split our great church.'"[49]

5

"Methodist Ministers Shatter Vacuum": January 1963

The statement was "meek and mild" by today's standards, but in the atmosphere of that day, it was like a bomb exploding within the Methodist conference and within the entire state.

—ROD ENTREKIN, "My Journey in Ministry," 2004

THE PUBLICATION OF Born of Conviction in the *Mississippi Methodist Advocate* on Wednesday, January 2, 1963, launched a battle of ideas in the media and also caused fallout in local congregations and communities; some of the local repercussions also made the newspapers. Every Mississippi daily newspaper reported on the statement the next day. By Thursday afternoon Bishop Marvin Franklin had declined comment, while four Meridian area signers quoted in front-page *Meridian Star* stories said the statement simply reflected the position of the Methodist Church. Wilton Carter explained, "This is not a rabid stand a few preachers have taken but what Methodists have believed all along. It is the position of the officials of the church." Ed McRae said the ministers had signed the statement "in order to open the door to discussion of the issues . . . without fear of recrimination."[1]

Discussion and recrimination ensued. Responses to the Twenty-Eight revealed a spectrum of attitudes among white Mississippians, from advocacy of civil rights movement concerns to the bitter opposition of the Citizens' Council and terrorist efforts to intimidate through threats and violence. The statement caused a huge controversy, and its publication and the range of public and private responses to it can be understood as a full-fledged argument on race relations, pastoral authority, and the purpose of the church among whites in Mississippi. This mostly one-sided early 1963 debate reveals the views of white Mississippians as they confronted the possibility their segregated world might change. Most of the public responders recoiled at the suggestion that the church might play any role besides supporter of the white supremacist culture, but the mainly private expressions of support revealed a substantial minority sympathetic to the signers' alternative witness.

Ed McRae (Figure 5.1) had been at Oakland Heights in Meridian, a new church on the western edge of the city, since 1960, and the congregation had built its church building and parsonage during his tenure. At 5:30 the morning after the statement appeared in the *Advocate*, he received a phone request from a reporter at the afternoon *Meridian Star* for a comment on why he had signed. Unsure how to respond, he told the reporter he would bring a written statement to the paper's offices in a couple of hours. When McRae delivered it, the reporter engaged him in further conversation, and to McRae's dismay, much of what he said orally found its way into a front-page story later that day. The signers' purpose, according to McRae, "was to stimulate thinking, not to push integration." When the reporter told him that "another Methodist minister in Meridian had declined comment and said

FIGURE 5.1 Ed McRae, 1960s. Courtesy of Ed and Martina Riley McRae.

he didn't even want his name near the story," McRae saw this as "typical of the type of fear of free expression that the statement is attacking."[2]

Public Responses: Voices for Change

Unlike the minister who declined comment, a few white Mississippi Methodists dared to speak publicly in support of Born of Conviction, including Mississippi Conference Lay Leader J. P. Stafford Sr. (Figure 5.2), of Cary, a small Sharkey County community in the Delta. Stafford, born near Winona, Mississippi, in 1893, had earned a master's degree in education from Peabody College for Teachers and was studying law at Ole Miss when trustees from the Cary Schools invited him to come there as superintendent. He began that job in 1919 with encouragement from the trustees to take the equality part of "separate but equal" schools more seriously. Cary had more black residents than white; it also had Chinese and Jewish residents. Stafford stayed in the superintendent's job more than thirty years; he also owned a successful cotton farm and paid his workers in real money

FIGURE 5.2 J. P. Stafford, 1960s. Courtesy of Emily Stafford Matheny.

rather than the standard sharecropping system practice of payment in scrip. In the early 1940s, he became associate lay leader of the Vicksburg District. His daughter Emily had recently married Robert Matheny, a young preacher in the conference. By 1944 Stafford had become lay leader of the Vicksburg District, and in 1947 he became the conference lay leader. In 1956, he told Bishop Franklin he wanted to step down from that post, but Franklin prevailed upon Stafford to stay as long as he remained bishop in Mississippi.[3]

Thoroughly convinced of the centrality of the Reformation concept of the priesthood of all believers, Stafford encouraged Mississippi Methodist laity to participate in a wide range of ministry activities in their congregations, rather than simply pay the bills and expect their pastors to do everything else. He promoted lay work in churches across South Mississippi, and the travel schedule led him to retire from the Cary Schools in the early 1950s, though he continued to farm. The conference paid his expenses, but he received no salary. He had an office in the Methodist Building in Jackson, seventy-five miles from his home, and usually spent a day or two a week there. In the 1950s he was elected to the General Church's Coordinating Council, and this increased his travel, expertise, and recognition as a lay leader in the Methodist Church. He played a central role in the founding of Methodist Men, a lay organization in the denomination, and helped many Mississippi congregations start local chapters.[4]

By 1963 Stafford was well-known and highly respected across the Mississippi Conference. Upon the release of Born of Conviction, he endorsed the statement and said, "It is hard for many of us to go along with the great Methodist Church and changing times, in matters of race, but this is an adjustment **Christians can make**." In a January 3 public letter to the signers, Stafford greeted them, "Welcome to the fold of those who are willing to stand up and be counted. There is still plenty of room left for others, and we hope many will join us. For our part we will not feel so lonesome any more." He also invoked the prophet Elijah: "In the future, there will be an answer for those who ask—Where are the Pastors of the Mississippi Conference? We can say there are at least '7000' (28) who have not 'bowed the knee to Baal'" and have rejected the Closed Society idolatry. Francis Stevens, a Jackson attorney and associate lay leader of the conference, also publicly approved of Born of Conviction.[5]

At a North Mississippi Conference Tupelo District preacher's meeting in Okolona on January 3, District Superintendent W. L. "Slim" Robinson presented the statement and asked for an endorsement. Twenty-three ministers "enthusiastically" voted to support it, and their names appeared in a

Clarion-Ledger story the next day. The other six present abstained. Robinson explained, "I felt it was one of the most comprehensive statements on the subject that I have read. A Methodist minister must go by the scripture, the position of the church and his own conscience." The endorsement request came as a surprise to the pastors present at the meeting, and some who supported it were not pleased that Robinson gave their names to the paper.[6]

One of the endorsers was E. S. Furr of Calhoun City. The publicity upset some of his church members, and one congregational leader told him he would have been ousted from the church if the people did not love him so much. June Murphree, a member of Furr's church and editor of the local weekly paper, mistakenly suggested in her next column that many signed or endorsed Born of Conviction "because the order was handed down to them from Bishop Marvin Franklin, through the District Superintendent." Furr did not experience any repercussions in the North Mississippi Conference and did not remember anyone leaving that conference because of this stand.[7]

The boldest Mississippi Methodist endorsement—stronger than Born of Conviction and quoted in full in the *Clarion-Ledger*—came from W. B. Selah, Jerry Furr's mentor and pastor of Jackson's Galloway Memorial. William Bryan Selah was born in 1896 in Sedalia, Missouri. His mother died when he was five weeks old, and a family in Kansas City adopted him. He graduated from Central Methodist College in Fayette, Missouri, and Yale Divinity School. In his early career in Missouri, he became known as an excellent preacher. This led to his appointment to St. John's M. E. Church, South in Memphis in 1937 and St. Luke's Methodist Church in Oklahoma City in 1941. In 1945, he arrived at Galloway, a prestigious congregation accustomed to going outside of Mississippi to find its pastors.[8]

Selah (Figure 5.3) soon won the respect and devotion of Galloway members, and he settled in to a long tenure there. Just after the early March 1958 controversy at Millsaps College involving Citizens' Council protest against integrationist views expressed in a campus event, Selah preached a moderate, gradualist sermon advocating a separate but equal approach to public education and expressing disagreement with the 1954 *Brown* decision. However, he insisted that people had the right to express dissenting views without persecution and called for freedom of the pulpit. He predicted reason and love would finally triumph in dealing with the race issue.[9]

His unsuccessful attempt to convince the Galloway Official Board to keep their church doors open to all in 1961 represented something of a shift in his views, but it was consistent with his faith in reason and

FIGURE 5.3 W. B. Selah, 1950s. Courtesy of J. B. Cain Archives of Mississippi Methodism, Millsaps College.

love. Subsequent events and his relationship with Jerry Furr pushed him beyond gradualism. Jim Waits visited Furr at Galloway just after the publication of Born of Conviction and recalls that Selah met him in the hall and said, "I saw your statement in the paper. The only problem is that it wasn't strong enough!"[10]

Selah released his statement commending Born of Conviction and its signers on January 6. He remarked, "They stuck their necks out without asking me to sign it. I was glad to receive requests to comment." He insisted that "for seventeen years I have preached the law of Christian love from the pulpit of Galloway Methodist Church" and proclaimed,

> We must seek for all men, black and white, the same justice, the same rights, and the same opportunities that we seek for ourselves. Nothing less than this is Christian love. To discriminate against a man because of his color or his creed is contrary to the will of God. Forced segregation is wrong. We should voluntarily desegregate all public facilities.

Echoing his 1961 statement to Galloway's Official Board, he added, "As Christians, we cannot say to anyone, 'You cannot come into the house of God.' No conference, no preacher, no official board can put up a color bar in the church," because Christianity is "an inclusive fellowship." Seconding the Twenty-Eight's call for pulpit freedom, he asserted, "The preacher must get his message not from the community but from Christ."[11]

A handful of state newspaper editors, including Hazel Brannon Smith, Ira Harkey, Hodding Carter III, and P. D. East, also supported the Twenty-Eight in print. Though he did not mention Born of Conviction, another North Mississippi voice joined the Twenty-Eight's rejection of resistance to change at any cost. In late January, Jack Reed, a Tupelo Methodist layman and president-elect of the Mississippi Economic Council, insisted in a public speech that Mississippians needed to face up to likely school desegregation, "keep every public school open," and avoid "directly or by implication [condoning] violence of any sort whatsoever."[12]

Mississippi native L. Scott Allen, a black Methodist minister and editor of the Central Jurisdiction's *Central Christian Advocate*, printed the full text of Born of Conviction in the February 15 issue. He called it "a refreshing breath of courageous Christian conviction." Though the number of signers was small, he celebrated the "deep fervor" of their statement, which "expresses the kind of Christian witness which has been characteristic of minorities who have changed the course of history many times."[13]

There is little evidence that Mississippi civil rights movement participants took much note of Born of Conviction, but Ed King, white Methodist minister and a leader in the Jackson Movement, later expressed deep appreciation for the stand taken by the Twenty-Eight. Victoria Gray, a black Methodist civil rights activist from Hattiesburg, responded to Methodist pastor Bertist Rouse's letter attacking the Twenty-Eight in the Hattiesburg paper; she praised the signers for speaking out against racial injustice even though they knew the price of taking such a stand in Mississippi. To her, to be "Born of Conviction" meant that one had to speak out.[14]

Public Responses: Segregationists in the Press

State senator and former Brandon mayor John McLaurin earned a reputation as a leading proponent of Closed Society massive resistance measures. In 1960, he helped push through an amendment to the appropriations bill for the state's colleges that prohibited paying any person who belonged to "'subversive' organizations such as the [American Civil Liberties Union], the NAACP, or the Communist Party." He played a central role in legislative efforts to block James Meredith's admission to Ole Miss, and he was a member of Governor Barnett's delegation at Ole Miss on September 30, 1962, the night Meredith officially arrived on campus and the riot ensued. McLaurin also belonged to Brandon Methodist Church, where Born of Conviction signer James Conner served as pastor. The senator responded to the Twenty-Eight publicly by asking Mississippians not to assume the signers represented the membership of the Methodist Church. Born of Conviction, he charged, was "calculated to stir racial strife and to destroy the society in which we are accustomed to living." He urged Mississippi Methodists not to "let a few men destroy our great church."[15]

In Pike County, the Summit Methodist Church's Official Board publicly condemned both "certain ministers" for "promot[ing] racial integration in our churches, schools and society" and J. P. Stafford, who "does not represent our laymen with his thinking." Insisting that "God will not smile on a mongrelized people," the church board added, "We are at peace and need to be left alone by those who would attempt to cause friction among us. 'God help us maintain this peace' is our prayer." Editor Mary Cain of the weekly *Summit Sun*, whose condemnation of James Meredith drew signer Bill Lampton's homiletical criticism at Pisgah Church three months earlier, saluted the Summit Methodists: "Their clearly presented statement leaves no doubt that our local church is blessed with real leaders."[16]

The most influential news voice in the state, the Hederman family-owned *Clarion-Ledger* and *Jackson Daily News*, accounted for almost 50 percent of the daily newspaper sales in South Mississippi, the area covered by the Mississippi Conference. The papers attacked the Twenty-Eight and their supporters. Jimmy Ward, a Methodist and editor of the afternoon *Daily News*, commented about "noisy" preachers who were "about to get out of hand," questioned whether Mississippi ministers truly lacked freedom of the pulpit, and suggested progress might be "better achieved with a return to old fashioned religion distinctly separated from the frills of new-fangled social and complex political theories." Because Born of Conviction invoked the authority of "the expressed witness of our Church" and Selah was pastor of Galloway, columnist Tom Ethridge quoted Galloway Church's namesake, MECS Bishop Charles Betts Galloway, who said in 1904 that two things regarding race "may be considered as definitely and finally settled: First: In the South there will never be any social mingling of the races. Whether it be prejudice or pride of race, there is a middle wall of partition which will not be broken down. Second: They will worship in separate churches and be educated in separate schools." The *Daily News* reprinted a 1932 article on MECS Bishop Warren Candler's view that "racial lines are ordained of God."[17]

Ethridge also asked, "Just where does Christian practice of 'equality' cease and un-Christian 'discrimination' end in a church, community or family?" Could Christians draw any color line between the races without being accused of "some degree of 'prejudice' and 'discrimination' which allegedly is sinful?" Later in January, Ward criticized Born of Conviction because it "caused Mississippians and millions elsewhere to think that the ministerial group was ready to pitch in the towel as far as the state's efforts to maintain racial integrity" and to give in to "agitators'" efforts to "[destroy] Mississippi's peaceful society and [convert] the state into one more integrated jungle of mahem [*sic*], rape and murder." The Hederman papers often derisively used the metaphor of race "mixing" to express their disdain at any suggestion that the current system of race relations needed repair.[18]

These standard views—that the Twenty-Eight had meddled in politics and secular matters and strayed from their calling to preach the Gospel and save lost souls; segregation and the supposedly historically peaceful race relations in Mississippi (now stirred up only because of outside influence) were ordained by God; and the signers had betrayed the holy cause of white Mississippi and sought to use the church inappropriately for political ends—arose frequently in January letters to the editor. Of twenty related missives published in the Jackson papers that month, all but one were critical of the Twenty-Eight (and occasionally Selah), with another five negative responses in the Meridian paper. The positive letter did not mention Born of Conviction but disagreed with the claim "that preachers should just stick to winning souls to Christ." The writer insisted "that if preachers cannot preach in a way that our daily lives are helped they might as well stop preaching." Only two directly supportive letters appeared in any Mississippi daily that month. One came in the Gulf Coast *Daily Herald*, written by Clara Mae Sells, a retired Methodist deaconess whose father and brother were Mississippi Conference ministers. She fully endorsed the statement and called for more open communication between the races. In response to Oliver Emmerich's January editorials in the McComb paper calling for free discussion on the race issue, a Kentwood, Louisiana, woman wrote expressing gratitude and invoking

Jesus's words in Luke 6:26: "Woe unto you when all men shall speak well of you. . . ." In her opinion, if there is no opposition to what ministers say or do, then they are probably not representing God very well.[19]

By that standard, responses to the Twenty-Eight proved the prophetic truth of their words. Some letter writers claimed Christian brotherhood was spiritual, not physical or social and thus did not entail any race mixing; one linked "spiritual purity" with "uphold[ing] racial integrity." Several also condemned the Methodist Church and its "integrationist" Sunday School literature and other publications, and a few explained the denomination's liberalism had led them to leave for spinoff Methodist groups like the Southern Methodist Church. Some claimed the Bible teaches segregation and distinguished between "biblical truths" and the Twenty-Eight's "personal opinions." One argued the ministers should be more concerned about the recent banning of prayer in public schools than any supposed racial injustice.[20]

Some called the signers Communist dupes. A writer suggested the churches of those demanding freedom of the pulpit "should rise as one man and 'free them of the pulpits' they now hold." Another letter asserted, "We may have to put up with a Negro in our university, but God have mercy upon a congregation who hasn't got enough of the spirit of God left in it to rid its pulpit of these sheep in wolves [sic] clothing who have openly denied the teachings of God's holy word." Mississippi Conference pastor Roy Wesley Wolfe said if pulpit freedom "means that laymen should be forced to pay a man's salary to stand Sunday after Sunday and shove integration down their throats, I do not believe in a 'free pulpit.' If it means to uncompromisingly proclaim the truth of God's Holy Word, I do believe in a 'free pulpit.' "[21]

Another attack came from MAMML. In its "Methodist Declaration of Conscience on Racial Segregation," released January 10 in response to Born of Conviction, MAMML charged that attacks on segregation were un-Christian, because segregation "has protected both races and allowed both their fullest development." MAMML claimed John Wesley founded Methodism because he "rejected ecclesiastical authoritarianism," and he "preached the witness of the spirit to the individual believer—there has never been any infallible source of authority within the Methodist Church." Born of Conviction and related national church statements showed "a developing spirit of authoritarianism." Ultimately, the church should not be seen as "an instrument of social revolution or control."

A *Meridian Star* editorial echoed this view by deploring the Twenty-Eight's meddling in politics and espousing the Social Gospel.[22]

The range of views expressed in the media represented a public argument about the meaning of Christian brotherhood, appropriate relations among human beings, and the purpose of the church, and this debate extended into local Methodist congregations. Born of Conviction cited the Methodist *Discipline*'s claim that the teachings of Jesus did not permit discrimination; the signers hoped the expressed witness of The Methodist Church would influence their church members. But numerous church readers saw it as scandalous for their ministers to call for race relations change in such a public way and upset so many white Mississippians. For many Methodist church members and some pastors, the commitment to "our Southern way of life" trumped the church's witness as expressed by the statement. By publicly advocating change in race relations, the signers had betrayed their families and their church (the conference and their congregations) and "bartered their loyalty to their own race, their state and to those who look to them for spiritual guidance."[23]

The Twenty-Eight's vocal opponents saw no tension between the segregated system and the Christian faith. The oft-repeated accusation of political and social emphases at the expense of the Gospel echoed the Southern Presbyterian doctrine of the "spirituality of the church," which maintained a strict dualism between spiritual matters (the proper realm of church attention) and secular matters (which the church should leave to civil authorities). In reality, this theological claim served to preserve the status quo and thus was inherently political and social. At best, therefore, critics were naïve—and at worst, dishonest—to accuse the Twenty-Eight of inappropriately offering theological commentary on "secular" affairs.[24]

Segregationist Responses in Congregations

MAMML's January statement included the assertion that a minister desiring freedom of the pulpit should "be ready to accept the consequences if what he says offends the consciences of those to whom he looks for support," and some of these inevitable reactions made the news. On January 10 the Official Board of Oakland Heights Church in Meridian voted on a motion to dismiss their pastor, Ed McRae. The motion failed, with a vote of thirteen for and nineteen against. A member of the anti-McRae faction said,

We do not believe in integration. We do not believe that all races are brothers as stated in the document signed by the 28 pastors. We believe in the freedom of worship and feel that we do not have this if we are forced to listen to a minister who has shown by his actions that he does not care about our Southern way of life but will betray part of his membership by signing what we believe is a politically inspired document.

Conditions at the church did not improve over the next few weeks, and in February the same board formally requested a pastoral change in June and declared they did not want the conference to appoint any other member of the Twenty-Eight as their pastor. Several other congregations passed resolutions echoing the latter demand.[25]

At Wesson and Galloway, served by signers Rod Entrekin and Jerry Furr (and vocal supporter Selah), more polite resolutions expressed respect for their pastors' "integrity of opinion" and leadership but claimed the published statements were "not necessarily the views and opinions of the individual members." Both churches asserted, "It is not un-Christian that we prefer to remain an all-white congregation" and cited "time-honored tradition," hoping its "perpetuation . . . will never be impaired." One church insisted the words of the Twenty-Eight, Sam Ashmore, and Selah were a "minority report" and called on the bishop or cabinet to publish the opposing "majority report" in the media. Another church's decree added disapproval of J. P. Stafford's public endorsement of the Twenty-Eight.[26]

Oakland Heights played by Methodist rules and waited until the end of the conference year in early June for McRae to move, but churches served by three of the signers entered the public argument by rejecting and ejecting their offending pastors immediately. One of the ousted pastors, James Rush, graduated from Duke Divinity School in 1962 and had served the Philadelphia Circuit, a three-church charge in eastern Neshoba County, for seven months. After the statement's release, Rush attempted to explain his Christian commitment to racial justice in his January 6 sermon and in the charge newsletter (which he hand delivered to church members), but strong segregationist sentiments in the community and a telephone campaign against him sealed his fate.[27]

The next week, three supportive church members informed Rush of a chargewide meeting of the Philadelphia Circuit to be held that evening; it was the first he had heard of it. When he arrived at the meeting, the door was locked, and church members did not want to let him in.

Upon gaining entrance, Rush was asked to recant and publicly remove his name from the statement; he refused. With Meridian District Superintendent James Slay presiding, the meeting culminated with a motion to remove Rush as their pastor; the vote was seventy to four in favor. One of those present, Lawrence Rainey, was elected later that year as Neshoba County Sheriff and later acquitted in 1967 of violating the civil rights of movement workers James Chaney, Andrew Goodman, and Michael Schwerner, murdered in Neshoba County in 1964. After the vote, Slay's insistence that Rush would remain on the charge until June caused an uproar. Rush remembers someone saying, "If the Methodist Church can't get rid of nigger lovers and Communists, then we can." Due to the vote, constant harassment, and threats of violence, James and Libby Rush and their infant son moved to Lake to his parents' home in mid-January, and by February 1, the conference had appointed another minister to the charge.[28]

At Byram, the second ousted pastor, James Nicholson, had endured an almost total congregational boycott in response to his October 1962 sermon after the Ole Miss riot. When he went public in January as a signer of Born of Conviction, church members again asked District Superintendent Willard Leggett to remove their pastor. Nicholson met with the church's Official Board, assured them he would move in June, and encouraged them to hold the church together until then. They insisted they would not pay his salary and would continue to boycott worship. In Leggett's view, Nicholson's support of Born of Conviction violated an agreement reached after his October sermon that he would say no more on the race issue; Nicholson denied making such a promise. Leggett decided the situation was irreconcilable and relieved Nicholson of his duties. Technically Nicholson remained pastor of the church and received some salary support from the conference, but Leggett appointed Hank Winstead, a neighboring pastor, as associate to conduct worship and regular pastoral duties. Leggett said Nicholson was free to "[administer] to any person who may request your service, provided it does not interfere with the services of the Church," but in effect, Nicholson was no longer the Byram pastor.[29]

At Pisgah in Pike County on Thursday, January 3, a local Citizens' Council member told Pastor Bill Lampton that a church meeting that evening would result in his dismissal from the congregation. District Superintendent Norman Boone did not allow a vote at the meeting, because Methodist polity does not involve congregational votes to decide on pastoral leadership. A few members said they would be at worship

Sunday, but others promised to stop all support of the church as long as Lampton remained. One church member insisted they would accept only preachers who believed in segregation. The next night, two tires on Lampton's car were slashed, and on Saturday church members informed him of "rumors of group action," which might result in damage to church property, and asked him not to be at worship on Sunday. He consulted with Boone, who left the decision up to him. Lampton feared the violence would spread, so he took his family fifty miles away to his hometown of Columbia and did not return. In explaining his departure to the press, he said, "It looked like I had another Ole Miss on my hands."[30]

Some Methodist pastors opposed to Born of Conviction used their pulpits to participate in the argument. Charles Duke, a graduate of Millsaps and SMU's Perkins School of Theology, was pastor of Broadmeadow Methodist, a North Jackson congregation. In his sermon on January 20, 1963, he proclaimed that Christians are born not of convictions but of the Spirit, and convictions without the Spirit destroy the unity of Christian people. Duke expressed puzzlement at the Twenty-Eight's concern about lack of freedom in the pulpit. He claimed he had always enjoyed that freedom but would never use the pulpit to "air my personal opinions or debate any issue." He resented the assertion that those who signed Born of Conviction had shown courage while nonsigning pastors were simply afraid. He said,

> I am not willing . . . to accept as the Christian position on race relations the theory that the Negro advances only in relation to his ability to force himself into social relations with the white race. I do not accept integration as an advancement for the Negro and I do not accept segregation as discrimination against the Negro.[31]

Then followed a common segregationist argument: in nature, animals remain true to their identity by sticking with their own kind. Birds of different species do not mix; different dog breeds are not improved by mating with each other. It is not discrimination to keep dog breeds separate, because that separation allows them to achieve their natural best. In human relations, "forced integration is unchristian since it inevitably results in abnormal conditions in which both races suffer and become less than their best." Christians should seek to develop the best in people, and trying to force unnatural mixing of the races would tragically result in less than the best for all involved. Copies of Duke's sermon were distributed around the conference.[32]

Spencer Sissell, the Jackson District Lay Leader and a member of Duke's church, expressed confusion in the *Advocate* as to Born of Conviction's meaning. While agreeing with the call to brotherhood, he added, "If they are saying that they advocate the mixing of the races in the local church, in the school room or socially, then I vehemently disagree with them." He affirmed freedom of the pulpit but insisted on the equal importance of "freedom of the pew."[33]

Private Segregationist Responses

The *Advocate* received some negative letters, all effectively private because editor Sam Ashmore almost never published letters to the editor. One Jackson Methodist pastor insisted that God "created every race and color and intended for man to stay that way" through "race purity." Another writer claimed the message of the Tower of Babel story in Genesis 11 was that "God created the races distinct from one another, and he scattered them all over the earth when they attempted to integrate and become as one."[34]

The Twenty-Eight also received critical letters from individuals. An acquaintance urged Inman Moore not to let the Communists "make you think you are 'going all the way' to be real Christian, when really this false teaching of theirs helps them to create a civil war in the U.S. and meantime they will take over and all Christians will be imprisoned or beheaded, etc." She knew he would recant publicly "when you see the true Bible teachings." Moore replied to her that Born of Conviction was "thoroughly in keeping ... with the teachings of the New Testament and the Spirit of Jesus Christ."[35]

A member of Summer Walters's congregation wrote him that the statement could not result in any good for the church and chastised him for signing it. Echoing arguments that Born of Conviction was "political" and Christians would not be damned to Hell if they sought alternatives to integrated schools, he vowed not to educate his children if an integrated school were the only option. He could not see how calls for integration had any connection to the Christian faith as he understood it. Wilton Carter received an anonymous letter that began, "Your recent action does not merit your being address Mr. or Rev [sic]." It attacked his statements to the press and concluded, "We are interested in seeing later reports along from you and other *sheep* (signers) of the *Methodist discipline resolution* . . . . Not once did any of you mention the *Bible*, which lays bare the fact that woe be unto them that sow *dissention* [sic] and the little 28 did just that and the harvest will be great with turmoil and hate."[36]

Private and Public Responses: Protect the Church and Don't Rock the Boat

Other writers criticized the Twenty-Eight for hurting the church. They expressed concern for white Mississippi Methodism as a whole and for the status of individual congregations in their local communities. A cluster of five Methodist churches cited the "incalculable harm" done to Mississippi Methodism by Born of Conviction and expressed the hope that leaders would provide proper guidance to help the church "fulfill its great destiny." Before 1963, some Mississippi Methodist pastors, including Jack Loflin at Bude in Franklin County, had been fairly honest in their congregations about their more open views on race relations. Loflin had known several Born of Conviction signers since his student days at Millsaps, and he and signer Bill Lampton were fraternity brothers. He attended Vanderbilt Divinity School with Jerry Trigg and Joe Way, and the list of potential signers developed by Jim Waits and others included Loflin's name. After the statement appeared, a church member well aware of Loflin's perspective on race asked him why he had not signed the statement, and Loflin replied that he had not been asked. The church member inquired how he would have responded had he been asked, and Loflin said he probably would have signed. As he later remembered it, the man replied, "I love you like a son, but [if you had signed it,] your ass would have been gone!" It was not acceptable for views similar to Born of Conviction to be made public beyond Bude Methodist Church.[37]

A member of Laurel's Franklin Church who identified himself as a friend of his congregation's founding pastor, Born of Conviction signer N. A. Dickson, wrote Sam Ashmore to disagree with the editor's claim that the Twenty-Eight spoke for "the vast majority of the clerical members of the conference." The correspondent had consulted several pastors and reported, "I won't say 'a vast majority' of all the ministers were opposed to the statement. But everyone with whom I have spoken did or indicated they would have declined the opportunity to affix their signature. None felt that it was good for the Church." Friends of Maxie Dunnam expressed disappointment at his "recent 'extracurricular' clerical activities," which had done "a great deal of harm to the Methodist Church."[38]

Bert Jordan of Jackson, an associate lay leader of the conference, said, "I do not understand why, in the face of magnificent progress, unparalleled growth in stewardship and unlimited opportunities, that we would bring down upon ourselves an unnecessary social crisis that lashes a staggering blow to the church and the unity of our people." Jordan wondered why ministers considering making controversial public statements would not first consult their church members or Official Board, "since they too strive to be Christian and are interested in any issue that involves the church they love." Jordan's critique was not necessarily segregationist. Concerns at the "incalculable harm" Born of Conviction would cause the church may have been a smokescreen for segregationist views, but some critics responded to the Twenty-Eight out of their intense (though misguided) love for the Methodist Church in Mississippi.[39]

The Official Conference Response

North Mississippi Conference pastor R. Glenn Miller wrote Ashmore that Bishop Franklin "should represent THE METHODIST CHURCH, and if he lets these boys suffer because they have convictions, then he has lost the respect of all of us." Roy Clark also wanted conference leaders, including the bishop, to offer a public response. Clark had not been asked to sign Born of Conviction, but on January 8, he met in Hattiesburg with "three or four [pastors] . . . identified with the power structure" who were also "men of social conscience." Working across conference political lines, they drafted a statement supporting "not necessarily everything that the Twenty-eight said" but defending "their right to say it and affirm[ing] the need for open conversation." They gained approval from a minister "very close to the power structure" and planned to seek signatures from a broad spectrum of conference ministers, but upon learning that the bishop and cabinet were meeting the next day, they agreed a declaration from that group would be better. Returning to Jackson, Clark took the Hattiesburg statement to the bishop and "asked him if he did not use this statement, to use one similar to it and to suggest that his cabinet issue it, which would say that we stand behind these young men . . . and their right to speak." The bishop took the statement and simply thanked Clark.[40]

Whether Franklin ever intended to take Clark's advice is not known, but something prevented it. Bishop Franklin and the Mississippi Conference Cabinet, including conference political leader Willard Leggett, released a response on January 14 that appeared in the January 16 issue of the *Advocate*. Their statement did not stand behind the Twenty-Eight and did not even mention Born of Conviction; it did not mention the right of ministers to speak their conscience or the need for open conversation on the race issue. The bishop and cabinet simply said, "We each declare anew our support of the doctrines and historic positions of the Methodist Church," but they also assured Mississippi Methodists that "integration is not forced upon any part of our Church." They closed by saying, "Our Conference has a great program in evangelism, education, missions and other areas. Let us move on to do the work of the Church, loving mercy, doing justly, and walking humbly with our Lord, pressing toward the mark of the prize of high calling of God in Christ Jesus." The bishop, cabinet, and many others in the conference—even some who questioned segregation—opposed anything that threatened the church's institutional success and standing in society. Many white Mississippi Methodists believed part of the church's purpose was to preserve the segregated system. By contrast, the Twenty-Eight's ecclesiology assumed the church had a duty to lead its members to speak out and stand against clear injustice, even if that meant possible backlash from the dominant culture.[41]

Perhaps the bishop and cabinet meant their affirmation of Methodist doctrines and historic positions as faint and implicit approval of Born of Conviction, because the Twenty-Eight quoted the *Discipline* and had asserted they were simply expressing the official Methodist position on the race issue. However, interpretation of the declaration of "support of the doctrines and historic positions of the Methodist Church" in the January 14 statement depended on one's perspective. J. Melvin Jones, senior pastor at Gulfport First Methodist (where Born of Conviction signer John Ed Thomas served as associate) wrote Sam Ashmore that the Twenty-Eight were mistaken to claim the words they quoted from the *Discipline* were the "official position of The Methodist Church." Because the quotation came from the Methodist Social Creed in an Appendix to the *Discipline*, Jones argued this made the words the "'unofficial' position" of the church. This strained interpretation ignored the fact that the General Conference, the only body with authority to speak for the Methodist Church, had approved the language. Those who agreed with

Jones's view could have read this sentence from the bishop and cabinet's statement as implying that Born of Conviction did not express "historic" Methodist views, and some of Bishop Franklin's critics claimed he shared Jones' opinion.[42]

If Bishop Franklin had offered public support—at least for the Twenty-Eight's right to speak—then some of the anger and bewilderment in the conference might have been allayed. Regardless of what the bishop and cabinet meant by their statement, signer Bufkin Oliver told Ole Miss professor James Silver that the Twenty-Eight considered it "a repudiation of what we had done." L. Ray Branton of Aurora Methodist Church in New Orleans wrote Bishop Franklin to say the January 14 statement was both tragic and ambiguous. It "can be interpreted only as an implied declaration of non-support for those who have had the courage to support the witness of our church in race relations." Conceding the risk involved in supporting the denominational position on race, Branton pressured Franklin to be courageous. If ministers who "are most vulnerable to reprisal" had taken the risk, "the great episcopal office of our church will be increased in stature by a similar witness." It was upon the race issue, he concluded, "that the church will stand or fall in our generation. If we fail here, we will have betrayed our Lord and our God. I ask your prayers that I will not fail. I pray you will not."[43]

The Millsaps College Faculty sent a confidential resolution to the bishop that expressed their disappointment in the January 14 public statement and urged him to offer both public and private support to the Twenty-Eight (sixteen of whom were Millsaps graduates). They also pressed him to encourage such persons to remain in Mississippi. The resolution mentioned Franklin's 1961 declaration in the *Advocate*, which counseled congregations to "insist that [their minister] be a prophet of God and not a panderer of meaningless platitudes," and claimed the preacher's role is to point the congregation "to the mind, the will, and the purpose of God." Franklin's response in a private letter to the secretary of the faculty voiced regret that they had passed judgment without discussing the matter with him and asserted he had always "exhorted laymen to insist that their ministers say what they honestly believe God would have them say, with the pew having the right to agree or disagree." In the October 1962 words of Sam Ashmore's editorial, Oliver, Branton, and the Millsaps faculty interpreted the January 14 statement from the bishop and cabinet as full of "pious platitudes" when "courageous witness" was needed.[44]

Private Sympathetic Responses

The Millsaps faculty's choice not to publicize its resolution to the bishop epitomizes a central element of the Born of Conviction controversy: most of the positive response to the statement remained private. J. P. Stafford told the Twenty-Eight, "When the shooting starts and you are far apart, maybe it will help to know that hundreds of consecrated laymen will applaud you, and countless others will wish you well in secret—that lack the courage and fortitude to come out into the open." The public applause he predicted did not materialize. In contrast to the overwhelmingly nega-tive, though not unanimous, public response, the many private letters sent to the signers ran four to one on the supportive side. Almost all of the negative letters came from Mississippi, but two-fifths of the positive letters came from secret well-wishers in the state.[45]

About thirty different organizations, groups, or individuals from Mississippi and beyond offered their support to the Twenty-Eight by sending them each a letter. The Mississippians included Ole Miss his-torian James Silver; Congressman Frank E. Smith (who had just lost a reelection bid due in part to his moderate approach to the race issue); J. P. Stafford, Episcopal priest and Ole Miss riot hero Duncan Gray of Oxford; and J. Reese Rush, lay leader of Wilton Carter's church at Lake and signer James Rush's father. Methodist individuals in several other states added their support, including Dean M. Kelley, a Methodist minister serving on the staff of the National Council of Churches. The denomination's General Board of Christian Social Concerns sent the signers a letter with signatures from a bishop and Clarie Collins Harvey, a black Mississippian and member of a Central Jurisdiction Methodist congregation in Jackson. All signers, along with Bishop Franklin, Sam Ashmore, and W. B. Selah, received a report that Born of Conviction had been read aloud at an inter-racial meeting of Kentucky Methodist ministers from the Louisville area who represented the black and white annual conferences. The group voted unanimously to send a letter of appreciation.[46]

Signers also received personal support from college and seminary friends, former mentors, pastors, and some church members and relatives of church members. Candler School of Theology professors E. Clinton Gardner and Theodore Runyon wrote to each of the recent Candler alumni among the Twenty-Eight. Runyon suggested, "The stand you have taken will be one of the most significant acts of your ministry, a minis-try directed to and for the very people who may now feel that you have somehow betrayed them. It is for them that you have done this. For you know that a church which simply says what we want to hear is of no more use to man than it is to God." Dow Kirkpatrick, pastor of First Methodist in Evanston, Illinois, had known seminarian Maxie Dunnam in the 1950s while serving in Atlanta and began his letter to Dunnam with pride: "You fellows have made news all over Methodism." Henry Clay, now of Laurel, the black Methodist pastor Dunnam had known in Gulfport, expressed his appreciation to Dunnam.[47]

Many supportive private letters came to the *Advocate* from Methodists within and outside of the state. A Gulfport layman predicted that Born of Conviction and Selah's statement would result "in awakening a great many people who have been afraid to speak out," and he was happy that "decent and responsible leadership" had risen to "replace the wrong kind that unfortunately has prevailed in recent months." A Memphis layman said the Twenty-Eight and Selah were "standing up for Jesus." The Executive Director of the Methodist United Nations Office requested copies of the January 2 *Advocate* for some UN friends "who need to have their hearts warmed by your courage." Bishop Franklin also received positive letters, including three from members of Maxie Dunnam's Gulfport congregation. Church members and pastors seldom applauded publicly. Another of Dunnam's church members admitted, "I am ashamed of my own silence, but my husband and I have tried not 'to rock the boat' since we chose to live here. So, I cannot tell you what it means to me to know that you and others like you are saying what I feel but do not have the courage to say."[48]

Roy C. Clark, pastor at Capitol Street Methodist in Jackson and a supporter of the Born of Conviction signers, understood well what could happen to people who publicly challenged the status quo in race relations. His brother-in-law, George Maddox, the Millsaps sociologist attacked by the Citizens' Council for taking his students to Tougaloo for integrated student forums in 1958, had chosen to leave the state. Clark had grown up in the Mississippi Conference parsonages of churches served by his preacher father, C. C. Clark, and he graduated from Millsaps in 1941 and Yale Divinity School in 1944. His appointment in 1953 to Capitol Street, one of the conference's top churches, drew criticism from some ministerial colleagues, but after a few initial difficulties, including a period of a few months in his first year when he lost his voice, Clark's ministry at the Jackson church had been quite successful.[49]

In his sermon on January 13, 1963, Clark reported that most of the laity with whom he had spoken since the January 2 publication of Born of

Conviction believed they could support segregation as followers of Christ. He had responded to them, "Support segregation as long as the *Lord* will let you." However, he added,

> the most pressing moral issue before us is: Do I and others like me, who sincerely believe by our light from Christ that justice and love require modification in the segregated way of life, have the same right to believe as we do and to express this belief and to work for it in appropriate ways without prejudice or reprisal against ourselves or our families?

Clark's affirmative answer acknowledged that Mississippians with such views knew they would suffer reprisal and thus usually kept silent as a result. The pastor at nearby Pearl Methodist, Bill Lowry, had agreed in December to sign Born of Conviction, but his name was omitted. At his church's Official Board meeting in late January, lay members spent several minutes criticizing the Twenty-Eight. Lowry remembers that one said, "I'm so proud our preacher did not sign that statement," followed by exuberant applause. Lowry did not tell his church members that he supported and had intended to sign Born of Conviction, and years later he termed it "the most embarrassing moment of my ministry."[50]

The results of the early 1963 debate caused by the publication of Born of Conviction remained unclear because few supporters of the Twenty-Eight spoke out. Just as Martin Luther King Jr. expressed frustration in his "Letter from Birmingham Jail" at the silence of white moderates and the white church in response to the civil rights movement, so also the silence of all but a few of the Twenty-Eight's supporters represented a moral failure and allowed public segregationist voices to drown out public support for the statement. However, the many private expressions of support from Mississippians verified the claim in the opening paragraph of Born of Conviction that at least some white Methodists in the state struggled with "the genuine dilemma . . . of Christian conscience" concerning race relations and shared the "anguish" at the current climate of massive resistance.[51]

"Answer[ing] for My Own Convictions"

The incredible intricacy of family and friendship ties in Mississippi virtually assures that any widespread conflict will strain personal relationships. The Born of Conviction controversy led to anguish, recriminations, and dialogue within families, even the families of some signers. Born in 1927, Jack Troutman grew up in Twin City, a tiny community in Central Mississippi's Leake County. By the time he was four his father had died, so his mother raised her children with the help of extended family in the area. They lived near Mt. Horeb Methodist Church and New Hope Baptist and attended each on occasion. Most of their relatives were Southern Baptist. In his childhood and youth, Troutman observed some incidents of real cruelty to blacks by whites, including members of his extended family. Something pushed him to be open to all people and all races, and he eventually considered himself a misfit on the race issue in Mississippi.[52]

Mississippi's segregationist governor, Ross Barnett, also grew up in Leake County, and Troutman's mother was Barnett's cousin. While in office in the early 1960s, Barnett hosted a family reunion at the Governor's Mansion, and Jack Troutman (Figure 5.4), now a seminary graduate and serving as a Mississippi Conference pastor, was invited to preach for a worship service at the event. He rejected virtually everything his distant

FIGURE 5.4 Jack Troutman, 1960s. Courtesy of Reverend Jack Troutman.

cousin stood for, and thus he turned down the invitation and refused even to attend.[53]

Late one December afternoon in 1962, two ministerial colleagues came to see Troutman at Big Point, showed him the Born of Conviction statement, and asked if he would sign. He agreed; it seemed the obvious thing to do. After the statement's release, Troutman's brother thought he had committed a crime against the family by participating in Born of Conviction. In response to bewildered questions from his mother, Troutman wrote her in February 1963 to explain his signature:

> I *will not* have to stand before the judgment bar of God and answer for anyone's soul but my own. I will have to answer for my own convictions and how I lead others ... to rid themselves of hatred and malice toward others regardless of race, color, or creed. ... In all of Christian history, it is not for the Christian to conform to public opinion but to let the love of God transform them into the personality of Jesus Christ who looked upon *all peoples* as of infinite worth. ... Who are we to blame for such "radical" beliefs? Jesus Christ, who was the most radical and unpopular preacher that ever lived.[54]

6

Congregational and Community Responses

BORN OF CONVICTION caused a large splash in the Mississippi press in January 1963 and a small ripple on the national level, including three *New York Times* articles in 1963 and some attention in mainline Protestant and denominational journals. The stories of the immediate departures of Bill Lampton and James Rush from their churches were widely covered in Mississippi; the January *New York Times* piece also included James Nicholson's exodus from the Byram Church. Mississippi newspapers reported on local church incidents occurring in response to their pastors' participation in Born of Conviction in the cases of Ed McRae, Wilton Carter, and Jerry Trigg, with more minor mentions of resolutions passed by the churches of Jerry Furr and Rod Entrekin (agreeing to disagree with their pastors), and James Holston (repudiation of their pastor's witness). Lampton's situation in Pike County received the most national coverage by far; several African American papers ran that story.[1]

Even in the churches that made the news, the published stories only scratched the surface of the responses to Born of Conviction and its signers. The Twenty-Eight served as pastors or associate pastors of a total of thirty-nine white Methodist congregations in twenty-three South Mississippi communities. The previous chapter focused more on the controversy as a battle of ideas in the public media. Beyond the news, church members and other persons in the places where the signers lived responded in a wide variety of ways, and here the attention concentrates more on relationships—broken relationships in some cases and polite detachment in others, but also some affirmation of relationship or struggle toward deeper connection between pastors and church members.

"Where the Old South Still Lives"

Summer Walters Jr. was born in 1935 at Sanatorium in Simpson County. His father worked in various jobs in South Mississippi and Alabama before the family settled in Forest Hill, a community on the southwestern outskirts of Jackson. In 1953 Walters graduated from Forest Hill High School; like fellow Born of Conviction signer Ed McRae, he played baritone horn in his school band. He considered attending Ole Miss or Mississippi State on a band scholarship; given the family's limited financial resources, he believed his only other option was to attend Hinds Junior College and live at home.[2]

In the summer of 1952, Walters attended a Mississippi Conference youth assembly at Copiah-Lincoln Junior College in Wesson and had a profound experience that planted seeds toward his eventual commitment to the ordained ministry. In addition, his family lived next door to the Forest Hill Methodist Church parsonage, and he got to know the church's pastors well, including John Cook and T. E. Nicholson, father of future Born of Conviction signer James Nicholson. When Cook went on vacation, he usually invited Millsaps philosophy professor and Methodist minister Bond Fleming to preach in his absence, and Walters developed great respect for Fleming and some Millsaps alumni he met at the conference youth assembly. Cook encouraged him to attend Millsaps, even though Walters told his pastor he had no interest in the ordained ministry. He applied, although he continued to pursue the band scholarship route at the state universities. Ultimately, the family worked out a plan for him to attend Millsaps that involved moving to a house near the campus so that Walters's mother could get a job in Jackson.[3]

Though he started Millsaps with the idea of becoming an engineer, Walters soon realized his vocation might be the ministry. In the summer of 1955, he worked as student assistant pastor at Main Street Methodist Church in Hattiesburg and had his calling confirmed. He also sang in the Millsaps Singers, and on a choir tour in the spring of 1956, the group made an unannounced stop at Rust College, the black Methodist school in Holly Springs, Mississippi. The two choirs sang for each other.[4]

A few years earlier at one of the Mississippi Conference youth assemblies, Walters recalled, a speaker asked the group, "When did you realize there was a world outside Mississippi?" Walters also heard Boston University philosopher Peter Bertocci speak at Millsaps, and he consulted Bertocci regarding seminary choice. Bertocci asked if he intended to stay in Mississippi for the rest of his life. His affirmative answer led Bertocci to suggest he consider going somewhere outside the South. Walters chose Yale Divinity School, but some members of the Conference Ministerial Relations Committee counseled against it because it was not in the Southeastern Jurisdiction and thus he might not come back to Mississippi. Walters wondered if they might not want him in Mississippi if he went to Yale. After the meeting, committee member Robert Kates told him to do whatever he thought was right. Roy Clark, also a committee member, had graduated from Yale, and if the highly respected pastor of Jackson's Capitol Street Church exemplified Yale products, then it seemed the obvious choice.[5]

Summer Walters and Betty Barfield met and became engaged while at Millsaps; they married in May 1957 and moved to New Haven that summer. They spent four years there, and Millsaps friend Jim Waits joined Walters as a student there in 1958. One highlight came when Martin Luther King Jr. spoke at Yale Divinity School in 1960. Walters's academic excellence caught the attention of his professors, including church historians Roland Bainton and Sidney Ahlstrom and Christian social ethicists Liston Pope and James Gustafson, all of whom encouraged him to pursue PhD studies. He stayed an extra year after completing his bachelor of divinity to do a master's degree, but part-time work at Methodist churches in Hamden and Bridgeport (the latter an interracial congregation) confirmed his calling to the parish ministry. So in 1961 the Walters family, expecting their first child, made plans to return to Mississippi. During the summer of 1955 while at Main Street Church in Hattiesburg, Walters had known Eva Pearl Williams, a widow who served as church secretary and volunteer Christian education director. She had since married Clyde Gunn, a Mississippi Conference pastor. When the Gunns learned of Walters's impending return, they arranged for Bishop Franklin to appoint him as associate pastor at Jefferson Street Church in Natchez, where Gunn had begun serving in 1960.[6]

In his last weeks at Yale, Walters (Figure 6.1) wrote a paper on Jefferson Street for Gustafson's Seminar in Sociology of Religion. He combined demographic, economic, and political data on Natchez with a discussion of the race issue, made use of the sociopsychological analysis of John Dollard's 1930s study of the Mississippi Delta town of Indianola, and described the recent efforts of the Citizens' Council, State Sovereignty Commission, and MAMML to maintain the "Southern way of life" in Mississippi. He concluded that "the racial problem penetrates into all

FIGURE 6.1 Summer Walters, 1961. Courtesy of Elizabeth B. Walters.

areas of life and has to be confronted." He anticipated a good working relationship with Clyde Gunn, with the two of them "serving as catalysts to the congregation in reference to social questions and taking the lead in these issues without completely jeopardizing our relationship with members of the church." Speculating that Jefferson Street Church had members who were "men of power" in Natchez, he foresaw the need to develop caring pastoral relationships with them in order to help them think in new ways about race relations "in light of their Christian convictions." Though his parents had warned them that things had gotten much worse in Mississippi since 1957, Summer and Betty Walters returned in June 1961, "hoping to work together for the improvement of human relations." He knew it would not be easy and might even involve suffering, but he envisioned a ministry in Natchez with all parties (including blacks) joining forces toward an orderly transition to a more just system.[7]

Because it had escaped the destruction of Union troops in the Civil War and boasted close to a dozen antebellum mansions, the city of Natchez marketed itself as a place "Where the Old South Still Lives." The annual spring pilgrimage included a tour of homes and a pageant glorifying the plantation life of the past. Isolated in the southwest corner of the state on the Mississippi River, white Natchez lived in what Robert Penn Warren called a "fantasia" in which it "worship[ed] the days of the more pleasant past" and "commodified history, convert[ing] it into the city's chief business concern."[8]

Jefferson Street Methodist Church, founded in the early nineteenth century and situated downtown a mile from the river, occupied an important place in that past. For a year and a half, Summer Walters immersed himself in the life of the 1,100 member congregation: he visited in members' homes and in hospitals when they were sick, worked with the youth group and Sunday School, participated in weddings and funerals, planned and led worship, and preached frequently. As hoped, he found Gunn to be a supportive mentor who treated him as a true colleague; like W. B. Selah and Jerry Furr at Galloway, they went fishing together on occasion. Although Walters spoke critically of the culture and thorough segregation of Natchez in a round robin letter to seminary friends one month before Born of Conviction's publication, he also expressed a sense of fulfillment in his work there and concluded with these words:

> While it is obvious that I have mixed feelings about the local situation, my commitment to the parish is more definite than ever. If Christianity is to be relevant to this generation, it seems to me that we must meet the people in the parish where they live and work and help them grapple with their problems. In this regard, I am most thankful to Yale not for the "how to" courses but for the academic courses through which a theological perspective was gained.

When he joined the Twenty-Eight, he reflected on how well the congregation knew him and had responded to his ministry. Aware that many church members would not agree with Born of Conviction, he hoped their respect for and relationship with him would remain strong.[9]

While this proved true in some individual cases, the church did not respond positively in early 1963. On Friday, January 4, the Official Board chairman presided at a three-and-a-half hour meeting of the Pastoral Relations Committee to decide what to do with their associate pastor. The next morning, the board chair told Walters he had three options: remove his name from Born of Conviction and follow that up with a written apology to the board and congregation; immediately leave the church;

or prepare to suffer the consequences for his support of integration. At the monthly board meeting on January 8, one man urged all members to withhold financial contributions to communicate their opposition to race relations change. Another member presented a signed petition asking that Walters not be reappointed to their church in June, but the motion for the board to approve it failed to pass. Walters determined that only ten of the fifty-eight present at the meeting had actually read the Born of Conviction statement. By the February board meeting, due to increasing concerns of harm to the congregation, the body passed a motion requesting that the bishop not reappoint Walters in June and affirming that he would not receive any financial support past June if the conference reappointed him there.[10]

At home the Walters family, now including their young son, received harassing telephone calls—some with death threats—that Walters eventually learned to ignore. One church member lectured Walters for an hour on the superiority of the white race, while others accused him of being a Communist, in spite of language to the contrary in Born of Conviction. Billy Yelverton, a former Ole Miss and professional football player and member of the church, told Walters if anyone threatened them to call him, and he would protect them. Privately, a few church members told Walters they agreed with him, while some others thought he had the right to sign the statement but believed the action was poorly timed. One man announced in a church meeting that Walters was no longer welcome in his home. Clyde Gunn, who supported his associate pastor but never clearly indicated if he agreed with Born of Conviction, had insufficient power to counteract the church's ruling clique. Although some church members continued to express private support and invited Summer and Betty Walters for meals in their homes, it was inevitable that Jefferson Street's first associate pastor would leave the church in June 1963.[11]

Harassment, Broken Relationships, "Ruining" Our Church

Most of the Twenty-Eight received harassment through anonymous phone calls, and several got threats of violence in other ways. James Holston's oldest daughter remembers that in Carthage on the morning of January 3, 1963, her younger brother answered the phone, listened a moment, and then with a puzzled look on his face asked, "Daddy, are we going to the Negro school today?" Wilton Carter later recalled getting two calls in Lake from someone who wanted to know if he wanted his son (only a few months old then) to marry "one of those niggers"; he also received a visit from a stranger from Meridian who questioned him at length on the statement and expressed opposition to it. In Sandersville, Ned Kellar recollects an unknown caller warning, "You boys are gonna be sorry you ever signed that nigger-loving paper." Kellar also received a veiled death threat from a marginal church member by way of a phone message taken by his wife Dot. Ed McRae got threatening phone calls in the middle of the night, and a cross was burned on his parsonage lawn while he and his wife and young sons were out of town. A man with a shotgun confronted signer Keith Tonkel in front of his parsonage in Gulfport. A recent seminary graduate in his first year at Guinn Memorial Church, Tonkel had been counseling a troubled church member who had connections to the Ku Klux Klan, and the church member intervened on Tonkel's behalf and convinced the armed visitor to leave. On another occasion, someone slashed the tires on Tonkel's car.[12]

A Jackson County law enforcement officer warned members at Caswell Springs Church of the possibility of violence against Jerry Trigg and his family by the Alabama Ku Klux Klan. Male church members took turns sitting through the night with a shotgun on their lap on the lighted front porch of the parsonage. Concerned more than usual on one night, church members told the Triggs they needed to leave town for a couple of days. Trigg called his parents in Quitman and said they were coming for a visit, and three carloads of church members escorted them up Highway 63 to Lucedale to be sure they were safely on their way. A few miles away at Big Point, men of Jack Troutman's church also guarded the parsonage and church building, often taking off work to do so. Some of them did not agree with their pastor's views, but they vowed to protect him and the church from violence. Men of signer James Conner's Brandon Church also guarded the parsonage there.[13]

In Neshoba County, James and Libby Rush experienced a range of trouble, from ridiculous to vicious. Someone drove cattle wearing cowbells around the Rush's parsonage in the middle of the night. At all hours, anonymous phone calls came and cars drove by the house. A male church member came by the parsonage in Rush's absence and verbally abused Libby Rush; this upset her so much that she required hospitalization. Though the doctor specified no visitors, another church member managed to get to her room and level more verbal abuse.[14]

James Holston and his family also endured harassment in Carthage. In addition to numerous phone calls and whiskey bottles strewn on their lawn, the Holstons received a rotten chicken from a church member. On one of his daily walks to the post office, Holston passed an unfamiliar man who nodded as he opened his coat to reveal a gun. Another man attempted to enter the parsonage when Holston's wife, Bennie, was alone there. The church had received the Holstons warmly when they arrived in June 1962, but Born of Conviction ruined that. The family's oldest daughter, who turned sixteen in May of 1963, remembers that in January,

> Life changed dramatically for our parents. Their social life within Carthage ceased to exist. Friends stopped calling and often would not even speak to them. They were pretty much ignored. People still came to church, but I got the feeling that many came out of a sense of obligation but not to listen to Dad's sermons . . . a few read while he preached.

Holston reported, ". . . the main harassment sought to make my ministry ineffective by devious means exercised by our most pious people." Several church members told him privately they supported his stand but could not say so publicly; other signers heard similar explanations. Some signers received no public support from any church member.[15]

In response to their pastor Marvin Moody's signature on Born of Conviction, several members of Oak Grove Church near Hattiesburg were shocked and hurt; they asked Moody why he had done such harm to them. At Scooba on the first Sunday after the statement's release, Powell Hall sensed a similar feeling in his congregation. He made a few remarks at the beginning of his sermon to explain Born of Conviction and his decision to sign it. As he told the story years later, an irate church member interrupted him and asked, "Preacher, do you want *them* to come here?!?" Surprised, Hall responded that he wanted God's will to be done. The man stormed out of the service and slammed the door.[16]

Thirty miles south at Soule's Chapel in rural Lauderdale County, in a meeting with their pastor, Joe Way, on Wednesday, January 9, angry church members accused him of trying to integrate the church, among other things. Because of the publicity connected with the statement, they criticized Way for not asking their permission to sign. Several people voiced other perceived faults of the pastor. After that, Way and his family were ostracized; no one associated socially with them, and church members came only for Sunday morning worship. As the Way family returned to the parsonage one Sunday in late January, their three-year-old daughter began crying as they entered the house. Way remembers that when pressed to explain her outburst, she said, "Nobody loves us anymore." Way later learned there had been discussion of removing them from the parsonage. A few church members told him privately that they disagreed with his views but believed in his right to express them. Some later apologized for how they had spoken in the January 9 meeting, but Way's opponents pressured those with any sympathy for the pastor to have nothing to do with him.[17]

At Brandon, signer James Conner faced a complex situation, because State Senator John McLaurin, a notorious segregationist who spoke publicly in opposition to Born of Conviction, belonged to the Brandon Church. The day after McLaurin's comments appeared in the news, Conner issued a statement to the congregation because Born of Conviction had "been widely misinterpreted and misunderstood, both as to meaning and purpose." He insisted he had not intended "to encourage or support the racial integration of the Brandon Methodist Church" but rather to oppose "all forms of '*discrimination*' in the church and society generally." He also asserted that in signing, "I did not mean to imply that I have been denied any freedom of expression in serving the Brandon Methodist Church, or any other Methodist Church." He closed with these words:

> Every minister, however, has the responsibility of forming his convictions intelligently, under God, in the searching of the Scriptures and much prayer; and every church has the responsibility to provide for such ministers the right to be heard without intimidation or fear.

Some members wanted Conner to leave the church immediately, but District Superintendent Willard Leggett refused and insisted Conner would stay until the normal moving time in early June after Annual Conference. John McLaurin, who ran for state attorney general later that year, boycotted worship most Sundays after the publication of Born of Conviction, but he came and received communion from Conner in a worship service just before Conner left the church.[18]

At a meeting members asked James Holston not to attend, the Carthage Church's Official Board unanimously passed a resolution censuring their pastor for his participation in the statement, among other reasons because of "the serious disruption of harmony in the local church without any apparent good being accomplished." They pledged continued loyalty to the congregation, "notwithstanding the strong disapproval of the Pastor's action," and published a brief statement to this effect in the Carthage paper. At Caswell Springs, eighty adult members (out of four hundred) signed a resolution informing Jackson County "that the views of the pastor, on integration, does [sic] not reflect the views of the total membership of the church." At Columbia First, signer and veteran pastor N. A. Dickson got a mixed response, from overt attempts to remove him as pastor to "open contempt" from some church members to personal support and commendation from others. In Dickson's view, church members remained confused "as to what should be done, resulting in nothing being done."[19]

The relationship between pastor and congregation is always complex, and in times of crisis it is tested—sometimes strengthened and at other times broken or made more ambiguous. On January 3, a prominent member of Maxie Dunnam's Gulfport church scratched gravel and raised a cloud of dust as he arrived in the church parking lot with a copy of the *Times-Picayune* story in hand. Storming in to Dunnam's office, the man expressed intense disappointment in his pastor, especially since Dunnam had meant a great deal to him personally. When the church member insisted he could not discuss it further then, Dunnam gave him a copy of the statement, and he left. This man continued to struggle with both the issue and the relationship; two weeks later he came in tears to Dunnam's home early in the morning and asked for forgiveness. He had read and reread the statement and recognized it as Christian conviction, though he couldn't commit to it. A few weeks later, in response to a sermon Dunnam preached on "the evils of conformity and the call of God to be transformed and to make a radical commitment to him," the same man raged in the narthex after the service and told a fellow church member, "As far as I'm concerned he's just tendered his resignation."[20]

Tensions at Oakland Heights Church in Meridian remained high during the weeks after Born of Conviction's publication, even though the January board meeting voted down the motion to expel their pastor, Ed McRae. More than a dozen active families in the congregation quit coming to worship and withheld their usual monetary contributions. When a woman in one of these families was hospitalized, McRae sought to maintain a pastoral relationship and stopped by to visit. Finding her asleep, he left his card. Later that day, her husband arrived at the parsonage and honked his horn repeatedly. McRae, his wife Martina, and their young sons stood in the driveway. The man refused to get out of his vehicle and shouted that McRae should never visit his wife again and that he wanted no connection with the pastor. McRae asked whether they might discuss the matter like Southern gentlemen, and he remembers the man replied, "You wouldn't make the pimple on a Southern gentleman's ass." He insisted that Mrs. McRae and their sons go inside, but she refused, fearing for her husband's safety.[21]

The lack of support from an older woman and pillar of the congregation hurt McRae much more. He saw her in the church parking lot a few days after the controversy began, and he hoped for some encouragement. Instead, she said he had ruined their church. He did receive some support in private; on Sunday, January 6, he made a brief statement explaining his stand and apologizing for any pain he had caused. After the service, he did not greet people at the door as he usually did but went to his office and cried. Knowing the pain he felt, three or four members sought him out and hugged him.[22]

Some responses by members can be described as simple denial. A woman told Maxie Dunnam she had decided to withdraw her support and move to another church. She said that she liked him, but he was ahead of his time. The time to speak would be when real trouble came. Dunnam suggested that the Ole Miss riot constituted trouble, and she replied that everything in that situation was wrong, but Meredith had no right to be there. At Oak Grove, Marvin Moody reported, "My situation has resolved itself; at least for the time being everybody seems ready to go ahead and 'bring the Kingdom in' (provided there are no negroes connected with it)."[23]

Like Oakland Heights in Meridian, several congregations announced publicly or communicated privately to conference officials that they did not want a member of the Twenty-Eight to be appointed as their next pastor. Although *Advocate* editor Sam Ashmore claimed in his preface to Born of Conviction that the signers "represent some of our best trained and most promising ministers" and that "they express the conviction of the vast majority of the clerical members of the conference," many Mississippi Conference laity and some clergy rejected the training and perspectives represented by this supposed majority. Born of Conviction elicited a wide range of local congregational responses. In some cases invitations to members of the Twenty-Eight to speak at other churches were withdrawn after the statement appeared. Collins Methodist Church cancelled a speaking engagement by Wilton Carter scheduled in January. Lamar Martin, the pastor, assured Carter that he had not wanted to cancel and would still be Carter's friend. The Collins Church, Martin explained, held no personal ill will against Carter and respected his beliefs. They had withdrawn the invitation to avoid misunderstanding; they did not want to appear to endorse Born of Conviction, because "to many a stand against discrimination means only full and complete integration." Not all invitations to the Twenty-Eight were rescinded. Jerry Furr preached for John Cook at Philadelphia First Church in Neshoba County on January 6, and Buford Dickinson preached a revival for Byrd Hillman at Buckatunna Methodist in Wayne County a few weeks later.[24]

"Preacher, Is There Any Way You Can Get Your Name Off That List?"

Buford Dickinson (Figure 6.2) grew up on a dairy farm in the Arnold Line community on the northwest edge of Hattiesburg. At Mississippi Southern College in the early 1950s, he met Maxie Dunnam, and they became close

FIGURE 6.2 Buford Dickinson, 1960s. Courtesy of Jean Dickinson Minus and Kathryn Dickinson.

friends. They roomed together when they went to Emory's Candler School of Theology, and both met their wives in Atlanta; each served the other as best man in their weddings. Dickinson met Jean Clegg, Candler Christian education student and daughter of Charles Clegg, the president of Young Harris College, a Methodist school in northeast Georgia. They married in 1957 and soon moved to Dickinson's first full-time pastoral appointment; her father joked that she had committed an unpardonable sin—marrying a Methodist preacher and moving to Mississippi. They spent five years in Meridian, where Dickinson started Druid Hills Methodist Church on the west side of town.[25]

In 1962 they moved about thirty miles west to Decatur, where the church received them enthusiastically. A block north of the church sat the campus of East Central Junior College, and many faculty and administrators at the school attended the Methodist Church. Although Jean Dickinson's father had always advised, "Be careful what you put your name on," Buford Dickinson signed the Born of Conviction statement along with his brother-in-law Ned Kellar and best friend Maxie Dunnam. He did not expect the statement to cause much controversy. Yet on January 3, 1963, as Jean walked with their two children to the drugstore she remembers seeing a church member who said, "I hear your husband has opened a can of worms. If I can help, let me know." The church's Official Board called a meeting a few days later and asked Dickinson to explain why he had signed the statement. The chair of the board allowed anyone to express anger or disappointment or whatever they felt. As Jean Dickinson Minus recalled it years later, at the conclusion of the open discussion, W. Arno Vincent, former president of the junior college, stood up and said, "You know, folks, if we want a minister to tell us what we want to hear, we don't need a minister. We can just tape record our own speeches and listen to them." At the end of the meeting, the board gave Dickinson a vote of confidence and asked him to speak to the congregation about Born of Conviction.[26]

As a pastor whose "gentleness let people know immediately that he cared for them," and whose "toughness let them know that he would get things done for them," Buford Dickinson already had close relationships with many in the congregation. One man invited him on a trip to his farm outside of town; when they arrived and got out of the pickup truck, the church member got his shotgun out of the rack in the cab. This bothered Dickinson, though he concealed his concern; the man explained he always carried his gun on the farm in case he encountered a snake. While they walked, Dickinson's widow and daughter recall, the man gently asked, "Preacher, is there any way you can get your name off that list?"[27]

Extended family members of several signers dealt with some fallout as a result of the statement, but Buford Dickinson's parents, Homer and Ella Ruth Dickinson, had to confront a problem not faced by others. For decades they had been members of the tiny Arnold Line Methodist Church where they had raised their children and played a central role in keeping the congregation alive. The pastor there in early 1963, Herbert W. Beasley, found Born of Conviction exceedingly offensive and made his displeasure known in a letter to Sam Ashmore, editor of the *Advocate*. Although his letter did not appear in the *Advocate*, Beasley made sure members at Arnold Line read it: he posted a mimeographed copy on the church bulletin board. Of the statement signed by the Dickinsons' son and son-in-law (Ned Kellar), he raged,

> This article is doubtless one of the most disgracing blows the Methodist Church has experienced in the past several years. I would like to say very emphatically, that if this article expresses the conviction of the majority of ministers in our conference, something is wrong somewhere. It is certainly not my feelings. I stand for segregation 100% because peace can better be maintained through segregation.

He quoted the Bible's injunction to "Follow peace with all men, and Holiness, without which no man shall see the Lord" (Hebrews 12:14) and insisted that the conviction expressed in the statement could not be of God "because it cannot bring glory to Christ." Ministers of the Gospel should limit their efforts to preaching salvation, and departure from that purpose only invited disaster. He closed by vowing to fight against Born of Conviction with all his strength, "for Christ's sake." Beasley, then in his second year as pastor of the church, moved to another church in June 1963.[28]

Although some churches rejected their pastors and refused to discuss the issues raised by Born of Conviction, others remained in relationship through dialogue and honest expression of feelings. There were few cases of unanimous response in any church, especially when private individual views are considered. Dickinson reported that his congregation was in a state of shock and some members wanted him to recant, while others argued he should be free to speak his mind.

After a Wednesday night prayer meeting at Caswell Springs, the church member who had gathered signatures against Jerry Trigg's view asked Trigg if he could show him any biblical references to support Born of Conviction, integration, and brotherhood. When Trigg offered to do so, the man withdrew the request and asserted he did not want to have to give up the Bible.[29]

Some pastors and at least one lay leader pushed church members to read the text of Born of Conviction together and discuss it. At Lovely Lane Church in Natchez, Elton Brown led some disgruntled members in such an exercise. He asked them to respond to various statements in the document with the question, "What's wrong with that?" By the end of the discussion, Brown sensed "they knew I was not wrong by having done it, but they still felt that I should not." On the Philadelphia Circuit, although two of the churches voted to dismiss James Rush, the third, Mars Hill, near the tiny community of Bogue Chitto in eastern Neshoba County, voted to keep him. Rush still had to leave the charge, but affirmation of him by Mars Hill was a moral victory and resulted from the leadership of Andrew Williamson, a farmer who had refused to join the Neshoba County Citizens' Council. His family included two ministers and two missionaries. At a meeting at Mars Hill, Mr. Williamson also read through Born of Conviction section by section and asked church members what was wrong with specific passages.[30]

On Sunday morning, January 6, Wilton Carter preached at Lake on the text, "No man who puts his hand to the plow and looks back is fit for the Kingdom of God" and affirmed his participation in the statement. That afternoon he met with the Official Board and explained that Born of Conviction's purpose was not to integrate the Lake Charge, that it expressed the official position of The Methodist Church, and that it primarily advocated fair treatment for all. The meeting maintained a civil tone, and afterward, Robert Logan, chair of the board and mayor of Lake, shook hands with Carter and pronounced the situation "satisfactory." Reese Rush, father of James Rush and lay leader of the church, strongly supported Carter, but several church members remained aloof. In spite of the official congregational approval, Carter did not feel comfortable preaching about race after that. An underlying current of tension lingered; many felt sorry for the Carters and thought they had been misled.[31]

At Wesson, the Official Board met and discussed the statement and their pastor's stand. Some complimented Rod Entrekin for sticking with his convictions, even though they disagreed with him and thought Born of Conviction was untimely. Although a vocal minority in the church tried to get him removed, they failed, both in January and in the late spring. Entrekin's stand and continued presence in the church created some soul-searching among church members. More disapproval came from people in other churches in the town, and some other signers confirmed similar experiences. In Natchez, Elton Brown reported that members of his church received calls from people they knew in churches of another denomination who said, "I saw that your preacher signed that statement in the paper; what are you all going to do about it?"[32]

Jack Troutman's (Figure 6.3) church members got similar calls. He had been at Big Point on the Gulf Coast for almost four years, and the church knew where he stood on the race issue. After the release of Born of Conviction, he brought copies of the statement to a meeting for church leaders to read; he also made a short presentation to them on why he had signed. A member told Troutman in the meeting that now he had seen the statement, he would have been disappointed if the pastor had not signed it. This led to a frank discussion on the problem of race in Mississippi. A few months later in a Bible study, in response to Troutman's explanation of the Apostle Paul's efforts to break down the barriers between Jew and Gentile in Galatians 3:28, a segregationist in the group wondered aloud if Paul's words might apply to the current racial conflict.[33]

At Keith Tonkel's church in Gulfport, some members spread false rumors that resulted in hurt feelings, but thanks to discussions between the pastor and church members, some people eventually changed their minds about the issue. Across town at Maxie Dunnam's church, some members supported his stand (most privately), while others demanded a retraction; the majority remained baffled by the situation. Later in 1963, the Official Board voted that if blacks came to worship, they would be denied entrance and seated in the Fellowship Hall so the pastor could talk with them. This disappointed Dunnam greatly, but he summed up the situation at Trinity in the fall of 1963: "We were one big family, and we lost that. But the church and I have both grown spiritually during this last year."[34]

As Ned Kellar tells the story in his 2010 autobiography, he took his usual place at a table in the Sandersville café the morning Born of Conviction made the news, and he was met with silence from people who usually greeted him warmly. His best friend in the community also shunned him. Their closest neighbors told Kellar and his wife they could not agree with Born of Conviction publicly because it would only cause misunderstanding in such a small town. This caused the Kellars much pain; he summed it up: "My experiences with bigotry had taught me that many [white] people hated black people, but this was the first time I had experienced such hatred directed toward me." Yet Kellar soon realized that "Others were hurt that their friend, the preacher, did not believe as they did."[35]

The two principal leaders of the Sandersville Church, Ned Dillard and Harvey Hinton, came to see Kellar the evening of January 3. Dillard expressed intense rage, while Hinton served as a peacemaker, though he wished Kellar had not signed the statement. Dillard demanded that Kellar make a retraction, but when he refused, Dillard remained angry but also expressed concern for both the church and Kellar. By the time the two men left the parsonage that evening, Kellar says Dillard had "accepted the fact that I could believe differently than he did, and we could still respect one another." They planned a congregational meeting on Sunday evening, January 6; Dillard would lead it.[36]

At the meeting, Kellar told the large crowd gathered in the church sanctuary that he had not thought Born of Conviction would cause a problem, although now he had a better understanding of their feelings. He reiterated his belief in the statement and claimed to be the same person they had come to know since his arrival the previous June. Now, however, they knew more about his views, and he reminded them that he had often preached on brotherhood and the love of neighbor. When he finished, Dillard asked him to leave so church members could talk it out. Dillard told Kellar later that evening that he had assured the meeting that what Kellar believed about integration did not matter as long as he did not preach about it. Dillard insisted to the church members that they would keep the church together and make it through the present conflict; this included Kellar continuing as their pastor.[37]

"I Don't Want You to Be Worried at All"

In 1949 and 1950, Denson Napier, a student at Mississippi Southern and a student pastor on the Waynesboro Circuit, often drove to Centreville to visit Jean Templeton, whom he would marry in August 1950. Because he was tall and balding with dark hair, when he walked down the street in Centreville occasionally people mistook him for the current Methodist pastor in town, Roy Clark. Napier enjoyed the mistaken identity and never corrected those who greeted him in this way. When he was ordained at Annual Conference a couple of years later, someone asked why Roy Clark was getting ordained again.[38]

Born in 1928, Napier grew up in Seminary, a small town in Covington County about twenty miles northwest of Hattiesburg. Upon graduation from Southern, the Napiers moved to Atlanta, where he attended Candler. When he finished seminary in 1954, he took his first full-time pastoral appointment at Sandersville. They moved in 1956 to Cary, the home of Conference Lay Leader J. P. Stafford, but a year later, Denson Napier succeeded his mentor Sam Barefield as director of the Wesley Foundation at Southern when Barefield left for a job with the denomination's board of education in Nashville. Convinced that campus ministry provided an ideal venue for transcending the limits of the Closed Society perspective, Napier invited Jameson Jones, editor of the Methodist student magazine *Motive*, to speak at Southern in 1958. Because many Mississippi segregationists viewed the national Methodist Church as much too liberal and *Motive* had a reputation for radical views, Napier expected a protest in response to Jones's appearance from some conservative students. He later remembered that he warned William D. McCain, president at Southern and a staunch segregationist, and McCain replied, "Who are they? If they protest, they won't be in this school any longer!"[39]

Napier stayed at Southern almost five years and raised funds for a Wesley Foundation building just off the Southern campus. The groundbreaking ceremony, led by Bishop Franklin, took place in March 1962. Finding the work with college students fulfilling, Napier planned to stay longer, but the February 1962 fire that destroyed the Methodist Church in Richton, a town in the county east of Hattiesburg, gave District Superintendent Brunner Hunt another idea. Hunt appealed to Napier to go to Richton as pastor and lead the congregation in their rebuilding effort; he accepted the challenge and moved there in June 1962. By the time he returned unexpectedly to the Southern Wesley Foundation in December 1963, the new Richton church building had been completed.[40]

Believing the statement was not only "Born of Conviction" but also "Born of Necessity," Napier agreed to sign without hesitation at the Hattiesburg meeting of potential signers in December 1962. On the morning after the statement hit the news in early January, Ben Stevens, president of the bank in Richton, Hattiesburg District Lay Leader, and a member of the Richton Methodist Church, asked his pastor to come to the bank. When they met, Stevens acknowledged that the two of them likely did not agree on everything, expressed concern for Napier and his family, and asked if he was worried in the wake of the Born of Conviction controversy. Both confident and pugnacious, Napier said no, and as he remembered it years later, Stevens continued, "I don't want you to be worried at all. If *anything* happens to the Methodist Church or to you or your family, all I have to do is call in a dozen loans, and I can stop anything." Led by Stevens and his wife, Arlean, the president of the Mississippi Conference Women's Society of Christian Service organization, many of the members of the Richton Church supported their pastor, though some remained unhappy.[41]

Some of the signers had little trouble in their congregations. In February, Inman Moore reported that members of Leggett Memorial in Biloxi took his participation in Born of Conviction quite calmly. Three miles northeast, Jim Waits wrote Bishop Franklin just over a week after the statement's release that "response here has been warm, and I have not felt more secure since I came to Epworth." Some of his church members privately expressed appreciation to him for the statement, though many said nothing. He also told the bishop, "If my preaching is to be dictated by the congregation, then I cannot preach at all. My people here understand that." When Waits visited one church member at his store, the man asked why he could not preach on something besides race on occasion.[42]

Also in Biloxi at Beauvoir Methodist, founding pastor and Born of Conviction signer Harold Ryker (Figure 6.3) reported little opposition to the statement. A few families left the church in January, which caused some criticism, but the response from most of the congregation was positive. Without focusing directly on integration, Ryker had "conditioned" his members over the seven years he had been there to be more open-minded on the race issue. In the weeks after Born of Conviction appeared, Ryker participated in the first integrated Methodist Christian Worker's School in Biloxi, held on Keesler Air Force Base. Only a few blacks attended, but there were no repercussions in response to the event.[43]

Though Maxie Dunnam experienced more protest in his Gulfport church, he also heard comments that encouraged him. On January 6, Bob Grimes, an adult Sunday School teacher at Trinity, said to his class, "I was impressed with the twenty-eight young ministers. Where were the *old* ministers? Why shouldn't our church speak? Why shouldn't Methodist ministers express themselves?" In a social gathering, Dunnam heard a couple in their early fifties from a Methodist Church whose minister did not sign the statement say they wondered why some ministers they

ORDAINED ELDERS—1961

It speaks well for Mississippi Methodism and its future, when such large numbers of young ministers consecrate themselves to Christ's work in The Methodist Church. The names of the 45 who were ordained are found both on page 90 and on page 91 in this Journal.

FIGURE 6.3 Mississippi Conference ministers ordained elder in 1961. Born of Conviction signers in picture: Ed McRae is top center (doorknob just to his left); just off his right shoulder is Harold Ryker (with wavy hair); just below Ryker and partially in front of his right side is Jack Troutman; just to right of center of picture, wearing glasses with light tie and holding paper over his heart is Bill Lampton. Others mentioned in book: Rayford Woodrick (see Chapter 10) is first row, far right; Nick Nicholson (signer James Nicholson's brother, see Chapter 10) is next to top row, second from right. Courtesy of Mississippi Annual Conference, The United Methodist Church.

knew had not signed it. A layman from another Methodist Church asked Dunnam, "What do you think my preacher will do—wait and see how the wind blows?"[44]

All of these examples are from the somewhat more open Gulf Coast. Support came in other places as well, much of it private and face to face. Mamie Ratliff Finger, wife of Millsaps President Ellis Finger and a member of Galloway in Jackson, visited Jerry Furr's wife, Marlene, and told her that in the face of criticism of Furr from some church members, she and her husband supported them. Jerry Furr got the most public support of all, because W. B. Selah, his senior pastor, released a statement not only endorsing Born of Conviction, but also speaking in stronger terms about the need for change. In consultation with Furr, some members of Galloway, including Dr. Noel Womack, Dr. Lewis Crouch, and Merle Mann, contributed funds to the conference for salary support for Lampton, Nicholson, and Rush, because their churches were no longer paying them; the bishop and cabinet approved the use of the money to pay the displaced pastors' salaries in full for the rest of the conference year. In a similar vein, a Jewish woman in Meridian who ran a day care center contacted Ed and Martina McRae in January and offered to keep their two sons, ages three and one, on a daily basis free of charge.[45]

An elderly church member wrote Wilton Carter at Lake, "I want to commend you on your stand it has been a long time since the truth has been told and I am really proud of you. We need more preachers of all denominations to proclaim the truths as written in the Bible." The man later told Carter that his family would back their pastor, and if they refused, he would disown them. At Ellisville, church leaders supported signer Bufkin Oliver, though some disagreed with his stand. Church attendance declined a bit, and one member insisted on boycotting worship as long as Oliver remained. But many members told Oliver the Twenty-Eight had done the right thing by signing the statement. He reported, "Some have expressed their own views on the issues which are good and show that they have been doing a lot of constructive thinking. I see evidences that many people are doing much soul searching and changing their attitude." In Natchez, a large man who worked at the tire plant shook Elton Brown's hand so hard one Sunday that he almost broke the pastor's fingers. Brown later recalled the man said, "Preacher, I wouldn't give a dime for you if you didn't stand up for what you believed." He came to see Brown that week and lamented how at every break at work he had to listen to hateful statements, racist jokes, and tough talk about what ought to be done to blacks.[46]

At Vimville, a small community near Meridian, signer Wallace Roberts had been pastor for two and a half years. A church leader expressed confusion and some anger to Roberts, but also assured him of their ongoing allegiance. Though church members disagreed with their pastor, they were intrigued by his stand and wanted him to say more about it. Congregational attendance at worship and contributions toward a new church building continued with no decrease, and the construction of the building proceeded on schedule in the spring of 1963.[47]

In many cases, the attitudes and actions of a few key leaders set the tone for a congregation's response. Thus Kellar, Roberts, Carter, Napier, Dickinson, and Oliver had more positive experiences, while signers such as Walters, Rush, Nicholson, McRae (Figure 6.3), Lampton (Figure 6.3), Holston, and Way suffered more because of negative leadership. At Lovely Lane in Natchez, Elton Brown's decade of pastoral experience played an important role in what happened there; in addition, Jack Sewell, chair of the Pastoral Relations Committee, suggested meetings between church members and Brown. Sewell did not agree with Born of Conviction and had fairly traditional Mississippi views on race, but as a lifelong Methodist, he believed in supporting the preacher. He also thought the world of Brown, and the two had long talks about Born of Conviction and became even closer friends as a result. Sewell's leadership played a central role in Brown's continued success and acceptance at the church, even though some members left.[48]

Although a step removed from the local level, in some cases the district superintendent's leadership played an important role in the future of signers in their congregations. Upset about Marvin Moody's participation, five members of Oak Grove Church went to see Hattiesburg District clergy leader Brunner Hunt after Born of Conviction appeared. Hunt read the statement out loud and paused after each paragraph to tell the men he agreed with it. A grateful Moody reported that Hunt had faithfully supported the pastors in his district. Brookhaven District Superintendent Norman Boone supported his two signers, Rod Entrekin and Bill Lampton, though Boone's efforts could not prevent Lampton's departure from Pisgah.[49]

Other district superintendents were critical in private or openly hostile to some signers. Inman Moore recalls the Seashore District's Tom Prewitt chastising him privately. In addition to allowing the vote to remove James Rush from the Philadelphia Circuit, Meridian District Superintendent Jim Slay reprimanded signers of the statement in front of their fellow pastors.

At a district preacher's meeting in January, when asked while presiding if he had read Born of Conviction, he replied he had not read it and would not allow anyone to read it to him. He added he did not worry about the signers, because their youth and education would allow them to start over in another profession.[50]

Some signers reported in 1963 that they got more negative response from fellow pastors in the Mississippi Conference than they did from their churches. Rod Entrekin told a February 1963 gathering of several of the signers, "I felt better after my Board meeting than I did after the preachers' meeting in Brookhaven." Some of the flak resulted from hard-core segregationist views like Herbert Beasley's, but conference politics also played a central role, as events at the May 1963 Annual Conference session confirmed.[51]

PART III

What Became of the Twenty-Eight?

7

Spoke Out, Forced Out?

Could I serve Sandersville for another year? I could,
but did I want to?

—NED KELLAR, *Sandersville,* 2010, remembering his 1963
thoughts

EDDIE STARR MET Ed McRae in the band at Pascagoula High School
and later lived with McRae's family to finish school there when his parents moved to Biloxi. He joined McRae and Jerry Furr as another of
Pascagoula First Methodist pastor Harland Hilbun's "preacher boys." At
Mississippi Southern, he met and married his wife, Betty; her maid of
honor, Ginny Selby, eventually married Rod Entrekin, already a full-time
pastor in the conference. At Candler School of Theology, long conversations with Professor Claude Thompson, a member of the NAACP, led
Starr to realize that "some of my thoughts and leanings were to more open
relations with people of color, too." After seminary graduation he served
Gulfport's Guinn Memorial and then became Roy Clark's associate pastor
at Jackson's Capitol Street Church in 1960. In October 1962 in the wake
of the Ole Miss crisis, the Starrs' two young daughters began reflecting
typical white racist attitudes, and the Starrs pondered leaving Mississippi.
Although Roy Clark supported Starr's commitment to new understandings in race relations, the lack of support from his district superintendent,
Willard Leggett, and from Bishop Franklin also motivated Starr to consider a transfer. By the time his friends Furr, McRae, and Entrekin had
signed Born of Conviction, Starr had agreed to a January 1 move to the
Pacific Northwest Conference. Sympathetic to the statement, he declined
to sign because he would leave before its publication.[1]

At the eleven Mississippi Annual Conference meetings between 1954
and 1964, 160 ministers were ordained elder, two-thirds with seminary
degrees. They represented a range of theological and political views and

formed a new generation in the conference. However, in those same eleven years, 105 ministers transferred out of the conference, while only thirty-six transferred in. Between 1960 and 1966, twenty-seven transferred in, while eighty departed, including seventeen who signed Born of Conviction—an average of more than eleven transfers out per year. Due to this exodus, the conference conducted a 1964 survey that identified frustration with the conference political leadership as the main reason for leaving.[2]

Many of the brief published mentions of Born of Conviction can be characterized as narratives of forced departure:

> . . . Walters joined the ranks of nineteen of the "Born of Conviction" signers who left their Mississippi churches, forced out either by order of the lay leadership or by unbearable hostility from the congregation.
>
> Retaliation was swift and severe. The salaries of three were discontinued immediately. . . . Pressures on fifteen were so great that they resigned and moved to other states. An official of the Southern Regional Council commented, "In the South we have a new class of DP's—displaced parsons."
>
> Most of the younger ministers were driven out of the state, as were many others who supported their stance.
>
> Literally all of [Rabbi] Nussbaum's circle of support—including most of the twenty-eight Methodist ministers—were soon compelled to leave the state.
>
> . . . when twenty-eight young Methodist ministers in Mississippi signed a mild statement regarding the University of Mississippi desegregation crisis, all of them were gone within the year.
>
> Twenty-eight Methodist ministers once lost their churches in Mississippi for a stand on the race issue.
>
> All the signers . . . were run out of Mississippi.

When James Rush published an article in a national Methodist magazine in 1967, the editors described him as "one of 28 Methodist ministers who left Mississippi a few years ago as an aftermath of civil rights activities." Aside from the varying degrees of factual accuracy of these eight statements, they show that Born of Conviction is usually cited by historians and others as part of a larger narrative: moderate whites in the Deep South (especially Mississippi) during the civil rights era who dared to speak against the tide on the race issue were forced out—of church, community, state, and region. The narrative includes Southern white clergy and implies the departures were all due solely to the race issue and direct pressure or even persecution. While there is truth to this narrative, a closer look at the experiences of the twenty-eight signers of Born of Conviction reveals more complexity. Of the twenty who left the state, some had no choice, while others departed voluntarily.[3]

The First Two to Leave

Aware that James Rush had been expelled from the Philadelphia Circuit, Inman Moore wrote him in early February to suggest that Rush meet with Bishop Franklin, and if the bishop "cannot give you much satisfaction, I would certainly consider a transfer." Moore noted that Rush's prospects for getting another Mississippi Conference appointment were "exceedingly difficult ... *unless* both Jim Slay and Bishop Franklin really go to bat for you." Slay, Rush's district superintendent, did not support Rush, and immediately after the January meeting when two of his three congregations ousted him, Rush had a disappointing meeting with Bishop Franklin. By the time Moore wrote him, Rush already sought transfer to another conference.[4]

James and Libby Rush and their son lived with Rush's parents in Lake for several weeks while he worked to find an appointment in another annual conference. He wrote to officials in Missouri and Indiana and called his uncle, Phil Grice, a pastor in the Southern California-Arizona Conference. In mid-February, he got an offer to move immediately to San Pedro, California, and serve as associate pastor at a 1,100-member church. The district superintendent there, S. Douglas Walters, was from Alabama originally. Mississippi pastor Mark Lytle, Rush's superintendent during his student pastorate at Millsaps, wrote a glowing letter to Walters explaining the situation and saying, "The Mississippi Conference can ill afford to lose these men but I must say that you will make no mistake in opening a way for James."[5]

Walters expressed one concern to Rush: he could not smoke, because churches in the West enforced the denominational rule against ministers smoking. Walters said, "Bishop Kennedy has had to have conferences with several [ministers] and has informed them they had better quit or go back to Texas or the South as we will not permit it in the West. I am saying this that you might pass it on to any of the Southern boys who might be anxious to join our Conference." A Methodist minister with more open views on race relations was unwelcome in most places in Mississippi, but Southern conferences ignored the no smoking rule.[6]

Rejected by most of their church people in Neshoba County and forced to leave their substandard parsonage and an annual salary of $3,600, the Rushes arrived in San Pedro almost out of money. They had not communicated their travel schedule with people at their new church. After staying at cheap motels on their cross-country auto trip, Rush decided to spend their first night in San Pedro at a nicer hotel. When he arrived at the desk, dressed down and unwashed, the desk clerk asked if he was a Methodist preacher. Surprised, he learned the church had reserved a suite for them. They soon moved into a redecorated parsonage, and Rush, twenty-five and not yet a year out of seminary, started work on March 1 at an annual salary of $5,000.[7]

Inman Moore Jr.'s Mississippi experience was quite different. The thirty-seven-year-old pastor at Leggett Memorial in Biloxi was in his fourteenth year in the conference, and his decision to transfer to the Southern California-Arizona Conference, while related to the response to Born of Conviction and the racial climate in Mississippi, was not due to expulsion from his congregation. Although a few church members protested his stance, he could easily have stayed. The race issue played a role in his decision, but Moore left primarily because of conference politics. He believed the Leggett group had abused its power and directed "a tight, well run political machine composed of untrained but shrewd men . . . not interested in men who are trained and may have ideas of their own." To him, this meant a "loss of vision and . . . the failure to wrestle with great ideas" in the conference. In such conditions, Moore decided, "my own ministry has run its course in Mississippi." Aside from political and philosophical differences with the conference power structure, Moore had personal reasons for leaving, too. His father, Inman Moore Sr. was one of Leggett's lieutenants. The son had sided with the opposition group, and he decided it was time to remove himself from that conflict.[8]

Just after the release of Born of Conviction, Moore and some clergy friends learned that Bishop Gerald Kennedy (Figure 7.1) of the Southern California-Arizona Conference was preaching on January 21 and 22 in New Orleans, and they arranged to meet with Kennedy after a service. Born of Conviction signers N. A. Dickson, Jim Waits, and Maxie Dunnam

FIGURE 7.1 Bishop Gerald Kennedy in 1961. Copyright, Archives, California-Pacific Annual Conference of The United Methodist Church.

made the trip with Moore, along with colleagues Warren Pittman and David McKeithen, Dunnam's pastoral mentor. With Dickson and McKeithen as primary spokesmen, they explained the current situation in Mississippi and told the bishop some of them might need to transfer to another conference. If so, would he be willing to receive them? Sensitive to the impropriety of actively recruiting ministers from another area, Kennedy expressed solidarity with the Twenty-Eight, but told them he considered Bishop Franklin a good friend. He could not promise anything at the moment, but if any of them wrote him, he would give them consideration. The bishop also mildly chastised the Born of Conviction signers for not informing Bishop Franklin beforehand. As Jim Waits remembers, Kennedy said, "If I am going to be involved in a crash landing, I'd like to be involved in the take-off."[9]

Moore and his wife, Nellie, had considered living in the West if they left Mississippi; he was stationed in Long Beach, California, in the Navy during World War II. Prior to the meeting with Kennedy, he contacted bishops in the Western Jurisdiction; he wrote Kennedy after the meeting.

By February 20, just after James Rush obtained his new position, Moore accepted a pastorate in Palmdale, California, in Bishop Kennedy's conference. The opening, at $100 less in annual salary than Leggett Memorial, resulted from the death of a minister, and it was Moore's position if he came by April. In a February 23 letter, Moore requested that Bishop Franklin approve his transfer as of April 15, the day after Easter, and the Moores moved then to Palmdale with their four children. In Bishop Kennedy's request to Franklin to approve Rush's transfer, he expressed personal concern for his episcopal colleague: "I wish I could see you and talk with you. I know you are having heavy burdens put upon you and you are always in my prayers." In his response approving the transfers of Rush and Moore, Franklin acknowledged the difficulties but expressed confidence that better days were ahead.[10]

Upon arrival in the Southern California-Arizona Conference, Moore was amazed at the warm welcome he received from ministers, even though he was an outsider. He compared this to the more closed atmosphere in Mississippi, where many ministers still saw W. B. Selah as an outsider, though he had been at Galloway for eighteen years. "Mississippi Methodism," Moore claimed, "is becoming a very provincial Methodism with an inbreeding quality that will ultimately destroy it."[11]

James Rush's departure from Mississippi fits the common narrative well: he spoke out and was forced out of Mississippi. Inman Moore was not forced out of his church and freely chose to leave. He assured Bishop Franklin that there "would not be a minute's trouble if you placed another one of the '28' here as pastor" at Leggett Memorial. The experiences of all who left range along this spectrum.[12]

Two to Indiana, Two to Florida, One to Oklahoma

The national Methodist monthly *Concern* printed a copy of Born of Conviction in its February 1963 issue and followed in March with Jim Waits's three-page article on the controversy, which gave attention to expressions of support for the Twenty-Eight, included a lengthy description of negative responses in the media and in some of the churches, and reported the ousting of Lampton, Nicholson, and Rush. Though Waits did not downplay the difficulties, he closed with hopeful words:

The 28 men, with three exceptions, are now on the job in their respective churches. . . . There is no despair, even among those

who have lost their churches. There is freedom, and assurance of
the work of the Holy Spirit. There is a fellowship of conviction, and
a centrality of purpose. In spite of the difficulties faced, the best
witness to the statement of conviction is that with only few exceptions, each man expects to continue his ministry in the Mississippi
Conference.

Some of the Twenty-Eight attempted to create the "fellowship of conviction" to which Waits referred. On February 13, twelve gathered at Galloway
senior pastor W. B. Selah's home in Jackson to meet with Dr. A. Dudley
Ward, Associate General Secretary of the Division of Human Relations
and Economic Affairs in the denomination's Board of Christian Social
Concerns. Ward encouraged them to stay in Mississippi. Those present
related their recent experiences plus news of other signers, and they discussed next steps, including another meeting in Hattiesburg two weeks
hence. Native Mississippian Will Campbell of the National Council of
Churches' (NCC) Southern Project of Racial and Cultural Relations corresponded with Waits to lend support, and his NCC colleague Elbert Jean
visited with several of the Twenty-Eight in mid-January.[13]

When Bill Lampton and his wife and infant daughter left Pisgah on
January 5, they spent the next few months in an apartment in Columbia,
his home town. Later in January the conference treasurer promised
Lampton his salary until June, and Lampton preached at least once during
those months at a church in the Brookhaven District. At the end of January
he still intended to take another pastoral appointment in Mississippi
in June, though he acknowledged the possibility of changed plans. He
received support and sympathy from many members of his home church,
Columbia First Methodist, where he and his family attended during that
time. Lampton had recruited the church's pastor, N. A. Dickson, to sign
Born of Conviction, and Dickson engaged Lampton to speak on the topic
"Keeping Your Faith" at a banquet honoring the graduating high school
seniors of that church in late March.[14]

By late April, Lampton had arranged with Bishop Franklin's cooperation to transfer to the Indiana Conference. He heard from the Mississippi
Conference Treasurer on May 1 that a portion of his April salary could not
be paid in full due to insufficient funds, and he wrote Franklin requesting
that money be allocated to pay him until he moved in early June. He feared
that because James Rush and James Nicholson had already left the state
and he was leaving, the conference saw no need to continue paying him.
In spite of rumors that he had received financial support from extended

family, he insisted his living came solely from his salary. In early June he took an appointment to start a new church in Indianapolis.[15]

Summer Walters also transferred to Indiana; he had vowed "to stay in Mississippi as long as possible," but the time to leave came sooner than he expected when he wrote those words in 1961. Even though it was early February before the Jefferson Street Official Board finalized its request that he not be reappointed there in June, Walters saw the writing on the wall. In late January, Bishop Franklin accused him privately of signing the statement to stir up trouble and embarrass the bishop. Franklin did not know where he could appoint Walters in Mississippi.[16]

At the recommendation of Roy Clark, pastor at Jackson's Capitol Street Church, on April 19 Walters wrote the bishops in five episcopal areas about the possibility of transfer: Oregon, Los Angeles (Bishop Kennedy), Dallas, Atlanta, and Indiana. A few days later, Bishop Franklin confirmed he had no appointment for Walters—the same news Roy Delamotte had received from his district superintendent in June 1955. Walters also heard from Bishop John Owen Smith in Atlanta, who expressed admiration yet gave no encouragement about openings in Georgia. A phone call from Bishop Richard C. Raines of Indiana on May 8 countered this bad news; Raines invited Walters to consult about a possible appointment. He flew to Indianapolis to meet with the bishop and cabinets of all three Indiana conferences. Later that month he returned to Indianapolis to meet the new pastor and lay leaders of the Roberts Park Church, where he was appointed associate pastor. In granting transfer, Franklin used language similar to his correspondence with Bishop Kennedy and admitted to Raines that he had experienced a great deal of tension. He also expressed sadness at losing Walters; he believed the young pastor had great potential.[17]

At the Indiana Conference session in June, Walters felt at home when the conference under Bishop Raines's leadership approved "A Statement on Race Relations," including quotations from and affirmation of Martin Luther King Jr.'s "Letter from Birmingham Jail"—a marked difference from Franklin's "episcopal laryngitis." The Walters family wrote to friends in July that they were now in a conference "where we might have the opportunity to serve God and His church more effectively." Walters later said, "We did not choose to leave Mississippi; Franklin and the Mississippi Conference chose for us to leave."[18]

While Lampton and Walters had to leave, Ned Kellar (Figure 7.2) and Wilton Carter (Figure 7.2) could have stayed at Sandersville and Lake for another year. In both cases, key lay leaders paved the way for a truce, in

ORDAINED DEACONS—1961

Unusually large classes of splendid, consecrated young men were ordained deacons and elders by Bishop Marvin A. Franklin on June 16 at the closing session of the 1961 Mississippi Annual Conference. There are 20 who were ordained deacons, and 25 who were ordained elders.

FIGURE 7.2 Mississippi Conference ministers ordained deacon in 1961. Born of Conviction signers in picture: Marvin Moody, first row, second from right; Ned Kellar, second row, far left; Wilton Carter, top row, far right. Others mentioned in book: Clint Gill (Chapter 9), top row, second from right; Wilson Brent (Chapter 10), top row, middle (with glasses). Courtesy of Mississippi Annual Conference, The United Methodist Church.

spite of their disagreement with Born of Conviction. As close friends, the Kellars and Carters conferred often about their futures during early 1963, discussing the pros and cons of leaving Mississippi. Kellar confirms in his 2010 autobiography that the issue was not whether he could stay but whether he *wanted* to do so, and Carter shared the same view.[19]

Carter and Kellar went together to Ministers Week at Emory's Candler School of Theology January 21–24, and Carter spoke with people from Florida, because he had known Florida Bishop James Henley's son in seminary. Kellar sought Bishop John Owen Smith's counsel. He had worked in the North Georgia Conference while in seminary, and the bishop knew him; at that point, he intended to stay in Mississippi at least another year. Smith wrote Kellar a few days later: "I know Mississippi needs you at this time and will continue to need you in the years to come. On the other hand, I feel that you have a right to be reasonably happy in your ministry." While in Atlanta, Kellar talked to several people, including G. Ross Freeman, a Candler administrator; David McKeithen of Mississippi; and pastors in South Carolina, Georgia, and Tennessee, each of whom sought an associate pastor for the coming conference year.[20]

Kellar explored a number of possibilities; some involved educational ministry on a church staff. McKeithen, pastor of Leavell Woods Church in Jackson, wrote in mid-February to say that his associate, William T. Gober, was leaving; would Kellar be interested in that position? Over the next two months as the result of his own inquiries or letters written on his behalf by Ross Freeman, Kellar heard from ministers in Georgia, South Carolina, North Carolina, Tennessee, Arkansas, the Canal Zone, Indiana, Southern California, and Florida. Another factor in Kellar's deliberations was that his wife Dot was pregnant with their first child. Did they want to leave Mississippi and be farther away from extended family? Did they want to raise a child in the current social and political climate in Mississippi?[21]

In the meantime, Wilton Carter's Florida connections enabled him to secure a transfer there by late March; he would begin serving in June as associate to Mississippi native and Millsaps graduate Caxton Doggett at Lakeland First Church. Carter encouraged Kellar to try the same conference, so Kellar wrote six Florida district superintendents. Responses were lukewarm; he heard from one superintendent that his chances were nonexistent. Kellar also experienced a struggle in his soul for weeks. He could stay at Sandersville another year, and he was still leaning that way in late March. But did he want to stay? What was the right thing to do? Then he received what he took as a sign: a mailing from MAMML with the text of four resolutions seeking to preserve segregation in The Methodist Church, approved at their March 21 Jackson meeting. This seemed to decide it.[22]

In early April, David Cathcart, senior pastor of First Church in Cocoa, Florida, invited Kellar to come for an interview at the church's expense. He took the first plane flight of his life to Florida; in spite of irrational worries about a crash, he survived the trip and liked what he saw and heard, including the offer of an annual salary more than $1,000 higher than Sandersville. Upon return home, he wrote Bishop Franklin on April 22 requesting a transfer. Bishop Henley wrote Franklin a week later and assured his colleague that he had actively sought to discourage Mississippi pastors from leaving their conference.[23]

So Kellar was set to go to Florida, or so he thought. At Mississippi Annual Conference in late May, his district superintendent, Brunner Hunt, saw him there on the first day and expressed surprise, thinking he had already left. Hunt told him Sandersville wanted him to stay and that was still possible. Hunt gave him a few hours to think about it. While considering, he encountered another minister who rebuked him for the problems Born of Conviction had caused. Kellar responded with fury, and when the exchange ended, he decided to go to Florida.[24]

Kellar's participation in Born of Conviction related to his departure, but conference politics played the most significant role in his decision. He had doubts about his prospects for advancement in a conference controlled by the Leggett forces. Seashore District Superintendent Tom Prewitt, a Leggett lieutenant, sought to alleviate that concern. Prewitt, at sixty-four a senior member of the conference, was a relentless evangelist (his prolonged altar calls at revivals were well-known) and recruiter of young men to the ordained ministry. Several pastors in the conference, including Willard Leggett, viewed him as their "father in the ministry." Rough-edged, forcefully persistent, and outspoken, he said at a preacher's meeting after Born of Conviction came out that if certain young preachers didn't watch out, there would be a "schasm" in the church.[25]

Yet Prewitt sought privately to be the paternal guardian of at least three of the signers, including Kellar and Carter, and of the eight signers in Prewitt's district, only one (Moore) left the conference in 1963, completely by his own choice. A key element of Methodist ministerial paternalism was the tradition of elders "taking care of" their charges. One's relationship with the elder was at least as important as one's ability to earn an appointment promotion through personal talents and hard work, and such care from the elder implied long-term loyalty from the younger minister. Prewitt spoke with Kellar about the possibility of starting a new church on the Coast and wrote him in early April, seeking a private meeting in the next week to discuss it further. He offered Kellar his help and implored him to keep their meeting and letters secret.[26]

Prewitt had met and corresponded with Wilton Carter a few weeks earlier and also offered him an appointment. Carter communicated his concerns about conference politics and his intention to leave Mississippi in person to Prewitt, who then wrote begging him not to leave. Regarding Carter's political concerns, Prewitt believed Carter had been prejudiced by persons opposed to the acknowledged leaders of the conference and wanted him to hear the other side. Prewitt assured Carter he would not be penalized for an honest stand such as his membership in the Twenty-Eight. Prewitt also asked Carter to tell no one of their correspondence.[27]

Carter found Florida quite attractive, but his primary reasons for leaving Mississippi were the conference political situation and the failure of conference leaders to acknowledge the crucial importance of the concerns expressed in Born of Conviction. He assured Prewitt he had indeed heard both sides of the story. Prewitt encouraged him to look honestly at the men leading the conference instead of accepting the opposition viewpoint. Carter had taken this advice and "simply [did] not find it feasible to go along with some of [the leaders'] policies." He believed the situation in Mississippi called for "the Church [to] spend her time at the job of being the Church," and thus far, Christians, including Methodists, had failed in that dire need. A year later in his response to the conference survey of ministers who had left, he explained, "If I could have found any encouragement from a single leader in the Mississippi Conference, not excluding the Bishop or my District Superintendent, assuring me that the cause of justice and brotherhood was the concern of the Methodist Church and that this would be a united effort wherein their support could be felt, I would be there to this day."[28]

Church members at Lake implored Carter to stay; they threw a party for the Carters on May 22 at the conclusion of the Wednesday prayer meeting. If he had responded favorably to Prewitt's paternal care, he could have also moved to a better appointment in Mississippi. In a letter to Bishop Franklin on March 27, Carter thanked him for coming to Lake the previous week to baptize the Carter's infant son. In a conciliatory tone in contrast to his letter to Prewitt two weeks earlier, he reported, "I appreciated the conversation with Dr. Prewitt, but as I told him, I cannot convince myself that we would be happy to stay in this Conference under the prevailing conditions. I do not mean to throw stones at any particular person. We will transfer with no bitterness towards anyone."[29]

In his seventeenth year of full-time ministry in the conference, James Holston (Figure 7.3) felt deeply committed to Mississippi and vowed at first to stay. He avoided responding to Ole Miss historian James Silver's January letter requesting information from the Twenty-Eight for fear such correspondence "would not enhance my position." However, he came to believe his involvement in Born of Conviction would mean concerted effort by pressure groups to undermine his ministry wherever he went in the conference. "In Mississippi," he said, "a Christian minister is free only as long as he is willing to run and bay with the pack." He considered church politics to be the "crushing blow," more important than the race question. Given the reaction of church members, he could not return to Carthage for another year. So in mid-March he sought to transfer; he explained to Georgia's Bishop Smith that "the hazards for [his] family" were too great to stay.[30]

FIGURE 7.3 James Holston, 1960s. Courtesy of Holston family.

Holston transferred to Oklahoma, and the family moved 555 miles from Carthage to Tulsa in June. Early in the trip, his sixteen-year-old daughter could not hide her sadness: "Leaving our culture, our relatives and our friends was tortuous. After patiently listening to my sobbing for a long while, Dad in a VERY stern tone told me to be quiet. My emotional ranting must have twisted the knife that had already penetrated his heart." Holston became pastor of Asbury Church, a year-old congregation meeting in an elementary school in Tulsa's southern suburbs. In the summer he wrote Silver, admitting he now felt "free to write" and that "it feels good to be out of Mississippi." Two years later he expressed ambivalence at having left and "admiration and sympathy for those still in Mississippi."[31]

A complicating factor in Holston's quest to transfer was his salary level, which made it more difficult for Bishop Smith to appoint him in Georgia, even though Holston expressed willingness to be considered for "any position that may be open." Of the seven signers who transferred out by the end of May, all but Holston and Moore were low enough on the appointment ladder that the conferences willing to take them had little difficulty with placement. Four became associate pastors, and one was appointed to start a new church; all received a raise in salary. These appointments caused little flak in the receiving conferences, because churches seeking associates were given freedom to choose their man and a new church represented a new slot in the system. The higher up the ladder, the more chance existed for hurt feelings by ministers already in a conference at the supposed favor shown a newcomer. Inman Moore benefited from a mid-year opening at Palmdale; bishops and cabinets prefer to move as few people as possible in such cases. Both Moore and Holston took salary cuts to make their moves. Holston's appointment at Tulsa Asbury lasted a year; in 1964 he began nine years at First Church in Moore, just south of Oklahoma City, and by the fall of 1965 his salary slightly exceeded what he had earned at Carthage.[32]

Mississippi Annual Conference 1963: Leggett Triumph

In a letter to Summer Walters just after the Born of Conviction statement appeared, Jim Waits wrote, "News from around the Conference is not so encouraging, though I believe most of the men will come out victorious in the end. I predict Conference will be *quite* exciting this year, and that even *politics* may take a back seat!" Roy Delamotte, the Mississippi

Methodist pastor who left in 1955 after his public protest against the conference's refusal to acknowledge the crisis of race relations, and the author of *The Stained Glass Jungle*, believed an annual conference should be "a dramatic public focusing of the highest thought and deepest conscience of Methodism," and the Twenty-Eight shared this theological understanding of the church's witness. The signers believed God had called them to speak publicly in response to "the grave crises precipitated by racial discord within our state in recent months, and the genuine dilemma facing persons of Christian conscience." This can be called the *conscience* perspective.[33]

Conference political leader Willard Leggett and his followers supported the maintenance of segregation in the state and the church, but they also saw the Twenty-Eight as attempting to wrest power from them and define new directions for the conference. Leggett lieutenant Tom Prewitt, the Seashore District Superintendent in 1963, told Jim Waits and Jerry Trigg they were inappropriately challenging the political leaders of the conference. Nolan Harmon's portrait of the annual conference as the "minister's church" and his image of the corporate individuality or culture of that Methodist body expresses Leggett's view of ministry and the church, the *traditional* perspective. The Born of Conviction statement struck a blow for the conscience perspective in the Mississippi Conference ideological battle, but the 1963 Annual Conference session was a decisive victory for the traditional perspective in at least three ways: the rejection of another conference minister's more radical civil rights witness, the General and Jurisdictional Conference election results, and the beginning of the exodus of many of the Twenty-Eight.[34]

The Born of Conviction controversy was not the most important race relations news in Mississippi during the first half of 1963. The Jackson civil rights movement, led by Medgar Evers and Tougaloo professor John Salter, had gained strength, spurred by a boycott of downtown merchants that began in December 1962. The majority of participants in the direct action campaign were students at Tougaloo College, the historically African American school on the northern edge of Jackson, and black high school students. When Bull Conner's police dogs and fire hoses in Birmingham made national news in April, the Jackson Movement gained added support from the NAACP. On May 21, a mass meeting with six hundred in attendance called for Mayor Allen Thompson, a member of Galloway Methodist Church, to meet with representatives of the black community to discuss their demands for hiring black police, establishing a biracial committee to deal with community concerns, and ending segregated public facilities and discriminatory hiring practices. When Thompson rejected these demands a few days later, demonstrations began, including the May 28 sit-in at the Woolworth's lunch counter by black Tougaloo students Anne Moody, Pearlena Lewis, and Memphis Norman. After Norman was beaten and kicked severely by a former Jackson police chief, John Salter and Tougaloo student Joan Trumpauer (both white) joined the two remaining at the counter. The white mob doused them with mustard, ketchup, and sugar. The resulting mass meetings and demonstrations led to hundreds of arrests. In early June the national NAACP withdrew its support for the demonstrations, and the Jackson Movement's momentum slowed. Then late on the night of June 11, Medgar Evers was assassinated in his carport.[35]

The direct connection between these events and the Mississippi Conference was Vicksburg native and Millsaps graduate Ralph Edwin King Jr., who knew nine of the Twenty-Eight at Millsaps and several others from conference activities in the 1950s. A graduate of Boston University School of Theology who had already been arrested in civil rights activities in Alabama, Ed King returned to Mississippi in mid-January 1963 to serve as chaplain at Tougaloo. His Mississippi Conference membership was still on trial, but Bishop Franklin had ordained him an elder in 1961. King also became a leader in the Jackson Movement, and he was present at the Woolworth's sit-in on May 28, just a few blocks away from Galloway Church, where the 1963 Annual Conference session had just convened. Arrested and jailed in the mass demonstrations that followed, King got out on bail in time to attend a Clergy Executive Session on May 31, the last day of conference, when the Board of Ministerial Training and Qualifications recommended "by a divided vote" that his conference membership be continued on trial. A lengthy debate ensued; King was not allowed to speak. Born of Conviction signer Powell Hall was among those who argued for King's continuation as a member, and at least four Leggett-aligned pastors spoke in opposition. The conference clergy voted eighty-nine to eighty-five to discontinue King's membership. At the invitation of Bishop Charles Golden, a black Mississippi native, King soon joined the Central Jurisdiction Mississippi Conference.[36]

At the same annual conference, Leggett forces swept clergy elections for 1964 General and Jurisdictional Conference delegates. Of the fourteen ministers elected to General Conference, Jurisdictional Conference, and reserve (alternate) delegates to Jurisdictional Conference, the first seven were all associated with Leggett, along with three or four of the remaining seven. Though the elections were not directly related to Born of Conviction or Ed King's case, Willard Leggett and his supporters stood firmly against such activities. The Leggett victory represented a resounding affirmation of him as leader of the conference and a clear rejection of both Born of Conviction (signed by "some of our best trained and most promising ministers" and symbolizing a different understanding of church, pastoral leadership, and Christian ethics) and of Ed King's more radical understanding of the church's role in social change. Conference politics was central at the 1963 Annual Conference session, and the traditional perspective, representing allegiance to the past, paternalism, continued segregation in church and society, and suspicion of seminary education, prevailed. It seemed Sam Ashmore had overstated when he said Born of Conviction represented the views of "the vast majority of the clerical members of the conference."[37]

J. P. Stafford had served faithfully and well as conference lay leader since 1947, but because of his support for Born of Conviction and a few forthright discussions of the race issue in his weekly *Advocate* columns, retaliation came in two ways at annual conference in May 1963. In the elections for 1964 General and Jurisdictional Conference lay delegates, Stafford, who had been chosen the first lay delegate to the past three General Conferences, was not even elected a Jurisdictional Conference delegate, failing to receive forty votes on any ballot when at least twice that many were necessary for election. In response to Born of Conviction and in preparation for the impending showdown on race at the 1964 General Conference, lay members chose MAMML member and Ross Barnett advisor John Satterfield to lead their delegation. James Conner observed Leggett supporters celebrating in the halls of Galloway after Stafford's defeat. There was also an attempt to vote Stafford out as conference lay leader, but this failed when Bert Jordan, the nominee to replace him, declined to run.[38]

Finally, by the time the 1963 Annual Conference session, described by one veteran pastor as "a combination of the Charge of the Light Brigade, the Battle of Manila Bay, and the Elegy in the Country Churchyard," adjourned, seven of the Twenty-Eight had transferred their membership to other annual conferences. Rush and Moore had already left, while the transfers of Walters, Lampton, Carter, Kellar, and Holston all became official at the Jackson meeting. Others left in the next few weeks, though none foresaw it on May 31.[39]

Southern California-Arizona and Iowa

Ed McRae knew by February that he would leave Oakland Heights in early June, but he planned to stay in Mississippi. His father-in-law, Martin Riley, an admirer and friend of Willard Leggett from the latter's days as pastor of Capitol Street Church in the late 1940s, spoke to Leggett, who asked Tom Prewitt to take McRae in the Seashore District. The appointment, North Biloxi, included a plan to start a new congregation to the east toward Ocean Springs. This may have been the situation that Prewitt offered first to Wilton Carter and then Ned Kellar. Shortly after his arrival in Biloxi, McRae got a phone call from a district superintendent in the Pacific Northwest Conference. His old friend Eddie Starr, now serving there, had told the district leader that McRae might want to leave Mississippi, so the offer came to move to Washington State. McRae declined, saying he was needed in Mississippi. The response, as McRae remembers it: "Have you ever thought that you could be needed somewhere else?"[40]

The McRaes agreed Washington was too far away from Mississippi and extended family, but they pondered the idea of serving elsewhere. McRae talked to several people, including his father-in-law, who advised him that if he could not mellow, he might as well leave. McRae called Jim McCormick, a Mississippi pastor who had just transferred to Southern California-Arizona, at the annual conference session at the University of the Redlands, and he promised to find McRae a position. Within an hour, Ray Ragsdale, senior pastor at Catalina Methodist in Tucson, phoned to offer a job as minister of education at the large church. Within twenty-four hours of that call, just two weeks after moving to Biloxi, McRae decided to request a transfer to the Southern California-Arizona Conference. By July 4, the McRaes and their two boys had moved to Tucson, where they stayed six years. After McRae got to know Ragsdale, he remembers kidding him, "Ray, I'm not sure about your leadership ability. You take a guy from Mississippi that you've never met and don't know anything about, sight unseen." Ragsdale responded, "Yes, but you signed that statement."[41]

When James Nicholson was forced out of Byram Church in January, his district superintendent, Willard Leggett, had not supported his stand but did make it possible for him and his family to remain in the Byram parsonage and receive a salary until another appointment could be arranged in May. Nicholson had unfinished business: he had not completed his seminary degree at SMU's Perkins School of Theology. R. Lanier Hunt, brother of Hattiesburg District Superintendent Brunner Hunt and on staff at the National Council of Churches in New York, visited Nicholson in Jackson in early January. Aware of Nicholson's plight and unfinished degree, Hunt arranged for scholarship funds from the Methodist Board of Christian Social Concerns to help pay tuition. Nicholson's wife Alice taught at Redwood High School in rural Warren County north of Vicksburg, and she and the children remained in Byram for that semester while Nicholson completed his degree in Dallas. He considered the opportunity a blessing and vowed to return to Mississippi, "to finish what we have started as long as it remains in my power." Brookhaven District Superintendent Norman Boone cleared the way to appoint Nicholson to Bassfield, and after Nicholson's ordination as elder at the conference session on May 31, his family moved there in early June.[42]

A few weeks later, fellow Born of Conviction signer N. A. Dickson, still at nearby Columbia, warned Nicholson that a black man intended to break the color line in worship at white churches in the area, including Bassfield Methodist. Nicholson, certain the man would be turned away at his church, feared a repeat of his Byram experience. He would have to take a stand and believed it best to transfer. He began calling bishops in other conferences, including Bishop Raines in Indiana, who invited him to come for an interview. Nicholson also contacted Bishop Gerald Ensley of Iowa, Chairman of the General Board of Christian Social Concerns; Ensley knew Nicholson's situation well because the board had helped fund his semester at Perkins and had sent a letter of salute to each of the Twenty-Eight in February. Iowa seemed the best option, and on Nicholson's fortieth birthday in August, the family moved to Truro.[43]

"There Can Be No Color Bar in a Christian Church . . ."

Jerry Furr hoped in late January that by the end of the year the Closed Society "will decisively be an experience of the past. . . . I see many reasons for great optimism in 1963." He vowed "to spend my life in my native state of Mississippi serving Christ through the Methodist Church." In March, Furr reported that twenty of the signers "would remain in Mississippi after the next annual conference." Furr's count implied eight leaving; one may have been Jack Troutman, whose plans to leave in 1963 fell through by May. But by the time Nicholson left in August, only fifteen signers remained at churches in Mississippi, and Furr had left.[44]

W. B. Selah experienced difficulties in the wake of his forceful support of Born of Conviction. He took much of the flak from some disgruntled church members, thus protecting Jerry Furr, his associate pastor. On Sunday, January 13, a week after issuing his statement to the press, Selah collapsed in the hall outside the sanctuary after cutting his sermon short and was hospitalized with a bleeding ulcer, though he soon recovered. Furr got strong, mostly private support from the more liberal members of the church. Many acquaintances condemned Furr, and a cross was burned on his lawn. The Galloway Official Board (with more than one hundred members) voted in the spring on a resolution related to the church's pastoral leadership; only eighteen voted against Selah's return for another year, but the vote on Furr, though still positive, was much more divided. Both Selah and Furr were returned to Galloway for 1963–4 when appointments were read at annual conference on May 31.[45]

The congregation's closed-door policy, passed by the board over Selah's objections in 1961 and reaffirmed in January 1963, had not yet been put to the test. That changed on June 9 (sixty hours before the murder of Medgar Evers), when after they were turned away from First Baptist, a group of five Tougaloo students came to Galloway for the 11:00 service. On the way to the sanctuary from his study, Selah noticed the commotion from a distance and sent Furr to investigate. A few minutes later Furr reached the chancel area as the choir finished its anthem and told Selah that the black students had been turned away by Galloway ushers. Selah shortened his sermon and made a brief statement,

> the gist of which was that I loved them, even the ones who disagreed with me on the race issue but that I could not serve a church that actually turned people away. I had been saying for 18 years that there can be no color bar in a Christian church and that all men, black and white, should be treated not on the basis of color but on the basis of conduct. Now I either had to repudiate my convictions or leave.

He resigned on the spot, and when he sat down, Jerry Furr also announced his resignation.[46]

After the service and in the next day or so, Furr tried to dissuade Selah from resigning, and this plea echoed repeatedly in the many letters Selah received in the days after June 9. However, Selah remained convinced that he must honor his promise to resign. Furr and Selah met with Bishop Franklin, who also implored Selah to stay. Franklin claimed there was no church in the conference to which he could appoint Furr; Selah insisted Franklin had to appoint Furr somewhere. Furr told the bishop he would serve anywhere but Galloway. This impasse led Furr reluctantly to seek a transfer, and Bishop Gerald Kennedy soon offered him an opportunity to start a new church in Las Vegas, then a part of the Southern California-Arizona Conference. Furr accepted, and less than a week after he and Selah resigned from Galloway, he transferred. Jerry and Marlene Furr arrived later that month in Nevada with their two young children.[47]

What Became of Them?

The three most prominent public supporters of Born of Conviction in Mississippi—Lay Leader J. P. Stafford, *Advocate* Editor Sam Ashmore, and W. B. Selah—were each born in the 1890s and had roots in the old MECS system but aligned themselves with a new understanding of church and race relations. All three paid a price for that choice. Stafford retired as conference lay leader as planned in 1964 but was denied the chance to represent Mississippi at the 1964 General and Jurisdictional Conferences because of his willingness to speak frankly about the need for change. Selah became vice president of his alma mater, Central Methodist College in Missouri, and a year later he retired, missing what would have been a glorious send-off from Galloway had he left there under normal circumstances.[48]

In 1965, a year before Sam Ashmore retired, the Methodist Press Association named him its Editor of the Year. The award, given only once, recognized the principled stand he and his wife Ann had taken in editing the *Advocate* for a decade. Yet negative reactions from many white Mississippi Methodists to Ashmore's editorials and choice to publish Born of Conviction and other articles led to subscription woes and financial struggles for the *Advocate* during his last years as editor. Ashmore, who got the paper out of debt when he took over in 1955, went without his salary on occasion in his final years there. The Publishing Committee for the *Advocate*, with clergy and lay representation from both white conferences, remained supportive of the Ashmores, and when he considered retiring in 1965, an outpouring of support encouraged him to stay. Methodists around the country, aware of the *Advocate*'s financial woes, sent contributions. Ashmore summarized the strain and realities of the work in 1964:

> In these tense times, when myth is substituted for reality; when character assassination is the order of the day; when men lose their pulpits for expressing their convictions; when repeated telephone calls in the dead of night voice ugly, whispered threats of violence and death; when crosses are burned on church property; when virtual silence is imposed with regard to existing evils; when Christian teaching is disregarded; the awesome responsibility of holding up the fundamental tenets of the church in the press becomes overwhelming.[49]

Selah, Ashmore, and Stafford joined the Twenty-Eight to represent the conscience perspective in the conference, filling the vacuum left by the failure of Bishop Franklin, Willard Leggett, and other leaders to do so. Stafford put it this way in a private letter in 1962:

> The race trouble is merely a symptom of our real sickness in this day when daring and duty to the future must be partners. ... I am a Mississippian. ... I was born and raised with all the prejudices of the times. BUT—a new day is here and we must have the courage to live in it or be the rear guard standing for what we cannot in conscience defend.

Selah returned on a couple of occasions to preach at Galloway in the years after his retirement and at least once gently reminded the congregation why he had left. Ashmore died in 1968, and Selah and Stafford died twelve days apart in May 1985.[50]

James Rush (Figure 7.4) remained at San Pedro for two years. In 1964 he worked against California Proposition 14, which nullified the Rumford Fair Housing Act and was later struck down by the California Supreme Court. In 1965, he was assigned to found a church in the San Fernando Valley; he stayed three years. In 1968, concerned that their two sons did not know their roots, he and his wife decided to move back to the Southeast, and Rush transferred to the South Carolina Conference. He served as a local church pastor there the rest of his career and retired in 2001.[51]

FIGURE 7.4 James Rush, 2004. Author photo.

Inman Moore never regretted leaving Mississippi. The Palmdale Church integrated while he served there, and in both his appointments in the Pasadena District in the 1960s, he felt free to speak his conscience on social issues. He occasionally ruffled some parishioners' feathers without threat of losing his job. In 1970 he took a leave of absence and went to work as director of training and personnel for a company owned by a former church member. He retired from the ministry in 1975 and continued to work in business; he and his wife owned and ran the official souvenir shop for the Tournament of Roses for more than twenty years. Moore occasionally served a few months as an interim pastor and became active in Democratic Party politics. In 1999, after they had retired from their business, the seventy-five-year-old Moore became pastor of a small African American United Methodist Church in Pasadena and stayed five years. He later took a part-time associate pastor job and explained, "I flunked Retirement 101."[52]

After three years as a pastor in Indianapolis, Bill Lampton left the ordained ministry in 1966. He earned a PhD in speech communication from Ohio University and worked in higher education and hospital administration, including some time in Mississippi as Associate Director of Development at Millsaps College. He has since started his own communication company; based in Georgia, he works as a motivational speaker, leadership coach, and author.[53]

In August 1963, Summer Walters heard from Clyde Gunn, still senior pastor at Jefferson Street: "On this, the hottest day, temperature wise, state election wise, Conference wise, local church wise I want you to know I am about burned up and out. I'll ... tell you again that you are fortunate to be out of this mess." Walters agreed; he served out his career as a local church pastor in the South Indiana Conference. Although their Mississippi experience left scars, Summer and Betty Walters never regretted his participation in Born of Conviction. His younger brother Jon also lost a Mississippi church job due to the race issue: he was fired as music director at Clarksdale First Methodist in 1968 when his black friends in the community came to his voice recital at the church. Summer Walters's Indiana pastorates included six years at Gobin Memorial in Greencastle, where he followed Born of Conviction signer Jerry Trigg, and three years at Broadway Church in Indianapolis. In the late 1960s, he helped sponsor a migrant worker ministry in Johnson County. In the 1980s, he took part in his conference's witness against South African apartheid, and he and Betty traveled to South Africa to spend two weeks with a pastor there. Walters retired in 1998 and died in 2010.[54]

After serving two years as associate at Cocoa First, Ned Kellar founded a new congregation in nearby Rockledge, Florida, and remained there five years. As his children started school, he decided he did not want to itinerate any longer. In 1971 he began a thirty-two year career as a pastoral counselor at a mental health center in the same area; he also began a twenty-seven year part-time pastorate at the United Methodist Church on Merritt Island. In the late 1970s, he and his wife bought a house there. Kellar retired in 2003.[55]

Wilton Carter remained at Lakeland First for two years and served two other churches in Florida. In 1968 he became an Air Force chaplain; his various assignments over the next twenty-two years included Germany, and he kept his annual conference membership in Florida. His marriage to Dolores ended in 1974. He did enough counseling as a chaplain that he eventually earned a master's in marriage and family therapy, and after retiring from the Air Force, he worked at mental health centers in Oregon,

Wyoming, and Utah. He retired from the Florida Conference in 2000. In 2004, Carter said, "Once I broke out of [Mississippi], I never really did fit back into it properly because the world had opened." To his would-be mentor, Tom Prewitt, Carter made a mistake leaving the state; Carter disagreed.[56]

In 1965 in Oklahoma, James Holston had a massive heart attack at the age of forty-two, and he had subsequent cardiac events, all of which his daughter believes "were at least partially the result of a heart pierced by the pain of the conflicts that Mississippi created in it." He continued as a pastor until taking disability leave in 1986, preaching "God's demand for good-will and respect for all His children." He retired in 1989 and died at home on April 19, 1995, just a few miles away from the infamous Oklahoma City bombing the same day.[57]

After two church appointments in Tucson, Ed McRae spent the rest of his pastoral career in Southern California, mostly in the Santa Barbara District. He and Martina had encountered new perspectives on human relations and theology as young adults in the 1950s, and they found a home and "a much more open and free atmosphere for learning and expression of faith and involvement with the world" on the Southern California coast. W. B. Selah had told some of the Twenty-Eight they would remember Born of Conviction as the defining moment of their ministry, and that was true for McRae: it set the tone for his subsequent career. He found himself on "the wrong side" of many issues, from the Vietnam War to gay rights. He retired from active ministry in 1998. The McRaes have always believed they made the right decision to leave Mississippi; they have returned regularly to visit family and in recent years have been there several times to work on Hurricane Katrina recovery projects.[58]

James Nicholson never doubted his choice to leave Mississippi either. In Iowa, he spoke on occasion to church and community groups about his experience; his October 1962 sermon was published in a number of places. In 1965, he saw Dr. Henry Bullock, the Mississippian still serving as Editor of Church School Publications for the denomination, at a pastors' school in Iowa, and in their conversation Nicholson emphasized the importance of understanding "that 'the rabid segregationist' of the South is also our brother and that the church must also have a message for him." At Bullock's invitation, Nicholson wrote an article, "Jesus Does Not Exclude—He Includes," for the denomination's *Bible Lessons for Adults*. He also tried to raise money for a library for Rust College, the historically

FIGURE 7.5 Groundbreaking service for Trinity Methodist Church in Las Vegas, 1965. Jerry Furr is at far left. Courtesy of Trinity United Methodist Church, Las Vegas, Nevada.

black Methodist school in Holly Springs, Mississippi. His wife, Alice, died in 1974, and he married again in 1980. He continued as a pastor in Iowa until his retirement in 1986. In 2005, he organized a Born of Conviction reunion in Jackson, and twelve of the twenty surviving signers attended. Nicholson died in 2009.[59]

From 1963 to 1971, Jerry Furr (Figure 7.5) served as pastor of the church he started in West Las Vegas; he also got involved in the fight for racial justice in housing, voting rights, and public accommodations in Las Vegas. In 1967 Nevada Governor Grant Sawyer appointed Furr to chair the Nevada Equal Rights Commission, and for more than four years he played a key role in convincing the casinos and the Nevada Test Site to comply fully with federal equal employment opportunity laws. In 1971, Furr decided he "had given the church as much as they'd given [him]," and he left the ministry and the church. He believed his Sunday morning sermons were "no longer needed. . . . The things I did in Las Vegas outside the church were more important than what happened in the church." For the next thirty years, he and his wife managed a federally funded free obstetrics and gynecology clinic in San Francisco; it eventually became a private clinic for low income women. Though he believed creating and signing Born of Conviction was the right thing to do, he saw his work with the poor and minorities as more meaningful: "If I could ever have done anything like that in Mississippi, it would have been a lot better than Born of Conviction."[60]

8

Continuing Exodus

*All of us who know him are sorry that he must consider
leaving, but we are getting accustomed to departures, and
we understand them.*

—LEE H. REIFF, reference letter for Joe Way,
December 13, 1963

IN SPITE OF the controversy surrounding Born of Conviction, eleven signers remained at the same church after the May 1963 Annual Conference.
In every case, their congregations were willing for them to stay another
year, contradicting the "spoke out, forced out" narrative. Eight others
moved in 1963 to different Mississippi Conference local church appointments. Jerry Trigg, John Ed Thomas, Harold Ryker, Ned Kellar, Wilton
Carter, Inman Moore, and Wallace Roberts could have stayed another
year as far as their parishioners were concerned. The first three moved
to another Mississippi Conference church either because of the amount
of time they had already served at their 1962–3 appointment or because
they requested the change; Kellar, Carter, and Moore chose to transfer
out of Mississippi, and Roberts left to attend seminary. This means that
eighteen of the Twenty-Eight either stayed or could have stayed at their
churches another year after the statement's publication.[1]

So the "spoke out, forced out" narrative fully applies only to a few of
the signers, and eight of the Twenty-Eight never left the Methodist ministry in the Mississippi Conference. It is true, however, that by eighteen
months after Born of Conviction's publication, sixteen of the signers
had transferred to other annual conferences and two others had left the
state. In all, nineteen of the Twenty-Eight transferred to another conference and one other pursued ministry elsewhere for more than twenty
years. Of the twenty who left, participation in Born of Conviction played
a role in the departure of most, but not all. The stories of departure
continue.

Two Best Friends Depart for California

After the January 1963 Official Board meeting at Decatur that ended in a vote of confidence for their pastor, Buford Dickinson, the church lost only two or three members. Although his signature on Born of Conviction did not necessarily change church members' minds, they did "begin thinking seriously about the problem," and some "felt that the church should have something to say about race relations." Most still accepted him, and Dickinson was reappointed in May 1963. In the next few months he led the church to finish a building project.[2]

However, by the fall of 1963, Buford and Jean Dickinson had decided to leave Mississippi. For her the decisive moment came on the main street of Decatur where she and her children were watching a parade. As the band from the black high school marched by, she recalls that a five-year-old boy told her son, "You know, if we don't watch out, they're going to think they're as good as we are." She did not want her children, then five and three-and-a-half, to grow up in an environment that so thoroughly socialized children into the white supremacist worldview. Coupled with her husband's disappointment in the conference leaders who failed to be faithful to the Methodist witness on the issue of race and had not even supported the freedom of ministers to speak their conscience, the time seemed right to leave.[3]

Five of the Twenty-Eight, along with David McKeithen, Jim McCormick, and other Mississippi ministers, had already left for the Southern California-Arizona Conference, and Dickinson's best friend Maxie Dunnam was also considering it. Jim Slay Jr., son of Dickinson's district superintendent, had transferred there in 1960 and was serving in Phoenix; at his recommendation, Dickinson interviewed for an appointment to start a new church. That opportunity did not feel right, but O. Magee Wilkes, vice president at Claremont School of Theology, a Methodist school in California, came to see Dickinson in Decatur and offered him a position in the seminary's Development Office. Dickinson saw the move as an opportunity to pursue a PhD and took the job. His transfer was arranged by early December 1963 and effective on January 1, 1964.[4]

In the summer of 1964 at Claremont, Dickinson hoped the new bishop coming to Mississippi would "make a great difference, but I cannot get too optimistic about the future. In the past ten to fifteen years, too many trained ministers have left the state." A year later he said the race issue had played a part in his decision to leave, but "perhaps church politics discouraged me most. I was tired of the whole mess and glad to get out. No desire, at present, to return." He acknowledged both relief and guilt at having left Mississippi.[5]

At the news of W. B. Selah and Jerry Furr's departures from Galloway, a few of Maxie Dunnam's Gulfport church members told him Mississippi needed people like him to stay. Not everyone at Trinity welcomed Dunnam's reappointment for the 1963–4 conference year, but he knew he could stay a while. His district superintendent, Tom Prewitt, could not understand why he had participated in Born of Conviction. Prewitt and another Leggett supporter told Dunnam that he and the other signers had ruined their future in Mississippi. Conference politics bothered Dunnam, but in the fall of 1963, he described his main concern:

> How can I work within the framework of a closed society and improve it? How can I maintain the tenuous dialogue between myself and my congregation? I'm not afraid. Let people curse me. Let them threaten me. But if I go too far, then my people won't listen to me. Then I'm no longer an effective force and I'm lost to the cause.[6]

The Dunnam family vacationed in California in August 1963 and inquired about a possible transfer. He liked what he saw there, especially Gerald Kennedy. He had read the bishop's books, heard him preach, and met him in New Orleans a few weeks after the publication of Born of Conviction, and Kennedy represented a model of episcopal leadership and the church that Dunnam preferred to what he had experienced in Mississippi. Dow Kirkpatrick, formerly a North Georgia minister and now senior pastor of the renowned First Methodist Church in Evanston, Illinois, invited him to come there as associate pastor, but when Dunnam received an offer to start a new church in San Clemente, California, he leaped at the chance, especially because of Kennedy and the presence of friends in that conference. Five days after Dickinson's transfer, Bishop Kennedy wrote Bishop Franklin for Dunnam's transfer, which became effective on February 10, 1964.[7]

In 1965 Dunnam wrote, "At times I wish I were back [in Mississippi] in order that I might participate in the cause; yet these feelings are overcome when I think of what was done and what could have been done." He believed the Mississippi Conference political situation had diminished the effect of Born of Conviction and that if things had been different, there might have been a "united Methodist statement" in response to the Ole Miss riot. The Dunnams experienced a new freedom in San Clemente. In their home, they did something they had not felt able to do in Gulfport: host the visiting family of Henry Clay Jr., a black pastor from the Central Jurisdiction Mississippi Conference with whom Dunnam had become friends in the late 1950s.[8]

After their arrival in California, both Dickinson and Dunnam spoke on the situation in Mississippi to audiences aware of the Chaney, Goodman, and Schwerner murders in Neshoba County in June 1964. Dunnam told the story of Born of Conviction, while Dickinson focused on white resistance to race relations change. He described the difficulties experienced by a Methodist clergy colleague who did not sign Born of Conviction but took a stand against a proposal in his Meridian congregation to prevent blacks from attending worship. Dickinson interpreted Mississippi events and attitudes "in light of our own trouble on the West Coast," and Dunnam said that although there was "blatant 'inhumanity to man'" in Mississippi,

> . . . there are subtle forces of hate at work in Southern California whose destructive powers are being strongly felt. . . . Therefore, though speaking specifically about the situation in Mississippi and my experiences there, let none think smugly that he is removed from involvement, or free from blame and guilt. The eruption of a racial crisis in one section of the country is a pointed finger at every man who has contributed to a system that has robbed a good portion of our population of their rights as citizens, and . . . *of their dignity as children of God.*[9]

Three More in 1964

About 20 percent of Jerry Trigg's church members had publicly censured his Born of Conviction stand in January 1963, but by the spring lay leaders at Caswell Springs requested that he be appointed there for another year. Although the traditional four-year stay in the same appointment was not an ironclad rule, District Superintendent Tom Prewitt invoked it; Trigg moved to Leggett Memorial in Biloxi at the 1963 Annual Conference session. Before Inman Moore left there in April, he assured Bishop Franklin that another member of the Twenty-Eight could be appointed to the church with no problems. Trigg had wanted to serve at Leggett for a while, and he was also determined to stay in Mississippi, especially because so many fellow signers had departed or seemed headed in that direction.[10]

Shortly after Trigg arrived in Biloxi, Prewitt told him there had been opposition to sending him to Leggett. As long as Trigg did not cause more trouble, things would be fine. To Prewitt, this meant something similar to what Willard Leggett expected of James Nicholson at Byram in the fall of 1962: no further public discussion of the race issue. But to Trigg, part of his commitment to stay in Mississippi involved representing the nonsegregationist perspective in some white Mississippi Methodist pulpits. On November 24, 1963, his sermon entitled "Who Killed President Kennedy?" grieved at reports that schoolchildren in Biloxi and elsewhere in Mississippi had "clapped their hands for joy" at news of the president's death. He quoted lyrics from Oscar Hammerstein's "You've Got to Be Carefully Taught" from *South Pacific* to illustrate how prejudice develops. He also scheduled E. Stanley Jones, world-renowned missionary and leader of the Christian Ashram movement, to preach a revival at Leggett. Tom Prewitt objected and told members of the church's Official Board that Jones was an integrationist and a Communist. Though Trigg protested, the board rescinded the invitation, making it the second time in a year that plans to bring Jones to Mississippi failed.[11]

Although the church was growing, there was enough dissatisfaction with Trigg among persons of power in the congregation that by the spring of 1964 the Pastoral Relations Committee voted six to three for him to move. Tom Prewitt agreed and told Trigg there was no place he could be appointed in Mississippi; he should move to a state where his liberal preaching would be accepted. Prewitt had sought to convince Ned Kellar and Wilton Carter to stay a year earlier, but Trigg did not fit Prewitt's idea of a Mississippi Conference pastor.[12]

In 1963 and 1964 Trigg spoke on the topic of the church and race relations in the Iowa and Northwest Indiana Conferences. By April 1964, he had received offers to transfer to Iowa, Southern California-Arizona, Florida, and Indiana. When he went as an observer to the Methodist General Conference in Pittsburgh late that month, he was still undecided. Bishop Richard Raines of Indiana and James Armstrong, pastor at Broadway Methodist in Indianapolis, cornered Trigg and argued that of all the offers he had received, the most challenging and best fit for his talents was to work in Indianapolis at Brightwood Methodist, where he would be involved in ministry in an interracial neighborhood in the inner city. Trigg ultimately accepted this offer. Bishop Raines wrote Bishop Franklin for Trigg's transfer, which became official on May 29.[13]

Jack Troutman signed Born of Conviction during his fourth year at Big Point, his first assignment out of seminary. He had found the rural church in the southeast corner of the state less and less of a challenge, and by mid-1962 he got permission from Tom Prewitt to start a new congregation in nearby East Moss Point. The fledgling church met in a union hall, but after Born of Conviction made the news, a union official requested that the new church not meet there anymore. The loss of the first meeting place, coupled with other difficulties, meant that the new church project failed.[14]

Concerned at the rejection some of the Twenty-Eight had experienced and the public requests from some churches that none of the Twenty-Eight be assigned to them, Troutman had also heard rumors that the conference power bloc had vowed signers would have difficulty getting new appointments. He knew he could stay at Big Point; he also believed he was capable of a bigger challenge and feared he would be passed over for better appointments in Mississippi. He and his wife visited with Jim and Patricia McCormick in West Jackson in the spring of 1963; the McCormicks spoke of their plans to move to Arizona to start a new church in Scottsdale. Although the Troutmans had deep roots in Mississippi, their views on race made them wonder about the future there, and he had previously considered moving to the Southern California-Arizona Conference. He arranged an interview with Bishop Kennedy, and when he arrived at the bishop's Los Angeles office, he remembers that the person who ushered him in said, "Bishop Kennedy, here's another one of those Mississippians."[15]

Kennedy steered him to the pastor of First Methodist in Tucson, who needed an associate. Troutman returned home and waited for final word, communicating plans for the transfer to Mississippi Conference officials, but in May the appointment fell through. So he stayed another year at Big Point. In the spring of 1964, a district superintendent invited him to start a new church in Mesa, Arizona, and with his May 29 transfer, Troutman became the eighth member of the Twenty-Eight to move to that conference, joining a larger group of pastors from his home state facetiously called the Mississippi Mafia. Like Troutman, several of them started new congregations. In 1965, he said, "My new location has certainly [provided] much more freedom to voice convictions weekly. I felt that I stayed as long as my witness was effective, taking into consideration the fact that we had no backing by conference leaders (a few helped)." The area's population growth in those years, along with a clergy shortage, meant most of the pastors who came from Mississippi were quite successful in the Southern California-Arizona Conference.[16]

Marvin Moody (see Figure 7.2) was born the second of three children in 1935 in Kosciusko, Mississippi, where his father worked as a sharecropper. In 1939 the family moved to Marion County, where Moody and his brother and sister grew up. They regularly attended the Methodist church in Columbia, the county seat; the Moodys also went every summer to the Frost Bridge Holiness Camp Meeting in Wayne County near the Alabama line. The family had played a role in the meeting's founding in 1896, and as a teen, Marvin Moody felt a call to the ordained ministry there. At Mississippi Southern College in the 1950s, he was involved in the Wesley Foundation and saw its director, Sam Barefield, as an important mentor. Known for his intellect, sense of humor, and love of practical jokes, Moody excelled as a student leader and was selected for membership in Omicron Delta Kappa as a junior. He spent a summer in Brazil through an International Farm Youth exchange program. After graduation in 1957, he studied at SMU's Perkins School of Theology. He met his wife, Pat, in Dallas. Upon finishing seminary in 1961, Moody was appointed to Oak Grove Methodist, near Hattiesburg.[17]

In October 1962, just after the riot at Ole Miss, the Oak Grove Church Men's Club hosted Forrest County Circuit Clerk Theron Lynd as their guest speaker. At the dinner, Lynd, notorious for his refusal to allow blacks to register to vote and his lack of cooperation with the US Justice Department's attempts to investigate his office, referred to maverick newspaper editor P. D. East of Petal as "a known Communist." Marvin Moody told East of this accusation, and East demanded in writing to Lynd that he either "apologize to the [church's Men's Club] or be prepared to prove his charges." Lynd reacted by calling some of the men in the church. In January 1963, these same men stirred up the most trouble in response to Moody's participation in Born of Conviction, but when they learned of his plans to return to school, this alleviated some of the pressure on Moody. He departed in June, appointed to pursue further graduate work at SMU. Moody felt a particular calling to campus ministry, and when no such appointments were available to him in Mississippi the next year, he took a job as campus minister at Midwestern University in Wichita Falls, Texas, transferring to the North Texas Conference in May 1964.[18]

"Where Are You Transferring?"

After sixteen years, Bishop Franklin's tenure as leader of the white conferences in Mississippi ended with his 1964 retirement. Episcopal elections held across the church at jurisdictional conferences that July resulted in the election of Millsaps President Ellis Finger, along with Edward J. Pendergrass Jr., of the Florida Conference, who was assigned as the new bishop in Mississippi, supervising both white conferences. When Pendergrass arrived in August 1964, he already knew of the exodus of ministers from the white Mississippi Conference.[19]

Jim Waits had no significant difficulties at Epworth Church in Biloxi as the result of Born of Conviction, and he remained there until June 1965. He briefly considered transferring to Southern California-Arizona and accompanied Maxie and Jerry Dunnam to visit various Mississippi exile clergy friends in Phoenix and Los Angeles in August 1963. In early 1964, he had a visit from Ed and Martina McRae, settled by then in Phoenix, but he had decided to stay in Mississippi. In response to Galloway Church's turning away Bishop Charles Golden (black) and Bishop James K. Mathews (white) from worship on Easter Sunday, March 29, 1964, and the repeated refusals by many white churches in Jackson to admit integrated groups to their services, Waits declared in his April 5 sermon, "Let the Church *be* the Church! The sanctuary of the Church is not a fortress, a symbol of racial bitterness. It is a house of prayer for all the nations. The doors of the Church must exclude no one—they are obliged by the very nature of the Church to welcome every child of God." Waits spoke freely in sermons, but most conference ministers could not do so in April 1964; many did not agree with Waits's views.[20]

Known for his subtle humor and satirical wit, Jim Waits enjoyed lampooning the "wacky logic of white supremacy" in the Closed Society. In January 1964, Lorne Greene, Michael Landon, and Dan Blocker of the television show "Bonanza" cancelled a scheduled appearance in Jackson when they learned seating at the event would be segregated. Jackson Mayor Allen Thompson then called for a boycott of "Bonanza." Waits chose the persona of "J. S. Duckey," a tongue-in-cheek reference to the segregationist claim that everything in Mississippi was "just ducky," to comment in a letter to the *Clarion-Ledger* in late February:

> Another drab week has passed without Bonanza. Tell me again, now, just what is the difference between white and Negro boycotts?

Of course the dilemma would never have arisen if we pure white Christians had been attending our segregated worship services on Sunday evenings.

Faithfully yours,

J. S. Duckey

930 Davis Street, Biloxi, Mississippi

P.S. Rumor has it that some Jackson citizens have lowered their shades and watched Bonanza anyway. Shouldn't these turncoats be investigated?[21]

In the next few months, Duckey commented again on the Bonanza boycott, expressed mock concern at folk singer Joan Baez's concert at Tougaloo College to an integrated audience, and ridiculed the Citizens' Council's opening of a segregated private school in Jackson, always closing with "Faithfully yours." In a satirical criticism of Billy Graham's appearance to an integrated audience of thirty-five thousand in Birmingham on Easter Sunday 1964, Duckey said he would no longer read Graham's newspaper column and suggested that support for all Baptist churches in Mississippi should be withdrawn "until he quits that mixing." He added a jab at the response of Jackson Methodist churches to the ongoing church visits campaign led by Tougaloo's Ed King, in which integrated groups sought, beginning in June 1963, to attend worship at white churches:

I may even join the Methodist Church. No bishop is going to tell them what to do! That's what I like—a Church that sticks to its guns—turn people away and have them arrested if possible. After all, we can't let a little thing like the Bible and the example of Jesus stand in the way of our Southern way of life. Thank goodness at least the Methodists have steadfastly guarded our pure white Christian faith.

Waits later referred to the letters as "the most original writing I've ever done."[22]

In June 1965 Waits (Figure 8.1) married Fentress Boone of Jackson, and they moved to Illinois, where he entered a master's program in political science at the University of Chicago and took a job as associate pastor in a suburban Chicago Methodist church. His conference membership remained in Mississippi; he was appointed to attend school. He went thinking he wanted to teach political science but determined it was

FIGURE 8.1 Jim Waits in Chicago with young friend, c. 1966. Courtesy of James L. Waits.

not his calling. He explored possible jobs in the broader church (e.g., the NCC or the Methodist Board of Social Concerns) but told a Mississippi friend in February 1967, "We have not given up the idea of a Mississippi pastorate, but apparently there will be no specific information about that until I commit myself to return." In early May, he wrote the same friend, "Just a note to let you know that the die is cast—will be rejoining you in Mississippi in June!" He conferred with Bishop Pendergrass a number of times; with his experience and training, he wanted to serve in an urban area. Upon learning he would be appointed to a rural church, he called Pendergrass to negotiate a different assignment. When the bishop refused and Waits stood fast in his rejection of that placement, he recalls that Pendergrass asked him, "Where are you transferring your membership?" Waits called Ellis Finger, president of Millsaps during his student days and now bishop of the Nashville area, to explore possibilities there. Roy Clark, formerly pastor at Capitol Street Church in Jackson and officiant at the Waits's wedding, was moving to Nashville as senior pastor of West End Church, near Vanderbilt University. Arrangements were soon finalized for Waits to transfer to the Tennessee Conference and begin work as Clark's associate in June 1967.[23]

Waits and seventeen other Born of Conviction signers transferred out of the Mississippi Conference in the 1960s, and they were joined by many who did not sign the statement. A total of thirteen left for Southern California-Arizona, and fourteen went to one of the three Indiana conferences. Hubert Barlow and Roy Eaton, the two who had agreed to sign Born of Conviction and then backed out a week before publication, ended up in the North Indiana Conference. In 1964, Barlow, by then pastor at Quitman, tried hard to keep his church from voting formally to close their doors to blacks and put a policeman on the door. The church was split on the issue, but when the proposal passed, Barlow told District Superintendent Jim Slay that he could not continue to lead a congregation that took such a stand. In his transfer request to Bishop Franklin, he said "I owe my life to Mississippi Methodism and trust you will understand that I feel a sense of responsibility to it. But after a long time of struggling to raise a remnant to oppose the radicals I see little fruit or hope from my labors."[24]

In 1968, Roy Eaton followed. Although race relations played a role in his decision, he later sounded the familiar refrain that problems with conference leadership, the departure of so many talented clergy, and the increasing control by the conference political machine all led him to leave. Barlow invited him to be his associate at a Fort Wayne church, and Eaton agreed. Others from Mississippi who went to the Indiana Conference (renamed South Indiana in 1969) included Robert Hunt, son of District Superintendent Brunner Hunt, and his brother-in-law, Paul Kern, along with Charles Ray Gipson, who used surveys and sermons from members of the Twenty-Eight as sources for a 1968 master's thesis about preaching on controversial issues.[25]

Conference Gadfly

Below Powell S. Hall Jr.'s senior picture in the 1947 Central High School yearbook, someone wrote "Est rara avis" ("is a rare bird"). Born in Jackson in 1929, he began life by showing one of his signature characteristics—persistence. Despite the prediction of doctors that he would not survive a difficult birth and his poor health in early childhood, he eventually thrived. Growing up in West Jackson, he developed a love of astronomy and gained a reputation as a formidable opponent in arguments. A childhood friend remembered in 2008, "Arguments with [Powell] were not like arguments with other boys. He could challenge my arguments better than anybody. ... I didn't win many arguments about astronomy. Mostly, I learned from him." One of Hall's children describes him as having "the annoying habit of always being right."[26]

Hall went to college at Emory University in Atlanta and remained for seminary. In 1953 he married Julia Hewitt in Durham Chapel on the Emory campus with Candler's Dean William R. Cannon officiating. The two had known each other since seventh grade. Her father, Purser Hewitt, had risen since the 1920s from sports reporter to managing editor and then executive editor at Jackson's *Clarion-Ledger*. His father, W. A. Hewitt, retired in the mid-1940s after twenty-eight years as pastor of Jackson's First Baptist Church; Julia grew up hearing her grandfather preach every Sunday and eating Sunday dinner at his home. She asked her grandfather's permission to marry Powell Hall, and the elder Hewitt approved, telling her that some Methodist preachers needed good Baptist girls for wives. A doctor told Hall at a premarital medical checkup that he would not be able to have children, but he continued proving doctors wrong: Mrs. Hall bore their first child in 1954, and by the end of 1961, they had five.[27]

During his thirteen years as a pastor in Mississippi, Powell Hall was the conference gadfly. A fellow minister called him "a genius—probably one of the smartest guys we ever had." Known as an incisive preacher, scholar, and stickler for the Methodist *Discipline*, Hall often rose at conference sessions to raise a point of order or offer an alternative view on a proposed action. This behavior earned him the reputation as a maverick and thorn in the side of conference leadership. He spoke adamantly in favor of continuing Jackson civil rights movement leader Ed King's conference membership in 1963, even though the Leggett forces had aligned against King. Bishop Pendergrass, who presided over the conference from 1964 to 1972, once told a group of ministers that though they thought he disliked Hall, he actually respected Hall greatly.[28]

Hall's willingness to speak and act according to his conscience, along with what some perceived as an air of intellectual superiority, often resulted in him becoming, in his own words, *persona non grata* at his churches. In addition to reactions to his early 1960s sermon at Lake protesting the treatment of Horace Germany, the white minister who had started a school for black pastors, and the response he received at Scooba to his participation in Born of Conviction, difficulties continued at subsequent appointments. At Sandersville, where Ned Kellar patched things up after the initial negative reaction to Born of Conviction, things did not go well for Hall. Soon after he arrived in June 1963, he went to visit a church member who lived with her sister. The Presbyterian sister had not yet met Hall; she answered the door and slammed it in his face because she thought he looked like a relative of President Kennedy. Just prior to the annual conference session in May 1964, Bishop Franklin offered Hall a better appointment if he would transfer to the Memphis Conference, but Hall believed his calling was to stay in Mississippi.[29]

In Hall's view, this refusal resulted in his being "sent to Coventry" about a month after the 1964 Annual Conference, when he was moved to Kingston, a church in Adams County ten miles southeast of Natchez. Arriving early in July, he soon offended the most powerful man in the congregation because of his associations with some people in the community, his identification with organizations sympathetic to civil rights, including the Mississippi Council on Human Relations (MCHR), or things he said in sermons. The church ceased paying his salary, and the instigator of this punishment came each Sunday and read the newspaper or slept during Hall's sermons but also watched the offering plate to make sure no one deposited any money. To replace the lost income, Julia Hall worked at the County Welfare Department. In the summer of 1964, Powell Hall applied for the position as executive director of the MCHR, which would have meant leaving the parish ministry and moving to Jackson. Both he and Jim Waits applied; Waits was the first choice but was not willing to accept without the bishop's approval. Pendergrass refused to do this when he first arrived, and thus neither Waits nor Hall took the job, because both wanted to keep their status as Methodist clergy.[30]

Southwest Mississippi was a hotbed of Ku Klux Klan activity; two black churches were burned near Kingston during Freedom Summer the month the Halls arrived. Law enforcement officers in Natchez often harassed Hall. On one occasion he showed up at fellow Born of Conviction signer Elton Brown's parsonage on the northeast edge of Natchez in an attempt to escape being followed by police. Hall's persecutors knew his red Rambler station wagon well, so Brown assisted Hall by allowing him to leave the car there and driving him back to Kingston. One evening a

FIGURE 8.2 Powell Hall, 1960s. Courtesy of Cathy Hall Shelton.

group of night riders terrorized the Hall family by driving back and forth in front of the isolated parsonage and firing guns.[31]

Hall (Figure 8.2) and his family survived their eleven months at Kingston and moved in June 1965 to Sandy Hook, a three-church Marion County charge near the Louisiana line. Although a cross was burned on the lawn of the charge's Kokomo Church, Hall had a much more pleasant experience there. In 1967, he moved to Silver Creek in Lawrence County; another cross was burned there during his tenure. Hall continued as a board member of MCHR. In 1968 he moved to Vaughan, a small community on the eastern edge of Yazoo County about forty miles north of Jackson. By this time, Mrs. Hall worked as a teacher and got a job in the Yazoo County Schools. In the fall of 1969 when the US Supreme Court issued the *Alexander v. Holmes* decision requiring real school desegregation in Mississippi, whites in Vaughan resolved at first to stay in the public schools. That changed in December, the month before integration, and a segregation academy sprung up in a few weeks, with virtually all of Hall's church members opting to send their children there. The five

Hall children remained in the public schools, and Julia Hall taught at a formerly all-black school. This unpopular stand resulted in yet another move in June 1970.[32]

The new appointment was forty miles west across Yazoo County to Satartia, a three-church charge. The Halls' three oldest children were able to attend Yazoo City High School, where integration had worked much better. But years of struggle and moving from one rural appointment to another had taken their toll, and Powell Hall worried about the effects on his family. In 1964 he had met Charles Marker, a New Jersey Methodist minister in Mississippi with a group of college students to assist rebuilding a black church that had been burned by the Klan. In the spring of 1971, Marker, now a district superintendent in the Southern New Jersey Conference, invited Hall to take an appointment in his district, and in June 1971, the Halls moved to Point Pleasant, on the Jersey Shore.[33]

Although this added Hall's name to the list of Born of Conviction signers who left Mississippi, his departure was not the result of that stand, because he remained in the conference for eight years after its publication. An analysis of Hall's pastoral appointments in Mississippi shows that conference leaders kept him in small, rural, low-paid appointments. Throughout the 1960s, the salary at all of Hall's appointments ranged around $4,000; it appears that at least one of his moves involved a salary cut, not to mention the failure of the Kingston Church to pay his salary for most of the 1964–5 conference year. His appointment to Satartia in 1970 came with a raise of more than $1,000, putting him at $4,900; Born of Conviction signer N. A. Dickson was the district superintendent. His transfer to Harvey Memorial Church in Point Pleasant, a congregation of almost six hundred members, came with a raise to $8,100, a salary he might reasonably have expected by that point in his career.[34]

Powell Hall's characteristic dogged persistence led him to stay in the Mississippi Conference longer than almost any other pastor would have under similar circumstances. His frequent moves—seven different appointments in nine years, in five of the six districts in the conference—indicate a problem. Was he punished for stands he took, including Born of Conviction? Did conference leaders continue to appoint him to small churches in hopes he would leave Mississippi? Hall admitted, "I may have been in something of a depression in some of those little country churches. I may not have been very effective as a pastor because of that." Both Dickson and Bishop Pendergrass supported his transfer.[35]

Leaving and Coming Home

In April 1963, Bufkin Oliver reported to Ole Miss professor James Silver that most of his Ellisville congregation had "responded in a splendid way" to his participation in Born of Conviction, but he expressed gloom at the climate in Mississippi and added, "In fact, at the supper table, my wife and I talked about transferring to another state. . . . My own thinking is about fifty-fifty for staying or leaving. I don't want to run from a fight for what I know is right, but I have a wife and four children who are also involved. Two of my children are Korean-American." The Olivers worried about possible prejudice against their two adopted children, still preschoolers, as they grew up in Mississippi. Oliver remained ambivalent; he was reappointed to Ellisville in May 1963, and he could have stayed. His older son, fifteen at the time, later said, "They loved him there." By late June, however, he had arranged a transfer to the Southern California-Arizona Conference. He expressed gratitude to Bishop Franklin for two decades of service in his home state and offered prayers and best wishes for the Mississippi Conference.[36]

At forty-five, Bufkin Oliver (Figure 8.3) invested himself fully in his assignment to start a new church in Tempe, Arizona, but he found it difficult and psychologically draining. Unlike his colleagues from the Twenty-Eight who loved the Southern California-Arizona Conference and life in the West, Arizona was a shock to him. After two years in Tempe, he moved to Huntingdon Park, California, where he served as an associate pastor, but that appointment did not suit him well either. In his older son's view, Oliver was never happy out of Mississippi, and he admitted he should have stayed. Within a year of his departure, he applied for a chaplain's position at the Mississippi state mental hospital at Whitfield.[37]

That attempt failed, but on January 1, 1967, Oliver transferred to the North Mississippi Conference, returning to his home state and service as pastor-in-charge of a church, Central Methodist in Columbus. He and his wife had left Mississippi because they saw little hope for change in race relations there. During his six years in Columbus, however, things changed enough that when a couple of black students from Mississippi

FIGURE 8.3 Bufkin Oliver, 1960s. Courtesy of Oliver family.

State College for Women started coming to Central, Oliver immediately quashed the mild resistance from some in the church.[38]

The seventh of Leroy and Callie Husband Roberts's eight children, Wallace Roberts was born in Meridian in 1932. His mother, the youth Sunday School teacher at Bonita Methodist Church just east of Meridian, taught her own children as well as Paul Ramsey, future renowned Christian ethicist and son of the pastor who served the church from 1930 to 1932. Thirteen of her students became Methodist ministers. Wallace Roberts joined the air force in 1950. In 1954, his older brother Waddell, a Methodist minister and Army chaplain, died in a helicopter crash in Korea. After completing his military service, Roberts married Barbara Jean Thompson that same year and worked at a Meridian appliance store. He soon discerned a call to the Methodist ministry, and in 1957 he served the Carlisle-Rocky Springs charge southwest of Jackson and enrolled at Millsaps College. When he graduated in 1960, his family, now including a daughter, moved to the Coker's Chapel Church at Vimville near Meridian and not far from the Bonita Church. Roberts also worked part-time as music director at the local high school.[39]

Roberts's name does not appear on the list of potential signers drawn up by Born of Conviction's creators in the fall of 1962; he heard about the statement in the Meridian District and agreed to sign. Shortly after it appeared, the tires on his car were slashed. Later that month, he and his brother Ken drove to Jackson and were harassed by a Mississippi Highway Patrol car on the way. A Klansman from the Bonita community wrote Callie Roberts a letter blaming her for her son's witness in signing the statement. Wallace Roberts got wind of it and came by her house for several days to intercept the mail; she never saw the accusatory letter.[40]

Although Coker's Chapel church members were willing for Roberts to stay on as their pastor, he had planned for some time to attend seminary at Emory, and in June 1963 the family moved to Georgia, where he took a student appointment. Painfully aware of the rejection of many of the Twenty-Eight by the conference political power bloc and convinced he would not be welcome in the Mississippi Conference, in 1966 Roberts transferred to the North Mississippi Conference. He was appointed to Grace Church in Greenville, where he stayed seven years.[41]

Roberts and the other six Meridian District pastors who signed Born of Conviction all found their district superintendent, Jim Slay, at best nonsupportive and at worst publicly hostile, but they had an advocate in Meridian: Robert Matheny, the pastor of the district's largest church, Central Methodist. Bob Matheny was not invited to sign the statement. Unlike his wife's father, Conference Lay Leader J. P. Stafford, he did not speak out publicly for Born of Conviction. He did support the signers privately, and several confided in him. Matheny unsuccessfully urged his friend Slay to stand by them. He also met with the bishop in a futile attempt to convince Franklin to provide more courageous leadership. Matheny's most public witness in support of the Twenty-Eight occurred in a downtown Meridian barber shop that January. As his son Jim, present at the shop, later recalled, the barber cutting the elder Matheny's hair opined to some other customers, "They oughta take all those nigger-lovin' Methodist preachers out and lynch them." His haircut unfinished, Matheny got up from the chair, took his son by the hand, and told the barber as he departed that no one who wanted to lynch Methodist preachers was going to use a razor on his neck.[42]

Later that year, with the Jackson church visits campaign constantly in the news, leaders at Matheny's downtown Meridian church posted ushers at the doors to turn away any black visitors or integrated groups. He lobbied lay leaders privately to open the doors of the church, and several were sympathetic. Their fears won out, however, and the church remained closed. Eight-year-old Jim Matheny observed some ushers standing on the front steps facing outward just before the service began one Sunday and asked them if they were coming in to church. One told him their job was to remain outside. The closed-door policy began to wear on the elder Matheny; in February 1964 he wrote Bishop Raines of Indiana regarding the possibility of a move there. By May he agreed to a transfer to the Northwest Indiana Conference. As his widow and son later remembered it, in announcing his departure during worship at Central, Matheny said his moment of clarity had come one Sunday as he gave the invitation to communion, "Whosoever will, may come." He "saw the silhouettes of the [ushers] patrolling back and forth on the other side of the stained glass windows" and knew he could not in good conscience give such an invitation in a church that would not open its doors. A few weeks after the Mathenys moved, Central Church's Official Board voted to change their policy and welcome visitors regardless of race.[43]

In 1967 Bishop Pendergrass invited Bob Matheny to return to Mississippi. Bishop Raines balked at approving the transfer until he learned Matheny would be appointed to Capitol Street Church in Jackson. Raines's son Richard Jr., a Methodist minister from Detroit, had knelt in silent witness at the altar rail during worship at Capitol Street on November 10, 1963, and prayed the church would open its doors; it finally did so on March 13, 1966. Matheny remained in Mississippi for the rest of his career and twice served as a district superintendent.[44]

A Divided Church

In the spring of 1963, Born of Conviction signer Joe Way (Figure 8.4) knew he would have to leave Soule's Chapel in early June. Way remembers that at a Meridian District preacher's meeting in January, Superintendent Jim Slay publicly condemned Born of Conviction and compared the signers to "an old goat walking on the railroad track. When the train approached, the goat felt he had as much right to the track as the train, so he lowered his head and charged. Now you have to admire the old goat's courage, but you sure have to question his mental ability." Slay vowed to do nothing to help signers receive a pastoral appointment for the coming year.[45]

FIGURE 8.4 Joe Way, 1960s. Courtesy of Joseph C. Way.

Way had graduated from seminary in 1960, and after a year as pastor of Pleasant Hill in the Meridian District, he moved to Soule's Chapel, near Lauderdale and the Meridian Naval Air Station. When invited to sign Born of Conviction in late 1962, he knew he had to do it. The negative response at Soule's Chapel coupled with Jim Slay's lack of support led Way to explore alternatives, including transfer to another conference, further graduate study, or the military chaplaincy. Brookhaven District Superintendent Norman Boone promised Way an appointment in his district, and Roy Clark (see Figure 2.2) invited him to be his associate at Capitol Street. Way's move to Jackson in June 1963 began the most demanding and rewarding year of his career.[46]

Roy Clark's approach to pastoral leadership on the race issue involved working behind the scenes for change, and he believed "you have to meet people where they are." As he understood it, "The problem was how to be faithful to your convictions and yet pastoral enough to stay in relationship to people in order to talk to them. People knew where I stood on race relations, but I had a relationship with them." In 1963, Capitol Street Church had more than two thousand members with a wide range of views on race, including both Garner Lester, Citizens' Council member and president of the segregationist MAMML, and my father, Lee H. Reiff (see Figure 2.2), Millsaps religion professor, liberal Mississippi newcomer, and supporter of the civil rights movement. Many members were caught in the middle, and Clark and Way spent much pastoral energy hearing their private struggles. Way said,

> I provided an outlet for honest conversation to those who were really struggling over the issue. Some parishioners told me they would deny under oath that they ever spoke to me about integration. They did so in order to protect their job and family, but they were desperate to talk to someone who could help them honestly deal with it.[47]

Clark and Way made a good pastoral team, but the partnership was short-lived. Clark had begun his eleventh year at Capitol Street, and the pressured environment of early 1960s Mississippi had taken a toll on him and his family. He told Bishop Franklin that if an opportunity arose for him to move to another conference, he would be interested. The chance came after June 9, when W. B. Selah and Jerry Furr resigned from Galloway, the other white downtown Jackson Methodist church. Franklin and Galloway's Pastoral Relations Committee had difficulty finding a new senior pastor but finally convinced Born of Conviction signer Jerry Trigg's father-in-law W. J. Cunningham, originally from the North Mississippi Conference but then at St. John's Church in Memphis, to come. The move necessitated a new pastor at St. John's, and Roy Clark moved there. The transfers were effective September 2, 1963.[48]

When the change was announced at Capitol Street on August 11, there was no word on Clark's replacement. Although appointment decisions belonged to the bishop and cabinet, the church's Pastoral Relations Committee believed their status was important enough to have a say in choosing their new pastor, and they shared the names of two ministers they thought were excellent possibilities with their former pastor and current District Superintendent Willard Leggett. He told them he knew more about the church than the committee but promised to cooperate with them. When the bishop named Seth Granberry, pastor of Main Street Church in Hattiesburg and a key lieutenant in Leggett's conference political organization, as the new pastor, congregational reaction was divided. On August 26, the Official Board voted 39 to 35 to ask the bishop to rescind the appointment. Board Chair R. E. Jordan told the press the vote "was not a protest of Rev. Granberry but a protest of the method used in making the transfers." Leggett claimed Granberry "was appointed at the request of the great majority of the congregation," and the appointment prevailed.[49]

The conflict continued at the September 16 Official Board meeting with the introduction of a resolution criticizing Leggett's conduct and asking Bishop Franklin to reprimand Leggett and instruct him to deal in good faith with Capitol Street, "to refrain from interference in its internal affairs, and to desist from actions and consultations calculated to encourage factions within our membership." It also asked the bishop to "do all things necessary . . . to insure that ministers and laymen of the Methodist Church in the Mississippi Conference may conscientiously oppose the policies and actions of [Leggett] without fear of intimidation, reprisal, or vindictive criticism of their integrity and actions." After lengthy discussion, a motion passed to adjourn without voting on the resolution, and the board never acted on it.[50]

When Granberry arrived in early September, he invited Joe Way to resign, but Way refused. "From that day forward," Way said, "there were two distinct groups operating under the name of one church." Official Board meetings were "wrestling matches" between the moderate/liberal and conservative factions. As one of the Twenty-Eight, Way symbolized race relations change, a new Methodism, and opposition to Willard Leggett. Granberry represented Leggett's authority as conference leader, the old Southern Methodism, and segregation, even though he was more of a moderate on the race issue. At a dinner that fall, he asked church leaders to tell him which way they wanted to go regarding the maintenance of segregation. His indecision and the ambivalence of moderates among church leaders aided the conservative faction and segregationist forces outside the church and resulted in a continuing closed door policy and occasional arrests of integrated groups testing it, even though Granberry claimed after the first arrests on October 6, 1963, that the church had not requested them. At the behest of Granberry and others, church doors were often locked during worship. For Way, a low point came on Easter Sunday, March 29, 1964, when Jackson police arrested an interracial group seeking to attend services at the church. Seven seminary professors made up part of the group, including Everett Tilson, author of *Segregation and the Bible* and Way's favorite teacher at Vanderbilt.[51]

During that year, Way received threats on his life, silent late-night phone calls, and harassment by some parishioners. He and his wife joined a few other Capitol Street couples in a semiclandestine group (an "underground church") that met in homes for mutual support and study of such works as Dietrich Bonhoeffer's *The Cost of Discipleship*. Way sought to engage the more segregationist members in dialogue, gently pushing them to question their attitudes. Knowing he would need to leave Capitol Street in June 1964, he again explored options, including the well-worn path to the Southern California-Arizona Conference. The air force approved his application for the chaplaincy and stationed Way and his family in Tucson, Arizona, that summer. Granberry also left then to become the Seashore District Superintendent.[52]

What Became of Them?

Seminary administration proved to be Buford Dickinson's calling. Between 1964 and 1981 he held positions of increasing responsibility at Claremont School of Theology; he also earned a PhD in homiletics from the school. In 1978 he applied for the presidency of Millsaps College but was told by a Mississippi Conference friend that some still viewed his participation in Born of Conviction as a strike against him. In 1981 he became president of the Methodist Theological School in Ohio, the institutional home of several of the seminary professors arrested at Capitol Street on that Easter Sunday in 1964. He remained there until 1985, when he entered the hospital for what doctors thought was a kidney stone. Instead they discovered cancer, and in a few weeks, he died at fifty-one.[53]

Maxie Dunnam's departure from Mississippi opened a new world for him; he sees it as crucial to his subsequent development: "I don't believe I could have made the contribution to the whole church that I have made, had I stayed." In Southern California, Dunnam experienced a new way of doing church beyond traditional Mississippi Methodism. After four years in San Clemente, he moved to a large suburban church in Anaheim. In 1970, he received a call from C. R. Ridgway, a leading layman at Galloway Memorial, about coming back to Mississippi as senior pastor at the Jackson church. Galloway had endured a great deal of conflict in the 1960s, including the dramatic resignations of Dr. Selah and Jerry Furr in 1963, the departure of several hundred members to the new Riverside Independent Methodist Church in 1965, and a failed proposal to use space at Galloway for a Head Start program in 1968. The invitation represented an important step toward unity to leaders of the conservative and liberal factions at the church—all had agreed Dunnam was the best choice for their new pastoral leader. Assured it was a done deal, Dunnam committed to return to Mississippi, but Bishop Pendergrass did not approve the plan. Some Galloway leaders believed Willard Leggett convinced the bishop not to bring one of the Twenty-Eight back to Mississippi, but Pendergrass may simply have wanted to end the tradition of Galloway's choosing pastors from outside the conference.[54]

In 1973, Dunnam took a position at the United Methodist Church's Board of Discipleship in Nashville, directing the Upper Room Fellowship, a new programmatic arm of the denomination's daily devotional publication, *The Upper Room*. In 1976 he was named its World Editor, and directed all the organization's publications and ministries, which eventually included the Academy of Spiritual Formation, the journal *Weavings*, and the Emmaus Walk. He has authored numerous books, preaching commentaries, and spiritual formation workbooks.[55]

In 1981 he transferred his conference membership to Tennessee, and the next year he became senior pastor at Christ United Methodist Church (UMC) in Memphis, which necessitated a transfer to the Memphis Conference. He remained twelve years, until he assumed the presidency of Asbury Theological Seminary in 1994 and transferred membership to the Kentucky Conference. In 2004 he retired, and he and his wife moved back to Memphis. In 2010 when Memphis Christ UMC's senior pastor left unexpectedly, Dunnam served for ten months as interim pastor. He then became executive director of Christ Church Global and helped create an extension site for Asbury Seminary at the Memphis church in 2013.[56]

Jerry Trigg spent five years in Indianapolis churches; he organized a community council in Brightwood that developed programs for all regardless of race. In 1969 he moved to a church in Clarksville, Indiana, and in 1974 he became pastor of Gobin Memorial in Greencastle on the edge of the DePauw University campus. In 1980, Bishop Melvin Wheatley of the Rocky Mountain Annual Conference contacted Maxie Dunnam, whom he had known in California, about coming to the largest congregation in United Methodism's Western Jurisdiction, First UMC in Colorado Springs. Dunnam declined but recommended Trigg, who moved to the church in December of that year. He remained until his retirement in 2002. Recognized as a leader in the city, he received numerous awards, including the NAACP's Outstanding Religious Leader and recognition for outstanding community service from the Urban League. Trigg died in May 2015.[57]

By late 1964, the congregation Jack Troutman started in Mesa, Arizona, had grown to three worship services. The church's social justice involvement included members working at a summer day school for Mexican, African American, and Native American children. When Troutman left Grace Church after nine years, it had one thousand members. He followed Maxie Dunnam at West Anaheim in 1973, and after two years there he spent the rest of his career in Arizona, with pastorates at large churches in Phoenix, Sun City, and Mesa First Church. He retired in 1991 and remained in Mesa. Though he loved his Mississippi parishioners, the Desert Southwest proved to be his land of opportunity: "Coming out here was just the best thing I ever did."[58]

Marvin Moody remained as campus minister at Midwestern University for three years. He then did some further graduate study, and his wife began work on a PhD in English at the University of Texas. He transferred his conference membership to Southwest Texas and served as pastor at Decker for more than three years beginning in 1968. In 1972, Moody withdrew from the United Methodist ministry, taking voluntary location, and the Moodys moved to Syracuse, New York, where Pat Moody took a university teaching job and he began selling real estate. He managed a realty company from 1976 to 1980 and then owned his own agency. He died at age forty-six at his summer home in Cazenovia, New York, on March 17, 1982.[59]

While serving as Roy Clark's associate at West End Church in Nashville, Jim Waits became friends with Vanderbilt Divinity School professor James T. Laney. When Emory's Candler School of Theology chose Laney as dean in 1969, Waits followed him there, serving as assistant dean and then associate dean. In 1976, he transferred his conference membership back to Mississippi. After Laney became president of Emory University, Waits was named dean at Candler in 1978 and remained in that position until 1991. He then moved to Pittsburgh to serve as executive director of the Association of Theological Schools in the United States and Canada, which accredits and supports the work of graduate schools in theology. In 1998 he returned to Atlanta as president of the Fund for Theological Education, whose main mission is to offer "programs for diverse young adults exploring a call to ministry." He retired in 2003. His mentor, former Capitol Street Church pastor Roy Clark, was elected a bishop in 1980 and presided over the South Carolina Conference, including signer James Rush, until retirement in 1988.[60]

Powell Hall remained at Harvey Memorial UMC on the Jersey Shore for five years, and then served two other appointments in Southern New Jersey before transferring to the West Virginia Conference in 1980. His appointments there included a five-year stint at McDonald Memorial in Man. He retired in 1994 and moved with his wife to Hermitage, Tennessee; he died in 2008. He remained convinced that leaving Mississippi in 1971 was the best choice for his family, but Powell and Julia Hall were never the same after they left Mississippi—they had lost something they could not recover.[61]

When Bufkin and Elizabeth Oliver left Central Church in Columbus in 1973, their time in Arizona and California was a distant memory, and they were happily committed to life and ministry in the North Mississippi Conference. He later served appointments in Pontotoc, Hernando, and Corinth. In the late 1970s Oliver was diagnosed with prostate cancer, and eventually it affected his health enough that he retired at age sixty-five in 1982. Ever the preacher, he managed after retirement to serve a part-time church outside of Hernando. Anticipating his inability to be present at worship, he tape-recorded a sermon for his congregation to use the Sunday he entered the hospital for the final time. Three days later on January 16, 1985, twenty-two years after the publication of Born of Conviction, Oliver died.[62]

In 1973, Wallace Roberts (Figure 8.5) followed Bufkin Oliver as pastor of Central Church in Columbus. Known as a gifted evangelist, he and his

FIGURE 8.5 Wallace Roberts, 1986. Courtesy of Mark Roberts.

younger brother Ken, an accomplished vocalist, often led revivals together. In 1978 he applied to become the executive director and on-air host of the *United Methodist Hour*, a radio program based in Hattiesburg and sponsored by the Mississippi Conference. He still worried that Willard Leggett would stand in the way of the move, but the ministry's board hired him and Leggett eventually supported him. Under his leadership the *United Methodist Hour* expanded its reach, including the development of a thirty-minute weekly television program. Born of Conviction signer Keith Tonkel did a weekly Sunday School lesson for the *United Methodist Hour*. In 1988 Roberts was diagnosed with a rare form of cancer and died in November. A few months later the Mississippi and North Mississippi Conferences merged to form the present Mississippi Annual Conference. Roberts never regretted signing Born of Conviction and was proud of his stand, though he seldom talked about it. He believed the Christian Gospel necessarily included the struggle for human equality and justice. His brother remembers that he often said, "You accuse me of preaching just the Social Gospel; let me suggest something to you: take the Social Gospel and bridle [it] to the Holy Spirit and ride that horse to heaven."[63]

When Joe Way left the state in 1964 for the air force chaplaincy, he kept his membership in the Mississippi Conference and returned each year for the annual conference session as a continuing "means of witnessing." During his first few years away, he felt unwelcome at annual conference; some ministers asked what he was doing there and expressed displeasure upon learning he was still a conference member. In 1987, Way retired from the air force and returned to Mississippi, requesting a local church appointment. In his view, the appointment offered did not give him credit for his lengthy ministerial experience, so he served as a chaplain at the VA Hospital in Gulfport for the next five years. In 1992, he became the fourth member of the Twenty-Eight to serve Leggett Memorial Church in Biloxi, where he stayed a year. He served a year at Lumberton and then two years at Caswell Springs, where Jerry Trigg was pastor in 1962–3. While there, Way did not tell church members that he had also signed Born of Conviction. In 1996, he retired from the conference and eventually moved to Texas. He also never regretted his participation in the Twenty-Eight and believed he could not have lived with himself if he had not signed the statement. Though he felt forced to leave Mississippi in 1964, he came to see it as a good thing: "It set me and my family free. I, my wife and children had much greater opportunities and experiences than we could ever have had in Mississippi."[64]

The twenty members of the Twenty-Eight who left Mississippi did so for many reasons, ranging along a spectrum from true "force" and virtually no choice to relatively free choice. Their exodus cannot be explained as simply a case of "the closed society [battering] the outspoken young preachers upon the anvil of public opinion," though most experienced some battering. To varying degrees, roughly a dozen of the twenty who left Mississippi could have stayed, and if they all had, Born of Conviction would not be so commonly cited as an illustration of the "spoke out, forced out" narrative.[65]

The early 1963 declaration closed with a commitment to "STAND TOGETHER IN SUPPORT OF THESE PRINCIPLES." Sociologist Jeffrey Hadden's study of the church's struggle to respond to the racial crisis in the 1950s and 1960s offers insight into the process of clergy involvement in conflict situations. A group of clergy defines and gathers to discuss a serious social problem, and their interaction results in a shared sense of commitment to a cause. They see an opportunity to act as a group on their convictions, but once they take controversial action, they need positive reinforcement in order to maintain their commitment. Hadden surveyed many of the Twenty-Eight after the Born of Conviction controversy and interviewed a few of them, and he decided their main problem was not enough positive reinforcement. They were physically separated from each other, and the storm created by their statement proved greater than they expected. Hadden concluded, "In short, in the moment of crisis, each of the clergy stood alone, with little reinforcement, and with lingering doubts as to whether he had done the right thing."[66]

Hadden offers a more complex explanation than "spoke out, forced out" for the departure of so many of the signers; his assessment bears some similarity to that stereotypical explanation and confirms it to an extent. He does not mention the conference political situation or the private support received by the signers, and given the limits of his coverage of Born of Conviction, he also did not examine the various reasons for the departures of signers. Like most of the published references to Born of Conviction, his emphasis on the exodus of so many signers privileges the dominant narrative of departure but ignores the most important omission in that story: eight signers kept their commitment to "stand together" and remained in Mississippi.[67]

9

A Mind to Stay Here

The real heroes of that story are not the ones of us who
left ... but the ones who stayed. They're the heroes.
—JEAN DICKINSON MINUS, 2004

SOME BORN OF Conviction signers were truly forced out of Mississippi
by a combination of congregational and local community resistance, plus
lack of support from the bishop and their district superintendent. Others
left primarily because of the cultural environment of the Closed Society,
and several others, tired of the battles and disappointed in the failure of
conference leadership, departed mainly because of the political climate in
the Mississippi Conference. Connected with the last reason, several chose
a different leadership model, for example, Bishops Kennedy or Raines
instead of Bishop Franklin and Willard Leggett. In the midst of this exodus, on May 30, 1963, in response to a motion by Jerry Furr (unaware at that
point that he would soon be leaving) and seconded by Maxie Dunnam, the
conference approved creation of a committee "to study why 44 seminary-
trained men have transferred out of the Conference in the last five years."
Eual Samples, a minister associated with the Leggett group, moved "that
a committee be named, or the one previously ordered, to make a study of
why seminary men have remained in the Conference." Some ministers
felt strongly that the conference was well rid of those who were leaving
(including, eventually, both Furr and Dunnam) and were content to continue their ministry in Mississippi free of embarrassments like Born of
Conviction.[1]

The eight signers who remained in the conference did so out of a
strong sense of commitment to the witness they had made, but like their
departing comrades, their stories are varied and complex. How did each
one negotiate the embattled landscape of white Mississippi Conference
Methodism in order to stay?[2]

"As If John Wayne Were a Methodist Preacher"

Nathan Andrew Dickson was a fighter known for his blunt speech and quick temper. In the 1970s, Bishop Mack Stokes interrupted a report Dickson was making at a Mississippi Annual Conference session to ask how much longer the report would last. Dickson slammed his notebook shut and curtly replied, "It's over, Bishop." A friend who knew him in the 1960s said he "relished interaction short of combat" and compared him to Clark Gable. Rob Gill, son of Dickson's protégé Clint Gill and a Mississippi United Methodist minister himself, describes Dickson "as if John Wayne were a Methodist preacher."[3]

Dickson's father Nathaniel was a wealthy entrepreneur in the 1920s; he opened theaters featuring films and traveling Vaudeville shows in Arkansas, Oklahoma, and Texas oil-boom towns. This involved a transient life for his wife, son, and daughter. The 1929 stock market crash and sub-sequent Great Depression ruined the elder Dickson financially. He and his brother joined with a few others and became successful bank robbers. Known as the Dickson Gang, they pulled heists from Texas to the Florida Panhandle. Nathaniel Dickson insisted they not practice their craft in Mississippi, but someone in the gang broke that rule in January 1932 by borrowing Nathaniel's car and robbing the Bank of Columbia. Because the car belonged to him, Nathaniel Dickson was charged with the crime, and his then fourteen-year-old son attended the March trial at the court-house in Columbia. A bank teller present at the holdup testified Nathaniel Dickson was not the robber, and others said he was in Picayune at the time of the incident. However, N. A. Dickson heard talk during a recess that the powers-that-be in Columbia wanted his father found guilty as an example to prevent other robberies. Upon conviction, the elder Dickson posted bond and remained free pending appeal. In November 1932 he robbed a Pascagoula bank and died from gunshot wounds when a posse found him in swampland across the Alabama line.[4]

N. A. Dickson's mother had separated from his father; she and the children were living in Picayune. After Nathaniel's death, they settled in her home town of Bassfield. Her family did not treat her son well; he sometimes lived with black sharecroppers in the community, and he left home in the summers for work to help support his mother and sister. Thus it is no surprise that he "pulled for the underdog. . . . He'd always been an underdog all his life. So he fought for them. . . ." He discerned a call to ordained ministry while studying entomology at Mississippi

State in the late 1930s, transferred to Millsaps, and met his future wife, Mary Myers.[5]

Returning from seminary in 1948, he founded two churches and eventually led four to build or renovate buildings. He also soon aligned with the anti-Leggett forces in the conference, opposing what he saw as an abuse of power. In 1961, Brunner Hunt, superintendent of the Hattiesburg District and a Leggett opponent, convinced the bishop to appoint N. A. Dickson to Columbia First Church, a significant promotion. Hunt and Franklin had no idea they were asking him to return for the first time in almost thirty years to the town where he had observed his father's trial for bank robbery and to serve as pastor to some of the people who were determined to convict his father, regardless of the truth. But Dickson went, because the assignment was one occasion when Bishop Franklin defied Willard Leggett's wishes in appointment making.[6]

Though there was controversy in the church in response to Dickson's participation in Born of Conviction, it was not severe; he remained at Columbia First until 1966. He said good-bye to close friends—signers James Holston and Inman Moore, along with nonsigners Dorsey Allen and David McKeithen—as they left Mississippi. Dickson (Figure 9.1) was "driven not to be driven out." He was called to ministry in Mississippi; if a person believed in something, he should stay and fight for it. In 1965, he listed his reasons for staying: "This is home. Too much in debt to get away from lending agencies who know me. I have 'run' from some things in life but chose not to run from this one; I like a fight now and then . . .; people let me remain."[7]

In spite of any residual prejudice against him because of his father's past, Dickson's abilities as a pastor and community leader won him great respect in Columbia. One of the leading families was the Lamptons, embattled signer Bill Lampton's parents, and in the midst of the Born of Conviction controversy, they expressed gratitude to him for supporting their son. Dickson modestly claimed in 1965 that his effectiveness as pastoral leader had been "curtailed" because of his participation in the statement, but he joined with an interracial group of leaders in Columbia to help the town negotiate the rough waters after the passage of the 1964 Civil Rights Act and the 1965 Voting Rights Act. He believed that in late 1962, signing Born of Conviction was the most strategic witness he and other ministers could offer, but now almost three years later, he had an opportunity that ministers who had left did not:

FIGURE 9.1 N. A. Dickson, 1960s. Courtesy of Dickson family archive.

The same statement is not needed today, in my opinion. Its spirit . . . needs to be incorporated in statements and stands made in local communities by school boards, city & county officials, etc.; more than the clergy should be speaking out, taking stands, saying "we will comply," "ours will be a law-abiding community," etc. We can help in this & in my opinion [it] would be more effective.[8]

When Dickson met Bill McAtee, the new Presbyterian pastor in town in May 1964, the two connected immediately. In Marion County, they saw radical segregationists (including the Klan) and white political and business leaders who were fearful and slow to move; there was also an active SNCC contingent and a chapter of the Mississippi Freedom Democratic Party (MFDP) organizing the black community. In March 1965, the city and county school boards refused to take action to comply with the Civil Rights Act, even though this would result in loss of federal funds. In response, Dickson and McAtee joined with three black ministers in the county—I. C. Pittman, a Methodist serving as Director of the Mississippi

Rural Center in Lampton, and two Missionary Baptists, L. Z. Blankinship and Amos G. Payton Sr.—to create an informal biracial leadership group. They met regularly and advised the new white mayor of Columbia, E. D. "Buddy" McLean Jr., a member of McAtee's church who pledged to be the mayor of all the town's citizens, both white and black.[9]

When McLean took office in early July 1965, the City School Board again failed to sign a compliance agreement or submit a voluntary desegregation plan, so Dickson and McAtee pushed the white community beyond denial to deal with the crisis constructively. On July 17 they urged twenty-eight Columbia businessmen to lead "a large and broad segment of the community [to insist publicly] on peaceful compliance so that order might be maintained and law be justly applied to all citizens." The result was a full-page ad in the Columbia paper on August 19 signed by 136 whites; it pledged obedience to federal law, even though "we may not approve" of all such laws, and added, "We insist that any person or group who assumes the role of punishing those with whom he or they disagree shall be found and punished to the maximum for their crime." Forty-six of the signers were Methodists, and Dickson reported, "[I] could not refrain from pointing out to them that their statement made the one of the '28' appear mighty mild . . . [I] got a few sheepish grins." McAtee and Dickson did not sign; they wanted it to be an expression of the will of long-term residents of the community. The statement got immediate results: the next week the Columbia School Board reconsidered and voted to submit a desegregation plan; they approved one on August 27.[10]

McAtee, Dickson, and the three black ministers advised Mayor McLean as tensions mounted in the summer of 1965. SNCC and MFDP led demonstrations and picketing efforts in the town, and someone—possibly the Klan—responded with violence, including firebombing the SNCC Freedom House. There were rumors of a Klan rally that would draw a counter-demonstration from the Deacons for Defense, a black armed self-defense group, but this never materialized. The mayor and the biracial ministers' group helped organize two mass meetings in September—one white, one black—with US Department of Commerce representatives. Each meeting elected twelve representatives to serve on a biracial Community Relations Committee that began meeting in October; N. A. Dickson served as a member. After two meetings, he said, "Wonderful things have come from them as men & women, white & negro have sat around table talking, listening, calling each other Mr. & Mrs., etc." One night that fall a young black man rode in a car with Dickson for two hours simply to talk;

it was the first time he had ever communicated this way with a white man. Dickson also served as an informal liaison between the MFDP and the mayor, and he helped the War on Poverty's Community Action Program get started in the town.[11]

Dickson kept Bishop Edward Pendergrass (Figure 9.2) informed about the efforts to mobilize town leaders. Born in 1900, Pendergrass was a stronger leader than Bishop Franklin. Arriving in Mississippi in the summer of 1964, he reportedly refused the Citizens' Council's offer of a Cadillac El Dorado, and he joined an ecumenical group to form Committee of Concern, which raised money to rebuild dozens of black churches burned as a result of Klan violence in 1964. During his first year in Mississippi, he received petitions from MAMML expressing opposition to Methodist participation in the National Council of Churches, strong displeasure at the supposed integrationist bias of church school literature, and firm insistence on maintaining segregation in white Mississippi Methodism and the structure of the national church.[12]

FIGURE 9.2 Bishop Edward J. Pendergrass, late 1960s. Courtesy of J. B. Cain Archives of Mississippi Methodism, Millsaps College.

In marked contrast to the response of Bishop Franklin and his cabinet to Born of Conviction in January 1963, Pendergrass and his cabinet issued a statement at the 1965 Annual Conference session firmly rejecting the MAMML perspective. Read aloud by the bishop in its entirety and published in the conference journal, it said the "race problem ... cannot be bypassed simply by assuming that the problem does not exist." Rather, Methodists sought to "face the problem and deal with it constructively." Commenting on the church visits campaign controversy, Pendergrass echoed language of the Born of Conviction statement concerning the "ownership" of the church:

> It should be apparent to any thinking churchman that no congregation can deepen the spiritual lives of its members and make an effective witness to Jesus Christ by placing special ushers at the doors of the church to select who will and who will not be allowed to participate in the worship services. After all, every church belongs to the Lord Jesus Christ, and His will and not ours must determine the answer to the question as to whom a church should be open.

When the bishop finished reading the statement, N. A. Dickson moved that "the Conference express its appreciation for the statement with a standing vote," and the motion passed.[13]

In late September 1965, Dickson asked Bishop Pendergrass to write letters of appreciation to five Methodist laypeople, including Mrs. I. C. Pittman, who directed Mississippi Rural Center with her husband, and W. T. Shows, a member of Dickson's church and the person most responsible for organizing prominent white citizens of Columbia. Dickson knew from experience how important the bishop's support could be for leadership efforts in race relations in 1960s Mississippi and how devastating it was when such support did not come; he believed Pendergrass would write the letters.[14]

The two men shared similar characteristics: both were plainspoken and had quick tempers. They also recognized each other as kindred spirits, and Dickson become a leader in the conference. When he left Columbia in 1966, he spent a year as pastor at Yazoo City First. Then Dickson and Willard Leggett (Figure 9.3) became codirectors of the conference's Action Crusade, a capital funds campaign to raise three million dollars for conference institutions. Pendergrass wanted to unify disparate elements of

CRUSADE DIRECTORS APPOINTED

FIGURE 9.3 J. W. Leggett Jr. and N. A. Dickson greet each other upon the announcement of their joint appointment as directors of the Mississippi Action Crusade in 1967. Courtesy of Mississippi Annual Conference, The United Methodist Church.

the conference, and his appointment of Dickson and Leggett sent a clear signal that it was time to heal political and race relations divisions. In 1968, Pendergrass appointed Dickson to his cabinet as superintendent of the Vicksburg District, and in preparation for the 1973 merger of the white and black conferences, Dickson continued his commitment to racial reconciliation by facilitating small gatherings of black and white clergy and laypeople in the district, simply for them to talk and listen to each other. In 1974, Dickson became the director of the Conference Council on Ministries. He served Centenary Church in McComb beginning in 1978, and in 1983, upon his retirement, he and his wife moved to Columbia, where he worked as a retired supply pastor for a few years at two small churches. He died in 2000.[15]

In 1965, Dickson wrote the much younger Jim Waits, then in gradu-ate school in Illinois, and urged, "You're still my leader and I want you to come on back home and get to leading!" Clint Gill (see Figure 7.2), who began his full-time pastoral career in 1963 and eventually became a clergy leader in the conference, said of Dickson,

> He influenced my life more than anyone else. Many thought of him as brusque, because he spoke his mind; he really did if he was irritated. But he was also a tender-hearted individual. He saw something in me that I didn't see, and he interacted with me in such a way that I began to see and believe it. He was the best district superintendent; he was able to build community with pastors in the district in a powerful way. . . . The people who served under him were better.[16]

Named Nathaniel at birth, Dickson changed his name to Nathan after his father died. Nathan the prophet, advisor to King David, spoke truth to power, while the disciple Andrew brought many people to Jesus. N. A. Dickson was also an encourager who "pulled for the underdog" and became mentor to and advocate for many in crisis, including W. O. "Chet" Dillard, an impoverished teenager in Pachuta whom Dickson befriended in the late 1940s. Dillard says Dickson "took me into his home, clothed me, fed me and enabled me to enter college. I became a naval aviator, district attorney, commissioner of public safety and a judge because of the personal sacrifice of an ordinary pastor and his family." In 2002 Dillard established the Dickson Order Endowment in memory of N. A. Dickson to honor Mississippi Conference ministers "who have served faithfully and blessed the lives of individuals in the churches they have served." The endowment's income funds seminary scholarships for persons preparing for pastoral ministry in Mississippi. Dickson, Dillard says, "believed in me when I didn't believe in myself."[17]

"No Need to Be [Frightened]"

James Sydney Conner was a consummate institutional church team player. Those who knew him well joked, "When a meeting is announced, James Conner gets his briefcase and heads for his car before they've said where it's being held." Respected for his reliability and commitment to the necessary bureaucratic workings of the annual conference, the district, and the local church, Conner served a number of Mississippi Conference leadership positions over his forty-year ministerial career, including chair of the Board of Ordained Ministry for eight years. In 1976 he told two ministerial candidates that the United Methodist *Discipline* and the conference journal would be their "bibles" when they became pastors. He helped develop conference camping and hiking programs and promoted continuing education for pastors.[18]

Given his strong commitment to the institutional church, one might expect Conner to have avoided doing anything to cause controversy in Mississippi Methodism in 1963, but his commitment to Personalistic Idealism trumped his institutionalism. Influenced by Emory philosopher L. E. Loemker, a Boston Personalist, Conner believed that personality was the highest form of existence and understood God as a person with a will and an infinite mind. God is also moral, and to believe human beings are created in God's image is to make a moral statement: we know good from evil because we are created *imago Dei*. Therefore, all human beings are equal, and we are obliged to treat everyone as created in God's image. David Conner remembers that years after the Born of Conviction controversy, he asked his mother about his father's decision to participate: "I understand he knew it was right . . ., but did he realize how angry people would get at him and how they would be threatened?" She responded, "I don't know if he ever thought of that. It seemed to him like such an obvious thing to do." A fellow signer remembers Conner simply as "a man of honesty and integrity," and another ministerial colleague describes him as "always trying to do what was right—sometimes in a plodding sort of way, but he was just a good guy."[19]

After Born of Conviction was published, Conner received a phone call from someone pretending to be a professor at Jackson State College, a black institution. Unaware the call was being audiotaped, he asked the caller if they had ever met at a MCHR meeting at Tougaloo. This led to a rumor that Conner had taught a course at Tougaloo. The Conners suspected the call and rumors to be the work of Citizens' Council members who sought to condemn him for his membership in the Twenty-Eight. Tougaloo served as the unofficial headquarters of the Jackson Movement, and most Jackson whites viewed it with negative emotions, ranging from confusion and disdain to outright hatred. In February 1963, Conner told Tougaloo President and MCHR Chairman A. D. Beittel that due to the controversy surrounding Born of Conviction, he would not be attending the Executive Committee and full council meetings that month. He assured Beittel he would continue his role with MCHR, including service as a vice-president and member of the Executive Committee.[20]

Conner stayed at Brandon until June, when he moved to Hawkins Church in Vicksburg. John Speed, pastor at Hawkins from 1961 to 1963, paved the way for the congregation to accept him. Conner's first year there passed without controversy, and he continued his involvement on the board of MCHR, where he got to know two Central Jurisdiction Mississippi Conference pastors: Henry Clay Jr. and Charlemagne Payne. The interracial and interfaith organization's purpose was to educate and communicate in order to create "a climate of opinion favorable to an expansion of opportunity for all the people of Mississippi, in economic, civic and cultural areas based on freedom from discrimination on grounds of race, religion or national origin." The group occasionally issued press releases or sent communications to members and sympathetic citizens seeking to counter segregationist propaganda. For example, just prior to the climactic days of the Jackson Movement demonstrations in late May 1963, MCHR issued a statement expressing disappointment at "the apparent unwillingness of Mayor Allen C. Thompson to set up a responsible bi-racial committee in the City of Jackson to consider the grievances of Negro citizens."[21]

During the church visits campaign controversy in Jackson, MCHR scheduled a panel discussion for January 28, 1964, on the topic "What Is Freedom of Worship in Mississippi?" In December 1963, Conner asked W. J. Cunningham, senior pastor at Galloway; Francis Stevens, attorney, associate lay leader of the conference, and member of Jackson's Broadmeadow Methodist; and Seth Granberry, senior pastor at Capitol Street, to participate on the panel with Rabbi Perry Nussbaum of Jackson's Temple Beth Israel; T. B. Brown, a black Baptist pastor in Jackson; and Father Bernard Law, editor of the Catholic state newspaper. The meeting, Conner told them, would be held at Tougaloo College, because it was "the only place that the group can meet unmolested at the present time." All three Methodists declined to participate; Cunningham's and Granberry's congregations felt besieged as the result of the church visits campaign, and Cunningham feared his participation would be "completely misunderstood . . . by some of my congregation."[22]

At Hawkins, Conner made no secret of his participation in MCHR, and it caused no trouble until the November 10, 1964, MCHR meeting received negative coverage in the Jackson press, including a mention of Conner as a vice president of the organization. The problem was not his membership per se but the publicity that church members viewed as reflecting badly on them in the Closed Society. The "repercussion and other 'back-lash'" in the congregation proved so intense that Conner wrote Episcopal priest Duncan Gray Jr., the new MCHR president, in December 1964 to resign his vice-presidency and Executive Committee membership, though he did not withdraw his MCHR membership. He explained that some church leaders could accept what happened and continue to work with him, but others "are angry enough to demand [my] immediate removal, or . . . are withdrawing their support, or perhaps their membership in the church." He saw the controversy as inevitable, and said, "Our people have got to find their way through the problems that face us, and accept the role that The Methodist Church will continue to play in it." As the only white Methodist on the Executive Committee and Board of MCHR at the time, he could not "take it upon [himself] to lead a 'one-man crusade.'" He knew Bishop Pendergrass had "an almost insuperable task ahead of him in clarifying and hardening the role of the church in the present crisis, and I want to play on his team, according to the signals he calls." This caution did not prevent Conner from participating in efforts to open lines of communication between white and black community leaders in Vicksburg.[23]

Conner (Figure 9.4) initially responded to the MCHR controversy in his church by explaining in a Sunday service that he believed some white people needed to be communicating directly with black people about a way forward in race relations. As the family ate lunch that day, he and his wife explained to their four children they would probably have to move again. Betty Conner Currey recalled in 2004 that their teenage son David responded, "Well, I'm not happy to be moving again. I hope someday we can stay longer at a church, but I was proud of you today, Daddy." On another occasion, David asked why they did not transfer to Colorado, where his father's sister lived. Conner did make some transfer inquiries; he called a seminary friend in the Florida Conference and spoke to Bob Matheny in Terre Haute, Indiana, about going there, but he pursued the matter no further. As expected, the Hawkins church requested that Conner move when conference rolled around in 1965.[24]

His new appointment was to Broad Street Church in Hattiesburg, but false rumors spread in that church that he had participated in the March 1965 civil rights march from Selma to Montgomery. He weathered that storm and had a successful ministry there, staying four years. As the annual conference session began in 1969, Betty Conner remained in Hattiesburg to pack, as they expected to move. She remembers that Hattiesburg District Superintendent G. Eliot Jones called to tell Conner about his new appointment to Grace Church in Natchez. In her husband's

FIGURE 9.4 James Conner, late 1960s. Courtesy of Heritage United Methodist Church, Hattiesburg, MS.

absence, Jones gave her the news and said, "He's proved now that he can stay." Conner's struggles at Brandon and Hawkins hindered his climb up the appointment ladder. In the 1970s, N. A. Dickson recommended to Bishop Mack Stokes that Conner be chosen for a district superintendent's opening. Stokes agreed Conner would do well in the post but lamented that his current salary was too low for him to be considered for the position.[25]

Conner spent five years at Natchez Grace, followed by four at Epworth Church in South Jackson. The supposed stigma of Born of Conviction continued to nip at Conner's heels: the effort to poison the well at Broad Street in 1965 came from someone in the Brandon Church, and as late as 1974, the Conners learned that someone from Brandon had called Epworth members in an attempt to prejudice the church against him. Both efforts failed. After five years at Petal UMC, just outside Hattiesburg, Conner retired in 1983 and served part-time as minister of visitation at Main Street in Hattiesburg, the church where he had belonged in his early life. In 1986 he had coronary bypass surgery, and complications caused his health to decline. His lungs gradually failed, and one night in June 1988, as his sons tell the story, "his color paled and his life began to ebb. Our mother, who had maintained a positive attitude through the preceding months, finally confessed to our father that she was frightened of what might happen next. With quiet confidence he whispered, 'No need to be.' "[26]

At his funeral in Hattiesburg, his friend and ministerial colleague Cecil Jones reminded the congregation of Conner's witness as a signer of the Born of Conviction statement and added that many of the signers had left Mississippi. Jones noted that "family and friends are proud that James Conner did not [leave]." Conner joined in Born of Conviction because of the failure of conference leaders to speak when a strong witness was needed. In the midst of his struggles to continue a viable ministry in Mississippi, in 1964 he found Bishop Pendergrass more willing to confront the problems facing Methodists, and that spurred his determination to remain. But according to Betty Conner Currey, the main reason he stayed was that in spite of the difficulties, James Conner "couldn't ever get the feeling that God wanted him to leave Mississippi."[27]

"We Remember You Signed . . ."

The personable, salt-of-the-earth country boy Delbert Elton Brown grew up in the small community of Hebron in Jones County. Born in 1927, after his 1944 high school graduation he attended Jones Junior College and left for the military in 1946. Stationed in Japan during the postwar occupation, the suffering he observed inspired him to enter the ministry, but he went to the University of Tennessee in 1947 to dodge his calling. He transferred to Millsaps College and made his commitment public in January 1949; he graduated in 1950 and moved on to Candler School of Theology in Atlanta. He returned to Mississippi in 1953 and served appointments at Sandersville, Chunky, and Pachuta. He married Juliette Tanner of Laurel in 1951, and they had three daughters. In 1961 he was appointed to Lovely Lane Church in Natchez.[28]

As a boy, Brown had played with the children of two black sharecropper families who lived on his family's farm, and by the mid-1950s, he was concerned about the plight of blacks in Mississippi and the growing white resistance to change. When he was invited to sign Born of Conviction, he did not hesitate; he also did not think it would cause controversy. This led to the commission of a cardinal marital sin: he neglected to tell his wife he had signed it. When news first spread of the publication, she was at the church practicing a solo for Sunday, and the organist mentioned the statement and her understanding of what it said. Mrs. Brown remembers joking, "That sounds like it came from a bunch of preachers who want to move." It was not until she saw her husband later that she learned he had signed it.[29]

Morgantown, the church's neighborhood, was known as "Klux's Den" by local blacks, and after Born of Conviction appeared, Brown found Klan literature left in the church entrance and strewn across the lawn on several Sunday mornings. He suspected a few church members were connected to the Klan. After events on a tense Saturday in downtown Natchez almost resulted in violent conflict between whites and blacks, Brown discarded his prepared sermon and told his gathered members the next morning that he did not believe God was pleased with what had happened. Half the church's members had moved there from other states and were not particularly upset by Born of Conviction, but between 1963 and 1966 some Lovely Lane leaders counseled inaction in response to civil rights controversy, claiming "that if everyone would leave these problems alone that [they] would soon die away." The church's task was to save souls, not to get involved in social issues. Brown responded "that everything that touches human society at any point has a religious significance," and the current crisis would not be resolved "unless good people began to exert the right influence."[30]

Brown's pastoral abilities and willingness to speak the truth resulted in his remaining at Lovely Lane after he signed Born of Conviction; with characteristic humility, he credits lay leadership: "I had some people who stood by me, and I was able to stay three more years." In the summer of 1964, with the Jackson church visits campaign still ongoing and rumors swirling of integrated groups possibly visiting Lovely Lane, he encouraged the Official Board to state publicly that "the doors of our church are open to anyone who comes to worship." They postponed the decision until the next monthly meeting. Attendance was high the night of the secret ballot vote, and as the secretary tallied the result on a chalkboard, it became evident the open door policy would pass by a two to one margin. Four men got up to leave, and Brown recalls that one exclaimed, "Y'all can have it and go to hell with it!" Brown reported that "about 28 (strange the number)" left the church; he visited every family rumored to be leaving. Most still departed, and in his view the church "had a better sense of purpose and unity . . . after we cleared those folks."[31]

When Brown left Natchez in 1966, Bishop Pendergrass asked him to go to the embattled Raymond Church, which in 1965 had come within one vote of approving a motion to withdraw from The Methodist Church. When news came the next year that one of the notorious Twenty-Eight would be their new pastor, thirty-five congregants withdrew their membership. Hearing this, Brown asked the bishop to reconsider; he "had fought the war already down in Natchez and didn't want to do it again." Pendergrass wanted to keep the church Methodist and believed Brown was the pastor to do it. If it didn't work out, the bishop promised he could move again in a year. Brown found a church paralyzed by fear and unwilling to take a stand as real Methodists. He challenged them to get off the fence and decide whether they were going to be true to their Christian faith. After one year, in June 1967 he surprised them by announcing on Sunday that he would move later that week. Repentant for the year's conflicts, several members came to see him before he left. A church leader told Brown his impending departure had waked them up, and they were now prepared to be a better church. Brown concluded he did more good for them by leaving than anything else he had done that year.[32]

James Conner had predicted privately in late 1963 that Brown might leave the conference. The frustrations of the year at Raymond led Brown to explore a transfer, and in 1967 signer Inman Moore, in California since 1963, invited him to come to La Crescenta Valley Church in the Pasadena District as associate pastor. Brown met with Bishop Pendergrass, who told him to go see about it, which he understood as tacit approval. He returned from the trip ready to transfer, but Pendergrass refused. He remembers the bishop said, "Under no circumstances will I release you. Elton, I'm trying to maintain a Methodist Church in Mississippi, and if all of you fellas continue to leave, then what have I got to work with?" Though disappointed at the time, in 2003 Brown (Figure 9.5) reflected, "I am glad I didn't, very glad I didn't, and I've often wondered if Providence was in it."[33]

Over the next eighteen years, Brown served at Purvis and at West Park Church in Jackson, as associate director of the Conference Council on Ministries while N. A. Dickson was the director, and six years at Wiggins. Similar to James Conner's experience, Elton Brown's ascent up the appointment ladder was likely slowed by his participation in Born of Conviction, but just as conference leaders had trusted him to revive a troubled church at Raymond, they later turned to him in another crisis. In January 1985, he returned to Natchez as pastor of Jefferson Street Church when their

FIGURE 9.5 Elton Brown, 2004. Author photo.

previous pastor was charged (and eventually convicted) of embezzling conference funds. He remained until his retirement in 1989. When he first arrived at Jefferson Street, he knew that although twenty-two years had passed, many current members had been there when the church had rejected Summer Walters in 1963. Brown recalls that several people in the church told him, "We remember that you signed that statement, and it's OK."[34]

"You're Here, and He's in Arizona"

At Wesson the mild controversy surrounding Born of Conviction soon dissipated, and Rod Entrekin remained. A small minority of members nursed lingering anger, resulting in a slight decline in attendance and collections, but most still accepted him even if they disagreed with the stand he took. He was reappointed to the church for the 1963–4 conference year, but with all the departures of fellow signers and other ministers from the conference, the bishop and cabinet made several mid-year moves to fill vacant churches. In October 1963, they decided to move Entrekin to Woodville. It meant a promotion for him, and the change had already been announced at Wesson. Brookhaven District Superintendent Norman Boone took him to a quarterly conference meeting at Woodville on October 23, just before he was to move, and as Entrekin later described it, during the meeting a member of the church "vowed that neither he, nor a considerable number of his friends, would accept me as their pastor. There were persons present who did not agree with his position, but no one spoke up." Deeply disappointed in the silence of church members who had supported the appointment, Entrekin told Boone on the way back to Wesson that night that he would not go to Woodville and would take a leave of absence if necessary. The Wesson Church was willing to keep him, so he remained.[35]

One day in the summer of 1964, Entrekin saw ants congregated around a spot of clear, sticky liquid (Karo Syrup) underneath the gas port of his 1958 black and white Chevrolet sedan. Without starting the engine, he called the local dealership, owned by a Catholic man who was not upset about Born of Conviction. An employee came to the house, took the gas tank off, and cleaned it out at the shop, then brought it back and reinstalled it. The same thing happened to the car of a nearby NAACP leader, and then someone shot into that man's house, which disturbed the Entrekins. Their two daughters had been sleeping in a front room, and they moved the girls to the back of the parsonage. Two years later, Entrekin learned that a Wesson neighbor, whose children had played with the Entrekin kids and who had always been cordial to him, was a member of the Ku Klux Klan.[36]

James Conner had also speculated that Entrekin might leave the conference, and in 1965, Entrekin admitted he had come close to doing so. Like most Methodist ministers, he had connections in other conferences, and one friend promised him significant assistance for a transfer should he choose to leave Mississippi. In the summer of 1964, he wondered what the future held for him in the Methodist ministry. In August an unusual opportunity arose. Entrekin's friend Howard Freeman had served four years as a chaplain at the Mississippi State Hospital, a psychiatric facility at Whitfield just east of Jackson, and had decided to pursue medical education and psychiatry. He encouraged Entrekin to apply for the resulting chaplain's opening. Entrekin was hired and began work on September 1 in a special appointment approved by the Mississippi Conference. He heard from the hospital's director, Dr. W. L. Jaquith, that a Methodist state legislator had pressured Jaquith not to give him the job because he was a member of the Twenty-Eight. Jaquith ignored the lobbying effort. Entrekin also discovered that fellow signer Bufkin Oliver, attempting to return to Mississippi, had applied for the position. Entrekin remembers Jaquith telling him he had been chosen over Oliver, among other reasons, because "You're here, and he's in Arizona."[37]

Entrekin came at a turning point in Whitfield's history. It had been segregated with strict racial divisions on its large campus housing four thousand patients, but the passage of the 1964 Civil Rights Bill forced changes. By 1965, he reported the hospital was moving toward full integration: "Consequently we now speak to integrated groups and render a personal ministry to mentally ill Negro patients and physically ill Negro employees." He was one of three chaplains—two white and one black—on the staff, and they worked as a team. The integration caused minimal problems with patients; the adjustment was more difficult for the employees.[38]

After more than a decade of ministry in Methodist congregations, Entrekin's new work took him to unfamiliar territory. His duties included relating to people with a wide range of mental illnesses; some underwent electric shock treatments. He held church services for patients and supported their family members. This new context of service proved a "rude awakening" to him and required many adjustments, but he soon gained the needed experience and expertise. As a pastor to an enclosed community, he offered a full range of ministry to residents and employees and gained a new appreciation for the Christian tradition of care and cure of souls.[39]

The Entrekin family lived in a house provided for them on the hospital grounds. The children attended local Rankin County public schools, and Ginny Entrekin taught first grade at Pearl Elementary. In 1965, the school integrated on a token basis, and she had two black girls in her class. She began teaching at Pearl High School in the fall of 1969. When the *Alexander v. Holmes* court decision mandated more full-fledged desegregation to begin in January 1970, she and some other white teachers at Pearl received notice of transfers to Carter High, the formerly all-black school in Brandon. All but Ginny Entrekin either quit or got jobs in other systems, and she was the only white teacher from Pearl to make the move to Carter. Some of her female colleagues at Pearl told her they were willing to teach at Carter, but their husbands would not permit it. As in many other Mississippi communities, a substantial number of white families in Rankin County sent their children to newly founded segregation academies; the Entrekin kids remained in the public schools. The Entrekins had support in this commitment: all the white doctors at Whitfield also kept their children in the public schools.[40]

In 1969, Rod Entrekin took a part-time United Methodist local church appointment at Greenfield, near the hospital, and he remained there twenty-two years. In 1991, after twenty-seven years at Whitfield, he retired from his chaplain's position. The Entrekins moved to Hattiesburg and became active members at Parkway Heights Church, the site of their 1956 wedding. In 2007, one of the two black women who had been Mrs. Entrekin's pupils in 1965 lived in the neighborhood where the Entrekins resided.[41]

In a talk to a 2004 gathering at Parkplace, an outreach ministry of Parkway Heights Church, Rod Entrekin (Figure 9.6) shared the story of his journey in ministry, recounting his experiences with the biracial Intercollegiate Council in college, the Born of Conviction controversy, and his decades of work at the State Hospital. In closing, he expressed appreciation for the United Methodist Church's "Open Minds, Open Hearts,

FIGURE 9.6 Rod Entrekin, 2004. Author photo.

Open Doors" campaign and reminded listeners of Washington Irving's *The Legend of Sleepy Hollow,* in which Rip Van Winkle "slept through a revolution." With characteristic modesty, he summed up his own story:

> Over the last fifty years, much of my ministry was simultaneous with the social revolution taking place in the South, accompanied with the environment of mental illness. Being involved in the social issues was not an act of courage on my part, but a matter of conviction. I would not have chosen the experiences I had, nor did I actively seek them out. I guess one might say they "just happened" and I SURVIVED.

Entrekin joined with twenty-seven colleagues in 1963 to call Mississippi Methodists to a new day in race relations, and he lived through a revolution. Perhaps it all just happened, but in the process he kept his commitment to serve as a Mississippi pastor in local churches and a state mental hospital for the next three decades.[42]

The Maverick

Of the eight signers who stayed in Mississippi, Denson Napier and Rod Entrekin were the two who spent much of their subsequent careers in ministries beyond the local church. They shared a subtle sense of humor and were good friends. In contrast to the mild-mannered, unassuming, and accommodating Entrekin, Napier was more gregarious and prone to sarcasm; at times he could be quite blunt. In their 2003 comments about Born of Conviction signers who left the state, Entrekin said, "I couldn't fault those that left. It would have helped if they had stayed, but I can't fault any of them," while Napier opined, "I don't know of a one of them that *had* to leave." Napier remembered talking with two ministers and a layman in 1963 about how difficult things were, how much hard work was needed, and how important it was for them all to stay in Mississippi. Eventually those three all left, and in later years, he joked to any of them back for a visit, "Here's one of the deserters!" But he knew the difficulties: he and his wife Jean briefly considered leaving in 1963.[43]

As a student at Mississippi Southern College in the late 1950s, signer Ned Kellar knew Napier as the director of the Wesley Foundation and described him as a "maverick" and "follower of 'the beat of a different

FIGURE 9.7 Denson Napier, 1960s. Courtesy of Sandra Napier Dyess.

drummer' [who] could be cynical and yet very caring." Such qualities made Napier (Figure 9.7) a natural in campus ministry, and when his successor at the Wesley Foundation transferred to Southern California-Arizona in late 1963, he accepted the invitation to return as director. It was a critical time to work with Mississippi college students, as big changes had begun. At the state Methodist Student Movement meeting at the Southern Wesley Foundation building in February 1964, the speaker was Everett Tilson, a seminary professor who was arrested a few weeks later as part of an integrated group attempting to worship at Jackson's Capitol Street Methodist Church. That summer, the Wesley Foundation hosted Freedom Summer workers, and some of Napier's students befriended them.[44]

Napier remained at Southern until 1969, earning a master's in college counseling in his spare time. He took a sabbatical leave and sold real estate in Hattiesburg for a few months before he began a job with the conference in early 1970. In 1965, Mississippi Methodists had established Mississippi Methodist Ministry as an alternative to the NCC's controversial Delta Ministry. It was based in Clarksdale and run by the

Killingsworth sisters, two missionaries. They retired in 1970, and Denson Napier began working for the organization, renamed Mississippi United Methodist Ministry (MUMM) and relocated to Jackson. The 1968 General Conference abolished the black Central Jurisdiction, and annual conferences in the same geographic areas had until 1972 to merge. Leaders in Mississippi Methodism knew this would not be easy. With support from the Fund for Reconciliation, started by the denomination in 1968 to promote justice for minority groups, Napier and staff partner Wayne Calbert, a black layman from Gulfport, planned and led biracial workshops for Methodists around the state to prepare them for the merger of the former Central Jurisdiction Mississippi and Upper Mississippi Conferences with the white Mississippi and North Mississippi Conferences, respectively. Even with those efforts, Mississippi United Methodists took until 1973 to merge, the last conferences in the denomination to do so. MUMM also promoted economic development work in the state to deal with issues of poverty, but its funding ran out by 1973.[45]

The Jackson Public Schools (JPS) had undergone more thorough desegregation in January 1970 after five-and-a-half years of the token Freedom of Choice plan. In 1972, JPS Superintendent Brandon Sparkman, familiar with Napier's work in the MUMM reconciliation program, hired him as part of a biracial team with Benny Richards to work in the schools in human relations. This included setting up dialogues between black and white students. After two years, the program was expanded with the support of federal Emergency School Assistance funds, and Napier directed a four-person biracial Community Relations Program, working with teachers, administrators, students, and parents. He functioned as a Protestant worker priest on the front lines of the emerging Mississippi society. It was part of a valiant effort, but whites in Jackson fled the public schools in droves in the 1970s. Fifty-four percent of JPS enrollment in 1968–9 was white; by 2001 that percentage had dropped to four. White parents who left JPS defended their decision by claiming the schools had declined, but Napier consistently told them that if they had stayed, it would have been different. In 2003, he saw this as analogous to ministers who left the conference in the 1960s and said, "They have to live with that."[46]

After five years at JPS, Napier returned to the local church as minister of program at Jackson's Galloway Memorial. In 1980, he left that position and took early retirement, struggling with alcoholism. He took his last drink in October 1981; in subsequent years he worked part-time as a recovery counselor at the Baptist Hospital in Jackson, "supporting many at life's lowest point, especially those who struggled with addiction." He came back from retirement to Galloway in 1982, remaining until 1988. He served at Magee for a year and two years as an associate director of the Conference Council on Ministries, and then at Canton UMC until his retirement in 1994. He lived with his wife in Jackson until his death in May 2010.[47]

In 2003, Napier recalled that shortly after the 1963 release of the Born of Conviction statement, his mother asked why he had signed it. He responded, "Mom, you always told me to sing a little song, 'Jesus loves the little children . . . red and yellow, black and white, they are precious in his sight.' When they grow up, they're no less precious than when they were little children." Napier did not see his signature as a turning point in his life but as a natural product of his upbringing. In 1965, he wrote, "The church should be at the forefront in leading people to a better understanding of and right relationship with all people." In signing the Born of Conviction statement, working with college students in the 1960s, seeking racial understanding and reconciliation through MUMM and his work at JPS, and helping persons recover from addictions, he made that belief central in his work as a Methodist/United Methodist minister for more than forty years in Mississippi.[48]

Bridge Builder

The oldest signer of Born of Conviction, Harold Ryker (see Figure 6.3) was born in 1906 in Hutchinson, Kansas. In the late 1960s he complained with humor about the depiction of the statement's signers as "young ministers." His family moved to the Mississippi Gulf Coast when he was seven, and save for his college years at Mississippi State and one year in Adams County, he spent the rest of his life on the Coast. He was the only signer who never attended seminary; he became a pastor at age fifty. He married Sarah Walker in 1934 and spent much of his adult life working in the retail and insurance businesses. A lay member of Biloxi First Methodist for decades, he served as a Sunday School teacher, youth counselor, and assistant to the pastor. He also invested his life in the community, working with Kiwanis, Boy Scouts, United Givers Fund, the National U.S.O., and other organizations.[49]

In February 1956, Ryker started a Methodist mission in a house in Northwest Biloxi; by the third Sunday, congregants gathered in the back

yard and he preached from the steps. By April, the district superintendent officially organized Beauvoir Methodist Church with Ryker as pastor, and its fast growth continued. The church constructed an education
building later that year and completed a sanctuary by Easter Sunday
1962. Ryker, ordained an elder as an approved supply pastor in 1961,
was still at Beauvoir when he joined the Twenty-Eight. Convinced the
race issue had to be confronted, not avoided, he proclaimed it made no
sense to "cross that bridge when we come to it and at the last minute
discover that it is not safe[.] No. We need to be doing some bridge building now."[50]

He told a young ministry intern in 1963 that his church members preferred he not discuss social issues; they wanted him simply to say God
loved them and everything was going to be all right. The folksy Ryker
assured whoever would listen that God loved them, but throughout his
career he also pushed church members and fellow pastors to continue
working toward racial reconciliation. Like James Conner, he was active
in the MCHR, and in the early 1960s he frequently hosted meetings for
interracial groups in his home because other places were not available.[51]

The Beauvoir Church would have kept him longer, but District
Superintendent Tom Prewitt, unhappy with Ryker's participation in the
Twenty-Eight, moved him in June 1963. In the wake of departures from
the conference, Ryker had barely settled at a new appointment in Biloxi
when he was moved again to Kingston in Adams County, the church
where Powell Hall had difficulty the following year. He returned to the
Coast in 1964, and in 1965 he followed Jim Waits at Epworth Church
in Biloxi. Ryker remained there three years, completing the Methodist
Course of Study to become a full clergy member of the conference. He
served Clermont Harbor, then Waveland, and finally Orange Grove before
poor health forced him to retire in 1974. Five years later, he died.[52]

Ryker and his wife had no children but always took a keen interest in
young people. He tirelessly supported Moore Community House, a Biloxi
community center working with families in poverty, and the institution
named a building after him. When his wife died, she left a bequest to
Beauvoir Church to support ministry with children and youth.[53]

In 1963 Ryker supplemented his statewide stand in Born of Conviction
with a manifesto in the local daily paper. Shunning the widespread practice of name calling and labeling people, he explained his view on race
relations: "I hope some day to be able to proudly wear the label—'I am a
Christian,' but I have got to clean out of the inside of the cup a little more

prejudice and pride. If I must hate something, let it be evil, arrogance, injustice, prejudice."[54]

"I'm Gonna Outlove These People"

Born in 1937, John Ed Thomas III was among the youngest members of the Twenty-Eight and one of five in his first year out of seminary at the time of the statement's release. He grew up in Woodville in the southwest corner of Mississippi. A lifelong Methodist, he credited Sunday School teacher Myrtle Neill with giving him the first hints of the injustices of the segregated system in Mississippi, and that consciousness grew in his time as a preministerial student at Millsaps College. In 1959, he married Margaret Ewing, daughter of James Ewing, president of Mississippi's Delta State College, and they moved to Atlanta, where he attended Candler and she taught high school choral music. They returned to Mississippi in June 1962.[55]

As the associate pastor at Gulfport First Church, John Ed Thomas endured the anger of his senior pastor, J. Melvin Jones, at his participation in Born of Conviction. Jones wished Thomas had cleared it with him, but the younger pastor knew Jones would have sought to dissuade him. Yet Jones also stood up for his junior colleague, deflecting much of the criticism from church members. Thomas did not enjoy the associate role, especially because he and Jones were quite different in pastoral style. Though he could have remained at First Church, in the spring of 1963 he told District Superintendent Tom Prewitt he wanted to move to a church of his own. Prewitt warned he would have to take whatever was offered.[56]

Thomas was assigned to the Satartia Charge in Yazoo County. Margaret Thomas's parents received an anonymous phone call claiming folks in Satartia were upset about it. At the invitation of the charge, the Thomases traveled to Satartia before moving day, expecting an informal meeting with members. When they arrived that evening, the lay leader asked Thomas if he wanted to speak to the group from the pulpit. He expressed surprise that they expected him to speak formally. He stood at a lectern in front of the pews; thirty people were present. Thomas remembered in 2003 that during the meeting, someone asked, "If you had it to do all over, would you sign the statement again?" He responded, "Yes, I'd sign it again." It was an election year, and a church member running for a county office walked out, saying he had heard enough. No one followed him. Before they adjourned for refreshments, Thomas told the group, "Folks, I'm assigned to be your pastor. I also want to be your friend, but friendship is a two-way street, and you're gonna have to meet me halfway." One man told him at the reception, "I came down here tonight ready to lynch you. But if you had answered that question [Would he sign the statement again?] any other way, I'd have had absolutely no respect for you."[57]

Representatives from the three churches voted thirteen to nine to accept Thomas as their pastor. He had some difficult times there; one night while he and Margaret were attending a revival service at another church, someone left Klan leaflets at their parsonage. On his first Sunday at one of the churches on the charge and in his presence, the adult Sunday School teacher criticized him for various misdeeds during a lesson. Thomas made no response but vowed to himself, "I'm just going to out-love these people." He eventually became friends with the Sunday School teacher and the man who had stormed out of the first meeting. Six months later he reported that things were going well as he and church members worked through the difficulties.[58]

In 1965, Thomas (Figure 9.8) returned to the Coast to serve at Gautier for four years, followed by four years at St. Paul Church in Ocean Springs and ten years at Parkway Heights in Hattiesburg. The Thomas children, two daughters and a son, were born during those years. While in his first year at Ocean Springs, at a board meeting to approve the church budget there was a serious proposal to withhold payment of the World Service apportionment, money that would go to the General Church Board of Global Ministries. The person who proposed the cut asserted the line item supported "liberal stuff." With characteristic calm, Thomas told the group that if they were not going to pay Methodist missionaries, they should not pay him either. The meeting ended in an impasse, and the next day a young and supportive church member tried to talk Thomas out of it, insisting he couldn't do that to his family. He would not back down, insist-ing on the importance of the principle involved. A week later, the board reinstated both the World Service apportionment and Thomas's salary. Throughout his career, he was known for his gentle wisdom and prin-cipled integrity.[59]

In 1983, Thomas returned to Gulfport First as senior pastor. In 1986, Bishop Robert Morgan appointed him as district superintendent of the East Jackson District, and he was elected a delegate to the 1988

FIGURE 9.8 John Ed Thomas, 1960s. Courtesy of Margaret Ewing Thomas.

General Conference. After the 1989 merger of the North Mississippi and Mississippi Conferences into one statewide annual conference, he was appointed senior pastor of First Church in Columbus in 1992 and remained there until retiring in 2002, when he moved to Hattiesburg with his wife. In 2006 he suffered a heart attack, and he died in November 2007. In their memorial tributes, Thomas's colleagues Claire Dobbs and Lovett Weems both emphasized his decisions to sign Born of Conviction and stay in Mississippi.[60]

In the summer of 1964, the Thomases spent a week at Lake Chautauqua in New York. He spoke with the main religion lecturer, who knew of the exodus of ministers from Mississippi. The man asked why he had not left, and Thomas remembered replying, "Because Mississippi is home, and I love the people, and there's no greater mission field anywhere than Mississippi is right now. Why should I leave?" In 2003, he added, "I think that's probably why we stayed—our roots were here, our love for the state is here, and no matter what we had to endure, we would tough it out, take it, and do the best we could."[61]

A Future in Ministry

The son of a nightclub drummer and a debutante, Keith Tonkel (see Figures 10.1 and 10.2) was born in New Orleans in 1936; he proudly calls himself a Cajun. Eight years later the family moved to Bay St. Louis, Mississippi. Tonkel's early Christian experience was in the Catholic Church, but he eventually became a Methodist, due to a conversion experience at a revival service preached by Bill McLelland, Jerry Trigg's pastor in high school years at Quitman. When he told his father of his calling to ordained ministry, the elder Tonkel reportedly said, "My God, son, there's no future in it!" Tonkel arrived at Millsaps College in the fall of 1954 with a Methodist license to preach in hand but almost no money. He sold his car, and President Ellis Finger arranged for scholarships. He majored in philosophy.[62]

On the day after he graduated in 1958, Tonkel was diagnosed with throat cancer; the prognosis included the possibility he would lose his voice or even his life. After a grueling series of operations and radiation treatments, he began his seminary education at Emory the following year. In 1962 he returned to Mississippi, appointed to Guinn Memorial Church in Gulfport, and six months later he agreed to sign the Born of Conviction statement at Maxie Dunnam's invitation. In spite of some distress and hurt expressed by some members, the church's response was "not so dramatic as we like to make it." Tonkel stayed seven years at Guinn, and in Gulfport he was involved in Head Start and the work of a Mennonite camp "which direct[ed] its whole effort toward helping the Negro move into the new society." He became foster parent to eight children and in 1968 married Pat Myrick. In addition to the foster kids, they were eventually parents to a son and two daughters.[63]

In 1967, Tonkel again spoke publicly in response to a race relations issue. The annual conference considered a resolution from the General Conference to eliminate the segregated Central Jurisdiction in preparation for the Methodist denominational merger with the Evangelical United Brethren. On the floor of a conference session with a fraternal delegation from the black Mississippi Conference present, John Satterfield, a leading lay spokesman, insisted there was no moral or biblical reason to end the segregated church structure. Appalled, Tonkel stood and replied there were only two reasons they should address it: moral and biblical. After the session, an older white woman told him she had changed her mind on the issue because of his words.[64]

In 1969, Tonkel moved to Jackson's Wells Memorial Church, a dying congregation in a transitional neighborhood a mile west of Millsaps College. He successfully pushed the remaining members to get involved in significant neighborhood ministry; the church gradually grew and became both socioeconomically and racially diverse. They assisted in the founding of Operation Shoestring, a community services organization. Since 1984, the church has sponsored WellsFest, an annual music and arts festival that has raised more than a million dollars for various ministries and community institutions.[65]

Tonkel wrote a weekly newspaper column for years and has published three books. He has participated for decades in the broadcast ministry of the conference's *United Methodist Hour* and preached revivals and spiritual life events at many churches both beyond and within Mississippi, including some of the congregations who announced in 1963 that they would not receive members of the Twenty-Eight. He is known for his thought-provoking authenticity in preaching as well as pastoral and personal relationships: "When people meet Keith Tonkel, when they hear him preach, what they experience is a person who is so genuine and has the gift to speak the truth. People perceive that he connects them to God."[66]

He had opportunities to go elsewhere, including large churches outside of Mississippi, but remained at Wells for the rest of his career. He "retired" at the required age of seventy in 2006 but stayed on as pastor of the church with the conference's blessing. Pat Tonkel died in 2011, and in 2013, Tonkel was diagnosed with cancer in the rear of his voice box and underwent chemotherapy and radiation treatments. In 2014 he underwent additional surgery and treatment.[67]

In 2007, Tonkel received the Emma Elzy Award for Racial Harmony, given by the Mississippi Conference Commission on Religion and Race for his decades of work at Wells. The presentation made no mention of Born of Conviction. Among other awards he has received is the Friendship Award from Jackson 2000, an interracial organization promoting racial reconciliation. The United Methodist Church's Foundation for Evangelism gave him the 2008 Distinguished Evangelist of the UMC Award and noted that "[h]e epitomizes grace, love, commitment, vision, integrity and openness to the movement of God's Spirit." Millsaps College named Tonkel its 2013 Alumnus of the Year. In his life, faith, and ministry, he has embodied a creative combination of personal piety and social justice.[68]

When asked in 1965 why he had remained in Mississippi when others were transferring and how he felt about those who had left, Tonkel replied,

> I understood this to be the original intention of the statement—to speak from within, and to stay in the area to work out the related difficulties (if any). Those who transferred have lost some of their real influence, but must be allowed to be human beings too! There's no doubt, however, that something of what this preacher thought to be the original intention of the statement is lost when signers move to other places.[69]

PART IV

Memory and Legacy

Assessing and Remembering
Born of Conviction

I would say that for me even though now I consider
it a very modest kind of effort and intervention, it has
been a kind of a touchstone for what I've seen as my
ministry in subsequent times, and I would bet that
most of the others feel the same way.

—JIM WAITS, 2003

After I left Satartia, ... this was put behind me, and
we went on to other things. ... It's kind of like a mosquito nip now; it stung and hurt a little bit then, but it
doesn't amount to anything now.

—JOHN ED THOMAS, 2005

AS MY 2003 interview with signers Elton Brown, Rod Entrekin, and John
Ed Thomas drew near its end, Brown—describing himself as "one who
has looked at this from the long haul"—asked his colleagues, "What positive benefit do y'all feel like came out of that thing, if any?" Beyond the
diverse stories of individual signers lurk questions of Born of Conviction's
significance in 1960s Mississippi and the way—more appropriately, the
ways—it is remembered and interpreted. Thus an analysis of the statement's impact is in order, but that leads to other complex issues: the
Mississippi Conference's recognition of the signers, the excavation of
memories surrounding Born of Conviction, the differences in perspective
on the experience between signers who left Mississippi and those who
stayed, and the efforts of Methodist/United Methodist leaders to help create a new Mississippi in the decades following the Born of Conviction
controversy.[1]

Prophets in Their Own Country

Central to the strategy of the authors of Born of Conviction was the idea that the words of native Mississippians would carry more weight with the intended audience, but much of the response to the signers' effort at prophetic speech illustrates Jesus's dictum that "Prophets are not without honor, except in their hometown, and among their own kin, and in their own house." Although the limited-invitations-to-sign argument won out in December 1962, in hindsight several signers admitted that more ministers should have been given the chance to participate. If a broader cross-section of clergy in the conference had signed, there still would have been controversy, but there would also have been more strength in higher numbers. In Mississippi, connections matter greatly, and Methodist laypeople would have considered the statement more seriously if more clergy had signed it. A possible corollary of the "spoke out, forced out" narrative is that Born of Conviction fell on deaf ears and thus did no good. In this interpretation, the manifesto was only a well-intentioned but naïve effort that slammed into an intractable wall and shattered.[2]

But most did take it seriously, even if they retaliated against it and the persons who published it. From this perspective, the attempt by the signers to push white Mississippi Methodists away from uncritical support of the white supremacist system succeeded, at least partially. On the simplest level, white Christians needed to talk with each other about race relations, and the Born of Conviction controversy served as a stimulus for creative dialogue. Breaking the silence was painful, but as Betty Conner Currey said in 2004, "I think it made people grow. They weren't happy about it at the time, but it made them think." Just a week in to the controversy, her husband James Conner wrote to a friend, "It has released a regular Pandora's Box of feelings, charges and counter-charges. But when you put off dealing with an issue, the longer you put it off, the more explosive the pressure becomes. If we can at least make a beginning in establishing an atmosphere in which people can disagree with one another without hatred and intimidation, we will have made a start." In 2003, John Ed Thomas said, "For those who were made angry, it allowed their anger to come out in the open, and they wouldn't heal until that had happened." The statement also affected troubled moderates who had remained tacitly complicit with the injustice in Mississippi. Thomas added,

I think there were a lot of quiet lay people who thought exactly as we did, and they had no voice in the church speaking out in their behalf. They weren't going to say anything, weren't going to shake the boat themselves. But it at least gave them encouragement and courage to hang with the church, even to feel good about themselves, to know that somehow there's somebody there who represents us and thinks like we do.[3]

Thus Born of Conviction contributed significantly to a crack in the united front of white resistance. Former moderate Mississippi Congressman Frank Smith, who heartily supported the Twenty-Eight, also experienced backlash for his approach to race relations, and in 1964 he said, "In my own personal brush with the politics of race, I think the leaders of the Citizens' Councils disliked more than anything else my refusal to reassure either them or my constituents that they were winning the fight for segregation, or that their tactics would ever win it." Born of Conviction testified, to people in and outside of Mississippi, to the lack of unanimity among Mississippi whites at the height of efforts by segregationists to hold the line. Changes in the system would not have come without the direct action of the civil rights movement across the state and throughout the nation, but change in the attitudes of rank-and-file whites also played some role in the success of the Mississippi black freedom struggle. Born of Conviction served as a catalyst for that attitudinal change.[4]

From an ethical and psychological perspective, the witness of Born of Conviction represented an ethic of justice approach to the situation, an emphasis on rights, rules, equality, and fairness. Aside from the clearly doctrinaire segregationist reaction of MAMML and some others, the negative responses of white Methodists can be understood as privileging an ethic of care, which values responsibility in relationships and protecting others from harm. However, here the circle of care extended only as far as white Methodism and white citizens in general, for the most part; thus "care" meant protecting the feelings of whites and the supposed health of the (white) institutional church by maintaining the peace. Ironically, as Mississippi civil rights leader Fannie Lou Hamer understood, this ultimately meant spiritual harm to whites on top of the physical and spiritual harm to blacks. Failure to love their black neighbors resulted in difficulty truly loving themselves. This white contingent stayed on the sidelines and shunned public statements or other revelations of dissenting views because they feared conflict and change. The Twenty-Eight violated that silence, and it felt like a betrayal to many of their church members.[5]

The frequent arguments against "forced" or "enforced" integration can also be read through this lens. The call for voluntary change assumed that whites should remain in control and determine the speed of social change: give them time, and they would do the right thing. But such gradualism had meant no progress in changing the lives of blacks; in fact, things had gotten worse for them due to massive resistance in the Deep South. There had to be force for any significant change to occur.

The same applied to change in the Methodist Church structure. At the 1964 General Conference in Pittsburgh when a group of black and white Methodists demonstrated outside the conference venue to call for an end to the Central Jurisdiction, Lee Reiff (see Figure 2.2)—Methodist clergyman, religion professor at Millsaps College, and a relative newcomer to Mississippi—offered the following analysis to supporters for change gathered there:

> Methodists outside Mississippi must realize that the situation here [in Mississippi] is unlike any they know. They must not interpret the situation here in terms of their own experience and be taken in by pleas for voluntarism from groups like [MAMML]. They must realize that the Mississippi brand of voluntarism and gradualism still means "never," and that progress of any sort is extremely unlikely here unless the Methodist Church issues a clear and authoritative command.

Born of Conviction co-author Jerry Furr echoed this view in 2004: the signers believed the church should embrace the call to a new day in race relations simply because it was "right and fair." The church had the "capacity to compel" people to change, and even though whites protested this change loudly and claimed it was unfair to them and hurt them, it "needed enforcement. You force people, and then they come to see [and say], 'Why didn't we do this sooner?'" White Mississippians needed a big push, and the courageous work of the civil rights movement provided most of the impetus for the 1964 Civil Rights Act and the 1965 Voting Rights Act. The Twenty-Eight pushed white Methodists toward acceptance of these necessary changes. Both Reiff and Furr understood that the voluntaristic argument placed too much confidence in human goodwill and did not account for human weakness, that is, sin.[6]

As moral psychologist Carol Gilligan makes clear, an ethic of justice alone can be too abstract, while an ethic of care alone can ignore clear mandates for justice. True care in this crisis time in Mississippi required forcing whites off the ledge of their fear and denial toward a more just social system that offered care for all persons. In this view, Bishop Franklin was not a segregationist—he operated out of the paternalistic model of care that valued peace in the church above all else and assumed that the institution's elders were charged with interpretive authority of Christian tradition and its application to life in the world, because they knew best how to care for the church and its members. If he understood how sick the society was (and there is evidence that he did), he did not grasp how fully intertwined the church had become with societal evil and how silence meant tacit and soul-crushing approval of the segregated system. He sought to protect the church, but the silent church effectively lost its authority. When it spoke at all, it resorted to the pious platitudes feared by Sam Ashmore in his editorial response to the Ole Miss riot. The signers of Born of Conviction proposed a different model of leadership for Mississippi Methodism—one best represented by Franklin's contemporaries Bishop Gerald Kennedy of Southern California-Arizona and Bishop Richard Raines of Indiana.[7]

From a theological viewpoint, the conflict was ecclesiological: a disagreement on the purpose of the church. Many well-meaning and institutionally loyal white Mississippi Conference Methodists saw Born of Conviction as an attack on their church, which they consciously and unconsciously understood as inextricably intertwined with the dominant culture. Thus a Jackson layman and lifelong Methodist told Sam Ashmore, "I love my church, but the action of some of our Ministers who apparently are trying to consolidate our church with politics, are taking my church away from me." In other words, the church should exist to confirm my unexamined assumptions about life in the world. But the Twenty-Eight knew the dualism between spiritual and political matters could not hold, and they offered a prophetic rejoinder. Reflecting on the controversy after his departure for Florida, Wilton Carter responded to the conference survey of its clergy exiles by exhorting the church to unite "for the cause of justice and mercy," which "will require her leaders ... to decide exactly what they expect the Church to be. My own wonder is, will the Church continue to be just a meeting place for 'good' people on Sunday, or will it serve as the mouthpiece of God?" A year later, Joe Way characterized Born of Conviction as "a voice in the wilderness which gave hope to many who were looking for some leadership in the time of darkness."[8]

The traditional, paternalistic, dualistic view of the church triumphed for the short term in the Mississippi Conference in 1963. Change eventually came to Mississippi Methodism, but the conference was exceedingly slow to recognize the value of Born of Conviction in that process.

Formal Recognition at Last

Shortly before ten o'clock on Sunday, June 9, the last day of the 2013 Mississippi Annual Conference session at the Convention Center in downtown Jackson, several hundred ministers and laypersons watched and listened to the Emma Elzy Award presentation. Given each year by the Conference Commission on Religion and Race, the award celebrates reconciliation by honoring persons who have contributed significantly to the improvement of race relations in Mississippi. On stage were eight signers of the Born of Conviction statement, along with Bishop James E. Swanson Sr., the first African American bishop assigned to any conference in Mississippi since the 1968 abolition of the segregated Central Jurisdiction, and the first black episcopal leader ever to preside over white Methodists in the state. Timothy Thompson, the bishop's administrative assistant (a clergy post) and also an African American, introduced the award recipients and characterized them as "bold individuals who took a stand when others could not, . . . when others would not." As their names were read aloud, a picture of each of the twenty-eight signers appeared on large screens in the hall, along with photos of J. P. Stafford, W. B. Selah, and Sam Ashmore. In addition to the eight signers present, seated down front were the wives of five of the signers on stage, plus the widows of four other signers. Another forty-five family members also attended, including twenty-five adult children of signers.[9]

This event commemorated three fiftieth anniversaries. The Twenty-Eight were nominated for the Elzy award to mark the fifty years since their witness. In addition, the conference invited Myrlie Evers to participate, and Bishop Swanson read a letter celebrating Medgar Evers's courageous leadership, because the coming week marked fifty years since his assassination. Mrs. Evers spoke to the gathering to express her thanks for the message of unity honoring her husband and his legacy, and then she posed for a photograph with the bishop, Thompson, and the eight Born of Conviction signers present (Figure 10.1). There was no mention

FIGURE 10.1 Emma Elzy Award presentation, June 9, 2013, left to right: Ed McRae, Rod Entrekin, Keith Tonkel, Ned Kellar, Bishop James E. Swanson, Myrlie Evers, Jack Troutman, Tim Thompson (bishop's assistant), Elton Brown (partially concealed), Maxie Dunnam, and Joe Way. Photo by Greg Campbell, courtesy of Mississippi Annual Conference, The United Methodist Church.

of the third anniversary: on this very morning in 1963, Galloway Church ushers turned away five Tougaloo students who sought to attend worship after they had been rebuffed at First Baptist, and Galloway pastors W. B. Selah and Jerry Furr resigned in protest.[10]

With only two-and-a-half days to complete all conference business, those who designed the award ceremony sought a balance between adequate commemoration of the occasion—celebration of both the Born of Conviction statement and the heroic leadership and vision of Mr. Evers—and the need to adjourn early that afternoon after completion of remaining agenda items. Thus two of the eight signers present, Maxie Dunnam and Keith Tonkel, were asked to accept the award for the Twenty-Eight. Dunnam spoke first and invoked words from the seventeenth-century Carmelite, Brother Lawrence: "God, you have outwitted me." Dunnam continued,

> Fifty years ago, some young men, now old men, signed a statement, and now this Annual Conference is saying "We appreciate that."

God outwits us. That's the story line of the Christian faith and
way: God continually outwits us. There've been times since that
occasion—many of us left the state—when I have been most, most
pleased with the faithfulness of people like Keith Tonkel who stayed
in the state, and there have been occasions when I have felt guilty
for having left and wondered what God was doing with that. But
God outwits us. When you think about the contribution that those
who left the state have made to the whole church, you know what
I mean when I say God outwits us. Two of those persons became
presidents of seminaries. Two of them became deans of seminaries; three of them became pastors of some of the largest churches
in the denomination. ... Others were not only in their General
Conference delegations, some of them led their delegations. God
outwits us.

At the end of his remarks, Dunnam expressed appreciation on behalf of
himself and Tonkel (Figure 10.2). The two shook hands with Mrs. Evers,
who had been standing behind them. After Mrs. Evers's speech and the

FIGURE 10.2 Maxie Dunnam speaks to the Mississippi Conference at the 2013
Emma Elzy Award Ceremony, with Keith Tonkel looking on. Photo by Greg
Campbell, courtesy of Mississippi Annual Conference, The United Methodist
Church.

photo, the conference sang "Blest Be the Tie that Binds" as the group left the stage.[11]

Signers and family members gathered in a nearby room, and a family member of one who stayed in Mississippi privately expressed anger and disappointment at the ceremony's lack of recognition of those who had remained in the state. Another such family member wrote, "And having one of the 28 who bailed out speak for the whole group was, I found, disrespectful of those who chose the more difficult path." Although Dunnam did briefly praise the signers who had stayed and offered the litany of accomplishments by those who had left as an example of triumph in the face of adversity through the power of God, the critics heard it as perpetuating the narrative that the Born of Conviction story centers on those who left the state.[12]

The conference had not intentionally slighted those who remained, and Tonkel had intended to speak briefly as their representative. However, he had recently undergone cancer treatments, and it remained uncertain until that morning whether he would even be able to attend. He chose not to speak because he felt the time pressure. The persons who planned the event could not know of the emotional minefield it would expose, and they were not responsible for the conference's lack of acknowledgment of the signers over the previous fifty years. This was the first time the Mississippi Conference had formally celebrated the 1963 Born of Conviction witness. Fifty years of pent-up feelings resulting from lack of recognition in Mississippi could not be put to rest with one thirty-minute ceremony, and the expressions of anger illustrate one of the central aspects of the Born of Conviction story: the experiential divide between the signers who left and those who stayed.[13]

Touchstone or Mosquito Nip? Divergence of Experience and Interpretation

In 2003, Jim Waits described his participation in the Born of Conviction statement as a "touchstone" for his ministry:

> Though it was a modest statement, it was that occasion when we knew that there was a reason for being a minister of the Gospel, and that there was a direct conflict between that and the ways of the world and the ways of society—and that was clear. What came out of that for me was . . . a sense that whatever you do in ministry and

whatever you do in the life of the church, it ought to go back and be tested by the scriptures and by theological perception.

This view resounded from other signers in 2004. James Nicholson said simply, "The most important thing I ever did was to sign that statement." Jerry Trigg called it "the defining moment of my ministry. ... My view of the ministry, my view of the church, my view of what my role is—it can [all] be defined by what we did there." In a 1963 letter to his former students among the Twenty-Eight, Candler professor Theodore Runyon predicted their participation would be "one of the most significant acts of your ministry."[14]

This interpretation of the experience is more prevalent among signers who left Mississippi. Compare John Ed Thomas's claim at the 2005 Born of Conviction reunion that his membership in the Twenty-Eight had become "like a mosquito nip" and "doesn't amount to anything now." He certainly valued the experience: "I'll always be proud of what I did, to take that kind of a stand. At that moment, I was so young, I didn't know whether it was courage or stupidity, but I sort of melded them together and put my name on the line and went forward, for what it was worth." But for him, it was not a touchstone; his proudest achievement was staying in the state "to serve the church here." The difference between those who left and those who stayed showed clearly at the reunion. With one exception, the eight Mississippi exiles at that event each took longer to tell their stories than the four present who stayed.[15]

For most of the ministers who left, Born of Conviction became the occasion for a new and exciting life in an environment much less confining than Mississippi; they benefited greatly from opportunities unavailable to them in their home state. Their new conferences not only recognized and valued their talents, but in most cases the embattled former Mississippians were celebrated as heroes for their January 1963 witness and given opportunities to tell their stories to sympathetic audiences. By contrast, Mississippi Methodists did not want to hear from the signers, at first because church members either remained angry or silent about the controversy, and later because it represented an embarrassment that they preferred to forget. Elsewhere, Born of Conviction was a hero story, and its participants were lauded and even lionized. In Mississippi, it soon became a "dangerous memory," something suppressed deep in the collective Methodist/United Methodist psyche and never acknowledged publicly.[16]

Thus the anger of family members and some of the signers who stayed is not only directed at those who left but is also an expression of long frustration at lack of recognition for their witness due to the collective burying of the story in Mississippi. The 1963 controversy was painful for all the signers, but those who stayed never spoke about their experience, for the most part. Clint Gill, close friend of both James Conner and N. A. Dickson, says that neither of them ever talked about Born of Conviction. In 2004 at Parkway Heights Church in Hattiesburg, Rod Entrekin told his story related to those 1963 events; it was the first time he had spoken of it in public in forty years. Keith Tonkel also had not talked about it; when the story made the news in 2005 related to the reunion of signers in Jackson, many members at Wells Church where he had served since 1969 learned about it for the first time.[17]

An Associated Press reporter in Jackson interviewed Tonkel for a story published the morning of the reunion, and she quoted his comments about having stayed when others left: "I said to them, 'I'm only signing this thing with the understanding we're committed to staying in Mississippi.' . . . How can you flesh out a conviction if you're absent? I thought our responsibility was to see what we can create that would be inclusive." Knowing that attendees had likely read the story, he began his remarks at the reunion with the claim that he had not sought the interview and the reporter had left out an important preamble that recognized the range of experiences: "Every single one of us in that group had to walk in their own integrity." Denson Napier avoided the reunion because he saw Born of Conviction as past history.[18]

The resentment comes as no surprise to some of the exiles. In 2004, Ed McRae commented, "It's true; I didn't have to leave Mississippi. I can understand that kind of judgment. You think of us as a group leaving—probably most of us wound up with a better life because we left. . . . It was almost like a stepping stone that we signed the statement. It was advantageous for my career." Inman Moore offered a similar view:

> I haven't so much heard it as I suspected that might be the feelings. The people that did stay, like Elton Brown and Rod Entrekin, they have never personally said it. And I've gone back to visit them. . . . But I think it's an understandable feeling. If I had been one, particularly that may have been dumped on and stayed and really felt the wrath of the powers that be, if I were in that position I might say,

"Well here I am, staying the course, and that Inman Moore is out in California basking in the sun."

In summary, those who left escaped the difficulties of Mississippi and got credit for their 1963 witness to boot, while those who remained in the state have only received kudos in recent years (some posthumously). The former left the state behind and proudly displayed the Born of Conviction badge of honor, while the latter kept their connection to Mississippi Methodism and in John Ed Thomas's words, put Born of Conviction behind them. Those who came from far away to the 2005 reunion did so partially to recover something they had lost, to relive a past struggle, and in some cases to deal with their own anger at a community that had rejected them, while those who came from within Mississippi struggled with different feelings. All had paid a price, but each individual story contained its own unique plot.[19]

Eight years later, as the group of signers and family members waited in the hall to go into the annual conference for the Elzy Award ceremony, a friend passed Margaret Thomas and congratulated her. She smiled and said with humor, "You know what John Ed would have said about this." In her view, Thomas did not think he deserved recognition for something he should have done anyway. In February 2006, I gave a lecture on Born of Conviction at Millsaps College to an audience of more than one hundred people, and Thomas, Elton Brown, and Rod Entrekin attended. When the lecture ended, I noted their presence, and they received a tremendous ovation. During the question period, Thomas said, "I appreciate your recognizing us, but there's a person here today who did a lot more than we did. Eddie King deserves our recognition." The audience then applauded Ed King, Mississippi civil rights movement leader and Thomas's Millsaps contemporary and ministerial colleague.[20]

When I interviewed Ed King a few months before talking with surviving signers who had left the state, he asked me to thank them for what they had done. This proved important to Ed and Martina McRae in California. He expressed some guilt at not being a good enough friend to King in the annual conference in the early 1960s, and she spoke of how she had been unwilling to put her body on the line as her Millsaps contemporary King and many others had done. They appreciated hearing of King's gratitude and his view that public words from white moderates played an important role in 1963 Mississippi. Given its particular time and context, Born of

Conviction played an important role in the larger ecology of myriad efforts to change race relations in the state (and more to the point, to change white attitudes toward blacks and their freedom struggle), and the signers deserved credit for that prophetic word. Yet the statement was only a first step on a long journey "to see what we can create that would be inclusive."[21]

Leading Mississippi Methodists toward a New Day

The Born of Conviction controversy came during the period of highest tension in civil rights era Mississippi, between 1962 and 1964. The community organizing, demonstrations, voter registration efforts, boycotts, influx of volunteers during Freedom Summer, and other work of the Mississippi movement all reached their peak during those years and played a crucial role in pushing white Mississippi and the US Congress toward significant changes. The white moderate call for gradualism in the 1950s and early 1960s was naïve; the needed radical campaign of the civil rights movement resulted in the rapid creation of the framework for a new societal structure in the mid-1960s: desegregation of all public facilities, voter registration for the vast majority of previously disenfranchised blacks, and eventual school desegregation.

It proved a difficult fight nonetheless. The Ku Klux Klan responded with intense violence: the 1964 Neshoba County murders, the 1966 killing of black civil rights leader Vernon Dahmer in Hattiesburg, other murders, and numerous bombings. White Mississippi political leaders still resisted, yet also cooperated to an extent and found ways to keep their power. The struggles also continued for Mississippi Methodism with the embarrassing publicity of the 1963–6 church visits campaign, demonstrations at the 1964 General Conference in Pittsburgh for an end to the church's segregated structure, the 1965 exodus of many MAMML sympathizers to the newly formed Association of Independent Methodists, the abolition of the Central Jurisdiction in 1968, and the eventual mandate for conference merger by the end of 1972.[22]

In the construction of this "new Mississippi," once the superstructure was in place, countless tasks remained to be completed bit by bit. Thus gradualism played a secondary role in the changes in Mississippi and the Deep South at that time. Ironically, although Bishop Marvin Franklin failed to lead the Mississippi Conference with courage during the Born of Conviction and church visits campaign controversies and could not understand the need for the radical actions of the movement, there was some truth in his words to the national Methodist press just before he retired: "The resident forces are the redemptive forces. It's going to take time." In 1965, Born of Conviction signer N. A. Dickson understood that a central role for whites and blacks alike involved making sure the changes mandated by new legislation would be implemented in their communities with a minimum of violence and conflict; it also involved learning to live together as partners across racial lines. As Mississippi Methodist minister Jack Loflin, who was not invited to sign the January 1963 manifesto, explained it forty years later, "What the church needed was not just someone to make a prophetic statement but [people] to get in the trenches and be examples to help the church deal with those issues on a daily basis."[23]

Many of the Twenty-Eight who left continued their witness for social justice in other places, and their stories, plus those of the ongoing efforts in Mississippi race relations by the eight who stayed, have already been told here. The signers who stayed had a great deal of company among Methodists—black and white, lay and clergy—in that struggle over the years following the 1963 controversy, and no account of the Born of Conviction story would be complete without some attention to the significant work "in the trenches" by Methodists to help create a new Mississippi from 1964 forward. This book has focused on ministerial leadership, so a few accounts of clergy experiences follow; they occasionally reveal aspects of laity experience. Countless more stories could be shared about other clergy and laity, black and white.

Clay Lee served as pastor at Quitman in the fall of 1962. Though invited, he chose not to sign Born of Conviction for several reasons. He did not think the statement was strong enough and later explained, "If you are going to say something and you know you're going to be crucified for it, make it stronger." He believed it would cause controversy, and his commitment to stay in Mississippi led him to pass on the opportunity and look for other ways to influence race relations change over time. He greatly respected those who did sign, including Elton Brown, whom he had known most of his life; Brown served as best man in Lee's early 1950s wedding.[24]

In the fall of 1963, W. J. Cunningham, newly arrived at Galloway as successor to W. B. Selah, asked Clay Lee to move there as copastor with him. Though Cunningham's vision of their professional relationship was sincere, Lee realized after he arrived that the pressures of ministry in the closed-door congregation prevented Cunningham from treating him as more than an associate pastor. On Easter Sunday 1964, when ushers refused to admit Bishop Charles Golden (black) and Bishop James K. Mathews (white) to worship at Galloway, church member Nat Rogers stopped Cunningham and Lee on the way to the sanctuary to ask the senior pastor what he should say to the bishops. As Cunningham tells the story in his 1980 book, he urged Rogers to admit the men to worship on his responsibility. When Rogers recoiled at this suggestion, Cunningham recalled turning to Lee for backup, but his associate walked away without response. In Cunningham's words, Lee told him the next day that "he thought the decision of the bishops' admission was mine and he should not become involved in it." Lee remembers the day differently, including Cunningham grabbing him in the hall to go speak with the bishops in the parking lot on the north end of the church building. Lee also recalls that Nat Rogers told the bishops he did not agree with the church's closed door policy. Bishop Mathews's published account says that he and Bishop Golden did not get to speak to the pastors.[25]

Feeling defeated by his seven-month tenure at Galloway, Lee requested a move in 1964. The cabinet sent him to a church with 750 members and a raise in salary. He was pleased with the appointment and looked forward to less tension than he and Cunningham had endured at Galloway. Thus in early June, Lee and his wife and five children moved from Jackson to First Church, Philadelphia, the Neshoba County seat. He later described it as going "from the frying pan to the skillet."[26]

Less than three weeks later on Sunday, June 21, while the new pastor prepared for the evening service in his church study, civil rights workers James Chaney, Andrew Goodman, and Mickey Schwerner were arrested just across the street, which set in motion what historian John Dittmer calls "the most depressingly familiar story of the Mississippi movement." They were executed that night south of town by Klan members and buried in an earthen dam in another part of the county. While the three were still missing, the white community publicly insisted it was a hoax perpetrated by movement leaders, but the FBI found their bodies in early August.[27]

Clay Lee later said, "I never have felt that my calling was to be one of the prophets that stood out front of a church and pushed the columns down," but he ruffled feathers in the community by supporting First Church member Florence Mars, longtime resident of the county who became a pariah because of her testimony to a federal grand jury in the case and her supportive relationships with the black community. In October 1964, he attended a Methodist Church meeting in Washington, D.C., where one of the speakers worked for the US Justice Department. Lee talked privately with the man afterward, because the speech had pricked his conscience, and the speaker recommended that Lee get in touch with the chief FBI investigator stationed in Neshoba, Joe Sullivan. Lee and his wife befriended Sullivan and his colleagues, also an unpopular thing to do. After months of investigation, on December 4 the FBI arrested nineteen men on federal charges of conspiracy to violate the civil rights of the murdered men.[28]

Everyone in the community had expected the arrests for weeks. As president of the small, all-white ministerial association in the area, Lee had convinced that group to write a statement in advance to be released when arrests were announced. They produced a brief declaration "as a matter of Christian conscience" that pledged to give "leadership to our community so that through this damaging and deteriorating experience of the past five months the results may be stronger character and deeper appreciation for those basic elements of democracy which have made our nation great." They expressed confidence that the leaders and citizens of the community would "respond to the present situation with respect to the cause of justice." Lee recorded the statement as soon as they wrote it, and the local radio station played it several times on December 4. Florence Mars saw it as strong and noted it was the first public acknowledgment of a "sense of shame and responsibility"— indeed, the first admission in the white community that a crime had been committed. Like the Born of Conviction statement, the wording may seem innocuous now, but in the climate of 1964 Neshoba County, these were important words.[29]

On Sunday, December 6, Lee preached a sermon entitled "Herod Was in Christmas" to his congregation, which that day included several out-of-state reporters. The "Herod spirit," he said, is "an evil resistant force which rises to destroy truth and love." It is "the spirit of bigotry," and the members of First Church and the citizens of Philadelphia would find no peace in Christmas while "the Herod spirit dwells among us." He did not mention the Klan but referred to "the events of the last five months." Over the next few months, he addressed the situation on several occasions in his preaching; his sermons were often reproduced and circulated, and according to Mars, "several people believed to be sympathetic with the Klan began to attend church more regularly to see what Clay was saying."[30]

When Bishop Edward Pendergrass first arrived in Mississippi in August 1964, he called Lee to say he was not just standing behind him—he was right beside him in this crisis in his ministry. Lee deeply appreciated the support. In 1966, he accepted an invitation to preach the baccalaureate service for the county high school, but the day before the service, he met with the school board because they had received threats that the school would be blown up if Lee preached. Before the meeting, he called the bishop for advice, and Pendergrass encouraged him to keep the engagement unless they cancelled the invitation. Thus he surprised the board by telling them he intended to preach for the service the next day, and they came to a stalemate—the board would not rescind the invitation, but they clearly did not want him to preach. Lee would not withdraw. They finally agreed that for the sake of the peace of the community, he would not preach, but they would say publicly that he had not withdrawn.[31]

Lee left Philadelphia in 1967 and served a number of other churches, including a twelve-year stint as senior pastor at Galloway, before he was elected a bishop in 1988. He retired in 1996, and in 2001, Bishop Kenneth Carder organized some events where his cabinet and other Mississippi Conference leaders visited civil rights movement sites in the state. The group went to Mt. Zion UMC, the African American church in Neshoba County that was burned by the Klan in June 1964 and that Chaney, Goodman, and Schwerner visited on that fateful Sunday, June 21. Bishop and Mrs. Lee, Ed King, and Florence Mars all attended this 2001 event; one of the speakers was Mabel Steele, the only surviving adult member of Mt. Zion who had been present for the church meeting on the night of the Klan fire. Various persons from the community attended, and one of them, John Steele, Mrs. Steele's son, had also been there that violent night. He asked to speak and said he recalled listening to the radio the morning the alleged conspirators were arrested and hearing a white minister say it was wrong "to shed innocent blood." The words had given the ten-year-old Steele hope in December 1964. He expressed regret that he had never gotten to meet that minister to thank him for his words. Bishop Carder said, "Well, now you have that chance. He's right here in the front row."[32]

Concluding his own telling of this story in 2003, Lee said, "There've been many times, not just in Philadelphia but in other places, where you wondered whether what you did was worth a plug nickel. You don't know. After thirty-seven years, I accidently found out that something makes a difference."[33]

Another Mississippi Conference minister who chose not to sign Born of Conviction was Wilson Brent (see Figure 7.2), who graduated from Asbury Theological Seminary in 1962 and took his first appointment that June at Kingston-Mars Hill, just south of Natchez. That fall, he met with other ministers to consider signing the statement. He agreed fully with the declaration but decided not to put his name on it because he had not yet dealt honestly with the race issue in his churches. That opportunity came in February 1963, when he said in his Race Relations Day sermon that he believed God expected love for all creation, including James Meredith. This caused no controversy at the Mars Hill Church, but at Kingston one angry member warned Brent that no one was indispensable.[34]

He moved to Wesley Church in Natchez in July 1963, and life for a Methodist preacher open to change proved difficult in that strife-torn city. Brent and his wife Charlotte suspected their phone was tapped, and he received anonymous death threats. Conflicts developed with Brent's church members over the race issue later in the year when he sought honestly to explore the implications for human relations of such biblical passages as "God is no respecter of persons" (Acts 10:34). After he discussed race in a couple of Sunday night sermons, in January 1965 three families threatened to leave the church if he mentioned the issue again. Things came to a head on Sunday evening, March 21, when during the service, church members grilled Brent concerning his beliefs on race relations. He sought to be honest with them, and the discussion got heated at times. The service lasted until 9:30 and ended with Brent inviting congregants to join him at the altar for prayer; many of those present did so. Though the discussion was difficult, he rejoiced at the result and wrote in his private journal that "God was greatly honored." A few days later, he talked at length with a man who had "allowed this race issue to rob him of his joy in Christ." Brent sought to help him come to a new understanding in light of his faith.[35]

Only one family left the church in the wake of that controversy, and Brent thought he would stay at Wesley another year. However, he learned at the 1965 Annual Conference that he was moving to Satartia. He spent a year there, followed by three years in Atlanta doing graduate work and serving as an associate pastor at a church where the climate proved much more open on the race issue. He returned to Mississippi in 1969 as pastor at Bonita in the Meridian area; he participated in several events where blacks and whites met to discuss improving relations and preserving the Meridian school system in the wake of more substantial desegregation resulting from the 1969 *Alexander v. Holmes* court decision. In 1971 he moved to Aldersgate, a growing congregation in North Jackson, and the church's ministry thrived for a couple of years. A conflict arose over the integration of the church-sponsored Boy Scout troop; the church's Board of Trustees voted to prohibit the black Boy Scouts' participation. Brent protested and brought the matter before the church's Administrative Board, where he argued that the church should keep its doors open to all. In spite of his strong statement, the board voted to support the trustees. Though he remained in the parish ministry a few more years, Brent was disillusioned by this defeat. He had found increasing satisfaction in counseling church members, and he eventually became a full-time pastoral counselor.[36]

Two of the Twenty-Eight—James Holston and James Nicholson—had younger brothers serving as Mississippi Conference pastors in 1962. Wilton Holston had concerns about some of the wording of the statement, and he chose not to sign. He remained in Mississippi as a pastor the rest of his career. Charles Warren "Nick" Nicholson (see Figure 6.3) was thirteen years younger than his brother James, and after graduation from seminary in 1961, he began his first appointment at Redwood, just north of Vicksburg. He came back ready to deal with the race issue, but he was not prepared for the intensity of resistance that had increased in Mississippi during his years in seminary.[37]

In December 1962, Nick Nicholson's brother James showed him a mimeographed copy of Born of Conviction. Nick read it and saw a list of those who had agreed to sign, and the two discussed it. The elder Nicholson did not ask his brother to sign, but the invitation was clearly implied. When the younger brother returned the piece of paper, James put it away and said no more. Though he agreed with the statement, Nick Nicholson had never been one to sign petitions. In the midst of the January 1963 controversy, he second-guessed his decision:

> I remember shedding some tears with [my wife] as I struggled in my own conscience. Am I rationalizing why I didn't sign it? Am I a coward? Or is this a better way for me to go? I never convinced myself I was a coward even though I questioned it, and emotionally it was tough, particularly when I saw [my brother] suffering because of it, and I didn't stand by him—I did stand by him, but I didn't sign with him.[38]

Nick Nicholson knew that integration was coming, and his goal was to help the Methodist people in whatever church he served face the changes in light of their faith. He knew transformation would be slow to come; he also knew that if the Methodist Church were to split, North and South, over this issue, he could not be part of a church that came into being to maintain segregation. He understood his role as a pastor or priest who would make it clear to his people where he stood on the race issue but would also stick with them to work on it. His brother had taken a different path: that of the prophet. In 2004, the younger Nicholson explained that the Twenty-Eight "were the ones who stood up, and without them it would have taken a lot longer. There is a need for the prophet, and if the prophet doesn't speak, you can sit in a hole forever. . . . Prophets pay a price." Priests play a different but still necessary role, in his view. They "stay in there and look after all the mundane things and look after the people, and I did my best to do that faithfully. My people knew where I stood and respected me for it."[39]

Playing the priestly role did not stop him from speaking when necessary. When he was pastor at Utica in 1964, one night after a meeting a church member confronted him about the liberal pronouncements of the national Methodist Church and the radical actions of Methodist ministers like Ed King, the Mississippi civil rights leader who had recently led protests at General Conference in Pittsburgh. Nicholson had lived in the same house with King at Millsaps College, and he refused to let his segregationist church member intimidate him. He recalls telling the man, "Eddie King has the right to demonstrate if he wants to." The other meeting attendees all left, and the argument continued until the church member's brother-in-law returned and asked if they planned to stay all night. The next day, Nicholson remembers, the brother-in-law came to see him and said, "Preacher, I just wanted to come by and tell you if you wanna go out there and whip that bunch, I'll help you." The memory arouses deep emotions in Nicholson: "He was telling me that I was right, and he was with me. And it gave me the courage to go on."[40]

In 1967, Nicholson moved to Burton Memorial Church in Gulfport, and in a sermon called "A Study in Black and White," he shared his own views on race and talked about the progress in race relations. It was a sermon he likely would not have preached in 1963, but change had begun. Nonetheless, some church members objected to the sermon and also did not want to use the Methodist Sunday School literature. He expressed his frustration with the ongoing racist attitudes to an older woman in the church, and years later he remembered her response: "Brother Charles, we've got to do some changing in the way we think." Staying in Mississippi to lead the Methodist Church in those years was difficult, but occasionally there were some "hallelujah moments." In 2004, Born of Conviction signer James Nicholson said, "I blew things out," and he described his brother as "one who was called to stay in Mississippi and build things up."[41]

Harmon Tillman's name appears on the list of potential signers drawn up by Born of Conviction's co-authors, but he was not asked to sign. A graduate of Millsaps College and Vanderbilt Divinity School, he returned to Mississippi in 1954 to serve a church while he also taught speech and coached debate at Millsaps; Jerry Trigg and Rose Cunningham were his star debaters in 1956. In 1962, he moved to Poplar Springs Drive Church in Meridian. There was a vocal minority in the church with ties to the virulently anti-Communist John Birch Society. In early 1964, the news of integrated groups seeking to worship at various white churches in Jackson disturbed the more conservative Poplar Springs Drive members, and they proposed to the Official Board that ushers (guards) be stationed at building entrances each Sunday and that the exterior doors should be locked once the service began, all in order to keep out "undesirables." Tillman opposed this and rallied enough lay support to prevent its passage. With the church in an uproar over the conflict, he preached a sermon explaining his views. He later summarized the sermon's argument: "I'm not trying to be a trouble maker, but this is the house of God, and we can't lock our doors. If there are people who want to integrate our services, seat them on the front row and let me preach to them. We can't say to anybody if they come that they're not welcome in our church to worship."[42]

The conflict continued through 1964, and the most vocal church members supporting Tillman paid a price, including Dr. Kinsman Ford, who suffered financially because of a concerted segregationist effort to boycott his dental practice. Other key supporters included Lawrence Rabb, Ivan Burnett, and George Warner, who assured Tillman of his support but said he did not want to stick his neck out for Tillman and then see his pastor leave the state. A faction in the church continued to oppose Tillman and sought—sometimes successfully—to cripple any aspect of the church's ministry that they saw as too liberal. Bishop Franklin offered to move Tillman in 1964, but he refused. However, he did inquire that same spring about transferring to Indiana, and Bishop Raines offered him an appointment but also told Tillman to stay if he thought he could do so. Tillman turned down the Indiana position and remained at Poplar Springs two more years.[43]

Bill Lowry and Rayford Woodrick both agreed to sign Born of Conviction, but their names were omitted. Lowry's experience at Pearl, when his Official Board praised him for not signing and he could not admit his true sympathies to them, caused him to feel he had failed as a minister of the Gospel. Like most white Methodist congregations in the state, Lowry's church resisted change and feared efforts to accomplish it. One Sunday morning in 1964 between Sunday School and worship, church members noticed a bus filled with black passengers pull up across the street. In Lowry's words, it "created absolute pandemonium—mothers running to gather up their children, men looking for something to defend the church with." The bus sat for a while, and finally someone walked across the street and discovered it was a church choir scheduled to sing at a black church in the area, but they were lost and needed directions. Several families had already gone home and missed the worship service.[44]

In such an atmosphere, Lowry says, pastors tried "to communicate strong convictions but [wrestled] with how to do that and yet at the same time not to cut off communication." They asked themselves, " 'How can I make a statement and not utterly destroy my ministry?' We had good people in our churches, good Christian people, but [most] had tunnel vision on this issue." A church member came to Lowry one day with a copy of a national Methodist magazine and angrily complained the cover picture showed an integrated choir. Lowry examined it and pointed out that the photo displayed the Council of Bishops of the Methodist Church. In the summer of 1964, Mississippi clergy exile Jim McCormick invited Lowry to come to Scottsdale, Arizona, to work as copastor at the new church McCormick had founded, and Lowry almost accepted the offer. Ultimately he decided his calling was to remain in Mississippi.[45]

In 1965, Lowry moved to Quitman and found church members there less consumed by the hysteria. However, conflict occasionally arose. One day blacks in the town picketed at the post office, and a crowd of whites gathered. Lowry and the town's white Baptist pastor went to the restaurant across the street, sat at a table in the window in clear view of those outside, and shared "a long cup of coffee." Their presence likely prevented white violence in response to the demonstration. The drama did not end there; a leader of the demonstration was the son of the Methodist church's long-time janitor. A group of church members pushed Lowry and the Official Board chair to call a special meeting to fire the janitor, but both men refused. By the time the regular board meeting occurred, cooler heads prevailed, and the matter was not mentioned.[46]

In 1969, Lowry moved to Hazlehurst, and within months, the *Alexander v. Holmes* court decision meant real desegregation in the schools there. A wealthy member of Lowry's church invested a large sum of money to develop the private Copiah Academy in Gallman, and white families fled the public schools in droves. Two church members approached Lowry and offered scholarships to send his children to the private school. Lowry thanked them but declined, even though his children would be in the minority in the public schools. Most church members respected the Lowrys' decision, though they disagreed. Barbara Lowry was one of two white teachers who taught at the formerly all-black school in Hazlehurst.[47]

The overarching theme of these stories is the difficult but partially successful effort to chip away at the petrified casing that protected the segregationist system in the 1960s. Critics rightfully insist that the systemic changes set in motion in those years have not led to complete justice for blacks, and race remains a difficult problem, not only for Mississippians, but also across the nation. However, many white pastors who stayed in the state in the 1960s and beyond deserve credit for their faithful attempts to lead their people toward the attitudinal changes necessary to face the new reality of a desegregating Mississippi.

For Mississippi Methodists, a major hurdle remained: how to accept and deal successfully with the dismantling of the segregated denominational structure. The 1968 union of Methodists with the Evangelical United Brethren to form the United Methodist Church played a significant role in the abolition of the Central Jurisdiction, and black and white annual conferences in the same geographical areas began the process of merger. The white Mississippi annual conferences took the longest to accept that reality, only approving merger with the black conferences in late 1972 as they faced a General Church deadline.[48]

Like societal desegregation in the state, the merger of black and white Methodists was accomplished only gradually. By 1970, the white and black Mississippi Conferences had begun working together in preparation for the merger. The story of Rayford Woodrick (see Figure 6.3), the other pastor who agreed to sign Born of Conviction but whose name was omitted and in his words "missed all the fun," and Bishop S. Thompson, a black Mississippi Methodist pastor, symbolizes the hope and difficulties of a new Mississippi Methodism. Typically, white and black Methodist pastors did not know each other, and the two met by chance at a 1965 parade in Forest, where Woodrick served Trinity Church and Thompson was at Lynch Chapel. They became close friends, and the Woodricks and Thompsons regularly visited each other's homes, though the Thompsons followed covert procedures when they came to the white neighborhood. At Thompson's invitation, Woodrick occasionally taught study courses and preached at Lynch Chapel. Woodrick could not reciprocate, but he did invite the black pastor to attend a Scott County Ministerial Association meeting at Trinity. The group was still all white, and thus Thompson's presence caused a stir. In the devotional Woodrick offered for the meeting, he pushed his colleagues a bit by reading them some excerpts from a sermon by Martin Luther King Jr. and then asking them to identify the preacher.[49]

The Thompsons took other risks. The initial desegregation in most Mississippi school districts involved "freedom-of-choice," where families could send their children to any school they chose; this resulted in only token desegregation and effectively continued white resistance. In January 1966, the Thompsons became the first black family to break the barrier in Forest; they sent two of their children to white schools. The Thompsons endured subtle and not so subtle persecutions. Their daughter Linda, a junior in high school suffered harassment, slurs, and ostracism from her classmates without a public complaint; she occasionally phoned Woodrick to vent her hurt feelings.[50]

Some of Woodrick's church members objected to their pastor's reputed role in the Thompson family's transgression of the color line. An opposition group met secretly to discuss possible responses: withholding contributions, boycotting worship, and removing Woodrick as pastor. Woodrick heard about these discussions because a black woman who worked in the home where the meetings were held relayed news to the Thompsons. Woodrick remembers Bishop Pendergrass told him, "I do not want people to get the idea they can run off Methodist preachers because of race. I want you to stay, but if you ever feel your life is in danger, let me know and we'll move you." Woodrick never felt that danger, and the situation improved enough that the church requested his return for another year. However, he decided to move.[51]

Woodrick and Thompson remained friends. The Woodricks moved to DeKalb in 1966 and occasionally drove across the state to Yazoo City to visit the Thompsons where they had moved. The two men were the first black and white pair of ministers to room together at a joint continuing education event for ministers in the black and white conferences in the early 1970s. Thompson was involved in the successful biracial efforts to ensure peaceful desegregation in Yazoo City, and as Woodrick remembers it, Thompson received threats from some radical blacks in the area as a result.[52]

In the years before the merger of the white and black conferences, the Central Jurisdiction ministers in Mississippi were more aware of what was happening in the white conference than vice versa. Henry Clay Jr., the black pastor who knew Maxie Dunnam in Gulfport, remembered in 2004 that his conference colleagues generally had two reactions to Born of Conviction: it was mainly affirming what the Methodist *Discipline* already said, so they did not see it as earthshaking. Yet, they were also concerned that the signers got such negative response and that so many of them left the state. Even in 1963, they expected the black and white conferences to merge eventually, and they did not want to lose sympathetic future colleagues.[53]

Some pastors in the Central Jurisdiction Mississippi Conference played roles in the Mississippi movement. In 1962, L. P. Ponder, pastor at St. John's Methodist in the Palmer Crossing community near Hattiesburg, opened his church to the movement and played a significant role in its development in that area. Victoria Gray, a key leader in the state movement, belonged to that church. Methodist pastor Clinton Collier became involved in the Neshoba County movement in 1964 and was known as "the most militant Negro in the county." A church he served in neighboring Kemper County was bombed in 1965.[54]

In July 1966, Henry Clay served as pastor of St. Paul Church in Laurel. His community involvement included membership in the local NAACP chapter and a vice-presidency of MCHR. After worship on Sunday evening, July 24, he and his wife and son tried to enter the Burger Chef, but a white man barred the door and insisted they go around to the side window where blacks had traditionally been served. The man did not own the restaurant nor work there, and since the passage of the 1964 Civil Rights Bill, the Clays had a confirmed legal right to use the main entrance. They reported the action to the police, and officers returned with them and insisted the man step aside. Clay remembers that as he walked to the counter, the man pointed at him and said, "Sambo, I'm gonna get you." Four nights later, a barrage of gunfire damaged the living room, kitchen, and office in Clay's parsonage; Effie Clay had been in the kitchen minutes prior to the shooting. The next day, as she cleaned up the broken glass, Klan leader Sam Bowers, a Laurel resident, pulled up outside the house and motioned for her to come out to the car. She declined, and he drove away. That fall, the Clays sent their third-grade son to a white school through freedom-of-choice; a few other black families in the neighborhood joined them.[55]

In 1967, Clay became a district superintendent in the black Mississippi Conference, and Allan Johnson, longtime NAACP member, followed him as pastor at St. Paul. During the height of the Klan terror campaign, the same parsonage was bombed just after midnight on November 15, 1967, causing massive structural damage. The white Jones County Ministerial Association, led by Methodist minister Wallace Mangum, "unanimously deplored" the bombing. Johnson responded to the attack by inviting Martin Luther King Jr. to speak at St. Paul, and King appeared there on March 19, 1968, just more than two weeks before his death.[56]

By 1973, these ministers and others in their conference became colleagues of the white Methodist ministers in South Mississippi through the merger of the two conferences; a similar merger took place in North Mississippi. Approving merger and then putting it into effect involved many difficulties, and though members of the black conferences celebrated this step, they remained concerned about being absorbed and then devalued in the new majority white conferences. As the former Central Jurisdiction Mississippi Conference said in a 1973 statement to the merged Mississippi Conference, "Merely declaring ourselves as one does not make it a reality." They worried that they no longer controlled their appointments and other aspects of their collaborative ministry, but they said, "We are conscious that through creative and meaningful participation our loss can become a real gain. We are, therefore, willing to lose ourselves in the larger structure, hopeful that through this process we may become stronger, not Black Methodist nor Black Christians, but Methodist and Christians."[57]

The conference kept a commitment to appoint at least one black district superintendent, and Henry Clay filled that role in the East Jackson District from 1980 to 1986. Wendell Taylor, a black pastor who served at Jackson's Central Church for many years and a leader in the Central Jurisdiction conference, continued in the years after the merger to remind the Mississippi Conference of its commitment to take the black churches seriously and to honor the legacy of the black conference, so that it would not simply be swallowed up and forgotten.[58]

When the Twenty-Eight published Born of Conviction on January 2, 1963, they could not foresee the extent of the controversy it would cause and the impending departure of so many of them from the Mississippi Conference. Those who remained in the state joined with many other Methodists, black and white, to refashion Mississippi Methodism into a church free from the fear and severe restrictions of the Closed Society. Much had changed for the better by the time of the 1973 mergers of the white and black conferences in Mississippi, yet much remained to be done. The spirit of the manifesto and the work of so many Methodists to improve race relations continue, through the legacies of Born of Conviction.

Legacies of Born of Conviction

The Christian ministry will always be in crisis.
Sociologists and historians can explain part of the crisis,
but the rest is inherent in the very soul of the Christian
tradition.

—E. BROOKS HOLIFIELD, *God's Ambassadors*, 2007

ANY SET OF events that clusters to form a story soon garners a wealth of interpretive understandings and seems to mean something different to each person who hears or reads it. The same is true of the ongoing legacies of such stories, and Born of Conviction is no exception.

Aside from his remarks celebrating the achievements of signers who left Mississippi and briefly praising the signers who had stayed, Maxie Dunnam had a bit more to say when he accepted the Emma Elzy Award for the Twenty-Eight at the Mississippi Conference event on June 9, 2013. He noted that though there has been progress since, the issues addressed by Born of Conviction in 1963 are "still with us." Referring to the statement's opposition to communism, he remembered that "people were trying to divert us from the central issues by accusing us of something else" and asserted that the tactic is still used. For instance, Pope Francis gets accused of being a socialist because of his advocacy for the poor, yet "unless we care for the poor we're not going to be representing the Kingdom cause that we pretend to represent." In Dunnam's view, equal access to public education remains a central justice issue, and he connected these ongoing causes with the legacy of Born of Conviction:

> My prayer is that . . . fifty years from now, maybe, an annual conference then will look back, and some of you will have taken a stand on behalf of those for whom God has extended preferential treatment, that is, the poor, and some of you will have taken a stand

on welcoming the stranger in our midst around the occasion of immigration, and some of you will see to it that we don't allow the zip code of a child to determine the kind of education that child gets [applause].[1]

The legacies of the white Methodist ministers' manifesto more than fifty years later include key changes in Mississippi Methodism, some stories of repentance and reconciliation, and consideration of the difficulties related to remembering the 1963 controversy. The statement has influenced subsequent generations of ministers, while pride and unresolved feelings persist among children of signers. The meaning of Born of Conviction was contested in late 2013 and early 2014 when a United Methodist leader invoked it as a symbol in a current church conflict. Finally, the church—clergy and laity alike—continues to struggle with its relationship to the world and with race relations as it seeks to understand and respond to Christ's ongoing invitation to follow him.

Ecclesial Repentance and Reconciliation

Bennie Holston, widow of signer James Holston, had doubts about coming to the 2013 Emma Elzy Award ceremony in Jackson: she feared the experience would aggravate old wounds. But she made the trip from Oklahoma, where she had lived since June 1963; her three adult children joined her. Her older daughter describes the family's reaction to the event:

> The pride in Dad's participation in Born of Conviction was always front and center for us, but the pain of the situation in Mississippi [and] leaving our family and friends was awful. However, standing in a room full of black and white Mississippi Methodists singing "Blest Be the Tie That Binds" was the perfect balm to assuage whatever scars still lingered from 1963. It made us realize that while Born of Conviction was a baby step in reaching the level of "WE" that exists in the Mississippi Conference today, it nevertheless helped jump start the process.[2]

The conference has changed a great deal since 1963. It includes black churches, white churches, Native American churches, Hispanic churches, along with several multiethnic congregations. The Conference United

Methodist Women's and Men's organizations are fully integrated and have had black presidents. Two African Americans have served as Mississippi Conference Lay Leader in recent years, and in 2012, the conference welcomed Bishop James E. Swanson, an African American, as their new episcopal leader. He followed a woman, Bishop Hope Morgan Ward, who led the body from 2004 to 2012. Every four years, the conference elects delegations to the General and the Jurisdictional Conference that represent the full range of its members. No one claims Mississippi United Methodists have solved all their problems in race relations, but Bishop Kenneth Carder, who led the conference from 2000 to 2004, insisted in 2003 that Mississippi was then ahead of most annual conferences in dealing with the issue because it was "moving beyond inclusiveness to reconciliation."[3]

The legacy of Born of Conviction includes changes in Mississippi United Methodism since 1963, but the unfinished transformation has taken a long time and has proven difficult. All the anger expressed and the pain experienced by church members, signers, family members, and others left enduring wounds, but some churches and individuals found ways to foster a healing process. A few years after they left Neshoba County for California, James and Libby Rush were invited back to the Philadelphia Circuit for a worship service in which they were received warmly with apologies from those present. When Rush transferred to South Carolina in 1968, he served under Bishop Paul Hardin, best known as one of the eight white religious leaders in Alabama whose 1963 public statement evoked Martin Luther King Jr.'s "Letter from Birmingham Jail." In the early 1970s in South Carolina, the bishop was upset at Rush's participation in the evangelical Good News Movement (sometimes critical of United Methodist leaders) and asked Rush to come see him at his office. During the meeting, Hardin wondered aloud why people could not simply support the United Methodist Church as an alma mater. Rush remembers replying, "Bishop, it's strange you should bring that up because when I took a stand on the Social Principles of our 'old mother,' I got kicked out of [Mississippi]. And nobody in the Southeastern Jurisdiction, including you, would touch us [the Twenty-Eight] with a ten foot pole." Hardin responded with emotion, "You know, you're right. Let me get down here on my knees and let us pray. I want to ask God's forgiveness for that."[4]

Several years after James Conner's 1965 departure from Hawkins Church in Vicksburg due to his involvement in MCHR, he returned there for a church event. A leader in the congregation came in tears to

Conner, confessed he had instigated Conner's removal, and apologized. The Soule's Chapel Church, where Joe Way endured ostracism and rejection from many church members in 1963, eventually declined and closed in 1989. In an early 1980s conversation with District Superintendent Bob Matheny, a leader of the congregation expressed sorrow for their treatment of Way and said he wished they had Way back as their pastor. Ed McRae accepted an invitation to Oakland Heights in Meridian to preach for the church's twenty-fifth anniversary celebration on April 29, 1984. During the event, he recalls, a woman who led the opposition against him in 1963 told him, "Ed, you were right, and we were wrong. We're sorry for what we did."[5]

There is no record of Bishop Franklin, Willard Leggett, or Tom Prewitt ever apologizing to anyone in the Twenty-Eight for opposing or failing to support them, nor did Charles Duke retract his 1963 segregationist sermon against Born of Conviction. However, Tom Prewitt retired in the 1960s and in later years regularly attended Wells Church in Jackson, where signer Keith Tonkel served as pastor and the congregation became interracial. Like other conservative conference leaders who remained active in the 1970s, Leggett and Duke eventually accepted the newly merged arrangement and adjusted their sense of what was good for Mississippi United Methodism to include the African American churches and their leaders. Duke served as administrative assistant to Bishops Mack Stokes and C. P. Minnick in the late 1970s and early 1980s, and Minnick remembers Duke as supportive of the conference's black churches. In Minnick's view, Duke often worked to reconcile opposing factions for the good of the church and sincerely sought to ensure that the conference might move away from its racist past.[6]

At a worship service during the 1983 Mississippi Conference session, visiting preacher Bishop William Boyd Grove of West Virginia called for inclusiveness and justice everywhere in the church. He closed the sermon by asking participants to hold hands in a large circle around the Galloway Church sanctuary, and the congregation, which included Willard Leggett, Charles Duke, black District Superintendent Henry Clay, and many other white and black Mississippi United Methodists, sang "We Shall Overcome." Two years earlier, John Satterfield, a leading lay voice for the maintenance of segregated Methodism in the 1960s, came to see Bishop Minnick at his office. Suffering from terminal cancer, Satterfield confessed to Minnick that though he had fought integration then, he had become convinced that he was wrong, because integration was working and would succeed because of the efforts of church people and other Mississippians. A few weeks later, Satterfield died of a self-inflicted gunshot wound.[7]

In recent years, some church bodies in Mississippi and surrounding states have attempted to repent of past sins in public ways. Galloway UMC in Jackson eventually welcomed Bishop Charles Golden (black) and Bishop James K. Mathews (white) to worship after they had been turned away on Easter Sunday 1964. On November 13, 2005, Mathews preached there, and the service involved congregational repentance for past sins and affirmation of the movement of God's grace, "even as we acknowledge the slowness with which we often allow it to shape our hearts and minds." Earlier that year, North Alabama United Methodists participated in a symbolic service "to demonstrate their repentance for past support of segregation in their state." On March 22, 2014, Second Presbyterian Church in Memphis commemorated the fiftieth anniversary of the day they turned away a pair of college students—one black and one white—from their worship service. That Sunday in 1964 marked the first of many occasions over the next year when integrated groups sought unsuccessfully to attend worship there in the Memphis Kneel-in Campaign. The 2014 event included an account of the kneel-ins by religious historian Stephen Haynes as well as remarks from Jim Bullock, the white student turned away fifty years earlier, and Carolyn Purdy, sister of Joe Purdy, the black student turned away.[8]

These efforts by whites who repent and seek racial reconciliation also require deeper consideration of issues of white privilege and the ongoing realities of race for blacks in the United States. Just as Dietrich Bonhoeffer spoke of the inadequacy of "cheap grace," so also superficial reconciliation will not suffice. Terrance Roberts, one of the nine black students who integrated Little Rock's Central High in 1957, observed in 2009,

> I would simply remind those who speak [of reconciliation] that to be reconciled there must have been some friendship or harmony then in existence that can now be restored. Perhaps it would be more fruitful to talk about how we can confront the past and learn from it, and in so doing begin to build a future devoid of those structures created to place white people at the top of some mythical racial hierarchy.[9]

Meaningful ritual acts of repentance depend on truthful stories of related past events. Though some who lived through the 1960s as adults know intellectually that the stories must be told, they are also reluctant to revisit those memories. Nick Nicholson, Born of Conviction signer James Nicholson's younger brother and a pastor in the conference beginning in 1961, reflected on this ambivalence in 2004:

> History has a way of casting light on events of the past and many times in enlightening ways that you couldn't see at the time because there was too much confusion; you need to go back and see it. What I'm saying is I hate to see all this dug up again, but at the same time I commend you for doing it because I think there's a place for it. I do rejoice when I see how much better things are now than they were.[10]

There is a difference in perspective between generations on efforts to consider past white Methodist sins in Mississippi. Some Baby Boomers who grew up in Mississippi Methodism long to hear and reflect on the full story. Rebecca Brent, daughter of Wilson Brent, another conference pastor from those years, wants "to fully understand the times I grew up in and the influences on my parents that had a big impact on my life." Mississippi Conference clergyman Jim Matheny, son of conference pastor Bob Matheny and grandson of J. P. Stafford (conference lay leader in the early 1960s and public supporter of the Twenty-Eight), believes his generation desires passionately to understand what it all means.[11]

As some in the state prepared to commemorate the fiftieth anniversary of Freedom Summer in 2014, Mississippi author Ellen Ann Fentress reflected on this phenomenon: "I'm a member of the cohort of Southerners in our fifties and sixties from once-notorious places. A number of us are drawn to returning to our hometowns' unsavory truths, their discussion no longer off-limits after 50 years. Yes, it has taken this long." The point for Baby Boomers, she says, is "to understand the people and culture to which we were hazy witnesses. Whether the adults spoke a word about the struggle or not—most especially if no words were uttered in the tense, dissolving assumptions of our childhoods—we absorbed the atmosphere. Our communities' parameters contoured our hearts and heads." Most who were adults—black and white—in those years, she says, kept silent about the difficult stories. In addition to the collective forgetting of the Born of Conviction story in Mississippi United Methodism since the 1960s, Jim Matheny offers another white Methodist example: when his father returned from Indiana to serve as pastor of Capitol Street Church in 1967, memories of turning away integrated groups at the steps of that church from 1963 to 1966 had already become repressed "deeply in the collective psyche." That painful recent history went unmentioned.[12]

Thus an important part of Born of Conviction's legacy centers on its meaning for subsequent generations of Mississippi United Methodist leaders, clergy and lay. The evidence for that phenomenon remains incomplete, because the story of the Twenty-Eight has only been told more widely in the last few years, but here is one glimpse.

Baptism at Caswell Springs

On November 26, 1962, Christopher Oris Cumbest was born to Maxine and Oris Cumbest, residents of the Cumbest Bluff area of northern Jackson County. Their church, Caswell Springs Methodist, welcomed Chris, the Cumbests' third child. The pastor, Jerry Trigg, co-authored and signed the Born of Conviction statement, which appeared in early January 1963, and though many church members did not protest, a group of eighty publicly disagreed with Trigg. In the early spring while the congregational conflict persisted, the Cumbests chose to present Chris for baptism—the only one of their four children baptized as an infant. Decades later, when Chris Cumbest had been a pastor in the Mississippi Conference for almost twenty years, his father confirmed what he had come to suspect: his parents had chosen infant baptism for him in order to show public support for Jerry Trigg and his witness.[13]

Trigg's impact on the Cumbest family continued long after he left that church in June 1963. Oris Cumbest began serving on the local school board around that time and with his quiet influence helped ensure the peaceful integration of the Jackson County schools. When Chris started school in 1968, he rode the first integrated school bus in the county with his two older siblings. Stories of the cross burned in Trigg's parsonage yard and of the Trigg family leaving town one night for their safety (escorted by Oris Cumbest and others) were part of the family lore as Chris grew up, and all the Cumbest children understood the ongoing importance of Trigg's ministry and example to their parents. The children also heard an account of an older family member (a law enforcement officer) confronting some blacks caught swimming in a creek location understood as reserved for whites, and they learned their father had taken a rifle out of the relative's hand to diffuse the situation.[14]

A little more than a year after his 1980 graduation from high school, Chris Cumbest married Sheila Rayburn and began working as a chemical operator at a nearby Morton-Thiokol plant. Early in October 1981, he attended the annual Salem Camp Meeting a few miles north of Cumbest Bluff. The preacher was Wallace Roberts, Director of Mississippi United Methodism's radio and television ministry, *The United Methodist Hour* (and unbeknownst to Cumbest, a member of the Twenty-Eight). At the end of his sermon, Roberts issued an altar call and included a specific invitation to anyone who felt led to pursue full-time Christian service. Cumbest responded and told Roberts he thought he might be called to the ministry but awaited some kind of sign from God. Roberts assured him that if he sought such a sign that strongly, he had already received it.[15]

Soon after, he told his parents he planned to quit his job and return to school to become an ordained minister. His father asked if he was sure he could not do anything else, and Chris took offense at first. His father explained, "If you can't do anything else, then it must be God calling, and he will sustain you through it, no matter what comes." He remembers his father then repeated some Jerry Trigg stories as part of their discussion. In the summer of 1983, Chris and Sheila Cumbest moved to a trailer park in Wiggins so he could attend a nearby junior college while she worked. Born of Conviction signer Elton Brown was pastor at Wiggins UMC, and he served as a mentor to the Cumbests. Brown may have mentioned his experience with the Twenty-Eight, but if so, it did not mean much to Cumbest at the time. Later as a student at the University of Southern Mississippi, he interviewed Brown for a sociology paper, and the veteran pastor spoke of ministers who had left and the tough times of the 1960s.[16]

Both the Cumbests finished college and Duke Divinity School, and he was ordained an elder while she became a diaconal minister and eventually a permanent deacon in the conference. In 2001, they were both appointed to Alta Woods UMC in South Jackson. That area of the city had transitioned in the 1990s from predominantly white to predominantly black. As senior pastor, Chris Cumbest saw that though the congregation still understood itself as white, the surrounding community presented many new opportunities for ministry. The staff reached out to the children of the neighborhood, welcomed them to the church's gym, and invited them to the youth group. Some church members protested, but Cumbest pointed out to them that because they built the gym decades earlier as a safe place for kids, then nothing had really changed except the skin color of the kids. The congregation got on board, and in 2004, a black associate pastor,

Eddie Spencer, joined Chris Cumbest in ministry there. The church also started a Sunday morning homeless ministry, called "Gravy and Grace." In January 2006, the Cumbests moved home to Jackson County for him to serve as Coordinator of Church Recovery as the Seashore District worked to overcome the devastation of Hurricane Katrina.[17]

When the reunion of signers and my research on Born of Conviction were publicized in the conference in 2005, Chris Cumbest saw a copy of the statement for the first time. He marveled at how many of the Twenty-Eight had influenced his life. In addition to his connections with Trigg, Roberts, and Brown, in his younger years he had heard Keith Tonkel preach revivals at Caswell Springs, and he knew Wilton Carter's family. Cumbest had worked as a colleague in the conference with Brown, Tonkel, James Conner, N. A. Dickson, Rod Entrekin, Denson Napier, and John Ed Thomas. He knew a few other signers as well, and once he learned of their participation in the statement, he connected in some way with all who were still living to thank them for their witness. In 2006, in a letter to Jerry Trigg, he wrote,

> Know that the times that may have been the hardest for you and your family have been used by God to call others into Kingdom work. Know that as long as I live the story of your witness in a small, somewhat insignificant, community in South Mississippi will always bear witness for the cause of Christ. Please know that I am eternally grateful for you allowing God to use your hands and witness that my life may be distinctly marked by God's grace and call.

A few hours after the 2013 Elzy Award presentation to the signers, Cumbest announced on Facebook that he carries a copy of the Born of Conviction statement with him as an important symbol for his ministry in Mississippi. Conference member Lisa Garvin said she also carried it with her, and another pastor, Rick Brooks, affirmed the idea and said he would do so, too.[18]

Dramatizing Family Experience

When James Holston moved from Mendenhall to Carthage in June 1962, the town and the Methodist Church there welcomed him and his family warmly. His oldest child, Debby, had just turned fifteen, and years later she remembered that for her and her younger sister and brother, their time in Carthage in 1962 was "the happiest six months of our growing up." That came to an end abruptly in early January. While out with some friends one afternoon with the car radio playing Fats Domino's rendition of "Blueberry Hill," she heard the local station interrupt the song with a news bulletin about the Born of Conviction statement. The announcer noted her father's participation, which made the report of more local interest to Carthage citizens. She had already sensed something brewing among her father and his like-minded Methodist clergy friends, but this was her first knowledge of the statement and her father's membership in the Twenty-Eight.[19]

Thus began a difficult time for her and her siblings. Her brother, a sixth grader at the time, endured a beating from some classmates at school. The Holston children do not remember any of their real friends or their families treating them any differently, but they were painfully aware of the ostracism their parents suffered. They also knew that their paternal grandparents strongly supported their dad, but their maternal grandfather did not. Though James Holston was, in his mother-in-law's view, like a son to them, his father-in-law refused to speak to him for several months after the statement appeared. That rejection had softened considerably by the time the Holston family left for Oklahoma in June 1963.[20]

Unlike the majority of children of the Twenty-Eight, Debby Holston was old enough to reflect deeply on her family's experience at the time. She had a strong sense of shared responsibility with her parents as the pastoral family in the Carthage church. James "Jimmy" Nicholson II, signer James Nicholson's oldest child (and the same age as Debby Holston), had a similar experience. When his father decided to preach the fateful October 1962 sermon at Byram in response to the Ole Miss riot, the elder Nicholson called his three children together and told them he was about to alienate himself from the congregation and community by preaching some unpopular things. He warned this would cause them problems. Decades later, the oldest son remembered responding as a good preacher's son would: "Dad, you've got to do what you've got to do. We're your kids, and we have to do what you believe." On the Sunday his father preached the offending sermon, the son sat in the choir and watched with horror as the expressions on the faces of many congregants turned angry. Outside after the service, he heard some men conspiring to retaliate against his father, and like most teenaged boys, his first inclination was to lash out at them. He refrained, because he was "a good preacher's kid."[21]

James Nicholson's warning of consequences proved true for his eldest child. Jimmy Nicholson, then a sophomore in high school, had joined the school's football team and played as a substitute lineman in every game prior to the offending sermon, but afterward, the coach kept him on the bench for the rest of the season, including the final game when every other player saw action. At school he was ostracized in the lunch room by football players he had thought were his friends, and he usually sat by himself. In the hall between classes, people harassed him, and after one incident, he appealed to the principal, who stood nearby. The man insisted he had seen nothing and that Jimmy Nicholson would have to take care of himself. Nicholson remembered that on a few occasions one football player stood up for him by telling the tormenters, "Hey! That's his daddy, not him."[22]

Jimmy Nicholson also remembered seeing an anonymous critical letter his father received after the publication of Born of Conviction, and when he mentioned it, his father said he should not be reading mail not addressed to him. The son insisted, "Dad, we're going through this together." That convinced his parents to let him read the letters, and he was gratified to learn that many were supportive. Several children of other signers did not share Nicholson's experience of the controversy because their parents did not talk to them about it much, if at all. David Conner, age twelve in January 1963 and the oldest of James and Betty Conner's four children, remembers that he stayed home from church due to illness the Sunday after the statement came out, and when the family returned home, his brother Tommy was upset and told him their father had signed a statement and everyone at the church was angry about it. The central shared memory of all three Conner sons comes from a January Sunday night after church services when they were home watching "Bonanza." The phone rang, and ten-year-old Tommy answered. The caller asked if his father was the preacher who signed that statement, and Tommy turned the phone over to his mother. The man told her that their parsonage would be dynamited that evening. Naturally concerned, the family spent the night at the home of some supportive church members. The threat of destruction proved false, but due to their absence from home that evening, the Conners' third son, John, made it to school that Monday morning without completing an important homework assignment. He had a valid excuse but did not feel free to use it, nor did he think his teacher would believe it. He endured her reproval in front of his classmates in teary silence.[23]

In 2004, David Conner regretted that he had never talked with his father, who died in 1988, about Born of Conviction. He suggested that his parents' reticence about that crisis "deprived us of the ability to work as a team." His mother learned of this later that year and eventually requested that each of her children receive a copy of both her taped interview for this book and the transcription of it. Rod and Ginny Entrekin's son David also reflected in 2009 that until recent years, his parents had not talked at all about their 1963 experience. Cathy Hall Shelton, daughter of signer Powell Hall, wished in later years that her father had said more to his five children to interpret his 1963 stand and the family's subsequent insistence on staying in the public schools after desegregation. Dolores Carter, signer Wilton Carter's wife in 1963, admitted in 2009 that she had only recently related the Born of Conviction story to her three children for the first time. The oldest was only an infant during the controversy, and the others were born after the Carters had moved to Florida. She told her adult children she was proud of their father's 1963 witness and her part in it.[24]

Elton and Juliette Brown's three daughters had a different experience. The oldest, Thais Tonore, nine years old in early 1963, remembers their parents gathering them together and saying, "Your daddy has signed a statement that says God created all men equal, and there are people who don't agree with that. We believe all people can worship God together, whether they are black or white. This may make some people mad around here, but we are fine, and we think this is what we're supposed to do."[25]

Many children of signers have unresolved feelings of pain and anger as well as pride surrounding their family experiences. A few have sought to deal with these emotions by writing memoirs or poems ranging from a few words to more than one hundred pages. Jacqueline Hall-Williams, Powell and Julia Hall's youngest child, wrote a poem to capture something of her sense even as a small child that her family was different and not accepted by the communities in which they lived; they moved seven times between 1962 and 1970 and endured the added stigma resulting from their remaining in the Yazoo County public schools. She understood as a young elementary schooler that what their father taught them—"that intelligence and correct reading of the Bible would eventually triumph"— was a truly dangerous idea in Mississippi. She consoled herself in those years with the conviction that her family's "redeeming value was our belief in civil rights," but her poetic effort also stemmed, in her words, from "the hope and the foolishness and the deep disappointment and sadness of many of us who were left as unintentional and unidentified wounded by the road to civil rights."[26]

The Halls' fourth child, Edwin, has worked on a memoir that offers profound theological, psychological, and prophetic insight into his own experience in the wake of "the twenty-eight paper" (as the Hall children called it). He became keenly aware of the fences that human beings build to separate themselves from people they deem as inferior. Outcasts remain on the wrong side of those fences, excluded by a "Domination System" that perpetuates the fence building. Edwin Hall says, "The twenty-eight paper made me into a person who can see fences that other people can't see, and a person who can't bear to be on the right side of them." In his view, Jesus was "the most insightful critic of the Domination System." In the ongoing spirit of efforts like the civil rights movement, Hall asks, "What kind of healing will be possible, once we do find a way to let all those fences down?"[27]

Kathryn Dickinson was not yet three when her father Buford signed Born of Conviction, and the family left the state before her fourth birthday. As she grew up in California, her family kept close ties with fellow Mississippi exiles the Dunnams, as well as David and Margaret McKeithen, Maxie Dunnam's mentors in Richton who left the Mississippi Conference in 1963. As an adult she has pursued a career in professional theater, and years after her father's 1985 death, she wrote a play, *Born of Conviction*, based on her family's Mississippi experience. It premiered at a Brooklyn theater in October 2010.[28]

The action rotates between 1960s Mississippi and a present day urban setting, with the main character, Kelly, appearing as a little girl in the former and as an adult single mother in her early forties in the latter. Some of the characters, including Kelly's father, Buford, "weave in and out of space and time." The 1960s action centers on Buford, a Mississippi Methodist preacher, his wife and two children, and his parents, and the story of their experiences as he signs the manifesto and deals with the reactions of his church and local community. The present-day action centers on adult Kelly's life with her boyfriend, Simon, and her fifteen-year-old daughter, as well as her struggle to deal with memories of her family's past. Dickinson employs language from James Silver's *Mississippi: The Closed Society* as well as the Born of Conviction statement in the play. She also uses the letter her real-life grandparents' pastor wrote condemning the Twenty-Eight, and he appears as a character in one scene.[29]

The other documents she uses are a tract entitled "The Kiss of Death" and an accompanying letter received by her father and the other twenty-seven signers in an anonymous communication postmarked in Memphis in January 1963. The tract is a typical "scientific" racist warning about the dangers of mingling "white blood" (which represents "more civilization," "science," and "creative intelligence") with "colored" ("back to the jungle forever"). It claims that "segregation is the law of God, not man" and that "Negro blood destroyed the civilizations of Egypt, India … It will destroy America!" It includes a drawing of a white woman kissing an apelike dark-skinned man (i.e., "the kiss of death"). The letter suggests to the recipients that "if you still believe as you have stated why not (if you have lovely young daughter [sic]) send her to a Negro school and demand that she be seated between to [sic] Negro boys her age. … The Kiss of Death will be your reward." Dickinson was both fascinated and repelled by the blatant racism of these documents her father had saved.[30]

In the play, adult Kelly struggles with her memories of the family's 1960s experience and also wrestles with how her experience of race affects her relationship with Simon, her fiancé, who is African American. The relationship is complicated by her concern that she is not setting a good example for her daughter, and she asks his cooperation in hiding their sexual relationship. These circumstances enable the couple and Kelly's daughter to talk about racial history in American society. Simon clearly loves Kelly, and near the end of the play he is overjoyed to learn she is pregnant with their child. Her ambivalence dissipates, and she commits fully to him.[31]

Dickinson's play reveals the absurdity of the "Kiss of Death" perspective, but it also grapples with Buford and his wife Mary's decision to leave Mississippi, as well as adult Kelly's main questions: "Can I bury those bones of Mississippi? Let my dad rest in peace?" In a climactic scene, the adult Kelly angrily asks her dead father (who has appeared to her) to explain why he left Mississippi, especially because he taught her about "conviction." He responds by relating a real-life incident from the Dickinson family, when they heard a five-year-old friend of Tim Dickinson's (Kathryn's older brother; his character is named Scott in the play) tell him that "if we don't watch out, them niggers are going to think they's just as good as we are." Kelly's father explains, "And it was then we said goodbye. We were dealing with the fear, but we just couldn't take you learning the hate. Then, Kelly, it was time for us to go."[32]

Dickinson's work of art has allowed her to explore her pride in her father's brave witness in Mississippi, her conflicted feelings about the family's departure to California, and her grief at her father's untimely death. Although many other children of signers suffered in 1963 and subsequent years and still deal with unresolved feelings from the whole experience, they have also expressed great pride in their fathers' (and mothers') witness. Elton and Juliette Brown's daughters each claimed their father's participation was true to his character: "It's always been 'Daddy does the right thing.' That's what we came to expect." "His signing that was just who they are." "I'm proud he did it; the Dad I know would do that." In a similar vein in 2009, Denson Napier's daughter, Sandra Dyess, said, "I am very proud; ... I feel very fortunate to have been reared the way I was to embrace differences ..., and Daddy's always been like that." In Deb Selden's words, James Holston's children

> agree that Dad's courage and Mom's unyielding support of him during the time before and following the publication of the Born of Conviction Statement have been the most powerful of all the influences of our lives. The experience shaped the core of our beings, our sense of justice, and above all deepened our faith in a good and just God. It has given us the courage to take the path less traveled.

In 1978, Jerry Trigg's son Mark (barely four when his family left Mississippi) expressed interest in and eventually chose to attend Millsaps College, his parents' alma mater. The choice pleased and surprised Jerry Trigg; he had assumed his son would have no interest in the school. Mark Trigg understands the choice as a way to claim and affirm his parents' legacy, and though he grew up in Indiana and now lives in Georgia, he considers himself a Mississippian.[33]

In spite of the difficulties experienced in the 1960s by Powell Hall's family due to their father's race relations stance and their choice to stay in the public schools in the rural communities where he was appointed, Hall's daughter, Cathy Shelton, says,

> I never wished that our parents had taken the community up on sending us to the segregation academy. I think we wore Born of Conviction as a badge of honor to hang on to—probably more than what it was in reality, but it's an identity. ... The decision

to do the right thing in the moment—that's what the church is supposed to do.

Her younger sister, Miriam Berele, understands her family's 1970 commitment to the Yazoo County public schools as "the purpose of our lives. If we ever considered for one second to go to the segregation academies, we would have been traitors to ourselves and to the army of the Lord." John Hall, the family's oldest child and now a computer scientist working on advancements in nanotechnology, said in 2009, "As a scientist, all my heroes were those who went against conventional thinking and revolutionized the way people see the world." His father's witness, he believes, shows "there can be people who stand up against the current and make a difference."[34]

Of the seventy-seven children of signers, only five have pursued ordained ministry for any length of time. David Conner began his pastoral career in the UMC and eventually changed to the United Church of Christ. When asked what his father's 1963 stand means to him, he replied, "It's always been something that I wanted to live up to . . ., a lure or goal that was held out there to me, by me, in my own mind, not by anyone else." He believes his father might regret that he feels such obligation, "but to me that was a great accomplishment, a courageous thing based solely on principle and faith, not any advantage it ever gained for him." It is part of David Conner's legacy as clergyman and human being.[35]

Shortly before James Holston died, his daughter Deb Selden faced a decision: whether she and her husband should take legal action against an employer who had mistreated their son who has Down syndrome. Her father told her that during the 1963 controversy, his father assured him by saying, "What's the point of having a conviction if you don't stand up for it?" The story inspired her to take the risks involved with the lawsuit, and they had committed to do so when the company backed down and made things right. David Entrekin continues to find inspiration in Rod and Ginny Entrekin's quiet example:

> I understand it was a deep sacrifice to do what they did. . . . Mom and Dad have stuck to their convictions, and I think it's proven that they put in their dues for heaven (I hate to say it that way). They met the standard, to me. If you ask them, they'll say you never meet the standard. But who else meets the standard to that extent? Some of my father's favorite passages are the Beatitudes. . . . I have no qualms

about saying [my parents] *are* the Beatitudes. . . . They have taken the Word and made it flesh.[36]

When Chief Petty Officer James Nicholson II retired from the US Navy in 2003, he found a way to honor his father both for his World War II service in the merchant marines and his 1962–3 race relations witness. He had always considered his father an exemplar of the navy's core values of honor, courage, and commitment, but he was puzzled as a child because whenever veterans were invited to stand and be honored at any public function, his father remained seated. Merchant marines were considered

FIGURE 11.1 Signer James Nicholson with his son, James Nicholson II, at the latter's US Navy retirement ceremony, 2003. Courtesy of James Nicholson family.

civilian sailors by the US government, not veterans. This changed with the Veterans Act of 1988 when Congress finally recognized their wartime service. Medals were struck to honor them, but merchant marines would have to buy them.[37]

At his retirement ceremony, the younger Nicholson told the stories of his dad's Born of Conviction witness and of the longtime lack of recognition for his merchant marine service, which had finally been rectified. Those two things, he said, had profoundly shaped his life. As he finished his remarks, he asked all the veterans present to stand. His father, long accustomed to the lack of recognition, remained seated, and so the son said, "Stand up, Dad. I've been waiting to see this all my life." His father stood, and then at his son's invitation, joined him in front, where the presiding navy captain pinned the elder Nicholson's merchant seaman medals on his coat (Figure 11.1). When he told this story in 2009, he concluded with tears in his eyes, "I finally got to see my dad stand."[38]

Competing Narratives: Born of Conviction and the United Methodist Church's Homosexuality Debate

During a break in the 2009 Mississippi Conference session, Maxie Dunnam spoke Friday evening, June 13, at a dinner sponsored by the Mississippi United Methodist Fellowship of Evangelicals. A blog account of the event on the organization's website said the group then had more than two thousand members, the largest annual conference group representing the Confessing Movement of United Methodism. That movement began in 1995 with a plea to the church to "confess, and be unified by, the apostolic faith in Jesus Christ" in response to perceived efforts to "challenge the primacy of Scripture and justify the acceptance of beliefs incompatible with [the church's] Articles of Religion and Confession of Faith." This call for a return to orthodoxy rejects practices that "rebel against the Lordship of Jesus Christ," such as "consuming the world's goods without regard for the poor; accommodating the prevailing patterns of sexual promiscuity, serial marriage and divorce; resigning ourselves to the patterns of racial and gender prejudice; condoning homosexual practice; and ignoring the church's long-standing protection of the unborn and the mother." Dunnam has been a leader in the Confessing Movement since its beginning, and in 2014 he served as an honorary cochairman.[39]

On that 2009 evening in Jackson, Dunnam addressed "three essentials for our resistance to worldliness in our time," the grace of God, faith in Christ and the authority of scripture, and the traditional Wesleyan emphasis on scriptural holiness. He asserted that God's grace is for all and the church must have ministries to all, including gays and lesbians. The church should welcome all but also confront sin as sin. He also insisted that the issue of homosexuality is tearing the church apart, and the root of the problem is lack of belief in scripture's authority.[40]

About an hour later, the annual conference session resumed with evening worship; a racially diverse crowd of more than one thousand attended. A central portion of the service, led by Born of Conviction signer Keith Tonkel, involved testimonies, in his words, "of joy and of pain. Some stories are easy; some are challenging and hard. All of the stories are the stories of the sons and daughters of God." They included a teen girl who lived in foster care, an interracial married couple, and finally, a lesbian couple—Connie Campbell and Renee Sappington. All were members of congregations in the conference and spoke of their difficulties but also the love and grace they had found in their churches. Campbell and Sappington closed by saying, "When you call God your father, you just don't get to pick and choose who your brothers and sisters are. God's doors are open even when the church's doors are not. The church doesn't always speak for God. We still have hope that this church will find the courage to follow Jesus' radical example and open its doors." When they concluded, Tonkel reminded the congregation that some stories are easy, but some are more difficult. He continued,

> If Jesus said "Whosoever," then we do need to deal with that, and in our deep hearts we need to understand that if God so loved the world, that whosoever believes should be included in the community. Sometimes that's not the easiest thing, but it's always the right thing. And if people misunderstand and if people put down what is of God and what is distinctly of the spirit of Christ, then that's a part of the cross that you bear, to be faithful to what we understand to be Christ-likeness. And so I think it's a call for us not to all understand or to agree at one time, but for us to say we belong to Christ and Christ leads and if we follow then all things will turn out well.

When Tonkel finished, a minister sitting in the audience said privately, "He's the only person in the Conference who could have pulled that off. Brilliant!!"[41]

Campbell and Sappington's story caught Tonkel off guard; he knew the service was about diversity and had agreed to lead that portion, but he was not involved in the planning. He claimed in 2014 that he still would have participated had he known who was speaking, though he suggested that kind of testimony is better done in a local church community than in a once-a-year large event. He has a fairly traditional view of marriage and family; he also takes membership in the body of Christ seriously. Tonkel's church has several gay and lesbian members, and thus he is willing to lead his congregation in prayer for a gay couple's relationship when they request it in worship. There are no easy answers to these issues of sexuality and the Christian faith, but ultimately the most important issue to Tonkel is how the body of Christ welcomes and includes all who come. In his report to the 2012 Charge Conference at Wells Church in Jackson, he said,

> It's easy to have a singular view of how churches should be and how church folks should do. When there is a call to be different, or to honestly include others in your love, then there are times when we are called to a new understanding of "inclusiveness," to offer blessings instead of curses, and to bring your personal understandings of all things to the very Spirit of Christ. The will to act prompted by God's love is easy and comfortable for some. It is hard and challenging for others. If we err, dear WellsFolk, let it always be because of what trying to live in love means.[42]

For Methodists in the early 1960s, the race issue was the biggest challenge facing the church, and it remains a crucial justice issue. Homosexuality has become the denomination's biggest conflict. On one side are those, including many of the surviving members of the Twenty-Eight, who believe the church should move to full inclusion and acceptance of gays and lesbians, with ordination rights and the blessing of same-sex marriages. They find support for this view in part from their understanding of the Bible's witness to the love of God. There is a larger contingent in the US and global UMC that holds to the views expressed by Dunnam: grace to all, but homosexual practice is sinful. In their view, any change in the church's teaching on this issue (that although all persons are "individuals of sacred worth," the UMC "does not condone the practice of homosexuality and considers this practice incompatible with Christian teaching"; and "self-avowed, practicing homosexuals" are not permitted to be ordained) would represent a denial of biblical authority. Dunnam has been a leading spokesperson in the UMC for this perspective since the 1980s. During the 2012 General Conference, a young UMC clergyperson referred to Dunnam in a blog post as one of the "grandfathers of the resistance movement."[43]

Because Dunnam is well-known in the UMC, when persons who are part of the full inclusion/acceptance group hear that he co-authored Born of Conviction, they often ask, "What happened to him?" From their perspective, the struggles for black freedom and for gay and lesbian liberation are analogous, and the legacy of Born of Conviction unquestionably includes full inclusion of gays and lesbians and acceptance of committed monogamous gay and lesbian relationships in the UMC. Yet Dunnam believes he has not changed much theologically, except to become more passionate and more explicitly orthodox. He remains committed to civil rights issues; most recently, as he indicated in his remarks at the 2013 Elzy Award ceremony, his main concern has been equal access to public education. He also believes it is possible for Christians to love and include gays and lesbians in the church and yet insist that the practice of homosexuality is sinful, and he has sought to live that out in his ministry.[44]

As more states legalize same-sex marriage, the UMC has struggled with ministers (and even a retired bishop) choosing openly to violate legislation passed at the 2004 General Conference prohibiting the church's clergy from performing same-sex wedding ceremonies. In November 2013, Frank Schaefer, a pastor in the Eastern Pennsylvania Conference, stood trial and was convicted for officiating at the 2007 same-sex wedding ceremony of his son. The church court suspended him for thirty days and directed him to determine during that time whether he would abide by the denomination's Book of Discipline "in entirety." On December 19, he refused to do so, and his conference considered that response sufficient for the surrender of his ministerial credentials. The next day, Bishop Minerva G. Carcaño of the California-Pacific Annual Conference issued a public invitation to Schaefer to come to her conference to be in ministry. She prefaced her offer by recalling that in 1963 (and 1964), Bishop Gerald Kennedy had welcomed to the same conference "8 Methodist pastors from Mississippi who had been condemned and ostracized by Methodists and others for standing against racial discrimination," and she claimed to be "following in the footsteps of Bishop Kennedy."[45]

In January 2014, Maxie Dunnam (one of those eight welcomed by Bishop Kennedy in the 1960s) publicly contested Bishop Carcaño's interpretation of the Born of Conviction legacy. He said only African Americans can judge if the debate about same-sex marriage is analogous to their past and present freedom struggle. Only they can decide if the fight in the UMC over church discipline compares appropriately to the struggle for voting rights and equality in education. More specifically, the bishop's explicit link to Bishop Kennedy and members of the Twenty-Eight troubled him:

> The differences seem clear. None of the 28 who signed the Born of Conviction statement were charged with violating the *Discipline* of our Church. In fact, in light of Bishop Carcaño's comparison, it is somewhat ironic that we were trying desperately to *support* the *Discipline*, not disregard it. The witness against racism in our *Discipline* was as clear then as the Church's present witness against same sex marriage and the ordination of professed practicing homosexual persons. We Mississippi 28 were not violating the covenant of our ordination; we were *upholding* it.[46]

Some of the Twenty-Eight applauded Bishop Carcaño's invitation. Jim Waits wrote her to praise the action "and its implications regarding our hopes for a broader inclusiveness of the church." Inman Moore replied to Dunnam's rejoinder to the bishop by calling his criticism of her words "terribly wrong"; he also invoked the inclusivity of the Christian gospel. He pointed to the stances of other mainline denominations that now allow the ordination of gays and lesbians, claimed that Methodist founder John Wesley violated Anglican church law on occasion, and asserted that the Bible "at its best has a neon sign flashing, 'To Be Continued.'" Dunnam read both responses, acknowledged their disagreements with him on homosexuality, but noted the larger concern of unity in the church, which he felt the bishop's invitation threatened. He also remained concerned about the failure of some UMC clergy to keep covenant because of their violation of the *Discipline*.[47]

Christian ministers, both clergy and lay, have always offered a range of understandings as to how Christians should witness to the world and what their message should be. Part of the legacy of Born of Conviction is that some of the Mississippi ministers who united in an alternative witness in 1963 disagreed in 2014 over the appropriate Christian witness on the homosexual issue. Both sides believe they have biblical mandates for their views. In the UMC debate, some on Dunnam's side accuse their opponents of conforming to the dominant culture rather than to Christian tradition; those arguing for radical inclusivity make similar claims (e.g., that condemnation of homosexuality is rooted in patriarchy). The words of church historian E. Brooks Holifield shed light on the impasse:

> The historian's temptation is to rummage through history labeling one set of clergy as the baptizers of culture and another set as its prophetic critics. I have tried to resist the temptation. In real life, all priests and ministers both affirm and deny; they legitimate cultural forms and subvert them; they follow now one side and then another of the paradox. The Christian ministry will always be in crisis. Sociologists and historians can explain part of the crisis, but the rest is inherent in the very soul of the Christian tradition.[48]

"Merely Declaring Ourselves as One Does Not Make It a Reality"

Born of Conviction signer Keith Tonkel intended to speak at the 2013 Mississippi Conference Emma Elzy Award presentation, but remained silent. Two days later, he shared the response he would have made on the stage, including thanks for the award and an acknowledgment that much remains to be done: "We have promises to keep, and miles to go before we sleep."[49]

Throughout the church's history, Christians have struggled to define their relationship to the dominant culture in which they live and to offer appropriate witness to their faith. As Holifield notes, the relationship has always been complex. In retrospect, the 1963 Born of Conviction controversy in Mississippi offers a clear case in which the majority of white Mississippi Christians, Methodist and otherwise, either affirmed an evil cultural form or kept silent about it, while a small number tried to support the movement's struggle to subvert it. Some spokespersons for the majority view insisted that the central "spiritual" calling of the church—to save souls—precluded involvement in such "political" matters as the efforts to change the segregated system. In spite of the strong resistance, the Twenty-Eight and some of their colleagues and lay supporters understood their responsibility as Christian ministers and disciples much differently.

When these clergymen were ordained, the bishop (in most cases, Franklin) laid hands on their heads and said, "Take thou authority as an elder in the Church to preach the Word of God." They understood the Christian ministry's responsibility for the care of souls *always* to include attention to the realities of human life in the world, and in early 1960s Mississippi, the spiritual and physical health of all Mississippians, white and black, required prophetic attention to race relations. Surely from the human side of the effort, salvation of souls is compromised if the church chooses, consciously or unconsciously, to ignore individual, interpersonal, and systemic social injustice.[50]

The Born of Conviction signers also knew their obligation to preach God's Word involved pastoral dimensions. Born of Conviction signer Rod Entrekin's son David, a United Methodist layman, articulated this in 2009 by citing the lengthy discussion of the power of the Spirit of God in Romans 8. He concluded, "If you have the Spirit of God, it means releasing all your fears. Racism is rooted in fear; it's irrational, and my dad understood that." Most white Mississippi Christians were consumed with fear in the 1950s and 1960s because the very foundations of their world teetered on the edge of destruction. As the Twenty-Eight and others knew, that world needed to crumble, and they sought to lead their people away from massive resistance to change and toward a world with new foundations. True faith allows one to put aside fear and to trust that whatever new world is coming, God will be present. To quote another New Testament voice, "There is no fear in love, but perfect love casts out fear." The white Methodist Church in 1960s Mississippi needed pastors willing to lead courageously and faithfully, along with church members willing to follow them and also to lead, as Conference Lay Leader J. P. Stafford well understood.[51]

As Holifield cautions, any sense of resolution to the dilemma of the relationship between the Christian faith and human culture always proves ephemeral. In the case of Born of Conviction, this is illustrated well by the response of persons reading the statement now. It seems so mild—its claims so obvious and acceptable to contemporary minds. Methodists and then United Methodists in Mississippi have gradually embraced its truth and moved toward inclusiveness and even some reconciliation. But American society and the American church are by no means "postracial"; the race issue abides, arguably as the thorniest problem in the United States. And as Terrance Roberts of the 1957 Little Rock Nine asserts, real reconciliation cannot come without truthful acknowledgment of the past and subsequent efforts to dismantle the ongoing system of racial hierarchy.[52]

In the 1960s in Mississippi and elsewhere, some well-meaning whites who believed integration was the answer failed to understand the depths of the system of white privilege that existed then; now, most whites remain unaware of their participation in and complicity with that system, which is still firmly entrenched in American culture. This book has explored the difficulties faced by the Twenty-Eight and others who addressed the evils of the Closed Society; the evils of continuing systemic racism today lurk much further under the surface and partially penetrate the consciousness of most white Americans only when a Trayvon Martin or a Walter Scott is killed and the dialogue on race intensifies for a while.[53]

This systemic reality continues to affect the church. In response to the 1973 reminder from the former Central Jurisdiction Conference representatives that the formal uniting of black and white conferences was only a beginning, Mississippi United Methodists have made progress toward true merger. The perspectives of African Americans in the conference vary on this ongoing issue. One view comes from Dora S. Washington, a lay member of Jackson's Anderson UMC, retired Jackson State University professor and administrator, and participant since the late 1960s in interracial efforts to fashion a new Mississippi. In the 1980s she became involved as a leader beyond her local church, and in 2014, she chaired the Annual Conference Planning Committee. She first served as a lay delegate to General Conference from Mississippi in 1992, and she remembers that then the bishop "had to continually remind the [conference] to be inclusive in its voting." Since that time, she believes Mississippi United Methodists have made progress in race relations on the conference level.[54]

Indeed, Mississippi Conference sessions and district meetings are integrated and seem fairly inclusive, and the commitment to include blacks in the leadership continues. However, in the view of some African American Mississippi United Methodists, the concerns raised in the 1970s and 1980s by leaders of the old Central Jurisdiction Mississippi Conference—that the black churches and leadership would simply be swallowed up by the white conference without sufficient recognition of the heritage and gifts of black churches and leaders—have never been fully addressed.

As a black student pastor in the Central Jurisdiction's Upper Mississippi Conference while at Rust College in the early 1970s, Ludrick

Cameron participated in initial discussions on merger with leaders of the white North Mississippi Conference. Upon graduation from Gammon Seminary in 1974, Cameron returned to an appointment in the Mississippi Conference, newly constituted due to the merger of the white and black bodies in the southern half of the state. He served on the conference program staff from 1978 to 1983 and as a district superintendent from 1998 to 2004, and he is now retired. In his view, true merger is "yet to be. We have not really merged, and the pain and hurt are still there." For the most part, he says, pastoral appointments are still made on the basis of race (with only an occasional cross-racial assignment), and in many ways, the conference has failed to be a truly "*United* Methodist Church." To the extent this is true, it is the result of both the dominant white perspective's blindness to what full inclusivity might mean and to larger systemic problems in the UMC that result in a failure to deal creatively enough with the realities and needs of the many small congregations, both white and black, in the conference and throughout the denomination.[55]

In 2004, the UMC's General Commission on Religion and Race did a leadership audit of the Mississippi Conference, and the report expressed surprise at the diversity in conference leadership. It also acknowledged that the conference still needed a long-range plan "with a time line for implementing open itinerancy and cross-racial/cultural appointments," including preparation of local congregations for such appointments. The report recommended "That the conference leadership hold 'listening sessions' where racial/ethnic persons can share their pain and frustration as well as their vision for the future. Responding to the concerns of racial/ethnic persons can help to alleviate their feelings of being unheard and powerless." In the church's protracted struggle against racism, progress has been made, yet there is still a long way to go toward the goal of God's justice in race relations.[56]

It is fitting to celebrate the witness of the many brave persons in Mississippi—black and white—who put their lives on the line to seek change, including both civil and voting rights for all citizens, in an exceedingly dark and difficult time. The Born of Conviction statement played a small part in that effort and a larger part in the ongoing struggle to change white attitudes. The signers added their voices to the civil rights movement's resounding prophetic "No!" addressed to the evil system of social, political, and economic oppression of black Mississippians. In response, the intense resistance to change came from individuals and groups, but the underlying power of such resistance always comes from a deeper place, as Ephesians 6:12 (RSV) claims: "For we are not contending against flesh and blood, but against the principalities, the powers, against the world rulers of this present darkness, against the spiritual hosts of wickedness in the heavenly places." The fight against such evil will always require persons "born of conviction."

Acknowledgments

RESEARCHING AND WRITING a book is truly a communal effort, and I am deeply grateful to all the friends and family (old and new) who assisted me over the past eleven years.

A Louisville Institute Religious Institutions Grant made possible a year's sabbatical leave in 2005–6, with additional support from Emory & Henry College. Various funds at Emory & Henry supported this project, including the McConnell Scholarship in the summers of 2004 and 2009, the Fugate Fund in the summer of 2011, and a semester sabbatical in the fall of 2013. The Mednick Fellowship from the Virginia Foundation for Independent Colleges supported travel in the summer of 2007.

This book has benefitted from several archival collections and the dedicated people who staff them; the collections are all listed in the bibliography. Debra McIntosh at the Millsaps College Archives and J. B. Cain Archives of Mississippi Methodism at Millsaps deserves high praise and much thanks for her expert and prompt assistance to me over many years, and I owe much to the fine people at the Mississippi Department of Archives and History. I am also indebted to the signers who saved documents related to their experience and shared them with me. I greatly appreciate all my friends at Emory & Henry College's Kelly Library for their help over the years, especially archivist extraordinaire Robert Vejnar, who scanned and rescanned photos for me and saw the value in this project from its inception.

I had many occasions to present this research, including lectures at Emory & Henry and the Virginia Highlands Festival in 2005 and a Millsaps College Forum event in 2006. Church presentations include Glenn Memorial UMC in Atlanta (with Jim Waits) in 2009 and Emory

UMC in Emory, Virginia, in 2013. The Wesleyan Studies Group of the American Academy of Religion allowed me to offer papers in 2006 and 2010, and I also presented at the American Historical Association in 2008. It was a singular honor to participate in "The Civil Rights Movement in Mississippi," the Chancellor Porter L. Fortune Symposium in Southern History at the University of Mississippi in 2010. Thanks to Ted Ownby and his staff at the Center for the Study of Southern Culture, as well as to John Dittmer for his helpful response to my paper. Also in 2010 I had the privilege of participating in a talkback with playwright Kathryn Dickinson after a performance of her powerful work, *Born of Conviction*, at the Irondale Center in Brooklyn, New York.

Parts of this book have been reprinted with permission in revised form from the following works: "Born of Conviction: White Methodist Witness to Mississippi's Closed Society," in L. Edward Phillips and Billy Vaughan, editors, *Courage to Bear Witness: Essays in Honor of Gene L. Davenport* (Eugene, OR: Wipf and Stock, 2009); "Conflicting Convictions in White Mississippi Methodism," *Methodist History* XLIX, 3 (April 2011): 162–75; "'Born of Conviction': White Mississippians Argue Civil Rights in 1963," an earlier version of this book's Chapter 5, which originally appeared in *The Civil Rights Movement in Mississippi*, edited by Ted Ownby (Jackson: University Press of Mississippi, 2013); and "'Born of Conviction' Statement," *Mississippi Encyclopedia* (Jackson: University Press of Mississippi, forthcoming).

I received research assistance of various kinds from friends too numerous to list; I thank them all, especially Ray Branch, Lloyd Gray, A. Heath Jones III, R. Lee McKinzie, Joe Powell III, and Dora Washington. Special thanks to Emory & Henry students Chelsea Ruiz, Danielle Peterson, and Kelly Johnson, who transcribed interviews. The research, especially the interviews, required thousands of miles of auto travel through thirty-three states and meant many opportunities to receive hospitality in the form of lodging and meals from friends and family numerous enough to fill a small village. Thanks to all of you, especially Lynn Raley and Rachel Heard and their daughter Gillian, whose home has served as my Jackson headquarters for more than a decade.

Then there are those who offered valuable encouragement, advice, and in a couple of cases, friendly harassment, as in "Have you finished that book?" They include Rex Matthews, Paul Harvey, Jim Matheny, Mark Matheny, Emily Sanford, Lisa Garvin, LaRue and Ree Owen, Warren and Janis Black, Julia and T. W. Lewis, Sam Lane, Art Minton, Bob Ratcliff,

Kathryn Dickinson, Kristen Williams, Jim and Kathleen Sullivan, Steve Burnett, the late Will Campbell, the late Mac Bryan, Larry and Jean Harley, Steve Fisher and Nancy Garretson, Marcia and David St. Clair, Frank Buchanan, Bill Spencer, Lee Ramsey and Mary Leslie Dawson-Ramsey, Sara and Ed Phillips, Billy Vaughan and Joni Laney, Kathy and Jeff Irwin, and John and Donna Banks. Ed King deserves special recognition here for his wisdom and experience shared so generously not only with me, but also with countless civil rights movement scholars.

I am blessed with stellar colleagues at Emory & Henry College who have believed in me and enriched my life through this process. There are too many to name here, but special thanks to Fred Kellogg, Jim Dawsey, Adam Wells, Kathleen Chamberlain, Ben Letson, Jack Roper, Linda Dobkins, and Tal Stanley. In their turn, Deans Chris Qualls and David Haney both championed my work, and I am especially grateful to their predecessor Paul Blaney, who paid exceptional attention to this project from the beginning and has continued to express genuine interest. Ed Davis expertly fashioned the two maps for this book and endured my obsessive questions with his usual humor and grace. Beyond my campus, I thank the Ecclesial Repentance group, a diverse collection of scholars and pastors convened by Steve Haynes, for their insights and commitment to examining the intersection of Christian faith and justice in race relations—past, present, and future.

I am indebted to various leaders and staff members, past and present, of the Mississippi Annual Conference of The United Methodist Church for their support and assistance, including Steve Casteel, Woody Woodrick, Bishop Hope Morgan Ward, Tim Thompson, Connie Shelton, Tamica Smith-Jeuitt, David Stotts, and Bishop James E. Swanson Sr.

I am exceedingly grateful to members of the Twenty-Eight and their families for their courage in 1963. Many of them have assisted my work, especially Jim Waits and Maxie Dunnam; kudos to the late James Nicholson, who organized the 2005 reunion of signers. When I began this project, twenty signers were still alive. I regret that six—John Ed Thomas, Powell Hall, James Nicholson, Summer Walters, Denson Napier, and Jerry Trigg—have since died and will not see the finished volume.

Several persons read portions of at least one draft of the book or book proposal and offered valuable feedback, including Joel Alvis, Anne Burkholder, Bishop Roy Clark, Thomas Edward Frank, Stephen Haynes, Bishop Clay Lee, Jan Love, Bill Lowry, C. Dalton Lyon, Bill McAtee, LaRue Owen, Ed Phillips, Russell Richey, Peter Slade, Tal Stanley, Billy Vaughan,

Jan Wofford, students in my Church and World course from 2004–14, and Born of Conviction signers and their family members. I am especially thankful for the time, effort, expertise, and advice offered by these readers: Joe Crespino, Carolyn Dupont, Charles Eagles, Charles Marsh, Alan Miller, Charles Miller, Lee Ramsey, David St. Clair, and Lovett Weems. Writers need people who both support and encourage them *and* who are willing to offer honest critique. Professor Eagles served those dual roles best, and I am privileged to call him friend.

Thanks to Cynthia Read and her excellent staff at Oxford University Press, especially Glenn Ramirez. They have shepherded this project with grace and ease, all the while offering patient assistance to this novice author.

This book is dedicated to the three most important people in my life. My wife Betty faithfully listened to and talked with me through the struggles to wrestle mountains of information into a coherent story. Between 2006 and 2014 she read chapters from every draft out loud to me and served as my best critic. I would not have finished this book without her. And this is the place to say that our three children—Rachel (and her husband Luke and children Noah, Rosie, and Max), Sarah, and Joseph (and his wife Jenni) all bless my life beyond measure.

My parents, Gerry and Lee Reiff, deserve credit and blame for my relationship with Mississippi, which began in 1960 when Millsaps College hired Dad to teach religion. Their Christian commitment, love for others, and concern for justice have always inspired me. My mother's discovery of archival work as a vocation intrigued me, and as the Mississippi Conference archivist, she was with me when I first saw and photocopied the Born of Conviction statement in 1983. When I began this research, my dad served as a sounding board to help make sense of the stories and struggles in 1960s Mississippi and the Mississippi Conference's response to it all. They both read and commented on the manuscript at various stages.

Only a few hours after I finished writing the last chapter, my mother called to say that Dad's struggle with dementia neared its end, and four evenings later on September 6, 2014, he died, surrounded by his wife, his two sons, daughters-in-law, and grandchildren. I grieve that he did not live to see the book in print, but his example and wisdom undergird its pages.

Advent, 2014
Abingdon, Virginia

Text of the "Born of Conviction" Statement

BORN OF CONVICTION ...

(Note: The statement below was formulated by some of the younger ministers of the Mississippi Conference who are concerned over present trends of curbing the freedom of the pulpit. They represent some of our best trained and most promising ministers. We feel they express the conviction of the vast majority of the clerical members of the conference. We suggest you read the editorial "Freedom of the Pulpit" on the opposite page.)

***

Confronted with the grave crises precipitated by racial discord within our state in recent months, and the genuine dilemma facing persons of Christian conscience, we are compelled to voice publicly our convictions. Indeed, as Christian ministers and as native Mississippians, sharing the anguish of all our people, we have a particular obligation to speak. Thus understanding our mutual involvement in these issues, we bind ourselves together in this expression of our Christian commitment. We speak only for ourselves, though mindful that many others share these affirmations.

Born of the deep conviction of our souls as to what is morally right, we have been driven to seek the foundations of such convictions in the expressed witness of our Church. We, therefore, at the outset of this new year affirm the following:

I. The Church is the instrument of God's purpose. This is His Church. It is ours only as stewards under His Lordship. Effective practice of this stewardship for the minister clearly requires freedom of the pulpit. It demands for every man an atmosphere for responsible belief and free expression.

II. We affirm our faith in the official position of The Methodist Church on race as set forth in paragraph 2026 of the 1960 Methodist Discipline: "Our Lord Jesus Christ teaches that all men are brothers. He permits no discrimination because of race, color, or creed. 'In Christ Jesus you are all sons of God, through faith . . .' (Galatians 3:26)"

The position of The Methodist Church, long held and frequently declared, is an amplification of our Lord's teaching: "We believe that God is Father of all people and races, that Jesus Christ is His Son, that all men are brothers, and that man is of infinite worth as a child of God." (The Social Creed, Paragraph 2020)

III. We affirm our belief that our public school system is the most effective means of providing common education for all our children. We hold that it is an institution essential to the preservation and development of our true democracy. The Methodist Church is officially committed to the system of public school education and we concur. We are unalterably opposed to the closing of public schools on any level or to the diversion of tax funds to the support of private or sectarian schools.

IV. In these conflicting times, the issues of race and Communism are frequently confused. Let there be no mistake. We affirm an unflinching opposition to Communism. We publicly concur in the Methodist Council of Bishops' statement of November 16, 1961[*], which declares:

"The basic commitment of a Methodist minister is to Jesus Christ as Lord and Savior. This sets him in permanent opposition to communism. He cannot be a Christian and a communist. In obedience to his Lord and in support of the prayer, 'Thy Kingdom come, Thy will be done on earth as it is in Heaven,' he champions justice, mercy, freedom, brotherhood, and peace. He defends the underprivileged, oppressed, and forsaken. He challenges the status quo, calling for repentance and change wherever the behavior of men falls short of the standards of Jesus Christ."

We believe that this is our task and calling as Christian ministers.

FINDING AUTHORITY IN THE OFFICIAL POSITION OF OUR CHURCH, AND BELIEVING IT TO BE IN HARMONY WITH SCRIPTURE AND GOOD CHRISTIAN CONSCIENCE, WE PUBLICLY DECLARE OURSELVES IN THESE

MATTERS AND AGREE TO STAND TOGETHER IN SUPPORT OF THESE PRINCIPLES.

Jerry Furr	Marvin Moody
Maxie D. Dunnam	Keith Tonkel
Jim L. Waits	John Ed Thomas [Jon in original]
O. Gerald Trigg	Inman Moore, Jr.
James B. Nicholson	Denson Napier
Buford A. Dickinson	Rod Entrekin
James S. Conner	Harold Ryker
J. W. Holston	N. A. Dickson
James P. Rush	Ned Kellar [Keller in original]
Edward W. McRae	Powell Hall
Joseph C. Way	Elton Brown
Wallace E. Roberts	Bufkin Oliver
Summer Walters	Jack Troutman
Bill Lampton	Wilton Carter

[Reprinted by permission of the Mississippi Annual Conference of The United Methodist Church, publisher of *The Mississippi Methodist Advocate*. All material in brackets [] added by J. Reiff. *In IV, "Born of Conviction" as printed dated the bishops' statement as 1962 in error. Original mimeo copies of "Born of Conviction" have the correct date, 1961.]

Notes

INTRODUCTION

1. Martin Luther King Jr., "Letter from Birmingham Jail," *Why We Can't Wait* (New York: Harper and Row, 1963), 87–8, 93–4.
2. Re: Meredith as the "first known" African American student at Ole Miss, see Charles Eagles, *The Price of Defiance: James Meredith and the Integration of Ole Miss* (Chapel Hill: University of North Carolina Press, 2009), 20–1. *MMA*, January 2, 1963.
3. James W. Silver, *Mississippi: The Closed Society*, New Enlarged Edition (New York: Harcourt, Brace and World, 1966), 6, 61, and 58; *MMA*, January 2, 1963. "Segregation now, segregation tomorrow, segregation forever" comes from George Wallace's Alabama inaugural address on January 14, 1963.
4. *MMA*, January 2, 1963.
5. Samuel S. Hill, *Southern Churches in Crisis* (New York: Henry Holt, 1966), e.g., 115, 190–1; see also Samuel Southard, "Are Southern Churches Silent?," *Christian Century*, November 20, 1963, 1429–32; David Chappell, *A Stone of Hope: Prophetic Religion and the Death of Jim Crow* (Chapel Hill: University of North Carolina Press, 2004), 107.
6. Jane Dailey, "Sex, Segregation, and the Sacred after *Brown*," *Journal of American History*, 91 (1) (June 2004), 119–44; 122; Peter Slade, *Open Friendship in a Closed Society: Mission Mississippi and a Theology of Friendship* (New York: Oxford University Press, 2009), 6; Carolyn Dupont, *Mississippi Praying: Southern White Evangelicals and the Civil Rights Movement, 1945–1975* (New York: New York University Press, 2013), 5; see also Joseph Crespino, *In Search of Another Country* (Princeton, NJ: Princeton University Press, 2007), 319–20, n. 45, and Howard Dorgan, "Response of the Main-line Protestant Pulpit to *Brown v Board of Education, 1954–1965*," in Calvin M. Logue and Howard Dorgan, eds., *A New Diversity in Contemporary Southern Rhetoric* (Baton Rouge: Louisiana State University Press, 1987), 30–40.

7. Ed King, *The White Church in Mississippi*, unpublished manuscript, Part 3, 7–8.

8. Charles Eagles urges more attention to nonmovement experience and viewpoints in "Toward New Histories of the Civil Rights Era," *Journal of Southern History* 66, 4 (November 2000), 815–16. In addition to Marsh's *God's Long Summer* and others cited by Eagles then, recent works that do this include Jason Sokol, *There Goes My Everything: White Southerners in the Age of Civil Rights, 1945–1975* (New York: Alfred A. Knopf, 2006); Crespino, *In Search of Another Country*; Stephen R. Haynes, *The Last Segregated Hour: The Memphis Kneel-ins and the Campaign for Southern Church Desegregation* (New York: Oxford University Press, 2012), and Dupont, *Mississippi Praying*. Dailey, "Sex, Segregation, and the Sacred after *Brown*," 144; Marsh, *God's Long Summer*.

9. Knox M. Broom, "Memo," n.d. (January 1963), Ashmore (Dr. Sam E. and Ann Lewis) Papers (Ashmore Papers), box 1, folder 1, JBCA; Hill, *Southern Churches in Crisis*, 112; Joel L. Alvis Jr., *Religion and Race: Southern Presbyterians, 1946–1983* (Tuscaloosa: University of Alabama Press, 1994), 4–5, 46–7; Slade, *Open Friendship in a Closed Society*, 94–5, 119–22; and Dupont, *Mississippi Praying*, 187–8, 190, 220—see also Haynes, *The Last Segregated Hour*, 89–90, 132; D. Elton Brown to James W. Silver, January 29, 1963, James W. Silver Papers (Silver Papers), UMDASC, box 23, folder 9.

10. Wayne Flynt, *Alabama Baptists: Southern Baptists in the Heart of Dixie* (Tuscaloosa: University of Alabama Press, 1998), 465; *MMA*, January 2, 1963.

11. The United Methodist Church came into being in 1968; the proper name of the denomination between 1939 and mid-1968 was The Methodist Church. On denominational responses to the race issue, see Alvis, *Religion and Race*; Mark Newman, *Getting Right with God: Southern Baptists and Desegregation, 1945–1995* (Tuscaloosa: University of Alabama Press, 2001); and Gardiner H. Shattuck Jr., *Episcopalians and Race: Civil War to Civil Rights* (Lexington: University of Kentucky Press, 2000). Peter Murray's *Methodists and the Crucible of Race, 1930–1975* (Columbia: University of Missouri Press, 2004) explores the issue on the Methodist General (national) Church level. Slade, *Open Friendship in a Closed Society*, ch. 4, and Haynes, *The Last Segregated Hour* explore white Presbyterian responses in Jackson, Mississippi, and Memphis, while Dupont's *Mississippi Praying* looks at white Mississippi Baptists, Methodists, and Presbyterians in the civil rights era. Treatments of one Methodist conference or state conferences and the movement include Donald E. Collins, *When the Church Bell Rang Racist: The Methodist Church and the Civil Rights Movement in Alabama* (Macon: Mercer University Press, 1998); and James T. Clemons and Kelly L. Farr, eds., *Crisis of Conscience: Arkansas Methodists and the Civil Rights Struggle* (Little Rock: Butler Center for Arkansas Studies, 2007).

12. An extensive discussion of white clergy statements in the civil rights era comes in Chapter 4.

13. Jean Dickinson Minus interview.

14. The Good Friday statement, signed by five bishops, (two Methodist, two Episcopalian, one Catholic), a Presbyterian and a Baptist minister, and a rabbi, appeared in Birmingham papers on April 13, 1963; for the text, see S. Jonathan Bass, *Blessed Are the Peacemakers: Martin Luther King Jr., Eight White Religious Leaders, and the "Letter from Birmingham Jail"* (Baton Rouge: Louisiana State University Press, 2001), 235–6. King, "Letter from Birmingham Jail," *Why We Can't Wait*, 81, 83; re: "local people," see John Dittmer, *Local People: The Struggle for Civil Rights in Mississippi* (Urbana: University of Illinois Press, 1994).

15. King, "Letter from Birmingham Jail," *Why We Can't Wait*, 95.

16. Because I was nine, I have relied on my mother's memory of this event as well as my own, supplemented by Carter Dalton Lyon's account in his 2010 University of Mississippi dissertation, "Lifting the Color Bar from the House of God: The 1963–1964 Church Visit Campaign to Challenge Segregated Sanctuaries in Jackson, Mississippi," 237–8, to determine the date. The ministers, Gerald Forshey and Donald Walden, accompanied Tougaloo students Betty Poole, Ida Hannah, and Julie Zaugg. The cover image of Carolyn Dupont's *Mississippi Praying* may be a photo from that day, although she dates it October 27 on the basis of the photographer's records. There is a discrepancy between that dating and Lyon's account. My father is in the upper left corner of the photo and was the only person on the steps facing the visitors who was sympathetic to their attempt.

17. *MMA*, January 2, 1963; Marsh, *God's Long Summer*, 1.

CHAPTER 1

1. Paul Hendrickson, *Sons of Mississippi* (New York: Vintage, 2003), 47; "Mississippi: Is This America? 1962–1964," Episode 5, Season 1, *Eyes on the Prize*, directed by Orlando Bagwell (Blackside, Inc., 1987).

2. Richard Heitzenrater, *Wesley and the People Called Methodists* (Nashville: Abingdon Press, 1995), 214; re: American Methodist beginnings, see Russell E. Richey, Kenneth E. Rowe, and Jean Miller Schmidt, *The Methodist Experience in America*, Vol. 1 (Nashville: Abingdon Press, 2010), chs. 1–4; and Frederick A. Norwood, *The Story of American Methodism* (Nashville: Abingdon Press, 1974), 70–102.

3. On the "Southern accent" of American Methodism, see Russell E. Richey, *Early American Methodism* (Bloomington: Indiana University Press, 1991), ch. 4; Richey, *Early American Methodism*, 57–8; David Hempton, *Methodism: Empire of the Spirit* (New Haven, CT: Yale University Press, 2005), 133–4. See also Donald G. Mathews, *Slavery and Methodism* (Princeton, NJ: Princeton University Press, 1965); and J. Gordon Melton, *A Will to Choose: The Origins of African American Methodism* (Lanham, MD: Rowman and Littlefield, 2007).

4. John G. Jones, *A Complete History of Methodism as Connected with the Mississippi Conference of the MECS*, Vol. 1 (Nashville: Southern Methodist Publishing House, 1887), 24–6; Jones, chs. 3 and 4; *MCJ*, 1989, 385.

5. Richey et al., *The Methodist Experience in America*, 178–92; see also Norwood, *The Story of American Methodism*, 197–209; and Lewis M. Purifoy, "The Southern Methodist Church and the Proslavery Argument," *Journal of Southern History* 32 (3) (August 1966): 325–41.

6. Richey et al., *The Methodist Experience in America*, 217–18; *MCJ*, 1989, 389–91; Gene Ramsey Miller, *A History of North Mississippi Methodism, 1820–1900* (Nashville: Parthenon Press, 1966), 80–2; *Journal of the Upper Mississippi Conference, Methodist Episcopal Church* (1913): 10–11; Richey et al., *The Methodist Experience in America*, 363ff.

7. The Colored Methodist Episcopal Church changed its name to Christian Methodist Episcopal in 1954. Richey et al., *The Methodist Experience in America*, Vol. 1, 363ff., and Vol. 2 (Nashville: Abingdon Press, 2000), 488–95; see also Dwight W. Culver, *Negro Segregation in The Methodist Church* (New Haven, CT: Yale University Press, 1953), 60–78 (esp. 69); Norwood, *The Story of American Methodism*, 407–10; James S. Thomas, *Methodism's Racial Dilemma* (Nashville: Abingdon Press, 1992), ch. 3; Murray, *Methodists and the Crucible of Race*, ch. 2; and Robert Watson Sledge, *Hands on the Ark* (Lake Junaluska, NC: Commission on Archives and History, The United Methodist Church, 1975), 46–9, 90–7, 234–5. From 1784 to 1938, American Methodist bishops were elected by the General Conference(s).

8. Norwood, *The Story of American Methodism*, 410, and Thomas, *Methodism's Racial Dilemma*, 177; Culver, *Negro Segregation in The Methodist Church*, 75, 32–3; Culver, *Negro Segregation in The Methodist Church*, 72 and 180, Tables 2 and 3. See also Morris L. Davis, *The Methodist Unification* (New York: New York University Press, 2008).

9. Culver, *Negro Segregation in The Methodist Church*, 81–2, 78, 174; Thomas, *Methodism's Racial Dilemma*, 44–6; Culver, *Negro Segregation in The Methodist Church*, 70; Thomas, *Methodism's Racial Dilemma*, 53; Culver, *Negro Segregation in The Methodist Church*, 83–95; and Thomas, *Methodism's Racial Dilemma*, chs. 3–4; Thomas, 53. See Culver, *Negro Segregation in the Methodist Church*, 103, for evidence that in the early 1950s, most blacks wanted the Central Jurisdiction abolished.

10. Culver, *Negro Segregation in The Methodist Church*, 113–15; Culver, *Negro Segregation in The Methodist Church*, 81, and Thomas, *Methodism's Racial Dilemma*, 93–4. See William McClain's foreword to Phil Noble, *Beyond the Burning Bus* (Montgomery, AL: New South Books, 2003), 12.

11. *MCJ*, 1989, 389, 391.

12. *DMC*, 1940, ¶22.

13. Large congregations are given freer rein to choose an associate pastor (the appointment must still be approved by the bishop and cabinet). Also, local

churches and ministers have some say in the appointment process—less so during the years considered here than today.

14. Norwood, *The Story of American Methodism*, 251, 364. Though a few women served as pastors through most of Methodist history, they were not granted full clergy rights in American Methodism until 1956, and for years after, most Methodist clergy still referred to ministers as "men." The Mississippi Conference received its first female clergy full member in 1980. Heitzenrater, *Wesley and the People Called Methodists*, 142–7.

15. *DUMC*, 2012, ¶333.1, 338; for a discussion of the "go where sent" tradition, see Richard Heitzenrater, "Connectionalism and Itinerancy: Wesleyan Principles and Practice," in Russell E. Richey, Dennis M. Campbell, and William B. Lawrence, eds., *Connectionalism: Ecclesiology, Mission, and Identity* (Nashville: Abingdon Press, 1997), 23–38, esp. 31ff. See also Thomas Edward Frank, *Polity, Practice, and the Mission of The United Methodist Church*, rev. ed. (Nashville: Abingdon Press, 2006), on itinerancy, esp. 218–25.

16. Nolan B. Harmon, *The Organization of the Methodist Church*, 2nd ed. rev. (Nashville: The Methodist Publish House, 1953), 128–9; Russell E. Richey, *The Methodist Conference in America: A History* (Nashville: Kingswood Books, 1996), 13–14, 186–90.

17. For a discussion of the MECS Course of Study and changes made to it in the 1930s, see Sledge, *Hands on the Ark*, 203–4, 213; see also his interpretation of MECS provincialism, which included "'perverted nationalism,' sectionalism, and sectarianism," 192.

18. *MMA*, July 31, 1991; bulletin from Leggett's July 20, 1991, funeral, in author's possession; *MCJ*, 1990, 446; Mississippi Methodist Foundation, Inc., "Report of Consultant and Investment Manager, Dr. J. W. Leggett, Jr., April 27, 1990," Bishop E. J. Pendergrass papers, JBCA, box 1, folder 5.1; *JMC*, 1942, 66.

19. *MCJ*, 1972, 188–9; *Journal of the Missouri West Annual Conference* (1986): 170–1.

20. Buff Oliver interview; *North Mississippi Conference Journal* (1985): 295; *JMC*, 1940, 61; *JMC*, 1942, 60, 67; *JMC*, 1946, 68.

21. *MCJ*, 1989, 395–6; Betty Conner Currey and David Conner interviews; *JMC*, 1943, 44, 63, 71, 73.

22. Debra Holston Selden interview; *Oklahoma Conference Journal* (1995): 239–40; *JMC*, 1942, 68; *JMC*, 1943, 69; *JMC*, 1945, 64; *JMC*, 1946, 66.

23. *MCJ*, 2000, 255–6; Mary Myers Dickson, Marilyn Foxworth Dickson, and Mike Dickson (Dickson family) interview; *JMC*, 1943, 73; *JMC*, 1944, 55; *JMC*, 1946, 65; *JMC*, 1948, 72.

24. *JMC*, 1943, 7; *JMC*, 1947, 4, 39. General Conference delegates also represent their annual conference at Jurisdictional Conference and are joined by additional delegates elected to serve only at Jurisdictional Conference. Re: Leggett dominance, see Tyler Thompson, "Another Pilgrimage to Jackson," *Christian*

Century, April 22, 1964, 511–12—Leggett's name is not used, but the article refers to him and his power.

25. http://georgiainfo.galileo.usg.edu/topics/historical_markers/county/white/bishop-marvin-a.-franklin (accessed July 20, 2014); Roy Clark interview, 2003.

26. Roy Clark and Inman Moore interviews; Clark interview, 2003.

27. George T. Currey interview; Bishop Clay F. Lee interview, 2003; see also Roy C. Clark Oral History Memoir, 1965, John Quincy Adams papers, MCA, box 16, folder 6 (Roy Clark Oral History), 15–19.

28. *JMC*, 1951, 4.

29. Moore interview; *JMC*, 1955, 51–4; *JMC*, 1959, 4. I have used my own knowledge of Mississippi Conference political allegiances to identify Leggett men and moderates.

30. Description of the group's *modus operandi* is based on my own knowledge. Lee interview, 2003.

31. Inman Moore Jr., to George Berry, March 12, 1964, Inman Moore PP, written in response to the early 1964 Mississippi Conference survey sent to ministers who had left the conference; Rod Entrekin, interview, 2003; Jack Loflin interview; Arthur O'Neil, Jr. interview. Stories of personal attention received from Leggett abound, e.g., Travis Fulton e-mail to author, July 24, 2009.

32. Loflin interview and Lee interview, 2003; Wilton Carter to George Berry, March 31, 1964, Wilton Carter PP; and Elton Brown interview, 2003; Roy Clark Oral History, 19–20.

33. Jack Troutman interview; James and Libby Rush, James McCormick, William T. Lowry, George T. Currey, Jack Troutman, Rod Entrekin, and Maxie Dunnam interviews, 2004; O'Neil interview; *JMC*, 1961, 96. Born of Conviction signer James Nicholson said his pastor father did not like politics but accepted Leggett as leader of the conference. For more support of claims re: the Leggett power bloc, see Alan K. Waltz, *The Mississippi Annual Conference, Southeastern Jurisdiction* (Philadelphia: Board of Missions, Methodist Church, 1963); *JMC*, 1963, 135; and Norman U. Boone, "A Statement to the Pastors of the Brookhaven District," September 25, 1962, with letter to "Dear Fellow Minister" (n.d., November 1962?), Ned Kellar PP—a quote from Boone's statement: "I personally count it an insult for anyone to imply that if I vote in a certain way, I will be taken care of . . . AND it arouses *every* ounce of indignation in me when pressure is brought to bear upon me to vote for certain people with the warning that it would be best for me to do so."

34. Total full members in the local churches in the conference increased from 96,892 at the end of 1949 to 102,704 at the end of 1960—*JMC*, 1950, 190; *JMC*, 1961, 280. From 1946 to 1950, an average of six ministers were ordained elder per year, while from 1951 to 1955, the average ordained elder per year increased to more than eleven, and between 1956 and 1964, an average of sixteen ministers were ordained elder each year—*JMC*, 1945–62, Condensed Minutes, "Who

Have Been Elected Elders?" *JMC*, 1960, 28–9; *JMC*, 1963, 135. For more on the conference political situation, see Waltz, *The Mississippi Annual Conference, Southeastern Jurisdiction*, 47–9, 79, 85–6. George L. Berry to Wilton Carter, February 29, 1964, Carter PP; *JMC*, 1964, 152.

35. David E. Harrell Jr., in Harrell, ed., *Varieties of Southern Evangelicalism* (Macon, GA: Mercer University Press, 1981), 2.

36. *DMC*, 1944, ¶2172; Murray, *Methodists and the Crucible of Race*, 60; "Pillars of Peace" and "That Freedom May Not Perish," Bishop Marvin A. Franklin papers, JBCA, box 4, folders 6 and 3, n.d. (1944 or so). There is no evidence Franklin ever preached these sermons in Mississippi.

37. Franklin, *JDN*, February 20, 1949.

38. *DMC*, 1948, ¶2026 (emphasis in original); *DMC*, 1956, ¶2026. This 1956 addition figures prominently in the 1963 Born of Conviction statement.

39. Eagles, *The Price of Defiance*, ch. 7; see also Numan Bartley, *The Rise of Massive Resistance* (Baton Rouge: Louisiana State University Press, 1969 [1997]); Walter Lord, *The Past That Would Not Die* (New York: Harper and Row, 1965), 60–1; "The Church Considers the Supreme Court Decision," pamphlet reprinted from *The Church News*, Episcopal Diocese of Mississippi, August 1954; Will Campbell, *And Also With You: Duncan Gray and the American Dilemma* (Franklin, TN: Providence House, 1997), 124–44; Shattuck, *Episcopalians and Race*, 66–7.

40. Lord, *The Past That Would Not Die*, 61; Campbell, *And Also With You*, 155–6.

41. Neil R. McMillen, *The Citizens' Council* (Urbana: University of Illinois Press, 1971 [1994]), 18–19ff., 26–7; Hendrickson, *Sons of Mississippi*, 46; Silver, *Mississippi: The Closed Society*, 36 (quoting Hodding Carter II); Dittmer, *Local People*, 50–3. For the most complete treatment of Citizens' Council repression, retaliation, and membership recruitment, see McMillen, *The Citizens' Council*, 21–39, 211.

42. *MMA*, December 1, 1954; *MMA*, December 22, 1954. Re: the *Advocate* and the race issue in the late 1950s, see Ellis Ray Branch, "Born of Conviction: Racial Conflict and Change in Mississippi Methodism, 1945–1983," PhD diss., Mississippi State University, 1984, 75–6.

43. Charles C. Bolton, *The Hardest Deal of All* (Jackson: University Press of Mississippi, 2005), 68–9, 72; *SSN*, January 1955, 7; Bartley, *The Rise of Massive Resistance*, 56, and Lord, *The Past That Would Not Die*, 64–5; see also Hodding Carter III, *The South Strikes Back* (Garden City, NY: Doubleday, 1959), 41–8. In 1954, only 4 percent of eligible blacks were registered voters, and that percentage fell as the result of massive resistance (see Dittmer, *Local People*, 70–1). Dittmer, *Local People*, 59; Yasuhiro Katagiri, *The Mississippi State Sovereignty Commission* (Jackson: University Press of Mississippi, 2001), 4.

44. *MMA*, April 6, 1955; see also *MMA*, December 22, 1954; Edwin L. Brock, "Methodism's Growing Cleavage," *Christian Century*, August 24, 1955, 971–2; and Bartley, *The Rise of Massive Resistance*, 300.

45. *JCL*, April 27, 1955, 1, 10; *MMA*, May 11, 1955, 12–13; *JCL*, April 27, 1955; Barefield, "Report from the South," *Motive*, February 1956, 19 (emphasis in original).

46. *JMC*, 1951, 47, 74; Roy Delamotte, "Pastor's Report to the Baltic and Versailles Methodist Churches, 1951–55," Ken McCormick papers, Library of Congress, Manuscript Division (McCormick papers), box 23, folder 5; Delamotte, "Brief Summary of My Experience at Mississippi Conference 1955," September 20, 1955, McCormick papers, box 23, folder 5 (emphasis in original).

47. Delamotte, "Brief Summary . . ."; *JMC*, 1955, 63, 120; *JCL/JDN*, June 19, 1955.

48. Delamotte, "Brief Summary . . ."; *JMC*, 1955, 73. For another account of these events, see David T. Ridgway, *MMA*, July 19, 1961. Currey interview; Delamotte, "Brief Summary. . . ."

49. Elton Brown interview, 2003. This was one of Leggett's better known sermons.

50. Walter G. Muelder, *Methodism and Society in the Twentieth Century* (New York: Abingdon Press, 1961), especially ch. 10 and part 3.

51. *MMA*, January 25, 1956; *JDN*, January 30, 1956; re: Sullens, see David R. Davies, *The Press and Race* (Jackson: University Press of Mississippi, 2001), 86–8.

52. *DMC*, 1960, 26–7 (¶45); see also Murray, *Methodists and the Crucible of Race*, 84–7; Branch, "Born of Conviction," 59–60; *JDN*, June 12, 1957.

53. *JMC*, 1959, 132.

54. Katagiri, *The Mississippi State Sovereignty Commission*, 61–2; Dittmer, *Local People*, 60, 82; Katagiri, *The Mississippi State Sovereignty Commission*, 65–6, 70, 72–4; Dittmer, *Local People*, chs. 4–5; Martin Luther King Jr., "Letter from Birmingham Jail," in King, *Why We Can't Wait*, 83.

55. *JCL*, February 17, 1960, 1, 12; *MMA*, February 10, 1960, 1 (see, e.g., *DMC*, 1956, ¶174–5); see Branch, "Born of Conviction," 77–85 for a more detailed discussion.

56. Branch, "Born of Conviction," 79; *MMA*, February 24, 1960; *MMA*, January 27, 1960; *MMA*, February 10, 1960; *MMA*, February 3, 1960; *MMA*, February 17, 1960; *JCL*, February 17, 1960; *JCL*, March 4, 1960; *MMA* editorials and articles, all 1960: February 10; March 30; January 27; February 17; February 10; and February 17.

57. *MMA*, February 3, 1960 (emphasis in original); March 4 entry in Franklin's personal 1960 calendar, Franklin papers, box 1; *JCL*, March 4, 1960.

58. *JCL*, March 1, 1960. Selah was proven wrong in 1994, when Phillip Heidelberg, an African American, was appointed to serve the predominately white Wesley UMC in Ocean Springs and remained four years (*MCJ*, 2005, 76). *JCL*, March 1, 1960; *JCL*, March 24, 1960; *JCL*, March 1, 1960.

59. Branch, "Born of Conviction," 85; Stanny Sanders to Sam Ashmore, April 6, 1960, Ashmore papers, box 2, folder 6, and Ashmore to Sanders, April 8, 1960, box 2, folder 1 (emphasis in original).

60. *MMA*, April 20, 1960.

61. *JCL*, March 2, 1960.

CHAPTER 2

1. Silver, *Mississippi: The Closed Society*, 153; 66; Katagiri, *The Mississippi State Sovereignty Commission*, 132–3.

2. William G. McAtee, *Transformed: A White Pastor's Journey into Civil Rights and Beyond* (Jackson: University Press of Mississippi, 2011), 235.

3. Maxie Dunnam interviews; Dunnam e-mail to author, August 12, 2010; Kim Dunnam Reisman, "Expectation: The Shaping Power of the Future," speech to The Parlor Club of Lafayette/West Lafayette, Indiana, January 17, 2009, Kim Reisman PP.

4. Dunnam interview, 2004.

5. Jerry and Rose Trigg interview; Trigg e-mails to author, August 12 and September 16, 2010; Trigg interview.

6. Jerry and Rose Trigg interview; *MCJ*, 1993, 502–3.

7. Jerry and Rose Trigg interview.

8. James L. Waits interviews; Waits e-mails to author, October 1 and 8, 2010.

9. Waits e-mails to author, October 1 and 8, 2010; Waits interview, 2010. Interracial Methodist church events in Mississippi were rare but not unheard of prior to the 1954 *Brown* decision. Though Dyess took a risk in encouraging Main Street youth to attend the St. Paul event, Mississippi was not as "closed" as it would become after 1954—see Charles Eagles, "The Closing of Mississippi Society," *Journal of Southern History* 67 (2) (May 2001): 331–372. Main Street Church would not have hosted youth from St. Paul then.

10. Waits interview, 2003.

11. Jerry Furr interview.

12. Furr interview; Furr e-mails to author, September 18–20, 2010.

13. Furr interview.

14. James Nicholson interview.

15. Powell Hall interview. The comic strip was "Parlor Sink and Bedroom," by Billy DeBeck—Cathy Shelton e-mail to author and Miriam Berele e-mail to Cathy Shelton, October 29, 2011. The Jones book may have been *The Choice before Us* (New York: Abingdon Press, 1937); the passage quoted is Acts 10:34–5.

16. Rod Entrekin, "My Journey in Ministry," 2004, Rod Entrekin PP; Rod Entrekin interviews.

17. James and Libby Rush interview.

18. Dunnam interview, 2004; *JMC*, 1954, 74. Mississippi Southern College is now the University of Southern Mississippi. See Sam Barefield, portion of "Report from the South," *Motive* 16 (5) (February 1956), 19; Denson Napier and Jack Troutman interviews; *MCJ*, 2013, 156.

19. Ed and Martina McRae interview.

20. Gene Manning and Mary Lynn Johnson, portions of "Report from the South," *Motive*, February 1956; Branch, "Born of Conviction," 60; McRae interview;

re: integration of Lake Junaluska pool, see Bill Lowry, *The Antechamber of Heaven: A History of Lake Junaluska Assembly* (Franklin, TN: Providence House Publishers, 2010), 106–12.

21. Furr interview.

22. Clarice T. Campbell and Oscar Allan Rogers Jr., *Mississippi: The View from Tougaloo* (Jackson: University Press of Mississippi, 1979), 171. Two of the students, Robert Ezelle and Raymond McClinton, were moderate members of Jackson's Galloway Memorial Methodist Church during the turmoil of the 1960s, while a third, Caxton Doggett, became a Methodist minister known for his liberal views. Paul Ramsey, who became a renowned Christian ethicist at Princeton, also attended these meetings in the mid-1930s—see "A Brief Account of the Mississippi Intercollegiate Fellowship (1933–58), T. W. Lewis Papers, MCA, box 1, folder 2 (the Intercollegiate Council is also called Intercollegiate Fellowship in some references). Re: promotion of interracial dialogue by the YMCA and other organizations in the South in the 1920s and 1930s, see David M. Reimers, *White Protestantism and the Negro* (New York: Oxford University Press, 1965), 84–8; see also excerpt from H. M. Bullock to DMK [D. M. Key], "Suggestions relative to form V-1. Outline of Religious Program," 1936, R. A. Goodbread Papers, MCA, box 2, folder 15 (Goodbread Papers); George Maddox, e-mail to author, January 6, 2006.

23. Graduation dates of those who earned Millsaps degrees range from 1938 (James Conner) to 1960 (Wallace Roberts). Rod Entrekin to Don Fortenberry, November 17, 2004; and Entrekin, "My Journey in Ministry," August 2004, both Rod Entrekin PP; Campbell and Rogers, *Mississippi: The View from Tougaloo*, 171–2; see also "A Brief Account of the Mississippi Intercollegiate Fellowship (1933–58), Lewis Papers.

24. Wilton Carter interview. Fleming taught at Millsaps from 1945 to 1962 (*JCL*, July 2, 2009).

25. Jerry Trigg e-mail to author, September 16, 2010; Waits interview, 2010; Andrew Young, *An Easy Burden* (New York: HarperCollins, 1996), 56.

26. *MMA*, October 2, 1957.

27. "Interdenominational Discussion Groups" brochure, A. E. Cox Papers, MSUSCD (Cox Papers), box 1-B, folder 48; Millsaps, *Purple and White*, February 27, 1958; *MMA*, March 12, 1958; Jackson *State Times*, March 9, 1958; Dittmer, *Local People*, 62 and *JDN*, March 4, 1958; *JCL*, March 7, 1958. Additional accounts of the Millsaps event include McMillen, *The Citizens' Council*, 244–6; Branch, "Born of Conviction," 62–74; Silver, *Mississippi: The Closed Society*, 36; Robert Canzoneri, *"I Do So Politely": A Voice from the South* (Boston: Houghton Mifflin, 1965), 69–71; and Carter, *The South Strikes Back*, 180–6.

28. *JDN*, March 6 and 7, 1958. Re: Tougaloo-Millsaps relations and Ernst Borinski's Social Science Forums, see Maria R. Lowe and J. Clint Morris, "Civil Rights Advocates in the Academy: White Pro-integrationist Faculty at Millsaps

College," *Journal of Mississippi History* LXIX (2) (Summer 2007): 121–45. See also Dittmer, *Local People*, 61–2.

29. The other four future Born of Conviction signers at Millsaps that spring were Wallace Roberts, James Rush, John Ed Thomas, and Keith Tonkel. Jim Waits, "Race Discussion Causes Crisis," *Concern*, March 28, 1958, 3, 8; event brochure, Cox Papers, box 1-B, folder 48; *MMA*, March 12, 1958.

30. *JCL*, March 9, 1958.

31. Joseph Mitchell, *There Is an Election!* (Troy, AL: Leader Press, 1980), 70–1; *MMA*, March 12, 1958, 2; *JCL*, March 7, 1958.

32. *MMA*, March 12, 1958; *MMA*, March 26, 1958. For a discussion of Southern Protestant colleges and segregation policy during this era, see Kenneth K. Bailey, *Southern White Protestantism in the Twentieth Century* (New York: Harper and Row, 1964), 147–8. The Millsaps Board affirmed segregation as policy but avoided future tense—the Citizens' Council would have wanted "will always be . . ." added.

33. Branch, "Born of Conviction," 70–1; Maddox e-mails to author, January 6, 2006 and July 27, 2006. Finger showed Maddox the letter. Maddox taught at Duke for the rest of his career.

34. O. Gerald Trigg to Ellis Wright, March 11, 1958, Goodbread Papers, box 2, folder 15; *MMA*, March 26, 1958, 2.

35. Dittmer, *Local People*, 62; Branch, "Born of Conviction," 74; Malcolm Mabry to Finger, March 10, 1958, box 5, folder 1; J. Allen Lindsey to Finger, March 10, 1958, box 5, folder 1; and Clara Mae Sells to Finger, March 18, 1958, box 2, folder 15—all Goodbread Papers.

36. *JMC*, 1956–63, Condensed Minutes, "Who Have Been Elected Elders?"; Clark interviews; Troutman interview; Wilton Carter interview.

37. Troutman interview; Wilton Carter interview; Calvin Trillin, *An Education in Georgia: Charlayne Hunter, Hamilton Holmes, and the Integration of the University of Georgia* (Athens, GA: University of Georgia Press, 1992), 50–54.

38. Furr interview; Dunnam interview, 2004; Ed Starr e-mails to author, July 17 and 18, 2011.

39. Jerry and Rose Trigg interview.

40. Joe Way interview; Way e-mail to author, September 26, 2011; Ray Waddle, "Days of Thunder: The Lawson Affair," *Vanderbilt Magazine* (Fall 2002), 34–43. The matter was resolved in the summer of 1960 with the reinstatement of Lawson, and the faculty withdrew their resignations; Lawson had by that time transferred to Boston University. See also Taylor Branch, *Parting the Waters* (New York: Touchstone, 1988), 273–5, 278–80. Way e-mail to author, September 26, 2011.

41. Waits e-mail to author, October 1, 2010.

42. Ned Kellar interview; Ned Kellar, *Sandersville* (Bloomington, IN: Xlibris, 2010), 18–19.

43. Boone M. Bowen, *The Candler School of Theology ~ Sixty Years of Service* (Atlanta: Emory University, 1974), 112–16; SMU's Perkins desegregated in 1951, while Duke University's trustees approved the admission of blacks in 1961—David M. Reimers, *White Protestantism and the Negro*, 131 (he claims Candler integrated in 1963) and http://divinity.duke.edu/news-media/news/20130118integration (accessed July 20, 2014). The boundary image comes from Roy M. Oswald, *Crossing the Boundary between Seminary and Parish* (Washington, DC: Alban Institute, 1985).

44. McRae interview.

45. Powell Hall interview; http://newswirehouston.com/dr-horace-germany%E2%80%99s-sacrifice-1960-2010/ (accessed July 20, 2014). Germany was a Church of God, Anderson, Indiana minister and was investigated in 1960 by the Sovereignty Commission (see http://mdah.state.ms.us/arrec/digital_archives/sovcom/#basicfolder, hereafter MSSC Records, esp. 1-32-0-24-1-1-1). *JCL*, August 22, 1960 (1-32-0-39-1-1-1, MSSC Records); Silver, *Mississippi: The Closed Society*, 96; *JCL*, August 27, 1960, 1. See Germany's autobiography, *At Any Cost: The Story of a Life in Pursuit of Brotherhood* (Anderson, IN: Warner Press, 2001).

46. Powell Hall interview; fragment of Lake antilynching sermon from Powell Hall PP.

47. Dittmer, *Local People*, 86; see also Gilbert R. Mason, *Beaches, Blood, and Ballots: A Black Doctor's Civil Rights Struggle* (Jackson: University Press of Mississippi, 2000), ch. 5; Inman Moore, "One Man's Journey (A Statement on Civil Rights)," unpublished address, n.d. (c. 2004), Moore PP; *Pasadena (CA) Star-News*, June 18, 2005.

48. R. Inman Moore Jr., "Biloxi—The Beach—And the Clarion Call of Christianity," sermon preached at Leggett Memorial Methodist Church, n.d. (May 1, 1960?), Moore PP; *Pasadena (CA) Star-News*, June 18, 2005.

49. *JMC*, 1958, 74; 1959, 86; Dunnam e-mail to author, September 24, 2008; Henry Clay, Jr. interview; Dunnam interview, 2004.

50. Dunnam e-mail to author, September 24, 2008; Henry Clay interview; Dunnam interview, 2004.

51. Jerry and Rose Trigg interview; *JMC*, 1959, 86; "A History of the Caswell Springs United Methodist Church, 1875–1975," in author's possession; Trigg interview; Jackson *State Times*, March 17, 1961.

52. *JMC*, 1961, 102; Dittmer, *Local People*, 87–9. For discussion of the developing Jackson Movement and the Freedom Rides, see Dittmer, 87–99, and Charles M. Payne, *I've Got the Light of Freedom* (Berkeley: University of California Press, 1995), 107–8.

53. *JMC*, 1956, 73; Furr interview; *MMA*, February, 7, 1962; Dunnam interview, June 12, 2009.

54. *JMC*, 1959, 79; Furr interview; *JMC*, 1960, 101.

55. Furr interview; Richard L. Ridgway e-mail to author, June 7, 2011.

56. Dittmer, *Local People*, 90–9; and Payne, *I've Got the Light of Freedom*, 107–8; "From: Meeting of the Official Board, June 12, 1961," W. J. Cunningham/ Galloway Papers, folder 4, UMDASC.

57. "From: Meeting of the Official Board, June 12, 1961," W. J. Cunningham/ Galloway Papers, folder 4, UMDASC; Selah, Dr. W. B., "Galloway and the Race Issue," William Bryan. Selah Papers, box 1, folder 2, JBCA (Selah Papers); Ray E. Stevens, "Galloway Church History, 1956–1995," MDAH, 92.

CHAPTER 3

1. James Graham Cook, *The Segregationists* (New York: Appleton-Century-Crofts, 1962), 3—the other two were Alabama and South Carolina. William Doyle, *An American Insurrection: The Battle of Oxford, Mississippi, 1962* (New York: Doubleday, 2001), 18, 29, 31–2, 34; Lord, *The Past That Would Not Die*, 107–8; Eagles, *The Price of Defiance*, chs. 12–18. A timetable of events after the US Fifth Circuit Court of Appeals ordered Meredith admitted on June 25, 1962, is found in Silver, *Mississippi: The Closed Society*, 116–17.

2. Re: Sovereignty Commission and Citizens' Councils, see Katagiri, *The Mississippi State Sovereignty Commission* and McMillen, *The Citizens' Council*; re: organized Klan intimidation and violence, see David Cunningham, "Shades of Anti-Civil Rights Violence," in Ted Ownby, ed., *The Civil Rights Movement in Mississippi* (Jackson: University Press of Mississippi, 2013), 180–203. Carter II, Harkey, and Smith all won Pulitzer Prizes (Harkey and Smith in the 1960s for outspoken opposition to massive resistance). Re: *State Times*, see Davies, *The Press and Race*, 86–87, and Curtis Wilkie, *Dixie* (New York: Touchstone, 2001), 100. Cain published and edited the *Summit Sun* in Pike County—see Wilkie, *Dixie*, 55–62, 124–5, 205; Adam Nossiter, *Of Long Memory* (Cambridge, MA: Da Capo Press, 2002), 83; re: the Hedermans, see Dittmer, *Local People*, 64–5, and Davies, *The Press and Race*, 85–6, 115.

3. Lord, *The Past That Would Not Die*, 107–8, and Russell H. Barrett, *Integration at Ole Miss* (Chicago: Quadrangle Books, 1965), 57–60; Elizabeth Sutherland Martinez, ed., *Letters from Mississippi* (Brookline, MA: Zephyr Press, 2002), 19.

4. Re: Southwest Mississippi activity, see Dittmer, *Local People*, 99–115, and Payne, *I've Got the Light of Freedom*, 111–28; re: planning in early 1962 and COFO, see Payne, *I've Got the Light of Freedom*, 129–31, and Dittmer, *Local People*, 118–19; re: Jackson, see Dittmer, *Local People*, 116–17, 123–4; re: the Delta, see Payne, *I've Got the Light of Freedom*, ch. 5, and Dittmer, *Local People*, ch. 6.

5. *JMC*, 1962, 132–3.

6. Gregory Wilson, *The Stained Glass Jungle* (Garden City, NY: Doubleday, 1962); the 1955 controversy is discussed in chapter 1. *JMC*, 1955, 73; *Holston Conference Journal* (1980), 242. Both Mississippi Conference pastors from that era who

were later elected bishops stated to me unequivocally that the book was about Mississippi Conference politics (Lee interview, 2003; e-mail from Roy Clark to author, July 21, 2006). See also Norman U. Boone, "A Statement to the Pastors of the Brookhaven District," n.d. (September 25, 1962), Ned Kellar PP, which mentions the novel and its possible connection to the conference three months after publication.

7. J. Rayford Woodrick interview; Wilson, *The Stained Glass Jungle*; correspondence from Roy Delamotte to Milton C. White in M. C. White Papers, MCA, box 1, folder 2a; and Roy Delamotte to Clement Alexandre, October 31, 1959, and February 3, 1960, McCormick Papers, box 23, folder 4; Delamotte to Alexandre, May 21, 1957, and Delamotte, "Pastor's Report to the Baltic and Versailles Methodist Churches," box 23, folder 5; Betty Conner Currey interview.

8. Wilson, *The Stained Glass Jungle*; Delamotte to Alexandre, April 28, 1957, McCormick Papers, box 23, folder 5; Delamotte to Alexandre, December 7, 1957, box 23, folder 4; Thaxton Springfield to Ken McCormick, June 8, 1962, box 23, folder 6; see also letters from Hugh Herbert (June 14, 1962), John Wesley Hardt (June 21, 1962), and James Allen Kestle (July 9, 1962), all box 23, folder 6, and from Bishop Gerald Kennedy (December 14, 1961), box 23, folder 2, and Nat G. Long (August 19, 1962), box 23, folder 1; see also William E. Albright, Jr., "Stained Glass Jungle or Modern Aldersgate," *Christian Advocate*, March 28, 1963, 11–12: "If Jack Lee isn't typical of Methodism, the Rev. F. J. Worthington is."

9. Delamotte to Alexandre, May 21, 1957, McCormick Papers, box 23, folder 5; Delamotte to Alexandre, June 17, 1959, box 23, folder 4; re: "poorly kept secret," see Alexandre to Delamotte, October 27, 1959, box 23, folder 4.; Seth W. Granberry to McCormick, August 23, 1962, McCormick Papers, box 23, folder 1; see also Arthur M. North and Barry Shaw, "To the Council of Bishops of The Methodist Church from Two Ministers Who Visited Jackson, Mississippi, on the Weekend of November 3, 1963," November 8, 1963, Humphrey Papers, box 1 "Methodism in Mississippi" 1960/65, 1/3.

10. "Willard would have said he was doing what was best for the church," O'Neil interview; Mississippi Methodist Foundation, Inc. "Report of Consultant and Investment Manager, Dr. J. W. Leggett, Jr., April 27, 1990," Bishop E. J. Pendergrass Papers, box 1, folder 5.1; Jack Loflin and T. Jerry Mitchell interviews. Leggett worked after his retirement as executive director and later consultant and investment manager for the Mississippi Methodist Foundation until the age of eighty-two. James R. McCormick interview (his father, M. L. McCormick Sr., was a chief Leggett lieutenant; Jim McCormick was best friends with Willard Leggett's son, Willard Leggett III, also a minister in the Conference); Wilson, *The Stained Glass Jungle*, 318.

11. *MMA*, August 8, 1962; Pascagoula/Moss Point *Chronicle* (*PMPC*), June 22, 1962; Lowman Letter to Editor, *JCL*, June 18, 1962 (10-35-1-140-1-1-1, MSSC

Records); Jerry and Rose Trigg interview; Trigg Letter to Editor, *JCL*, June 26, 1962 (10-35-1-141-1-1-1, MSSC Records); Summer Walters e-mail to author, July 12, 2006; Millsaps College, *Purple and White*, March 16, 1956; Trigg e-mail to author, August 12, 2010.

12. "Myers G. Lowman, The Circuit Riders," mimeographed document, no author or date apparent (early 1960s?) in "NCC—Lowman and the Circuit Riders" folder, box 1, Humphrey Papers; re: the MFSA controversy, see Richey et al., *The Methodist Experience in America*, Vol. 2, 573–4 and Vol. 1, 419–23; also Muelder, *Methodism and Society in the Twentieth Century*, 213–28; "Myers G. Lowman, The Circuit Riders;" 7-0-2-69-1-1-1, MSSC Records; Ralph Lord Roy, *Communism and the Churches* (New York: Harcourt, Brace, 1960), 305; General Conference report, "Attacks Upon Churches and Churchmen," quoted in Muelder, *Methodism and Society in the Twentieth Century*, 225n42.

13. 7-0-4-31-1-1-1, MSSC Records; Katagiri, *The Mississippi State Sovereignty Commission*, 88, 92; 7-0-3-87-1-1-1, 7-0-2-69-1-1-1, 7-0-3-80-2-1-1 and 3-1-1, MSSC Records; see Eagles, *The Price of Defiance*, 172; R. Glenn Miller to Dear friends, April 19, 1961 in Cox Papers, box 1-A Circuit Riders; 7-0-3-87-1-1-1, MSSC Records; and Katagiri, *The Mississippi State Sovereignty Commission*, 92; Joseph E. Wroten, "Implications of the Violence at Oxford," *Concern*, December 15, 1962, 5 (10-86-0-24-1-1-1, 2-1-1, and 3-1-1, MSSC Records).

14. *JCL*, July 31, 1962 (10-35-1-143-1-1-1, MSSC Records); Jerry and Rose Trigg interview; Lum Cumbest et al. interview; MAMML *Information Bulletin*, September 1962; *DDT*, July 31, 1962; *MMA*, August 8, 1962; *DDT*, July 31, 1962; and *JCL*, August 1, 1962 (10-35-1-143-1-1-1, MSSC Records).

15. Jerry and Rose Trigg interview; MAMML *Information Bulletin*, September 1962; see 10-35-1-148-1-1-1, MSSC Records, for Lowman's response to the debate; see also M. G. Lowman to *The Mississippi Methodist Advocate*, August 14, 1962, and Henry M. Bullock to Ashmore, August 15, 1962, Ashmore Papers, box 1, folder 5.

16. Numan V. Bartley and Hugh D. Graham, *Southern Politics and the Second Reconstruction* (Baltimore: Johns Hopkins Press, 1975), 71; *DDT*, October 8, 1962; Dittmer, *Local People*, 139; Karl Wiesenburg, "The Oxford Disaster . . . Price of Defiance," *PMPC*, December 17–21, 1962; September 16 statement, Duncan Gray PP; see also William A. Pennington to Sam Ashmore, October 12, 1962, Ashmore Papers, box 2, folder 1.

17. Kellar, *Sandersville*, 123–4.

18. Boone, "A Statement to the Pastors of the Brookhaven District," n.d. (September 25, 1962), Kellar PP.

19. For the most thorough account of these events, see Eagles, *The Price of Defiance*, 314–23. The incident where Paul Johnson stopped Meredith on the campus is depicted in this book's cover photo.

20. Quoted in Dittmer, *Local People*, 140; see also Wilkie, *Dixie*, 104; and Eagles, *The Price of Defiance*, 336–7.

21. For detailed accounts of the September 30 riot, see Eagles, *The Price of Defiance*; Doyle, *An American Insurrection*; Wilkie, *Dixie*, 95–112; and Dittmer, *Local People*, 138–42; this summary is drawn mainly from Doyle, *An American Insurrection*, chs. 7–15 and Dittmer, *Local People*, 140.

22. Kellar, *Sandersville*, 129; see Eagles, *The Price of Defiance*, 331, 334; McRae interview; Furr telegram to John Satterfield, October 1, 1962, John C. Satterfield/American Bar Association Collection, UMDASC, folder 201a.

23. Walker Percy, "Mississippi: The Fallen Paradise," in Patrick Samway, ed., *Signposts in a Strange Land* (New York: Farrar, Strauss, and Giroux, 1991), 49; "Oxford: A Warning for Americans," Jackson: Mississippi State Junior Chamber of Commerce, October 1962, printed in Bradford Daniel, ed., *Black, White and Gray* (New York: Sheed and Ward, 1964), 81–102; Silver, *Mississippi: The Closed Society*, esp. 122–33, 175–6, 188–9; Frank E. Smith, *Congressman from Mississippi* (New York: Pantheon Books, 1964), 305. There are numerous accounts of the reaction to JFK's death in Mississippi schools—see, e.g., Biloxi-Gulfport *Sun Herald*, November 20, 1983; W. Ralph Eubanks, *Ever Is a Long Time: A Journey into Mississippi's Dark Past* (New York: Basic Books, 2003), 61–2; *JCL*, November 27, 1963, 6; and Smith, *Congressman from Mississippi*, 315; see also Kevin Sessums, *Mississippi Sissy* (New York: St. Martin's Press, 2007), 123; and "Mississippi's Inheritance to Its Youth," Ashmore Papers, box 2, folder 4.

24. The "Call for Repentance" was published in *Christianity Today* on October 26, 1962, 35–36, and in *New South* in March 1963; *MMA*, October 17, 1962 (statement dated October 8); Percy, "Mississippi: The Fallen Paradise," 43; J. H. Mitchell to K. I. Tucker, October 22, 1962, Ashmore Papers, box 1, folder 7.

25. *Baptist Record*, November 15, 1962; *JCL*, November 16, 1962; *Baptist Record*, November 15, 1962; *MMA*, November 21, 1962.

26. Mabel Anne Ashmore Harjes interview; Donald Lewis interview; Shirley Harjes e-mail to author, October 19, 2014—the Ashmores' granddaughter believes (and offers evidence) that Ann Ashmore wrote many of the editorials and says the Ashmores consistently worked as a team. This claim was echoed by her mother (Mabel Anne) and cousin (Lewis).

27. *MMA*, October 10, 1962.

28. *Wall Street Journal*, October 3, 1962; James S. Conner to Frank E. Smith, January 11, 1963, Silver Papers, box 23, folder 9 (quoted in Smith, *Congressman from Mississippi*, 309); the "statement" is Born of Conviction.

29. Dunnam interview, 2004, and Dunnam e-mail to author, September 19, 2008; Douglas M. Strong, *They Walked in the Spirit* (Louisville: Westminster John Knox, 1997), 80–2; see "A Reply to His Critics from E. Stanley Jones," 1960, mimeo, Ashmore Papers, box 1, folder 5; Stephen A. Graham, *Ordinary Man, Extraordinary Mission* (Nashville: Abingdon Press, 2005), 355; Strong, *They Walked in the Spirit*, 84; Dunnam e-mail.

30. Dunnam e-mail to author, September 2, 2012; Dunnam interview, 2004; Dunnam e-mail to author, September 19, 2008; R. I. Moore (Sr.) to Bishop Franklin, November 3, 1962, BOP, box 1, folder 19; Dunnam interview and e-mails, September 19 and 22, 2008.

31. Kellar, *Sandersville*, 88; *DH*, September 15, 1962.

32. *JMC*, 1960, 101; Rod Entrekin interview, 2007; Charles Ray Gipson, "Preaching on Controversial Issues: A Study of Theory and Practice," Master's thesis, Perkins School of Theology, 1968, 55–7.

33. *MMA*, October 31, 1962, 8; Waits interview, 2003.

34. Jerry and Rose Trigg interview.

35. Jerry and Rose Trigg interview; *DH*, October 6, 1962.

36. *JMC*, 1959, 81; *JMC*, 1961, 99; re: 1961 civil rights organizing activity in Pike and Amite Counties, see Dittmer, *Local People*, 99–115; Charles M. Payne, *I've Got the Light of Freedom*, 111–31; and Bob Zellner, *The Wrong Side of Murder Creek* (Montgomery: New South Books, 2008), 150–72. Lampton declined to be interviewed for this book.

37. Gipson, "Preaching on Controversial Issues," 94–8.

38. James Nicholson interview; *Washington (Iowa) Evening Journal*, December 26, 2003; James Nicholson interview; *JMC*, 1958, 94; *JMC*, 1962, 104.

39. James Nicholson, "My Mississippi Experiences" (unpublished essay from James Nicholson PP), my emphasis.

40. James Nicholson to "My Beloved Friend the 'Duke'" (Earl Marlatt), February 1, 1963, Nicholson PP; Nicholson, "My Mississippi Experiences," and "Real Issues for These Times," *New South*, March 1963; the sermon elaborated on three of four points eventually included in Born of Conviction and used language from Ashmore's "Who Is To Blame for the Rioting?"

41. James Nicholson to James Silver, January 22, 1963, Silver Papers, box 23, folder 9; James Nicholson interview; *JMC*, 1962, 242.

CHAPTER 4

1. Furr interview; see also Waits interview, 2003.

2. Re: Southern clergy response in this era, Ernest Campbell and Thomas Pettigrew's study of Little Rock, *Christians in Racial Crisis* (Washington, DC: Public Affairs Press, 1959) and Jeffrey Hadden's *The Gathering Storm in the Churches* (Garden City, NY: Doubleday, 1969) offer sociological analysis. Works by historians include Chappell, *A Stone of Hope*; Michael B. Friedland, *Lift Up Your Voice Like a Trumpet: White Clergy and the Civil Rights and Antiwar Movements* (Chapel Hill: University of North Carolina Press, 1998), chs. 1–5; Paul Harvey, *Freedom's Coming: Religious Culture and the Shaping of the South from the Civil War to the Civil Rights Era* (Chapel Hill, NC: University of North Carolina Press, 2005), ch. 4; and Bartley, *The Rise of Massive Resistance*, 294–305;

see also Dorgan, "Response of the Main-line Protestant Pulpit to *Brown v. Board of Education, 1954–1965*"; Reed Sarratt, *The Ordeal of Desegregation: The First Decade* (New York: Harper and Row, 1966), ch. 10; "The Southern Churches and the Race Question," *Christianity and Crisis*, March 3, 1958, 17–28; *NYT*, July 5–8, 1959; Ralph McGill, "The Agony of the Southern Minister," *NYT Magazine*, September 27, 1959: 16, 57–60; and the Samuel Southard articles in *Christian Century*: "Are Southern Churches Silent?," November 20, 1963, 1429–32, and "The Southern 'Establishment,'" December 30, 1964, 1618–21. At the June 2005 reunion of Born of Conviction signers, Ross Olivier, a white South African Methodist minister then serving as pastor of Galloway Memorial United Methodist Church, said that with the publication of Born of Conviction, "a line was drawn in the sand; a marker was placed. It is written into the record as a defining benchmark document, like the *Kairos* document or the Barmen Declaration" (author's notes from 2005 Born of Conviction reunion; *JCL*, June 7, 2005). For the text of the Barmen Declaration, see http://www.sacred-texts. com/chr/barmen.htm, and re: the 1985 *Kairos* document's response to South African apartheid, see http://kairossouthernafrica.wordpress.com/2011/05/08/ the-south-africa-kairos-document-1985/ (both accessed June 16, 2014). For comparisons of early 1960s Mississippi to Nazi Germany, see Adam Nossiter, *Of Long Memory*, 67–9; Clarice T. Campbell, *Civil Rights Chronicle: Letters from the South* (Jackson: University Press of Mississippi, 1997), 177; Doyle, *An American Insurrection*, 95; and John D. Humphrey, "What Is Your Image of Man?," Address to Faculty and Student Body of Millsaps College, November 29, 1962, Humphrey Papers, box 1, Methodism in Mississippi, 1960–5.

3. Bishop Kenneth Carder interview, November 18, 2005. The four white and black annual conferences in Mississippi merged in the mid-1970s to form two, Mississippi and North Mississippi. In 1989, those two united to become the Mississippi Conference, including all United Methodists in the state. Martin Luther King's "Letter from Birmingham Jail," *Why We Can't Wait*, 93–9; Dupont, *Mississippi Praying*; Robert Paul Sessions, "Are Southern Ministers Failing the South?," *Saturday Evening Post*, May 13, 1961, 37, 82–8; Chappell, *A Stone of Hope*.

4. In addition to the statements described in the following text, ministers in Huntsville and Montgomery, Alabama; Chattanooga, Tennessee; and Charlotte, North Carolina issued proclamations during these years, and there were others—Bass, *Blessed Are the Peacemakers*, 11–12, and Bartley, *The Rise of Massive Resistance*, 296–7.

5. For an account of Mrs. Hamer's literal "speaking truth to power," see Marsh, *God's Long Summer*, 33–44; re: words and the civil rights movement, see Davis W. Houck and David E. Dixon, eds., *Rhetoric, Religion and the Civil Rights Movement, 1954–1965* (Waco, TX: Baylor University Press, 2006), esp. 1–6, and Vol. 2 (2014).

6. *NYT*, July 5, 1959; Newman, *Getting Right with God*, 159; Sarratt, *The Ordeal of Desegregation*, 265; Alvis, *Religion and Race*, 57–8—an attempt was made to rescind "A Statement to Southern Christians" in 1955, but the General Assembly passed it by a larger margin. Newman, *Getting Right with God*, 23–4, notes that other state conventions, including Mississippi, kept silent regarding *Brown*. See Marsh, *God's Long Summer*, 98–100, re: the story of how Douglas Hudgins, pastor of Jackson's First Baptist Church, left the national convention before the vote on *Brown* and communicated his opposition. He later explained that the church had no business dealing with this "purely civic matter." Murray, *Methodists and the Crucible of Race*, 70–2; *MMA*, December 1, 1954.

7. "The Church Considers the Supreme Court Decision," pamphlet reprinted from *The Church News*, Episcopal Diocese of Mississippi, August 1954; Gardiner H. Shattuck Jr., *Episcopalians and Race*, 66–7; Will D. Campbell, *And Also with You*, 138–40; re: the creation and dissemination of the statement, see Campbell, *And Also with You*, 123–44; see Eagles, *The Price of Defiance*, ch. 7, for the argument that Mississippi society had "closed" more firmly by 1955; Shattuck, *Episcopalians and Race*, 67. I found no mention of the diocesan statement in the Jackson daily papers.

8. *SSN*, December 1954; January 1955; February 1955; March 1955; and March 1956.

9. Collins, *When the Church Bell Rang Racist*, 25–31; Robert S. Graetz, *A White Preacher's Memoir: The Montgomery Bus Boycott* (Montgomery: Black Belt Press, 1998).

10. *SSN*, January 1957; Newman, *Getting Right with God*, 117; Reed Sarratt, *The Ordeal of Desegregation*, 271; Samuel Southard, "The Southern 'Establishment,'" 1621; *SSN*, January 1957; *The Call* (Holston Conference UMC newspaper), February 25, 2005; *Nashville Tennesseean*, January 10, 1957. For more on Clinton, see Wilma Dykeman and James Stokely, "Clinton, Tennessee: A Town on Trial," *NYT Magazine*, October 26, 1958, 9, 61–5.

11. Nashville *Tennessean*, January 10, 1957; *NYT*, July 5, 1959; Bartley, *The Rise of Massive Resistance*, 295; Richmond *News-Leader*, January 29, 1957, and *Times-Dispatch*, January 29, 1957; Bartley, *The Rise of Massive Resistance*, 295–6; *NYT*, July 5, 1959; *SSN*, February and March 1957; Ralph E. Cousins et al., eds., *South Carolinians Speak: A Moderate Approach to Race* (Dillon, SC: South Carolinians Speak, 1957); *SSN*, August 1957; Dorgan, "Response of the Main-line Protestant Pulpit . . .," 18–19; Cousins et al., *South Carolinians Speak*, 72; William Peters, *The Southern Temper* (Garden City, NY: Doubleday, 1958), 28–9; *SSN*, August 1958.

12. Campbell and Pettigrew, *Christians in Racial Crisis*, 19, 175n5; *Arkansas Democrat*, September 7, 1957. E. J. Holifield was the father of American church historian E. Brooks Holifield—Brooks Holifield e-mail to author, June 30, 2009. *Arkansas Democrat*, September 13, 1957. The interracial statement's signers included twelve Presbyterians, six Methodists, five each from the Episcopal and

Christian churches, four from the black CME Church, and one each from AME, Baptist, and Congregational bodies. For an essay written by a signer of both the Methodist and interracial statements mentioned here, see Sessions, "Are Southern Ministers Failing the South?"; Dorgan, "Response of the Main-line Protestant Pulpit . . .," 33–4. For more on segregationist Christian response in Little Rock, see Campbell and Pettigrew, *Christians in Racial Crisis*, 41.

13. *Atlanta Journal-Constitution*, November 3, 1957; Peters, *The Southern Temper*, 96; Bishop L. Bevel Jones interview; NPR story, October 26, 2007, http://www. npr.org/templates/story/story.php?storyId = 15643777 (accessed June 13, 2014); Dow Kirkpatrick, "The Methodist Church: It Reflects Culture as Much as It Reforms It," in "The Southern Churches and the Race Question," *Christianity and Crisis*, March 3, 1958, 17–28; *Atlanta Journal-Constitution*, November 23, 1958; *NYT*, July 6, 1959.

14. *Mobile Press-Register*, March 5 and 8, 1958; Collins, *When the Church Bell Rang Racist*, 39–45, 62.

15. *Dallas Morning News*, April 27, 1958; *SSN*, May 1958; Julian N. Hartt, "Dallas Ministers on Desegregation," *Christian Century*, May 21, 1958, 619–20; *SSN*, November 1957.

16. *SSN*, July 1958; Newman, *Getting Right with God*, 27 (see 90, 95, and 97 for discussion of the ways Southern Baptist leaders soon "retreated into silence" in Virginia), 99; Alexander S. Leidholdt, *Standing before the Shouting Mob: Lenoir Chambers and Virginia's Massive Resistance to Public-School Integration* (Tuscaloosa: University of Alabama Press, 1997), 97–8; "Virginians Are Told Segregation Is Sin," *Christian Century*, September 3, 1958, 990; Bailey, *Southern White Protestantism in the Twentieth Century*, 149.

17. "Southern Ministers Speak Their Minds," *Pulpit Digest*, December 1958, 13–17. Dorgan, "Response of the Main-line Protestant Pulpit . . .," 45–7, criticizes the survey's methods and says its results "ought to have been heavily qualified."

18. Ellen Blue, *St. Mark's and the Social Gospel: Methodist Women and Civil Rights in New Orleans, 1895–1965* (Knoxville: University of Tennessee Press, 2011), 161–87; Baton Rouge *Morning Advocate* May 7, May 9, May 14, and June 7, 1961; John M. Winn e-mail to author, June 20, 2014; Baton Rouge *Morning Advocate* May 21, 1961; Walker Knight, "Race Relations: Changing Patterns and Practices," in Nancy T. Ammerman, ed., *Southern Baptists Observed: Multiple Perspectives on a Changing Denomination* (Knoxville: University of Tennessee Press, 1993), 167–8. For more on the experiences of individual signers, see Southard, "Are Southern Churches Silent?," 1431.

19. John M. Winn Jr., e-mail to author, June 19, 2014. The claim of relative lack of difficulties for the Methodists is based on Winn's memory and appointment records (*Louisiana Conference Journal*, 1960, 45–6; 1961, 48–9; 1962, 50–1), which show no evidence of any significant moves by the signers right after the statement came out.

20. *SSN*, June 1956; *NYT*, July 8, 1959; Blue, *St. Mark's and the Social Gospel*, 169; Baton Rouge *Morning Advocate* May 7, 1961. For a discussion on the differences between Catholic and Protestant traditions relating to church and clergy stands on the race issue, see Dorgan, "Response of the Main-line Protestant Pulpit . . .," 44–5.

21. *NYT*, July 7, 1959. When reporter John Wicklein asked Methodist Bishop Bachman Hodge to comment for this story on Birmingham, the Bishop said the *Times* had no business exploring the issue and hung up after he advised Wicklein to "take care of your situation up there, and we'll take care of our situation down here."

22. Bass, *Blessed Are the Peacemakers*, 18–20, 233–4. The January statement was modeled on one composed by the Huntsville Ministerial Association in October 1962 (the same month Born of Conviction was written). Bass, *Blessed Are the Peacemakers*, 23–7, 235–6. Bass's book profiles the eight men who signed the April statement, including Methodist bishops Paul Hardin and Nolan Harmon.

23. Benjamin E. Mays, *Born to Rebel* (New York: Charles Scribner's Sons, 1971), 244–5. The Dallas statement and others also insisted on the need for the power of God to deal with the crisis at hand.

24. NPR story, October 26, 2007; Bevel Jones interview.

25. Ernest Q. Campbell and Thomas F. Pettigrew, "Racial and Moral Crisis: The Role of Little Rock Ministers," *The American Journal of Sociology* (March 1959): 510 (emphasis in original); Hartt, "Dallas Ministers on Desegregation," 620. For an example of the voluntarist view from a Mississippi Conference moderate minister, see David T. Ridgway, "The Methodist Church and Integration," *MMA*, March 16, 1960, and "Will Southern Ministers Continue to Be Misunderstood?" *MMA*, July 19, July 26, and August 2, 1961. Hartt, "Dallas Ministers on Desegregation," 620; Reinhold Niebuhr, *Moral Man and Immoral Society* (New York: Charles Scribner's Sons, 1932), 253.

26. Southard points to the institutional concerns of all parish clergy in "Are Southern Churches Silent?," 1430. Hartt, "Dallas Ministers on Desegregation," 620; Campbell and Pettigrew, *Christians in Racial Crisis*, 2–3; Hartt, "Dallas Ministers on Desegregation," 620. Minimal consensus and dissatisfaction characterized the Barmen Declaration—see Charles Marsh, *Strange Glory: A Life of Dietrich Bonhoeffer* (New York: Alfred A. Knopf, 2014), 223–5.

27. Examples of individual stories include Robert B. McNeil, *God Wills Us Free* (New York: Hill and Wang, 1965); J. Herbert Gilmore, *They Chose to Live* (Grand Rapids, MI: Eerdmans, 1972); Alvis, *Religion and Race*, 64–8, 70; and Dorgan, "Response of the Main-line Protestant Pulpit . . .," 22, 29. Re: the Mississippi rabbis, see Gary Phillip Zola, "What Price Amos? Perry Nussbaum's Career in Jackson, Mississippi," and Clive Webb, "Big Struggle in a Small Town: Charles Mantinband of Hattiesburg, Mississippi," both in Bauman and Kalin, eds., *The Quiet Voices* (Tuscaloosa: University of Alabama Press, 1997), 213–29

and 230–57; "The Church Considers the Supreme Court Decision," Episcopal Diocese of Mississippi, 1954; September 16 statement, Duncan Gray PP; "Call for Repentance," *Christianity Today*, October 26, 1962, 35–6; see also *MMA*, October 10, 1962, and October 17, 1962.

28. The date is confirmed by the 1962 Daily Suggester calendars of Maxie Dunnam and Jim Waits (Dunnam e-mail to author, September 3, 2012; and Waits PP and e-mail correspondence between author and Waits, July 22 and 31, 2009). The description of the site and surrounding area comes from my interviews and correspondence with Dunnam and my own visits to the location (which has changed greatly since the 1960s—the house described here burned down long ago; the Hintonville Road is now paved, and a concrete bridge spans the creek).

29. Silver, *Mississippi: The Closed Society*, 6.

30. Interviews with the four participants; Furr e-mail to author, September 18, 2010; Jerry and Rose Trigg interview.

31. *MMA*, January 2, 1963; Mays, *Born to Rebel*, 244.

32. *DMC*, 1960, ¶s 2026 ("The Methodist Church and Race") and 2020 ("The Methodist Social Creed").

33. Bartley, *The Rise of Massive Resistance*, 274–5; Bolton, *The Hardest Deal of All*, 68–9, 72.

34. Because Jerry Trigg had debated anti-Communist champion Myers Lowman eleven weeks earlier, it is not surprising they included the point against Communism. See also Katagiri, *The Mississippi State Sovereignty Commission*, 88–9, 93–4.

35. See Hartt, "Dallas Ministers and Desegregation," 620, for a discussion of the fallacy of divorcing "spirit" and "world" or "spiritual" matters from "political" matters (an effective response to the Southern Presbyterian doctrine of the "spirituality of the church.")

36. Two movement leaders who did take notice of Born of Conviction were Ed King (*The White Church in Mississippi*, Part 3, 7–8) and Victoria Gray (Victoria J. Gray to Bertist C. Rouse, January 14, 1963, Ashmore Papers, box 1, folder 4)—see ch. 5.

37. The Mobile statement discussed earlier in this chapter is also comparable, given the intensity of resistance in Alabama, but it was a more localized declaration. The release of Born of Conviction to the state wire services and the location of signers across South Mississippi ensured wider knowledge of the Twenty-Eight's witness.

38. Waits and Dunnam interviews.

39. Waits interview, 2003, and Dunnam interview, 2004, and subsequent conversations and correspondence. The November 1 date comes from the pocket calendars of Maxie Dunnam and Jim Waits, and Ned Kellar has an account of the November 1 meeting at Hidden Haven in *Sandersville*, 171–4, though he does not date it. James L. Waits Papers, Pitts Theology Library Archives, Emory

University (hereafter PTLA), box 1, folder 2; Dunnam interview, 2009. The evidence for the list of names of potential signers present includes Kellar's book, the handwritten list of potential signers, and Ed McRae's 1962 pocket calendar (McRae e-mail to author, July 7, 2011); Woodrick interview.

40. Roy Eaton letter to author, January 25, 2006—he and Barlow expressed similar views in their letters to Maxie Dunnam in late December 1962 (Dunnam PP). Collins, *When the Church Bell Rang Racist*, 39–45; Waits interview, 2003, and Dunnam interview, 2004; Eaton letter to author. There is conflicting evidence concerning the December 13 meeting, which I have dated based on specific statements in letters from Barlow (December 25, 1962) and Eaton (December 24, 1962) to Dunnam (Dunnam PP) and on Jim Waits's 1962 Daily Suggester calendar, Waits PP.

41. Eaton to Dunnam, December 24, 1962, and Barlow to Dunnam, December 25, 1962, Dunnam PP.

42. Of all the statements discussed in this chapter, the only ones signed by a group spread apart in a comparable land area were two of the Little Rock declarations—one with ministers in fourteen cities, and the other signed by ministers of the North Arkansas Conference.

43. "Full-time ministry" in most cases means time served after graduation from seminary, but three of the signers had not completed seminary by late 1962, and one of those (Harold Ryker) never attended. Ed McRae, James Conner, Keith Tonkel, and Harold Ryker were not born in Mississippi. *JMC*, 1963, Statistical Tables, 236ff (of the signers, Dickson was also the highest paid that year).

44. The number considered (fifty-eight) represents everyone whose name appears on the statement or on the Waits list mentioned, plus one other person who told me he was approached. Woodrick interview; William T. and Barbara Lowry interview.

45. Jack Loflin's name appears on Waits's list of potential signers, but he was never asked (Loflin interview). Wilson Brent and George Currey interviews; draft text of a *Life* magazine article by Ron Bailey (never published), Dunnam PP; McRae interview; Ed Starr e-mail to author, July 17, 2011.

46. Jerry and Rose Trigg interview; Elton Brown interview, 2003; Kellar, *Sandersville*, 174–5.

47. "Signatures—12/27/62," in Waits Papers, PTLA, box 1, folder 2; James Nicholson interview; *MMA*, January 2, 1963.

48. Waits to W. L. Robinson, December 31, 1962, and Bill Pennington, December 31, 1962; Waits to John Hall (AP reporter—unbeknownst to Waits, he was Born of Conviction signer Powell Hall's younger brother) and Cliff Sessions (UPI reporter), both January 4, 1963, all in Waits Papers, PTLA, box 1, folder 8. The Oxford Call for Repentance got some national coverage but only a brief news story in the Jackson papers (*JCL*, October 8, 1962).

49. Walters interview; Summer Walters e-mail to author, January 25, 2006.

CHAPTER 5

1. *MMA*, January 2, 1963; *JCL*, January 3; *JDN*, January 3; *MS*, January 3, 1963.

2. McRae interview; *MS*, January 3, 1963.

3. Emily Stafford Matheny interview; *MCJ*, 1985, 328–9; Mark Matheny e-mail to author, June 27, 2011; *JMC*, 1942, 13; 1944, 9; 1947, 11, 4, 49; Emily Stafford Matheny interview.

4. Emily Stafford Matheny interview; Mark Matheny e-mail to author, June 27, 2011; Elise Matheny Eslinger e-mail to author, June 28, 2011; *Journal of the General Conference*, 1956, 325. For more on Stafford, see *MMA*, December 2, 1959.

5. *MMA*, January 9, 1963, 11 (emphasis in original); *JCL* and *JDN*, January 4, 1963; Summer and Betty Walters Papers, JBCA, box 1, folder 3 (Walters Papers)—see I Kings 19:18; *MMA*, January 9 and subsequent issues; *JCL*, January 6.

6. *JCL*, January 4, 1963, 14; Waits to W. L. Robinson, December 31, 1962, Waits Papers, PTLA, box 1, folder 8; *JCL*, January 4; E. S. Furr interview.

7. E. S. Furr interview; *Calhoun City Monitor Herald*, January 10, 1963.

8. *Journal of the Missouri West Annual Conference*, 1986, 170–1; Selah video, July 1983, Selah Papers. St. John's became a Methodist Church in 1939 due to the merger of the MEC, MECS, and Methodist Protestants.

9. *MMA*, April 9, 1958, 8–9.

10. Waits interview, 2003.

11. *Tupelo Daily Journal*, January 7, 1963; *JCL*, January 7, 1963.

12. *DDT*, January 6, 1963; *Lexington Advertiser*, July 18, 1963; *PMPC*, May 15 and 22, 1963; *The Petal Paper*, February 1963; see also *MEJ*, January 11 and 18, 1963; *Deer Creek Pilot*, January 18, 1963; and *PMPC*, May 15 and 22, 1963; *JCL*, January 7, 1963; *JCL*, January 23, 1963, also *MS*, January 30, 1963. Reed's speech drew harsh criticism from the Citizens' Council: *JCL*, January 25, 1963.

13. "Mississippi Methodism Refreshed," *Central Christian Advocate*, February 15, 1963, 3.

14. King, *The White Church in Mississippi*, Part 3, 7–8; Victoria J. Gray to Bertist C. Rouse, January 14, 1963, Ashmore Papers, box 1, folder 4. Rouse's letter appeared in the *Hattiesburg American* on January 9, and his letter and Gray's response appeared in *The Petal Paper*, February 1963. For more on Gray's role in the movement, see Dittmer, *Local People*, 127, 148, 181–4.

15. Eagles, *The Price of Defiance*, 192, 292–3, 320, 344, 354–5, 415; *JCL*, January 8, 1963; *JDN*, January 8, 1963.

16. *Summit Sun*, January 17, 1963; see also *Summit Sun*, January 10, 1963.

17. Susan Weill, *In a Madhouse's Din: Civil Rights Coverage by Mississippi's Daily Press, 1948–1968* (Westport, CT: Praeger, 2002), 256; *JDN*, January 3, 1963; *JDN*, January 4, 1963; *JCL*, January 7, 1963—Bishop Charles Galloway, "The South and the Negro," *Great Men and Movements: A Volume of Addresses*

(Nashville: Publishing House, MECS, 1914),316. Galloway's statement can be read as more descriptive than prescriptive. *JDN*, January 15, 1963.

18. *JCL*, January 10, 1963; *JDN*, January 25, 1963; *JDN*, January 8, March 22, 1963; *JCL*, January 15 and 16, March 22.

19. The letters date from January 6 to January 29, 1963, with seventeen in *JCL*. The clearest examples echoing the editorial arguments outlined here are found in *JCL*, January 23; *JDN*, January 9, 1963; and *JCL*, January 18, 1963. Ruth A. Wallace of Jackson wrote the positive letter (*JCL*, January 24, 1963); *DH*, January 7, 1963; *MEJ*, January 11 and 18, 1963; and January 30, 1963.

20. *MS*, January 8, 1963; *JDN*, January 9, 1963; *JCL*, January 18, 1963; *JDN*, January 16, 1963; *JCL*, January 9, 10, and 29, 1963; *MS*, January 8, 1963; *JCL*, January 10, 11, 24, 1963; *JDN*, January 9, 1963; *JCL*, January 10, 1963; *JDN*, January 16, 1963. *Engel v. Vitale*, the Supreme Court school prayer decision, came in June 1962.

21. *JCL*, January 23, 1963; *JCL*; January 10, 1963; *JCL*, January 24, 1963 (either the writer meant "wolves in sheep's clothing" or intentionally reversed it to imply they were both brainwashed and dangerous). Roy Wesley Wolfe, pastor of the Moselle Charge, in Charles Hills's "Affairs of State" column, *JCL*, January 8, 1963 (to Wolfe the "truth of God's Holy Word" meant segregation of the races).

22. *JCL*, January 11, 1963. The MAMML statement was written by Medford Evans, a Yale PhD in literature, the son of a Methodist minister, and part of the "chain of seniority" in the Citizens' Council who pursued a career in "organized racism," (McMillen, *The Citizens' Council*, 125–6). Although Wesley did defy Church of England authority on occasion, this was hardly his central motivation for founding the Methodist movement, and to suggest that the witness of the Spirit to the individual trumped any other source of authority for Wesley is absurd (see Heitzenrater, *Wesley and the People Called Methodist*, esp. chs. 2–3 and 10, 318). *MS*, January 10, 1963.

23. *JCL*, January 23, 1963.

24. For a discussion of the spirituality of the church in the context of the Presbyterian Church in the United States response to the race issue, see Alvis, *Religion and Race*, 4–5, 46–7; Slade, *Open Friendship in a Closed Society*, 94–5, 119–22; Dupont, *Mississippi Praying*, 187–8, 190, 220; and Haynes, *The Last Segregated Hour*, 89–90, 132. Slade and Dupont focus specifically on Mississippi Presbyterian responses.

25. *JCL*, January 11, 1963; *MS*, January 11, 1963; H. H. Buchanan to Bishop Franklin, February 11, 1963, BOP, box 1, folder 19; Pine Springs (*JCL*, February 16, 1963) and Meridian Wesley (Louis R. Wolfe to Bishop Franklin, February 22, 1963, BOP, box 1, folder 19).

26. *JCL*, January 31, and January 15, 1963 (the Wesson resolution copied Galloway's almost verbatim, BOP, box 1, folder 19). T. V. Nichols Jr. to Bishop Franklin,

January 20, 1963; Cleveland Welch and Mrs. E. J. (Reba) Welch (Bogue Chitto Charge) to Bishop Franklin, January 12, 1963, BOP, box 1, folder 19.

27. Gipson, "Preaching on Controversial Issues," 84–5; newsletter in Silver Papers, box 23, folder 9.

28. *Neshoba Democrat*, January 10, 1963; Rush interview; collection of handwritten vignettes, February 1963, Maxie Dunnam PP; "Why Did You Transfer from the Mississippi Conference?," Rush PP. The Mars Hill Church gave Rush a vote of confidence—see *NYT*, January 19, 1963. A portion of Rush's account is included in Silver, *Mississippi: The Closed Society*, 59–60. For more on Rainey, see Florence Mars, *Witness in Philadelphia* (Baton Rouge: Louisiana State University Press, 1977), 76–9, 132–5, 188–92. *JMC*, 1963, 113; Rush to Silver, January 17, 1963, Silver Papers, box 23, folder 9; Julia Hall to Libby Rush, January 20, 1963, Rush PP.

29. Unlike those of Rush and Lampton, Nicholson's dismissal was not reported in the Mississippi press in January; it was mentioned in Claude Sitton's *NYT* story on January 19, 1963. James Nicholson, "My Mississippi Experiences," unpublished, n.d. (mid-1960s?), Nicholson PP; J. W. Leggett Jr. to James Nicholson, January 11, 1963, Nicholson PP; James Nicholson interview; Nicholson to Silver, Silver Papers, box 23, folder 9; Nicholson, "My Mississippi Experiences"; Henry Winstead interview.

30. Lampton to James Silver, January 30, 1963, Silver Papers, box 23, folder 9; collection of vignettes from February 1963 meeting, Dunnam PP; *JCL*, January 9, 1963; *MEJ*, January 7, 1963; *JCL*, January 9, 1963.

31. *MCJ*, 1991, 423–4; Charles Duke, "Born of the Spirit," preached January 20, 1963, enclosed with March 1963 letter, John and Margrit Garner Letters, MDAH.

32. Duke, "Born of the Spirit."

33. *MMA*, January 16, 1963.

34. Roy Wolfe to Ashmore, January 3, 1963; J. N. Harris, Olive Branch, MS, to Ashmore, January 17; both in Ashmore Papers, box 1, folder 1.

35. Grace Jones to Moore, n.d. (early January 1963) and his January 17 response, Moore PP.

36. Robert B. Haltom to Walters, January 9, 1963, Walters Papers, box 1, folder 3; Anonymous to Wilton Carter, January 9, Carter PP (all emphases in original). Born of Conviction refers to one biblical passage and cites the teachings of Jesus.

37. Gulde, Shiloh, Lodebar, Holly Bush, and Pelahatchie Churches, n.d., BOP, box 1, folder 19 (see *JCL*, January 24); re: honesty in congregations on race relations, see Hadden, *The Gathering Storm in the Churches*, 190; Jack Loflin interview; list of potential signers, James L. Waits Papers, PTLA, box 1, folder 2.

38. E. U. Parker Jr. to Ashmore, January 5, Ashmore Papers, box 1, folder 1. The letter was copied to Dickson and Robert Hunt, the Franklin Church pastor and son of District Superintendent Brunner Hunt. Editor's note at beginning

of Born of Conviction, *MMA*, January 2, 1963; Martha and Grady Jackson to Dunnam, January 5, 1963, Dunnam PP.

39. *MMA*, January 16, 1963.

40. R. Glenn Miller to Ashmore, January 10, 1963 (emphasis in original); Ashmore Papers, box 1, folder 4; Roy Clark Oral History Memoir, 30–2; Roy C. Clark to Robert Kates, Stewart Smith, and Homer Peden, January 4, 1963, and Clark to Peden, February 4, 1963, Roy C. Clark PP. On January 13 Clark preached a sermon on Born of Conviction and quoted the response statement in full— "Coming to Grips with the Real Issue," Houck and Dixon, eds. *Rhetoric, Religion, and the Civil Rights Movement*, Vol. 2, 307–15. While referring to "recent events," the response statement does not mention race or any other specific issue; it affirms "full and free expression of Christian convictions by ministers and lay-men with mutual respect for one another." Born of Conviction signer Jerry Trigg tried to collect signatures from other pastors in the conference on a state-ment expressing mild support for Born of Conviction, but the effort never got off the ground—see Trigg to Furr, January 2, 1963, Ashmore Papers, box 1, folder 2.

41. *MMA*, January 16, 1963; see also *DH*, January 15, 1963; and *JCL*, January 15, 1963. The "integration is not forced" language referred to Amendment IX of the Methodist Church's constitution, passed by the General Conference in 1956 to allow for voluntary merging of Central Jurisdiction Annual Conferences with white conferences.

42. *MS*, January 3, 1963, 1; Jones to Ashmore, January 4, 1963, Ashmore Papers, box 1, folder 1. Some claimed Bishop Franklin shared Jones's view—see Martin Deppe, notes for "Mississippi Journal," Deppe PP, and Deppe e-mail to author, February 6, 2012. It is true that the statements in paragraphs 2026 and 2020 were not church "law," i.e., "not binding upon members and clergy in a juridical sense," but they were official—Darryl W. Stephens (an author-ity on the Methodist Social Creed and Social Principles) e-mail to author, November 10, 2006. See Ed King's interpretation of this statement in his *White Church in Mississippi* manuscript, III, 19–24.Though the choice of the word "historic" leaves one wondering, I read the Bishop and Cabinet's state-ment as "Yes, what Born of Conviction quoted is in the *Discipline*, but let's move on."

43. Bufkin Oliver to Silver, April 9, 1963, Silver Papers, box 23, folder 9 (see also Waits, "To Live in Controversy," *Concern*, March 1963, 10); L. Ray Branton to Franklin, January 16, 1963, Walters Papers, box 1, folder 3; see also James McKeown to Franklin, January 15, 1963; and Dean M. Kelley to Franklin, February 20, 1963, both BOP, box 1, folder 19.

44. Paul D. Hardin, Faculty Secretary, to Franklin, January 25, 1963; and Franklin to Hardin, February 8, 1963, MCA, Faculty Meeting Minutes, Memos, and Reports, box 1, folder 1962–1963 (the resolution was written by history professor

Ross Moore); the Franklin column quoted appeared in *MMA*, October 25, 1961; *MMA*, October 10, 1962.

45. The Twenty-Eight received national press coverage, both in church press (e.g., "Methodist Ministers Shatter Vacuum," *Christian Century*, February 20, 1963, 229–30) and secular (*NYT*, January 19, 1963). The four to one positive ratio is based on all the letters I found in archives and the personal papers of the signers, with 108 different positive missives and twenty-six negative. Of the latter, more than half were sent to the *Advocate* and found in Ashmore Papers, box 1, folder 1. J. P. Stafford to "Dear Brothers," January 3, 1963, Walters Papers, box 1, folder 3.

46. Walters Papers, box 1, folder 3; re: Frank Smith's story, see his *Congressman from Mississippi*. The Kelley letter is found in Ashmore Papers, box 1, folder 4; Kelley's book, *Why Conservative Churches Are Growing* (New York: Harper and Row, 1972), has become a classic. Vernon Chandler to Sam Ashmore, January 16, 1963, Ashmore Papers, box 1, folder 4.

47. E. Clinton Gardner to Wilton Carter, January 22, 1963, and Theodore Runyon to Carter, January 17, 1963, Carter PP (Kellar, Troutman, and Dunnam received the same letters); Kirkpatrick to Dunnam, February 11, 1963; and Henry C. Clay Jr., to Dunnam, February 27, 1963, Dunnam PP.

48. J. L. Henderson to Ashmore, January 8, 1963; Ensley Tiffin to Ashmore, January 24, 1963; Carl David Soule to Ashmore, January 13, 1963; all Ashmore Papers, box 1, folder 4; Louis Doleac family to Franklin, February 15, 1963; James Lawrence James to Franklin, January 11, 1963; and Nettie Beeson to Franklin, n.d. (January 1963); see also Tex S. Sample to Franklin, January 11, 1963; Arthur M. O'Neil Jr. to Franklin, January 16, 1963; and William M. Justice to Franklin, March 21, 1963; all BOP, box 1, folder 19; Meg Marcow to Dunnam, January 6, 1963, Dunnam PP.

49. Clark interviews; Lee interview, 2003; *JDN*, May 3, 1954.

50. Roy C. Clark, "Coming to Grips with the Real Issue," January 13, 1963, Houck and Dixon, *Rhetoric, Religion, and the Civil Rights Movement*, Vol. 2, 307–15; see also *JCL* and *MS, January* 15; Lowry interview.

51. Martin Luther King Jr., "Letter from Birmingham Jail," *Why We Can't Wait*, 87–8, 93–4.

52. Troutman interview.

53. Troutman interview; Troutman to James Silver, Silver Papers, box 23, folder 9.

54. Troutman interview; Jack Troutman to "Dear Mother," February 8, 1963, Troutman PP (emphasis in original).

CHAPTER 6

1. *NYT* (Western Edition), January 19, 1963; *NYT*, June 29, 1963; *NYT*, June 30, 1963; see also *Washington Post*, January 4 and 7, 1963; "Methodist Ministers Shatter Vacuum," *Christian Century*, February 20, 1963, 229–30; Jim L. Waits,

"To Live in Controversy," *Concern*, March 1, 1963, 8–10; "Mississippi Methodists Lead in Attack on Segregation," *Presbyterian Outlook*, January 21, 1963, 3–4; *Birmingham World*, January 12, 1963; *Atlanta Daily World*, January 18, 1963; *Baltimore Afro-American*, January 19, 1963; *Pittsburgh Courier*, February 2, 1963.

2. "Chronology of Estelle Styron Walters," Walters Papers, box 2, folder 1; Summer Walters e-mail to author, June 22, 2005; Walters interview; McRae interview.

3. Walters interview; *JMC*, 1947, 69; 1950, 66; 1951, 70; 1952, 65.

4. Walters interview; Summer Walters e-mail to author, April 10, 2007.

5. Summer Walters e-mail to author, July 10, 2006; Walters interview.

6. Walters interview; Elizabeth B. Walters, "One Person's Journey," paper for S562, Indiana University School of Social Work, n.d. (1978?), Walters Papers, box 3, folder 18; Summer Walters e-mail to author, December 18, 2009.

7. Summer Walters, "Some Thoughts on the Witness of Jefferson Street Methodist Church, Natchez, Mississippi," Walters Papers, box 2, folder 2; John Dollard, *Caste and Class in a Southern Town* (Madison: University of Wisconsin Press, 1988 [first published 1937]); Summer Walters e-mail to author, November 21, 2009; Elizabeth B. Walters, "One Person's Journey," Walters Papers, box 3, folder 18; Walters, "Some Thoughts on the Witness . . .," 33, 28.

8. Jack E. Davis, *Race Against Time: Culture and Separation in Natchez since 1930* (Baton Rouge: Louisiana State University Press, 2001), 15.

9. Summer Walters, "Recent Developments in Jefferson Street's History," n.d., (1962?), Walters Papers, box 7, folder 59; *JMC*, 1963, 304; Summer Walters e-mails to author, October 30, 2008, and November 3, 2008; Walters interview; "Hello to all," December 2, 1962, Walters PP.

10. Summer Walters, "My Ministerial Experiences in Mississippi 1961–1963," September 1963, Walters Papers, box 2, folder 3 (this account differs slightly from Walters's letter to James Silver, June 18, 1963, Silver Papers, box 23, folder 9); Waits's notes on February 13, 1963 meeting at Selah home, Waits Papers, box 1, folder 10.

11. "My Ministerial Experiences in Mississippi;" Summer Walters e-mail to author, October 30, 2008; Walters interview; "My Ministerial Experiences in Mississippi."

12. Deb Holston Selden, "One Family's Response to the Born of Conviction Statement," unpublished memoir, 2007; Wilton Carter to James W. Silver, August 13, 1963, Silver Papers, box 23, folder 9; Wilton Carter interview; Kellar, *Sandersville*, 183, 186–7; McRae interview; Tonkel interview, 2003; Ron Bailey, unpublished *Life* article draft, October 1963, Dunnam PP.

13. Jerry and Rose Trigg interview; Jerry Trigg e-mail to James Nicholson, May 31, 2005; Troutman interview; Tommy Conner interview.

14. Rush interview; James Rush, "What Has Happened to Me," included with January 17, 1963 letter from Rush to James Silver, Silver Papers, box 23, folder 9.

15. Selden, "One Family's Response …"; James Holston to James Silver, n.d. (Summer 1963), Silver Papers, box 23, folder 9; "One Family's Response …"; Selden interview; Moore interview.

16. Marvin Moody to James Silver, February 12, 1963, Silver Papers, box 23, folder 9; Powell Hall interview (emphasis in Hall's telling of the story); Thelma Briggs McConnell et al. interview.

17. Joseph C. Way to James Silver, January 18, 1963, Silver Papers, box 23, folder 9; Way to author, April 21, 2004; Way to James Silver, June 17, 1963, Silver Papers, box 23, folder 9.

18. *JCL* and *JDN*, January 8, 1963; James S. Conner statement, January 9, 1963, Cox Papers, box 1-B, folder 50 Methodist—28 (Miss.), emphasis in original; Betty Conner Currey interview (she believes Leggett's partial support of her husband may have been out of loyalty to her, since she had been his secretary in the late 1940s).

19. Holston to James Silver, n.d. (Summer 1963), Silver Papers, box 23, folder 9; "Statement of Position of the Official Board of Carthage Methodist Church," January 6, 1963, BOP, box 1, folder 19; *The Carthaginian*, January 10, 1963; *PMPC*, January 17, 1963; N. A. Dickson response to "Questionaire to the 28," n.d. (late 1965), Waits Papers, box 1, folder 14.

20. Maxie Dunnam, "From Symptoms to Malady in Race Relations," unpublished sermon, n.d. (1965?), Dunnam PP.

21. *MS*, January 11, 1963; McRae interview.

22. McRae interview.

23. Collection of written vignettes, Dunnam PP; Marvin Moody to Maxie Dunnam, January 12, 1963, Dunnam PP.

24. H. H. Buchanan to Bishop Franklin, February 11, 1963, BOP, box 1, folder 19; *MMA*, January 2, 1963; Lamar Martin to Wilton Carter, January 10, 1963, Carter PP; *Neshoba Democrat*, January 3, 1963; Byrd and Sara Hillman interview.

25. Dunnam interview, 2004; Jean Dickinson Minus interview.

26. Minus interview.

27. *California Pacific Annual Conference Journal*, 1985, 160–1; Minus interview. This story is used in Kathryn Dickinson's play, *Born of Conviction*, discussed in Chapter 11.

28. Herbert W. Beasley, "To the editor of the Mississippi Methodist Advocate and the preachers that expressed their feelings in the advocate [*sic*] in the article 'Born of Conviction,'" January 9, 1963, Ashmore Papers, box 1, folder 1; Minus interview; *JMC*, 1962, 103; 1963, 104.

29. Dickinson response to "Questionaire to the 28," n.d. (late 1965), Waits Papers, box 1, folder 14; J. and R. Trigg interview. Signer Marvin Moody told this story in a sermon at Oak Grove on Race Relations Sunday in February 1963 (Gipson, "Preaching on Controversial Issues," 100), as did Maxie Dunnam in "Mississippi: Some Reflections," a talk he gave in California in 1964 or

1965, Dunnam PP; see also Ardis Whitman, "How the Civil Rights Struggle Challenges Our Churches," *Redbook*, August 1965, 134; and Kenneth Cauthen, *I Don't Care What the Bible Says: An Interpretation of the South* (Macon, GA: Mercer University Press, 2003).

30. Elton Brown response to "Questionaire to the 28," n.d. (late 1965), Waits Papers, box 1, folder 14; D. Elton Brown to James Silver, January 29, 1963, Silver Papers, box 23, folder 9; Jerry Williamson interview; *NYT*, January 19, 1963; A. W. Martin Jr., "The Lawson Affair, The Sit-ins, and Beyond," unpublished paper; A. W. Martin e-mail to author, April 15, 2008.

31. Luke 9:62; *JDN*, January 7, 1963; Wilton Carter interview; Carter to James Silver, August 13, 1963; Dolores Carter interview.

32. Collection of written vignettes recorded in February 1963, Waits Papers, box 1, folder 10; Entrekin response to "Questionaire to the 28," n.d. (late 1965), Waits Papers, box 1, folder 14; Brown to James Silver, January 29, 1963, Silver Papers, box 23, folder 9.

33. Jack Troutman to James Silver, June 19, 1963, Silver Papers, box 23, folder 9; Troutman, "Why My Statement?" handwritten document in Troutman PP; Ron Bailey, unpublished *Life* article draft, October 1963, Dunnam PP.

34. Tonkel interview, 2003; Tonkel to James Silver, February 14, 1963, Silver Papers, box 23, folder 9; Collection of written vignettes, Waits Papers, box 1, folder 10; Dunnam response to "Questionaire to the 28," n.d. (late 1965), Waits Papers, box 1, folder 14; Ron Bailey, unpublished *Life* article draft, October 1963, Dunnam PP.

35. Kellar, *Sandersville*, 181–2, 187, 191.

36. Kellar, *Sandersville*, 187–8.

37. Kellar, *Sandersville*, 197–203; Kellar interview.

38. Clark interview, 2007; *JMC*, 1949, 63; Sandra Napier Dyess interview, 2012; Denson Napier interview.

39. Napier interview; Sandra Dyess interview, 2012; *JMC* 1954, 75; 1956, 74; 1958, 77; 1959, 81.

40. *MMA*, March 7, 1962; Denson Napier interview; *JMC* 1964, 108; *MMA*, August 28, 1963.

41. Denson Napier to "Dear Cousin" (John Hawkins Napier III), July 27, 1963, Napier PP; Napier interview (emphasis in Napier's story); Dyess interview, 2009; collection of written vignettes, Waits Papers, box 1, folder 10; Napier response to "Questionaire to the 28," n.d. (late 1965), Waits Papers, box 1, folder 14.

42. Inman Moore Jr. to Bishop Franklin, February 23, 1963, BOP, box 1, folder 19; Jim Waits to Bishop Franklin, January 11, 1963, Waits Papers, box 1, folder 8; Waits to David Carpenter, United Press International, September 11, 1963, Waits Papers, box 1, folder 8; Waits to James Gustafson, January 24, 1963, Waits Papers, box 1, folder 8; Waits interview, 2003.

43. Ryker to James Silver, March 27, 1963, Silver Papers, box 23, folder 9; Ryker response to "Questionaire to the 28," n.d. (late 1965), Waits Papers, box 1, folder 14.

44. Collection of written vignettes, Dunnam PP. Although most of the signers were young, Harold Ryker, the oldest, was fifty-six.

45. Furr interview; *JCL*, January 15, 1963; *JCL*, January 7, 1963; David Womack e-mail to author, May 1, 2010; W. E. Lampton to Bishop Marvin Franklin, May 1, 1963, BOP, box 1, folder 19; McRae interview and Ed McRae to Summer Walters, July 22, 2005.

46. C. D. Parker to Carter, January 8, 1963, Carter PP; Wilton Carter interview; H. Bufkin Oliver to James Silver, Silver Papers, box 23, folder 9; Elton Brown et al. interview.

47. Ken Roberts interview; Wallace Roberts to Bishop John Owen Smith, March 8, 1963, Bishop John Owen Smith Papers, PTLA, box 4, folder 5.

48. Brown et al. interview; Janice Sewell Williams to author, July 30, 2005; Jack Sewell to *The Methodist Story*, December 7, 1964, BOP, box 2, folder 1.

49. Marvin Moody to James Silver, February 12, 1963, Silver Papers, box 23, folder 9; Moody to Lee H. Reiff, January 25, 1963, Lee H. Reiff PP; Inman Moore Jr., to Norman Boone, January 18, 1963, and Inman Moore Jr., to B. M. Hunt, January 18, 1963; Lampton to Silver, January 30, 1963, Silver Papers, box 23, folder 9; Rod Entrekin interview, 2003.

50. Moore interview; Joseph C. Way to author, April 21, 2004; Way to James Silver, January 18, 1963, Silver Papers, box 23, folder 9; see also February 1963 vignette collections in Dunnam PP and Waits Papers, box 1, folder 10, and Rush interview.

51. Collection of vignettes, Dunnam PP; see also Harold Ryker to James Silver, March 27, 1963, Silver Papers, box 23, folder 9.

CHAPTER 7

1. Ed Starr e-mails to author, July 17 and July 18, 2011; *JMC*, 1958, 74; 1960, 93; Starr e-mails to author, July 17 and July 18, 2011; *JMC*, 1963, 100.

2. *JMC*, 1954–66; *JMC*, 1964, 152. I heard several stories of ministers leaving the conference because of their dissatisfaction with the Leggett power structure (e.g., Rush, Dickson family, Betty Conner Currey and George Currey, and Moore interviews). See Thomas Stevens Burnett, "Ministerial Roles and Institutional Restraints: The Mississippi Conference of the United Methodist Church," D.Min. Project, Claremont School of Theology, 1976.

3. Davis, *Race Against Time*, 200; Sarratt, *The Ordeal of Desegregation*, 237; Randy J. Sparks, *Religion in Mississippi* (Jackson, MS: University Press of Mississippi, 2001), 237; Zola, "What Price Amos? Perry Nussbaum's Career in Jackson, Mississippi," in Bauman and Kalin, *The Quiet Voices*, 252; Campbell, *And*

Also With You, 141; Canzoneri, *"I Do So Politely,"* 142; Young, *An Easy Burden*, 56; James P. Rush, "Secularized Christianity: Salvation by Faith or Works?" *Christian Advocate*, March 23, 1967, 7. Of the passages quoted, the first two are most accurate re: numbers but less so as to causes; the next two are exaggerated; and the final four (including the editorial description of Rush) are the most inaccurate. See also Gayle Graham Yates, *Mississippi Mind: A Personal Cultural History of an American State* (Knoxville: University of Tennessee Press, 1990), 265–6; Dittmer, *Local People*, 463–4, n. 62; Bailey, *Southern White Protestantism in the Twentieth Century*, 150–1; Friedland, *Lift Up Your Voice Like a Trumpet*, 102; and Bruce Hilton, *The Delta Ministry* (London: Collier-Macmillan, 1969), 177.

4. R. Inman Moore Jr. to James Rush, February 5, 1963, Inman Moore PP (emphasis in original); Rush interview; "Why Did You Transfer from the Mississippi Conference," Rush response to 1964 Conference survey, Rush PP.

5. Rush interview; Z. Glen Jones to James Rush, January 29, 1963; *JMC*, 1959, 90; Mark F. Lytle to S. Douglas Walters, February 6, 1963; Lytle to Rush, February 6, 1963, all letters Rush PP.

6. S. Douglas Walters to Rush, February 11, 1963, Rush PP. Methodist ministers were traditionally required to dedicate themselves "to the highest ideals of the Christian ministry with respect to purity of life in body, in mind, and in spirit, and to bear witness thereto by abstinence from all indulgences, including tobacco, which may injure [their] influence" (*DMC*, 1960, ¶306.5), but this was not enforced in many conferences by the 1960s. *DMC*, 1996 (see 176n2) changed the language slightly to call for "higher standards of self-discipline and habit formation in all personal and social relationships." See Frank, *Polity, Practice, and the Mission of The United Methodist Church*, 225–6, 228.

7. S. Douglas Walters to Rush, February 11, 1963, Rush PP; Rush interview; S. Douglas Walters to Rush, February 1, 1963, Rush PP; *JSCAC*, 1963, 112, 115. The 1962–63 Cabinet Work Sheet (Franklin Papers, box 3, folder 4) lists the Philadelphia Circuit at a salary of $3,000, plus travel and other expense money totaling another $1,000. Rush's memory of the salary as $3,600 may be accurate, as there were sometimes discrepancies between cabinet information and actual salary.

8. Moore interview; Inman Moore Jr., to George Berry, March 12, 1964, Moore PP (written in response to the 1964 Mississippi Conference survey).

9. Moore interview; Moore to Bishop Franklin, February 23, 1963, BOP, box 1, folder 19; Waits interview, 2003.

10. Moore interview; Moore to Bishop A. Raymond Grant, January 18, 1963, Moore PP; Moore to George Berry, March 12, 1964, Moore PP; Moore to Franklin, February 23, 1963; Bishop Gerald Kennedy to Bishop Marvin Franklin, February 11, 1963; Franklin to Kennedy, February 25, 1963; all these letters BOP, box 1,

folder 19; *JSCAC*, 1963, 112, 119. Moore's salary at Leggett Memorial totaled $6,532 (Moore to Bishop Grant, January 18, 1963).

11. Moore interview; Moore to George Berry, March 12, 1964, Moore PP.

12. Moore to Franklin, February 23, 1963, BOP, box 1, folder 19.

13. *Concern*, February 1963, 16; Waits, "To Live in Controversy," *Concern*, March 1963, 8–10; Waits's handwritten notes from the meeting, Waits Papers, box 1, folder 10; and Jerry Furr to Rod Entrekin, n.d. (early February 1963), Entrekin PP. I have found no record of the planned late February meeting in Hattiesburg, although it is possible Maxie Dunnam's handwritten notes with vignettes about experiences of the signers (Dunnam PP) came from it. Waits to Campbell, January 11 and 26, 1963, and Campbell to Waits, January 18 and February 5, 1963, Will D. Campbell Papers (Campbell Papers), USMMLA, box 8, folder 11; Elbert Jean to Alfred S. Kramer, January 15, 1963, Campbell Papers, box 38, folder 10.

14. W. E. (Bill) Lampton to Bishop Franklin, May 1, 1963, BOP box 1, folder 19; Lampton to Franklin, May 1, 1963; Lampton to James Silver, January 30, 1963, Silver Papers, box 23, folder 9; Steve Dickson e-mail to author, February 12, 2013, and list of potential signers, James L. Waits Papers, PTLA, box 1, folder 2; *Columbian-Progress* (Columbia, MS), April 4, 1963.

15. Lampton to Franklin, May 1, 1963, BOP, box 1, folder 19—re: Lampton's family's wealth, see, e.g., J. B. Cain to Summer Walters, June 11, 1963, Walters Papers, box 1, folder 3; Mrs. A. J. Spaulding to Franklin, May 22, 1963, BOP, box 1, folder 19; *JMC*, 1963, 100; *Indiana Conference Journal*, 1963, 1014.

16. Summer Walters, "Some Thoughts on the Witness of Jefferson Street Methodist Church, Natchez, Mississippi," 1961 paper for James Gustafson, Walters Papers, box 2, folder 2; Walters, "My Ministerial Experiences in Mississippi 1961–1963," September 1963, Walters Papers, box 2, folder 3; Walters e-mail to author, October 15, 2006 (dating based on Walters's 1963 Daily Suggester pocket calendar); Walters interview.

17. Summer Walters to Roy C. Clark, May 23, 1963, Clark PP; Summer Walters to James Silver, June 18, 1963, Silver Papers, box 23, folder 9; Walters interview; Walters e-mail to author et al., September 8, 2008; see Chapter 1 for Delamotte's story; Walters to Bishop John Owen Smith, April 19, 1963, and J. O. Smith to Walters, April 24, 1963, both J. O. Smith Papers, PTLA, box 4, folder 8; Walters interview; Walters e-mails to author, November 3, 2008 and April 18, 2008; Franklin to Raines, May 20, 1963, BOP, box 1, folder 19.

18. Walters interview; S. Walters e-mail to author, November 5, 2008; "My Ministerial Experiences in Mississippi 1961–1963," September 1963, Walters Papers, box 2, folder 3; *Indiana Conference Journal*, 1963, 994, 1096–7; Walters family to "Dear friends and relatives," July 11, 1963, Walters Papers, box 1, folder 3; Walters e-mail to author, November 20, 2009.

19. See Kellar, *Sandersville*, 237, 267–8, 289; W. Carter interview; D. Carter interview; Kellar, *Sandersville*, 263.

20. Kellar, *Sandersville*, 243–5; Wilton Carter interview; Kellar to Bishop John Owen Smith, January 29, 1963, and Bishop Smith to Kellar, February 4, 1963, both J. O. Smith Papers, PTLA, box 4, folder 8; G. Ross Freeman to Raymond A. Gray, February 13, 1963, Kellar PP; Kellar, *Sandersville*, 244.

21. See, e.g., G. Ross Freeman to Raymond A. Gray, February 13, 1963; W. Harold Groce to Kellar, February 18, 1963; Kenneth Goodson to Kellar, February 22, 1963, all Kellar PP; David H. McKeithen to Kellar, February 15, 1963, Kellar PP; various letters in Kellar PP; Kellar, *Sandersville*, 274ff.; Kellar, *Sandersville*, 243–5.

22. Bishop James W. Henley to Bishop Franklin, March 26, 1963, BOP, box 1, folder 19; W. Carter interview; *Florida Conference Journal*, 1963, 133; Kellar, *Sandersville*, 263, 267, 274–5, 272, 270–2. The mimeographed resolutions come from Kellar PP—they were not printed in the *Advocate* (see *MMA*, April 3, 1963); *JCL* and *JDN*, March 22, 1963.

23. Kellar, *Sandersville*, 275–285, 284–5; Franklin Papers, box 3, folder 4; Ned Kellar to Bishop Franklin, April 22, 1963; Bishop Henley to Bishop Franklin, April 29, 1963 and March 26, 1963, all BOP, box 1, folder 19.

24. Kellar, *Sandersville*, 289–290; *Florida Conference Journal*, 1963, 135.

25. Kellar, *Sandersville*, 265, 286; Summer Walters e-mail to author, November 2, 2008; George Currey interview; *MCJ*, 1990, 446–7; Waits interview, 2003 and J. Trigg interview.

26. The discussion of the paternalistic pattern is influenced by my interview with Jim McCormick, whose father was a Leggett lieutenant. T. O. Prewitt to Ned Kellar, April 4, 1963, Kellar PP.

27. T. O. Prewitt to Wilton Carter, March 13, 1963, Carter PP; Carter to James Silver, August 13, 1963, Silver Papers, box 23, folder 9; see also Carter to George L. Berry, March 31, 1964, Carter PP.

28. Kellar, *Sandersville*, 245; Wilton Carter to T. O. Prewitt, March 14, 1963, and Prewitt to Carter, March 13, 1963, Carter PP; Carter to George L. Berry, March 31, 1964, Carter PP.

29. W. Carter interview; *MMA*, June 5, 1963; D. Carter interview; Wilton Carter to Bishop Franklin, March 27, 1963, BOP, box 1, folder 19.

30. James Holston to James Silver, n.d. (Summer 1963), Silver Papers, box 23, folder 9; Holston response to "Questionaire to the 28," n.d. (late 1965), Waits Papers, box 1, folder 14; Holston to Bishop John O. Smith, March 15, 1963, Smith Papers, PTLA, box 4, folder 5.

31. *JMC*, 1963, 100; http://www.asburytulsa.org/Home/NewtoAsbury/AboutUs/History.aspx (accessed July 20, 2014); Holston to Silver, n.d. (Summer 1963), Silver Papers, box 23, folder 9; Holston response to "Questionaire to the 28," n.d. (late 1965), Waits Papers, box 1, folder 14.

32. Bishop J. Owen Smith to James Holston, March 19, 1963, and Holston to Smith, March 15, 1963, both Smith Papers, PTLA, box 4, folder 5; *Oklahoma Conference Journal*, 1964, 92, 322; Moore interview; Holston to James Silver, Silver Papers,

box 23, folder 9; Holston response to "Questionaire to the 28," n.d. (late 1965), Waits Papers, box 1, folder 14.

33. "Jim" (Waits) to Summer Walters, January 8, 1963, Walters Papers, box 1, folder 3 (emphasis in original); Delamotte, "Brief Summary . . .," McCormick Papers, box 23, folder 5—for Delamotte's story, see Chapters 1 and 3.

34. Waits interview, 2003 and Jerry Trigg interview; Harmon, *The Organization of the Methodist Church*, 128–9.

35. Re: the Jackson Movement in 1963, see Dittmer, *Local People*, 157–69; and John R. Salter Jr., *Jackson, Mississippi: An American Chronicle of Struggle and Schism* (Hicksville, NY: Exposition Press, 1979); Dittmer, *Local People*, 157–66. See Ed King, "Bacchanal at Woolworth's" in Susie Erenrich, ed., *Freedom Is a Constant Struggle* (Montgomery: Black Belt Press, 1999), 27–35. For Evers's May 20 speech explaining the grievances of the black community, see Myrlie Evers-Williams and Manning Marable, eds., *The Autobiography of Medgar Evers: A Hero's Life Revealed through His Writings, Letters, and Speeches* (New York: Basic Civitas Books, 2005), 280–2; re: the Evers case, see Bobby DeLaughter, *Never Too Late: A Prosecutor's Story of Justice in the Medgar Evers Case* (New York: Scribner, 2001).

36. Ed King interview; Marsh, *God's Long Summer*, 126–7 (see Chapter 4 for King's story); *JMC*, 1961, 95, 94; King, *The White Church in Mississippi*, Part III, p. 75; author's notes from Ed King remarks at Church Desegregation Oral History Roundtable, Chicago, October 5, 2008; *JMC*, 1963, 93; "From Journal, 1963 Miss. Annual Conference," typed account of Executive Session, BOP, box 1, folder 20; *GM*, 1964, 288.

37. *JMC*, 1963, 4. I have used my own knowledge of conference politics to identify Leggett associates. Ashmore's words in the introductory note to Born of Conviction, *MMA*, January 2, 1963.

38. Stafford's offending comments came in "Thoughts from a Quiet Corner" in his weekly *Advocate* Lay Activities column, especially January 9, 16, 23, 30, and February 6, 1963. *JMC*, 1963, 4; *JCL*, May 30, 1963. The number of votes necessary for election is a majority of those cast on any ballot; on the first lay General Conference ballot that year, 213 votes were cast, with 107 needed for election (*JMC*, 1963, 78). Clearly there was well-organized lay opposition to Stafford's candidacy. Jordan had spoken publicly against Born of Conviction in the January 16 *MMA*, but he refused to participate in the attempt to oust Stafford—Emily Stafford Matheny interview; Betty Conner Currey interview; *JCL*, October 24, 1964.

39. J. B. Cain to Summer Walters, June 11, 1963, Walters Papers, box 1, folder 3.

40. McRae interview.

41. McRae interview; *JMC*, 1964, 94; *JSCAC*, 1963, 129.

42. J. W. Leggett Jr., to James Nicholson, January 11, 1963, Nicholson PP; James Nicholson interview; Nicholson, "My Mississippi Experiences," n.d.

(mid-1960s?), Nicholson PP; R. Lanier Hunt to James Nicholson, January 23, 1963, Nicholson PP; James Nicholson interview; R. L. Hunt to Nicholson, January 23 and February 5, 1963, Nicholson PP; Charles Nicholson interview; James Nicholson to "My Beloved Friend the 'Duke'" (Earl Marlatt), February 1, 1963, Nicholson PP; *JMC*, 1963, 94, 102.

43. James Nicholson interview; Bishop F. Gerald Ensley and Clarie Collins Harvey to Summer Walters, February 26, 1963, Walters Papers, box 1, folder 3; Bishop Ensley to Bishop Franklin, July 23, 1963, and Official Notice of Transfer Out, both BOP, box 1, folder 20; *JMC*, 1964, 94; *South Iowa Conference Journal*, 1964, 62, 99.

44. Jerry Furr to James Silver, January 28, 1963, Silver Papers, box 23, folder 9; R. L. Hunt to Will Campbell, March 6, 1963, Campbell Papers, box 33, folder 13; Furr to Paul D. Hardin, January 29, 1963, MCA, Faculty Meeting Minutes and Reports, box 1, folder 1962–3; Troutman interview.

45. Furr interview; *JCL*, January 14, 1963, 1; *JMC*, 1963, 106. Selah had asked the Galloway Official Board to vote on whether they wanted him to stay or leave—see Selah, "Galloway and the Race Issue," n.d., Selah Papers, box 1, folder 2; Roy C. Clark to Eddie Starr, May 1, 1963, Clark PP.

46. "Galloway and the Race Issue," Selah Papers, box 1, folder 2. Ed King says Medgar Evers was involved in the spontaneous decision to send the students to Galloway on June 9, although he had previously avoided targeting the church due to his respect for Selah—author's notes on King remarks at Church Desegregation Oral History Roundtable, Chicago, October 5, 2008. Selah, "Galloway and the Race Issue"; Furr interview; for more on Selah's story, see W. J. Cunningham, *Agony at Galloway: One Church's Struggle with Social Change* (Jackson: University Press of Mississippi, 1980), ch. 1.

47. Furr interview; *1963 Letters to Dr. W. B. Selah*, Selah Papers; *JMC*, 1964, 93; *JSCAC*, 1963, 109, 120.

48. *Journal of the Missouri West Annual Conference*, 1986, 170–1.

49. See Ashmore Papers, box 1, folders 1, 3, 6–8, and 10; Mabel Anne Ashmore Harjes interview; see Marshall Grisham to "Brother Sam," September 8, 1965; and Audie C. Bishop to Ashmore, September 15, 1965, both Ashmore Papers, box 1, folder 8; see also Thad H. Ferrell to Ashmore, January 10, 1963, box 1, folder 4; Joseph Wroten to Ashmore, March 5, 1965; and Bishop Richard Raines (Indiana) to Ashmore, February 7, 1964, both box 1, folder 8; *MMA*, April 29, 1964.

50. J. P. Stafford to J. W. Fowler, August 16, 1962, quoted in Lowry, *The Antechamber of Heaven*, 111 (emphasis in original); see Selah's letter to *JCL* reporter Kevin Jones, July 11, 1984, Selah Papers, box 1, folder 4. As a member of Galloway in the late 1960s, I heard Selah remind the congregation of the circumstances of his resignation. *JDN*, November 20, 1968; *MCJ*, 1985, 328–9; *MMA*, May 22, 1985, and June 5, 1985.

51. Rush interview; *JSCAC*, 1965, 117; 1968, 104; *South Carolina Conference Journal*, 2001, 125.

52. Moore interview; *JSCAC*, 1970, 146; 1975, 128; *California-Pacific Conference Journal*, 2000, F-10; 2003, F-9.

53. *Indiana Conference Journal*, 1966, 767; *Millsaps College Catalog and Announcements*, 1973–4, 114; and 1975–6, 84; William Lampton, *The Complete Communicator* (Franklin, TN: Hillsboro Press, 1999).

54. Clyde Gunn to Summer Walters, August 6, 1963, Walters Papers, box 1, folder 3; Walters interview; Jon Walters e-mail to author, January 25, 2006; *South Indiana Conference Journal*, 1981, 156, 414; 1994, 152; 1995, 472; 1998, 124, 138; *Indiana Conference Journal*, 2011, 257.

55. Kellar interview; *Florida Conference Journal*, 1965, 119; 1970, 114, 127; 1971, 87; *GM*, 2003, 252.

56. W. Carter interview; D. Carter interview; *Florida Conference Journal*, 1965, 114; 1967, 154; 1968, 143; *GM*, 2000, 265; W. Carter interview.

57. Selden, "One Family's Response to the Born of Conviction Statement"; Holston response to "Questionaire to the 28," n.d. (late 1965), Waits Papers, box 1, folder 14; *Oklahoma Conference Journal*, 1987, 125; 1989, 129; 1995, 239–40.

58. McRae interview; *California-Pacific Conference Journal*, 1997, J-22; 1998, E-11; Ed McRae e-mail to author, May 26, 2012.

59. James Nicholson interview; Nicholson, "My Mississippi Experiences," n.d. (1963?), and "I Remember the Night I Died," n.d. (mid-1960s?), both Nicholson PP; James B. Nicholson, "A Trail through the Wilderness," *New South*, March 1963, 5–8. The sermon may have appeared in *The Christian Science Monitor* and the *Texas Methodist Reporter*. Henry M. Bullock to James B. Nicholson, April 28, 1965, Nicholson PP; Nicholson, "Jesus Does Not Exclude—He Includes," *Bible Lessons for Adults*, June–August, 1966; "The Man Who Dreams About a Library," *Together*, June 1965; *Iowa Conference Journal*, 1986, 449, 493; *JCL*, June 6 and 7, 2005.

60. http://tumclv.weebly.com/50th-anniversary.html (accessed July 20, 2014); Furr response to "Questionaire to the 28," n.d. (late 1965), Waits Papers, box 1, folder 14; Dennis Perea, Nevada Equal Rights Commission, e-mail to author, November 3, 2008; Annelise Orleck, *Storming Caesar's Palace: How Black Mothers Fought Their Own War on Poverty* (Boston: Beacon Press, 2005), 135, 153, 161; *JSCAC*, 1971, 167; 1972, 134; Furr interview.

CHAPTER 8

1. *JMC*, 1963, 102, 103, 104, 106, 107, 109, 110, 112; *JMC*, 1963, 104, 106, 109, 112; *MMA*, June 5, 1963, *JMC*, 1964, 109. The decisions to leave or stay involve the pastor, the district superintendents, and bishop, as well as the local church(es) involved. If the decision had been left up to the church(es) alone, eighteen signers could have stayed another year.

2. Minus interview; Buford Dickinson response to "Questionaire to the 28," n.d. (late 1965), Waits Papers, box 1, folder 14; *JMC*, 1963, 107; Minus interview.

3. Minus interview—Kathryn Dickinson relates this story in her play, *Born of Conviction*. Buford Dickinson, "Impressions of Mississippi," unpublished address given at Convocation at Claremont School of Theology, August 11, 1964, Dunnam PP.

4. The five that went to that conference in 1963 include Bufkin Oliver, whose story is told later in this chapter. Dunnam interview, 2004; *JMC*, 1960, 96; Minus interview; Bishop Gerald Kennedy to Bishop Marvin Franklin, December 4, 1963, BOP, box 1, folder 19; *JMC*, 1964, 93; *JSCAC*, 1964, 122.

5. Buford Dickinson, "Impressions of Mississippi"; Dickinson response to "Questionaire to the 28," n.d. (late 1965), Waits Papers, box 1, folder 14.

6. Ron Bailey, unpublished *Life* article draft, October 1963, Dunnam PP; Dunnam interview, 2004; Bailey, unpublished *Life* article draft.

7. Jim Waits e-mail to author, July 31, 2009; Ron Bailey, unpublished *Life* article draft, October 1963; Dunnam interview, 2004; Kennedy to Franklin, January 6, 1964, BOP, box 1, folder 19; *JMC*, 1964, 93; *JSCAC*, 1964, 121.

8. Dunnam response to "Questionaire to the 28," n.d. (late 1965), Waits Papers, box 1, folder 14; Dunnam interview, 2004.

9. Dickinson, "Impressions of Mississippi"—for the story of Dickinson's colleague, Harmon Tillman, see Chapter 10; and Dunnam, "Mississippi: Some Reflections," n.d. (1965?), both Dunnam PP; Dickinson response to "Questionaire to the 28; Dunnam, "Mississippi: Some Reflections," emphasis in original.

10. *PMPC*, January 17, 1963; *JMC*, 1963, 109; Jerry and Rose Trigg interview.

11. Jerry Trigg e-mail to Jim and Hilda Nicholson, May 31, 2005, and Trigg e-mail to author, June 20, 2012; Jerry and Rose Trigg interview; J. W. Leggett Jr. to James Nicholson, January 11, 1963, Nicholson PP; Trigg e-mail to author, June 20, 2012; *MMA*, December 4, 1963; Trigg e-mail to Jim and Hilda Nicholson, May 31, 2005; see "A Reply to His Critics from E. Stanley Jones," 1960, Ashmore Papers, box 1, folder 5. See Chapter 3 re: Maxie Dunnam's 1962 attempt to host a Christian Ashram in Mississippi.

12. Jerry and Rose Trigg interview. *JMC*, 1964, 254, shows more than one hundred new members received at Leggett Church in 1963, and *JMC*, 1965, 268, shows a comparable number for 1964. J. Trigg e-mail to author, June 20, 2012.

13. Jerry and Rose Trigg interview; flyer for "A North-South Dialogue on Race Relations," sponsored by the Board of Christian Social Concerns of the Northwest Indiana Conference, n.d. (April 1964?), Trigg PP; J. and R. Trigg interview; J. Trigg e-mail to author, August 20, 2011; Trigg response to Questionaire to the 28," n.d. (late 1965), Waits Papers, box 1, folder 14; Richard C. Raines to Marvin Franklin, May 14, 1964, BOP, box 1, folder 20; *JMC*, 1964, 94; *Indiana Conference Journal*, 1964, 46, 72.

14. Troutman interview; handwritten rough draft of Jack Troutman letter to James Silver, n.d. (June 1963), Troutman PP; *JMC*, 1963, 109; *JMC*, 1964, 104.

15. Troutman interview.

16. Troutman interview; *JMC*, 1964, 94; *JSCAC*, 1964, 118; Troutman interview; list of thirty-three former Mississippi Methodist pastors (from both white conferences) in Southern California-Arizona, n.d. (1974?), Troutman PP.

17. Allen L. Moody e-mail to author, July 25, 2012; *Columbian-Progress* (Marion County, MS), April 1, 1982; Gerald Walton e-mail to author, September 14, 2010; Allen Moody e-mail to author, July 27, 2012; *JMC*, 1960, 93, and 1961, 101.

18. Marvin Moody to James Silver, February 12, 1963, Silver Papers, box 23, folder 9; Dittmer, *Local People*, 179–80; Moody to Silver; P. D. East to Theron Lynd, P. D. East Papers, USMMLA, folder 1, Correspondence; for more on Lynd, see http://www.lib.usm.edu/legacy/archives/m027.htm (accessed July 19, 2014) and Gordon A. Martin Jr., *Count Them One by One: Black Mississippians Fighting for the Right to Vote* (Jackson: University Press of Mississippi, 2010). For more on East, see P. D. East, *The Magnolia Jungle: The Life, Times and Education of a Southern Editor* (New York: Simon and Schuster, 1960) and Gary Huey, *Rebel with a Cause: P.D. East, Southern Liberalism, and the Civil Rights Movement, 1953–1971* (Lanham, MD: Rowman and Littlefield, 1985). Collection of written vignettes recorded in February 1963, Waits Papers, box 1, folder 10; *JMC*, 1963, 105; Moody response to "Questionaire to the 28," n.d. (late 1965), Waits Papers, box 1, folder 14; *JMC*, 1964, 94; *North Texas Conference Journal*, 1964, 67, 76.

19. Mitchell, *There Is an Election*, 60; memo from JSC (James Conner) to Jim Waits, August 11, 1964, James Conner PP; Edward J. Pendergrass, "An Evaluation of Methodism in the Jackson Area," n.d. (Fall 1964), Humphrey Papers, box 1, Methodism in Mississippi 1960–5.

20. Jim Waits e-mail to author, July 31, 2009, and Waits Daily Suggester calendars for 1963 and 1964, Waits PP. For more on the Jackson church visits campaign, see Marsh, *God's Long Summer*, 131–41, Lyon, "Lifting the Color Bar . . ."; Dupont, *Mississippi Praying*, ch. 7; and Cunningham, *Agony at Galloway*, 55–60. Jim Waits, "Let the Church Be the Church," sermon at Epworth Methodist, April 5, 1964, copy in Entrekin PP (emphasis in original).

21. Stephen Whitfield, *A Death in the Delta: The Story of Emmett Till* (New York: Free Press, 1988), 68; Dittmer, *Local People*, 227; *JCL*, February 20, 1964.

22. *JCL*, March 2, 1964; April 10, 1964; October 26, 1964; and April 14, 1964; Waits interviews, 2003, 2009.

23. Jim Waits to "Dear Friends" (the Twenty-Eight), October 29, 1965, Waits Papers, box 1, folder 14; *JMC*, 1965, 109; Jim Waits to Lee H. Reiff, February 22, 1967, and May 5, 1967, Lee Reiff PP; Waits interview, 2003; *JMC*, 1967, 128; *Tennessee Conference Journal*, 1967, 93, 86.

24. Eventually nineteen Born of Conviction signers transferred out of the confer-
    ence; Powell Hall did not leave until 1971. *JMC*, 1964, 93; Barlow interview;
    Hubert Barlow to Bishop Franklin, June 2, 1964, BOP, box 1, folder 20.

25. *North Indiana Conference Journal*, 1968, 1797; Roy Eaton e-mail to author,
    January 25, 2006; *JMC*, 1968, 91, 110; *North Indiana Conference Journal*, 1968,
    1570, 1574; *JMC*, 1965, 95, and 1964, 94; *JMC*, 1968, 110; Gipson, "Preaching on
    Controversial Issues."

26. Powell Hall interview; Miriam Berele, "Memorial to My Father," unpublished
    memoir, 2009, Miriam Berele PP; *West Virginia Conference Journal*, 2009, 334–5;
    Berele, "Memorial to My Father"; Berele e-mail to author, August 13, 2012.

27. Powell Hall interview; Miriam Berele e-mails to author, August 11 and July 29,
    2012; Berele, "Memorial to My Father"; Powell Hall to author, May 10, 2006.

28. Jack Loflin interview; Woodrick interview; *JMC*, 1963, 93; Williamson interview.

29. Powell Hall interview. See Chapter 2 for the story of Hall's sermon at Lake and
    Chapter 6 for the Scooba Church's response to Hall's participation in Born of
    Conviction. *JMC*, 1963, 104.

30. Powell Hall interview; *JMC*, 1965, 98; James S. Conner to Duncan M. Gray Jr.,
    July 1, 1964, and Gray to Conner, July 13, 1964, both in James Conner PP.

31. Powell Hall interview. Elton Brown related the story of Hall's Red Rambler and
    attempts to avoid harassment at the Born of Conviction reunion in June 2005.
    Julia Hall is convinced that the family would have suffered even more harass-
    ment were it not for the intervention of a man in Natchez who felt indebted to
    her father. Re: the climate in Natchez and Adams County in those years, see
    Dittmer, *Local People*, 216, 353–62, and Hendrickson, *Sons of Mississippi*, 19–32,
    222–30.

32. Powell Hall interview; *JMC*, 1965, 100; 1967, 132; *MCJ*, 1968, 119. Re: the
    January 1970 desegregation of schools in Mississippi, see Bolton, *The Hardest
    Deal of All*, ch. 7.

33. Powell Hall interview; Cathy Shelton interview; *MCJ*, 1970, 126; 1971,
    120; see Willie Morris, *Yazoo: The Integration of a Deep Southern Town*
    (New York: Harper's Magazine Press, 1971); *Southern New Jersey Conference
    Journal*, 1971, 54.

34. *JMC*, 1960, 230; 1961, 246; 1962, 260; 1963, 286; 1964, 224; 1965, 286; 1966,
    216; 1967, 252; 1968, 232, 247; *MCJ*, 1970, 263; 1971, 292; and *Southern New
    Jersey Conference Journal*, 1971, 116.

35. Powell Hall interview.

36. H. Bufkin Oliver to James Silver, April 9, 1963, Silver Papers, box 23, folder
    9; *MMA*, July 5, 1961; Oliver interview; *JMC*, 1964, 94; *JSCAC*, 1963, 109,
    129; H. Bufkin Oliver to Bishop Marvin Franklin, June 25, 1963, BOP, box 1,
    folder 20.

37. Oliver interview; Troutman interview; *JSCAC*, 1965, 194; Oliver interview; Rod
    Entrekin interview, 2007.

38. *JSCAC*, 1967, 110; Oliver interview; *Journal of the North Mississippi Conference*, 1967, 75, 85.

39. Ken Roberts interview; *JMC*, 1930, 101; 1931, 80. Ramsey was a senior in high school when his father came to Bonita. He graduated from Millsaps in 1935 and taught there from 1937 to 1939 (Lindsey, *Methodism in the Mississippi Conference, 1920–1939* [Jackson, MS: Hawkins Foundation, 1980], 143, 161). *MMA*, August 4, 1954; *JCL*, August 15, 1954; *MCJ*, 1989, 409; James Harrison interview; *JMC*, 1957, 76; Millsaps, *Purple and White*, March 6, 1958; *JMC*, 1960, 96, 60; Wallace Roberts to Bishop John Owen Smith, March 8, 1963, Bishop John Owen Smith Papers, PTLA, box 4, folder 5.

40. James L. Waits Papers, PTLA, box 1, folder 2; Ken Roberts interview; James Harrison interview.

41. Ken Roberts interview; Wallace Roberts to Bishop John Owen Smith, Smith Papers, PTLA, box 4, folder 5; *North Georgia Conference Journal* 1963, 87; 1964, 85; and 1965, 86; *JMC*, 1966, 101; *Journal of the North Mississippi Conference*, 1966, 71.

42. Joe Way letter to author, April 21, 2004; Jim Matheny, "Image, Identity, and Repression in Southern Church Experience," paper for Brooks Holifield, Candler School of Theology, 1977, Jim Matheny PP. Re: signers confiding in Bob Matheny, see, e.g., Joseph C. Way to Bishop Franklin, January 18, 1963, BOP, box 1, folder 19. In the early 1980s, I heard Bob Matheny, then my district superintendent, discuss his fruitless efforts to push Slay to support the signers. Emily Stafford Matheny interview; Jim Matheny, "Image, Identity, and Repression . . ."; Jim Matheny interview; Jim Matheny e-mail to author, April 7, 2014.

43. Jim Matheny and Emily Stafford Matheny interviews; Robert Matheny to Bishop Franklin, May 14, 1964, BOP, box 1, folder 20; *JMC*, 1964, 94; *Northwest Indiana Conference Journal*, 1964, 65, 74; Jim Matheny e-mail to author, August 3, 2013, and E. S. Matheny interview; Jim Matheny, "Image, Identity, and Repression. . . ."

44. Emily Stafford Matheny interview; Lyon, "Lifting the Color Bar . . .," ch. 11; Howard H. Spencer and John B. Garner, "To All Methodist Bishops Serving in the United States," March 16, 1966, Lee Reiff PP; *JMC*, 1967, 127, 135.

45. Joseph C. Way to author, April 21, 2004. Of the seven signers in the Meridian District, three left Mississippi in the next few months, three (including Way) moved to a different Mississippi Conference church in June, and one was reappointed to the same church in June. All left Mississippi, though Wallace Roberts returned from seminary to the North Mississippi Conference in 1966, and Way, who never transferred his membership out of the conference, returned to serve in the state in 1987.

46. Way interview; Way to author, April 21, 2004—the Soule's Chapel response is described in Chapter 6; Joseph C. Way to James Silver, January 18, 1963, and June 17, 1963, Silver Papers, box 23, folder 9; Joseph C. Way to Bishop Franklin,

January 18, 1963, BOP, box 1, folder 19; Way to author, April 21, 2004; *JMC*, 1963, 106.

47. Clark interviews, 2003, 2007; *JMC*, 1963, 264. My family attended Capitol Street from 1960 to 1964. Way to author, April 21, 2004.

48. Lee H. Reiff to "Dear Folks," August 17, 1963, Lee Reiff PP; Clark interview, 2003; Cunningham, *Agony at Galloway*, 5–12; *JMC*, 1964, 93, 108. Galloway considered Clark as a candidate for Selah's replacement in June 1963—see Clark's typed memo dated June 17, 1963 (likely never sent) that lists conditions to be met in order for him to go there (e.g., "I must be free to preach my convictions."), Clark PP.

49. Lee H. Reiff to "Dear Folks," August 17, 1963, Lee Reiff PP; "Resolution, Official Board, Capitol Street Methodist Church," n.d. (September 1963), Lee Reiff PP; *JCL*, August 31 and September 1, 1963. The Resolution asserted that Leggett's statement to the press was not true, and my father's August 17 letter also said this.

50. "Resolution, Official Board, Capitol Street Methodist Church," n.d. (September 1963), Lee Reiff PP; Joseph C. Way to "Dear Sir," November 2, 1963, Way PP; Lee H. Reiff to "Dear Folks," September 21, 1963, Lee Reiff PP.

51. Way to author, April 21, 2004; re: Granberry's quietist approach to the race issue, see Marsh, *God's Long Summer*, 135–7. Way to author, April 21, 2004. There is evidence Granberry was willing to open the doors of the church if sufficient lay support developed, but according to one unnamed source, Willard Leggett put a stop to that—Roy C. Clark to Warren Pittman, May 18, 1964, Clark PP. Marsh, 135–6; Lee H. Reiff to "Dear Folks," November 9, 1963, Lee Reiff PP; Way to author, April 21, 2004. For a full account of Capitol Street's response to the church visits campaign, see Lyon, "Lifting the Color Bar . . ."; for accounts of the Easter 1964 arrests at Capitol Street, see Carter Dalton Lyon, "Easter in Jackson, Mississippi, 1964," *Methodist History*, January 2011, 99–115; and Thompson, "Another Pilgrimage to Jackson." For more on Tilson, see Houck and Dixon, *Rhetoric, Religion and the Civil Rights Movement, 1954–1965*, Vol. 1, 362–8.

52. Way to author, April 21, 2004; Jim Livesay to Lee H. Reiff, October 18, 1964, Lee Reiff PP. My parents participated in the underground church group. Lee H. Reiff to Roscoe S. Strivings (District Superintendent, Phoenix, Arizona), December 13, 1963, Lee Reiff PP; *JMC*, 1964, 46, 104.

53. *JSCAC*, 1968, 130; *Pacific and Southwest Conference Journal*, 1973, 242; *California Pacific Annual Conference Journal* 1985, 160–1; Jean Dickinson Minus interview; see Maxie D. Dunnam, *Exodus: Communicator's Commentary* (Waco, TX: Word, 1987), 172–3.

54. Dunnam interviews, 2004, 2009; *JSCAC*, 1968, 128; Cunningham, *Agony at Galloway*, 61–7; Lee H. Reiff interview; Dean and Gloria Miller interview; Dunnam interview, 2009. I heard the story of Leggett's lobbying against

Dunnam from two different longtime Galloway members, but Dunnam doubts the claim. Leggett had more influence on Bishop Franklin than he ever had on Bishop Pendergrass. See Frank, *Polity, Practice, and the Mission of The United Methodist Church,* 201.

55. *JSCAC,* 1973, 135; 1976, 148; Dunnam interview, 2004; Dunnam e-mail to author, June 28, 2013.

56. Dunnam interview, 2004; *Tennessee Conference Journal,* 1981, 105; *Memphis Conference Journal,* 1982, 85, 94; *Kentucky Conference Journal,* 1995, 76; Dunnam e-mail to author, June 28, 2013; *Commercial Appeal,* July 21, 2010; Dunnam e-mail to author, June 28, 2013.

57. Trigg response to "Questionaire to the 28," n.d. (late 1965), Waits Papers, box 1, folder 14; *South Indiana Conference Journal,* 1969, 99; 1974, 117; 1981, 132; *GM,* 1981, 748, 750; Dunnam interview, 2004; *GM,* 1981, 754, 705; "O. Gerald Trigg, Ambassador-at-Large, Colorado Springs of Faith," Trigg PP.

58. *East Valley Tribune* (Arizona), July 31, 2004; Jack S. Troutman to James B. Nicholson, February 23, 1965, Nicholson PP; Troutman response to "Questionaire to the 28, n.d. (late 1965), Waits Papers, box 1, folder 14; *JSCAC,* 1973, 129; 1975, 141; *Pacific and Southwest Conference Journal,* 1982, 104; *Desert Southwest Conference Journal,* 1986, 67; 1991, 50; Troutman interview.

59. *North Texas Conference Journal,* 1966, 60; 1967, 60; *Southwest Texas Conference Journal,* 1969, 73; 1972, 55; Allen Moody e-mail to author, July 27, 2012; Marvin D. Moody obituary, Marion Co. (MS) *Columbian-Progress,* April 1, 1982.

60. Waits interview, 2003; *Tennessee Conference Journal,* 1969, 99; *MCJ,* 1976, 87; www.ats.edu and www.fteleaders.org (both accessed July 19, 2014).

61. *Southern New Jersey Conference Journal,* 1979, 250; *West Virginia Conference Journal,* 1980, 80; 1993, 401; 1994, 160; Powell Hall interview; Berele and Hall-Williams interview.

62. Oliver interview; *North Mississippi Conference Journal,* 1973, 127; 1974, 94; 1979, 107; 1982, 108; 1985, 295.

63. *North Mississippi Conference Journal,* 1973, 125; 1978, 102; Ken Roberts interview; James Harrison interview; *MCJ,* 1989, 409; Mark Roberts e-mail to author, June 14, 2013; James Harrison interview. The timing of the merger of the two conferences meant that Roberts never officially returned to the Mississippi Conference, though he served in the state for twenty-two years upon his return from seminary. Ken Roberts interview.

64. Joseph C. Way to James B. Nicholson, February 9, 1965, Way PP; Way to author, April 21, 2004; *MCJ,* 1987, 156; 1989, 200; 1992, 415, 437; 1993, 456; 1994, 216; George Sholl e-mail to author, May 13, 2011; *MCJ,* 1996, 184; Way e-mail to author, August 1, 2013; Way to author, April 21, 2004.

65. Silver, *Mississippi: The Closed Society,* 58.

66. "Born of Conviction," *MMA,* January 2, 1963 (emphasis in original); Hadden, *The Gathering Storm in the Churches,* 190–2 (quote on 192).

67. Hadden, *The Gathering Storm in the Churches*, 189–93. I tried to consult the late Hadden's papers in order to review the data he collected on Born of Conviction, but they have not been preserved—Elaine M. Hadden e-mail to author, November 28, 2005.

CHAPTER 9

1. This chapter's title comes from John Egerton's *A Mind to Stay Here: Profiles from the South* (New York: Macmillan, 1970). *JMC*, 1963, 84–5.
2. "Remained in the Conference" is important, because signer Wallace Roberts left Mississippi in 1963 to go to seminary only; he returned to the state in 1966 for a full-time appointment but transferred his membership to the North Mississippi Conference, due to the Mississippi Conference political situation and Willard Leggett's ongoing power. A different qualification excludes signer Joe Way from this list of those who stayed—he kept his membership in the conference, but as a US Air Force chaplain, he served outside Mississippi from 1964 to 1987.
3. Clint Gill interview; William McAtee interview; Rob Gill interview.
4. Steve Dickson e-mail to author, February 12, 2013. The teller who testified was T. Foxworth, father of Richard Foxworth, who later married N. A. and Mary Dickson's daughter, Marilyn. *Hattiesburg American*, January 4, 1932, and March 4, 1932; *Pascagoula Chronicle*, November 11, 1932.
5. Steve Dickson e-mail to author, February 12, 2013; Steve Dickson interview; *MCJ*, 2000, 255–6; Dickson family interview.
6. Dickson family interview; *MCJ*, 2000, 255–6; Steve Dickson e-mail to author, February 12, 2013.
7. Dickson family interview; Allen left Mississippi in the late 1950s and McKeithen in 1963 (both to Southern California-Arizona); McAtee interview; Dickson family interview; Dickson response to "Questionaire to the 28," n.d. (late 1965), Waits Papers, box 1, folder 14.
8. Written vignettes recorded in February 1963, Waits Papers, box 1, folder 10; Dickson response to "Questionaire to the 28."
9. McAtee interview; McAtee, *Transformed*, 96–106.
10. McAtee, *Transformed*, 107; N. A. Dickson to Bishop Edward J. Pendergrass, September 29, 1965, with enclosures, BOP, box 2, folder 1; Dickson response to "Questionaire to the 28"; McAtee *Transformed*, ch. 6; *Columbian-Progress*, August 19, 1965, copy in BOP box 2, folder 1; Dickson response to "Questionaire to the 28"; McAtee, *Transformed*, 118–20.
11. McAtee, *Transformed*, 123–6; re: the Deacons of Defense, see Akinyele Umoja, *We Will Shoot Back: Armed Resistance in the Mississippi Freedom Movement* (New York: New York University Press, 2013); Dickson response to "Questionaire to the 28."

12. N. A. Dickson to Bishop Edward J. Pendergrass, September 29, 1965, BOP, box 2, folder 1; collection of letters to John Burnett from Mississippi Conference ministerial leaders during Pendergrass's tenure, Pendergrass Papers, box 4, folder 3; Bishop Earl G. Hunt Jr. to John Burnett, Pendergrass Papers, box 1, folder 5–1; *JCL*, September 18, 1965, copy in MSSC Records, 9-25-0-15-1-1-1. Committee of Concern eventually developed a broader focus and changed its name to the Mississippi Religious Leadership Conference. For more on Mississippi Conference involvement with Committee of Concern, see Branch, "Born of Conviction," 171, 184–5, 198–9.

13. *MMA*, January 16, 1963; *Christian Advocate*, July 1, 1965, 24; *JMC*, 1965, 81–2, 119–21, 120.

14. N. A. Dickson to Bishop Edward J. Pendergrass, September 29, 1965, BOP, box 2, folder 1.

15. Collection of letters to John Burnett, Pendergrass Papers, box 4, folder 3; *JMC*, 1966, 116; 1967, 135; MMA, June 24, 1967; *MCJ*, 1968, 124; 1974, 106; 1978, 103; 1983, 101; Dickson family interview; *MCJ*, 2000, 255–6.

16. The average age of Born of Conviction signers was 32.6; Dickson was forty-four in January 1963. Dickson response to "Questionaire to the 28"; Clint Gill interview—Gill was Seashore District Superintendent from 1983 to 1988.

17. Steve Dickson interview; McAtee, *Transformed*, 96; Dickson family interview; Dickson Order Endowment web page, http://ms-umf.org/index.php?q = dickson-order.html (accessed July 19, 2014); *JCL*, January 25, 2003.

18. *MCJ*, 1989, 395; David E. Conner interview. The "briefcase" description has been credited to J. B. Cain and to N. A. Dickson. My future wife and I were the candidates—the 1976 meeting took place in Conner's office at Epworth UMC in Jackson. *MCJ*, 1989, 395.

19. The definition of Personalistic Idealism is paraphrased from David Conner's explanation (he has a ThD in philosophical theology). David Conner interview; Waits interview, 2005; Woodrick interview.

20. Betty Conner Currey interview; James S. Conner to A. D. Beittel, February 1, 1963, James Conner PP.

21. Betty Conner Currey interview; *JMC*, 1963, 112; MCHR to "Dear Sir" with four-page prospectus from COFO on Freedom Summer, May 1964; MCHR "Immediate News Release," May 20, 1963; and MCHR "Purpose and Policy" statement, from MCHR Constitution, adopted May 20, 1963, all from James Conner PP.

22. James S. Conner to W. J. Cunningham, December 17, 1963; Conner to S. W. Granberry, December 6, 1963; Conner to Francis Stevens, December 6, 1963; Conner to Duncan M. Gray Jr., December 24, 1963; W. J. Cunningham to Conner, December 20, 1963; all letters in James Conner PP.

23. *JDN*, November 11, 1964 (MSSC 2-79-2-21-1-1-1); James S. Conner to Duncan M. Gray Jr., December 4, 1964; and MCHR letter "To the Members of the

Board of Directors," November 5, 1963, both James Conner PP. Conner to Gray, December 4, 1964.

24. Betty Conner Currey interview; David Conner interview.

25. *JMC*, 1965, 102; *MCJ*, 1969, 103; Betty Conner Currey interview.

26. *MCJ*, 1974, 104; Betty Conner Currey interview; *MCJ*, 1978, 107; 1983, 101; *MCJ*, 1989, 395, and David Conner interview.

27. *MCJ*, 1989, 395; David Conner interview; Betty Conner Currey interview.

28. Elton Brown interview, 2003; Elton Brown to author, August 12, 2013; *JMC*, 1953, 63; 1954, 77; 1956, 72; 1961, 109.

29. Brown interview, 2003; Elton and Juliette Brown interview.

30. Davis, *Race Against Time*, 198; Brown et al. interview; D. Elton Brown to James W. Silver, January 29, 1963, Silver Papers, box 23, folder 9.

31. Brown interview, 2003; Brown response to "Questionaire to the 28," n.d. (late 1965), Waits Papers, box 1, folder 14; Brown interview, 2003; Brown response to "Questionaire to the 28."

32. Brown interview, 2003; *JMC*, 1966, 116.

33. James S. Conner to Elbert Jean, December 6, 1963, Campbell Papers, box 54, folder 23; Moore interview; Brown et al. interview.

34. *JMC*, 1967, 134; *MCJ*, 1971, 129; 1974, 106; 1978, 111; 1985, 140; Lee interview; *MCJ*, 1989, 200; Brown interview, 2003.

35. Rod Entrekin interview, 2003. There were more mid-year moves in 1963–4 than in any other year in that era, involving eight separate sets of changes (all but one directly connected to the departure of at least one Born of Conviction signer)—*JMC*, 1964, 108–9. Entrekin, "My Journey in Ministry," and Rod Entrekin to Mr. and Mrs. Tom Miller, Woodville, October 28, 1963, both Entrekin PP.

36. Rod Entrekin interview, 2011; Brown et al. interview. He learned of his neighbor's Klan involvement from *JDN*, n.d. (February 1966), MSSC Records, 6-53-0-46-1-1-1.

37. James S. Conner to Elbert Jean, December 6, 1963, Campbell Papers, box 54, folder 23; Entrekin response to "Questionaire to the 28," n.d. (late 1965), Waits Papers, box 1, folder 14; W. B. "Bill" Jones to "Dear Rod," May 5, 1963, Entrekin PP; Rod Entrekin interview, 2003; *JMC*, 1965, 97.

38. Entrekin, "My Journey in Ministry"; Entrekin response to "Questionaire to the 28."

39. Entrekin, "My Journey in Ministry."

40. Entrekin, "My Journey in Ministry"; Rod and Ginny Entrekin interview.

41. Entrekin, "My Journey in Ministry"; Rod and Ginny Entrekin interview.

42. Rod Entrekin to Don Fortenberry, November 17, 2004, Entrekin PP; Entrekin, "My Journey in Ministry" (emphasis in original).

43. The character descriptions are mine, supplemented by Dyess interviews. Rod Entrekin interview, 2003; Napier interview (his emphasis); S. N. Dyess to author, May 24, 2009.

44. Kellar, *Sandersville*, 152–3; Napier interview; *JMC*, 1964, 108; *JCL*, February 16, 1964; Patricia Collins guestbook entry for Napier online obituary, *JCL*, May 11, 2010, and Patricia Collins interview.

45. Aubrey Lucas e-mail to author, August 19, 2013; Napier interview; *MCJ*, 1969, 88; 1970, 121. In 1968 the denomination's name changed to United Methodist Church due to the merger with the Evangelical United Brethren. Murray, *Methodists and the Crucible of Race*, 213, 215–16; Branch, "Born of Conviction," 179–80, 216, 244, 272–3, 280–1, 302–3; Murray, *Methodists and the Crucible of Race*, 188–9, 200–1, 228–30. For more on the Delta Ministry and white Mississippi Methodist objections to it, see Findlay, *Church People in the Struggle: The National Council of Churches and the Black Freedom Movement, 1950–1970* (New York: Oxford University Press, 1993), chs. 4–5, and Murray, *Methodists and the Crucible of Race*, 213–214. The most complete account of the merger is in Branch, "Born of Conviction," ch. 9; see also Murray, *Methodists and the Crucible of Race*, 228–230.

46. Bolton, *The Hardest Deal of All*, chs. 5–7, esp. 141–2; Napier interview; *MCJ*, 1972, 94; Lee Reiff to Joe Reiff, February 10, 1973, and Joe Reiff to Lee and Gerry Reiff, February 13, 1973, author's PP; Napier interview; Bolton, *The Hardest Deal of All*, 221—see also 174–5.

47. *MCJ*, 1977, 101; 1980, 98; 1982, 99, 108; 1989, 206, 212; 1991, 228; 1994, 200; Napier interview; *JCL*, May 11, 2010; *MCJ*, 2010, 209.

48. Napier interview; "Jesus Loves the Little Children," written by C. Herbert Woolston with music by George F. Root, 1913; Napier response to "Questionaire to the 28," n.d. (late 1965), Waits Papers, box 1, folder 14.

49. Lee Reiff interview; *MCJ*, 1980, 199–200.

50. *MCJ*, 1980, 199–200; http://personalpages.bellsouth.net/b/u/bumc2113/history.html (Beauvoir UMC Church History, accessed August 11, 2013—no longer available); *MMA*, April 18, 1956; October 18, 1961; and May 9, 1962; *JMC*, 1961, 95; Harold Ryker to James Silver, March 27, 1963, Silver Papers, box 23, folder 9; *DH*, January 18, 1963.

51. Richard Creel e-mail to author, July 18, 2013; Charles Nicholson interview; *MCJ*, 1980, 200.

52. Ryker response to "Questionaire to the 28," n.d. (late 1965), Waits Papers, box 1, folder 14; *JMC*, 1963, 109 (but see *MMA*, June 5, 1963, 9—Ryker was appointed to Pine Grove-Merrill, then shifted to North Biloxi when Ed McRae left just weeks after moving there, then moved again on July 22, 1963, to Kingston: *JMC*, 1964, 109); *JMC*, 1964, 105; 1965, 107; 1965, 94; 1966, 100; 1968, 122; *MCJ*, 1969, 101; 1973, 107; 1974, 92; 1980, 200.

53. *MCJ*, 1980, 200; Marilyn Perrine interview.

54. *DH*, January 18, 1963; also in Ryker to Silver, March 27, 1963.

55. John Ed Thomas interview, 2003; Margaret Thomas interview.

56. Margaret Thomas interview; *JMC*, 1962, 109; John Ed Thomas interview, 2003.

57. *JMC*, 1963, 112; Margaret Thomas interview; Margaret Thomas e-mail to author, August 16, 2013; John Ed Thomas interview, 2003.

58. Margaret Thomas interview. The vote to accept a new pastor is not normal Methodist procedure. John Ed Thomas interview, 2003; James S. Conner to Elbert Jean, December 6, 1963, Campbell Papers, box 54, folder 23.

59. *JMC*, 1965, 107; *MCJ*, 1969, 101; 2008, 200–1; LaRue Owen e-mail to author, August 19, 2013.

60. *MCJ*, 1983, 113; 1986, 145; 1987, 7, 119; 1992, 441; 2002, 178; 2008, 200–1; Claire Dobbs, sermon for Thomas funeral service, November 26, 2007; Lovett Weems, "Squandering Leadership Potential?," Lewis Center for Church Leadership "Leading Ideas" blog (www.churchleadership.com/leadingideas), January 16, 2008.

61. Margaret Thomas e-mail to author, August 16, 2013; John Ed Thomas interview, 2003.

62. *JCL*, January 21, 2006; author's notes from Fellowship for Evangelism award dinner, November 1, 2008; Tonkel blog post, July 30, 2013, http://wellschurch.org/blogs/keiths-blog (accessed July 19, 2014); Millsaps College news release, October 22, 2002.

63. Millsaps news release, October 22, 2002; *JMC*, 1962, 109; Keith Tonkel interview, 2003; Tonkel response to "Questionaire to the 28," n.d. (late 1965), Waits Papers, box 1, folder 14; *JCL*, January 21, 2006.

64. Tonkel interview, 2003; *MMA*, June 24, 1967; *JMC*, 1967, 111.

65. *MCJ*, 1969, 97; *JCL*, January 21, 2006; http://wellschurch.org/www.wellsfest.org (accessed July 20, 2014). As a Millsaps College student, I joined Wells in 1975 and attended for eighteen months. From 1982 to 1985, Tonkel was my colleague in West Jackson when our churches were part of a cooperative ministry venture.

66. Tonkel interview, 2003; Tonkel, *Finally the Dawn* (Kansas City: E. L. Mendenhall, 1959); *Heart Stuff* (Jackson: Wells Church Press, 1995); and *God Stuff* (Jackson: Wells Church Press, 2011); JCL, January 21, 2006—the quote comes from what I said about Tonkel to the reporter.

67. Tonkel interview, 2013; *MCJ*, 2012, 217; "Get Well Keith Tonkel" Facebook page; Tonkel e-mail to author, August 23, 2013.

68. *MCJ*, 2007, 151; author's notes on 2007 Elzy Award presentation. The failure to mention Born of Conviction simply reflects the presenter's lack of awareness of the Born of Conviction controversy. Foundation for Evangelism Banquet award program, November 1, 2008; *Millsaps Magazine*, Winter 2014, 71.

69. Tonkel response to "Questionaire to the 28."

CHAPTER 10

1. Brown, Entrekin, and Thomas interview, 2003. "Excavation of memories" is suggested by Ellen Ann Fentress, "Ending 50 Years of Silence about Mississippi's Freedom Summer," *The Atlantic*, June 19, 2014, http://www.theatlantic.com/politics/archive/2014/06/excavating-memories-of-the-freedom-summer-in-mississippi/373025/ (accessed July 24, 2014).

2. Mark 6:4. Six responses to the questionnaire Jim Waits sent to all signers in 1965 included some statement regarding the value of giving more ministers the opportunity to sign: Brown, Dickinson, Napier, Ryker, Trigg, and Troutman responses, all Waits Papers, box 1, folder 14.

3. Jerry Trigg response to "Questionaire to the 28," n.d. (late 1965), Waits Papers, box 1, folder 14; Betty Conner Currey interview (see also Buford Dickinson response to Waits "Questionaire to the 28"; Moore interview; McRae interview; and Rod Entrekin interview, 2003); James Conner to Lee H. Reiff, January 11, 1963, Lee Reiff PP; John Ed Thomas interview, 2003.

4. The "crack" image and similar analogies abound, both in interviews with signers and in literature on the period, e.g., Tonkel interview, 2003 ("little tiny bit of a crack"); Wilton Carter interview (a "break in the ice"); and McMillen, *The Citizens' Council*, 40 (the "dike analogy," which motivated massive resistance thought, i.e., that "the region was only as strong as its weakest component"). Smith, *Congressman from Mississippi*, 117.

5. Carol Gilligan, *In a Different Voice: Psychological Theory and Women's Development* (Cambridge, MA: Harvard University Press, 1982), 73. For examples of this care/peace perspective, see the statement of the Summit Methodist Church Official Board, *Summit Sun*, January 17, 1963; Bert Jordan's "I Do Not Understand" essay, *MMA*, January 16, 1963; and E. U. Parker Jr. to Ashmore, January 5, Ashmore Papers, box 1, folder 1 (all three discussed in Chapter 5). Ed King also explores the desire to maintain peace in his unpublished *White Church in Mississippi* manuscript. Re: Mrs. Hamer's views, see Marsh, *God's Long Summer*, 23, 31, 33, and 46.

6. Lee H. Reiff (author's father), "Some Features of Methodism in Mississippi" and "A Personal Opinion," (n.d., early May 1964), prepared for a gathering of Methodists demonstrating for change in the segregated church structure at the 1964 Methodist General Conference in Pittsburgh, Lee Reiff PP; re: General Conference protests, see *NYT*, May 3 and 4, 1964; and *Chicago Sun-Times*, May 3, 1964; Furr interview.

7. Gilligan, *In a Different Voice*, 163–74. For evidence of Franklin's understanding of societal injustice, see "Pillars of Peace" and "That Freedom May Not Perish," Franklin Papers, box 4, folders 6 and 3, n.d. (1944 or so); *MMA*, October 10, 1962.

8. Hillman interview; A. K. Ellzey to Ashmore, February 14, 1963, Ashmore Papers, box 1, folder 1; Wilton Carter to George L. Berry, March 31, 1964, Carter PP; Way response to "Questionaire to the 28," n.d. (late 1965), Waits Papers, box 1, folder 14.

9. Thompson's words from the conference video of the event, transcribed by the author. Signers present included Elton Brown, Maxie Dunnam, Rod Entrekin, Ned Kellar, Ed McRae, Keith Tonkel, Jack Troutman, and Joe Way. Wives present were Juliette Brown, Jerry Dunnam, Ginny Entrekin, Martina McRae, and Ruth Way. Widows present were Betty Conner Currey, Jean Dickinson Minus, Bennie Holston, and Margaret Thomas. The signers' names were read by the cochairs of the Conference Commission on Religion and Race, Stephen Cook (an African American) and Kathy Price, both pastors in the conference.

10. *MCJ*, 2013, 49–50.

11. *MCJ*, 2013, 49–50; author's transcript from event video.

12. Both statements were addressed to me; the speakers will remain anonymous. The second comment came in an e-mail after the event.

13. Keith Tonkel e-mail to author, June 4, 2013; Tonkel interview, 2014. When twelve surviving signers gathered in Jackson for a reunion on June 6, 2005, they attended part of the afternoon session of the Mississippi Annual Conference, and Bishop Hope Morgan Ward briefly acknowledged their presence, though she did not use the words "Born of Conviction statement" in her remarks.

14. Waits interview, 2003; James Nicholson interview; Jerry and Rose Trigg interview; Theodore Runyon to Carter, January 17, 1963, Carter PP (Ned Kellar, Jack Troutman, Maxie Dunnam, and possibly John Ed Thomas and Keith Tonkel all received the same letter).

15. John Ed Thomas, speaking at Born of Conviction Reunion on June 6, 2005, transcribed from the event video shot, edited, and provided to all participants by Paul Walters. The remarks of signers who left averaged more than eleven minutes, while those who stayed averaged just more than five minutes.

16. Carter, Dickinson, Dunnam, Furr, Kellar, Lampton, McRae, Moore, Nicholson, Rush, Trigg, Troutman, Waits, Walters, and Way all flourished professionally after they left—some more than others. In my judgment, exile came with varying degrees of anger, unresolved feelings, and even grief, especially for Hall, Holston, Moody, and Walters, while Oliver (who soon decided his departure had been a mistake) and Roberts both spent most of their remaining careers in North Mississippi. For three (Lampton, Furr, and Moody), life outside Mississippi eventually meant their departure from the ordained ministry. Re: opportunities to tell their stories, I have the text of speeches made by Dickinson, Dunnam, Nicholson, and Walters soon after they left, and others made similar talks. Re: "dangerous memories," see Johann Baptist Metz, *Faith in History and Society: Toward a Practical Fundamental Theology*

(New York: Seabury Press, 1980), 88–118. The lack of public acknowledgment of Born of Conviction gave it a mystique in the eyes of my preministerial friends—including Syd Conner (son of James) and Jim Matheny (grandson of J. P. Stafford)—and me at Millsaps in the mid-1970s. To us, the Twenty-Eight represented the epitome of a prophetic stand—a refusal to be conformed to the prevailing culture of both society and church.

17. Clint Gill interview; Rod Entrekin and Keith Tonkel remarks at Born of Conviction reunion, June 6, 2005.

18. *JCL*, June 6, 2005; Tonkel remarks at 2005 reunion. Elton Brown told me at the reunion of Napier's comment.

19. McRae interview; Moore interview. For other discussions of the struggles of persons who left Mississippi in those years, see Dittmer, *Local People*, 70, 202–3; Silver, *Mississippi: The Closed Society*, 81–2; and Wilkie, *Dixie*, 19.

20. I overheard Margaret Thomas's comment; John Ed Thomas died in 2007. Margaret Thomas interview; Millsaps Forum Lecture, February 17, 2006.

21. Ed King interview; McRae interview; *JCL*, June 6, 2005.

22. Dittmer, *Local People*, 247–52, 283–5, 180–91, 391, 417–18; Crespino, *In Search of Another Country*; Lyon, "Lifting the Color Bar . . ."; Branch, "Born of Conviction," 151; *NYT*, May 3 and 4, 1964; see also *Chicago Sun-Times*, May 3, 1964; Murray, *Methodists and the Crucible of Race*, 228; Branch, "Born of Conviction," 193–97, 219–22; Murray, *Methodists and the Crucible of Race*, ch. 7; Branch, "Born of Conviction," 295, 307–10, 313, 319.

23. Re: "new Mississippi," see Dittmer, *Local People*, ch. 18. Eric D. Blanchard, "The National Council in Mississippi," *Christian Advocate*, August 13, 1964, 3; Dickson response to "Questionaire to the 28"; Loflin interview.

24. *JMC*, 1962, 107; Lee interview, 2003.

25. *JMC*, 1964, 108; Cunningham, *Agony at Galloway*, 55–7; Lee interview, 2003—Lee did not recall Cunningham asking for his opinion; Lee interview, 2014, and Lee e-mails to author, August 8, 2014; James K. Mathews, "Easter in Jackson," *Christian Century*, April 15, 1964, 478. For the most thorough historical account of that day at Galloway, see Lyon, "Easter in Jackson, Mississippi, 1964," esp. 106–7.

26. Lee interview, 2003; *JMC*, 1964, 246, 232, 248, 103; Clay F. Lee Oral History Interview, conducted by Orley B. Caudill, July 8, 1980, University of Southern Mississippi Center for Oral History and Cultural Heritage, http://digilib.usm.edu/cdm/compoundobject/collection/coh/id/4521/rec/12 (accessed August 3, 2014; Lee-Caudill interview).

27. Lee-Caudill interview; Dittmer, *Local People*, 247, 283; Mars, *Witness in Philadelphia*, 85–92.

28. Lee-Caudill interview; Mars, *Witness in Philadelphia*, 142–3—for Mars's account of Lee's support, see 145–7, 176–7. One of the many reasons why Florence Mars was ostracized in Philadelphia was her refusal to accept the hoax theory. The

state did not charge the men with murder then, but one of the surviving conspirators, Edgar Ray Killen, was convicted of the murders in 2005.

29. Lee-Caudill interview; Mars, *Witness in Philadelphia*, 142–3, 146.

30. Lee-Caudill interview; Mars, *Witness in Philadelphia*, 146; *NYT*, March 8, 2014; Mars, *Witness in Philadelphia*, 176–7.

31. Lee interview, 2003; Lee-Caudill interview; see also "Memories of Bishop Edward J. Pendergrass," Pendergrass Papers, box 4, folder 3.

32. L. Gregory Jones and Kevin R. Armstrong, *Resurrecting Excellence: Shaping Faithful Christian Ministry* (Grand Rapids, MI: William B. Eerdmans, 2006), 36–8; Lee interview, 2003.

33. Lee interview, 2003.

34. *JMC*, 1962, 111; video interview of Wilson Brent by Richard Felder, March 31, 2010 (Brent-Felder interview), Wilson Brent PP. Brent likely attended the November 1, 1962, meeting at Hidden Haven and/or the December 13 meeting in Hattiesburg. Rebecca Brent e-mail to author, January 25, 2011.

35. *JMC*, 1964, 109; re: Natchez tensions in 1964–5, see Dittmer, *Local People*, 353–62; Brent-Felder interview; Wilson Brent Journal, January 5, 1965; March 21, 1965; and March 25, 1965, Brent PP. His papers also contain notes on index cards that he prepared for the March service.

36. Brent-Felder interview; *JMC*, 1965, 110; 1966, 116; *MCJ*, 1969, 99; 1971, 129; 1975, 98, 107; 1976, 96; 1978, 98. Due to racial transition beginning in the late 1970s in Aldersgate's neighborhood, the church eventually became an African American congregation. *Raleigh News & Observer*, June 11, 2010.

37. Shirley S. Holston to author, July 21, 2004; *JMC*, 1961, 109; Charles Nicholson interview.

38. C. Nicholson interview.

39. C. Nicholson interview.

40. C. Nicholson interview; re: General Conference protests, see *NYT*, May 3 and 4, 1964; and *Chicago Sun-Times*, May 3, 1964.

41. *JMC*, 1967, 140; Charles Nicholson interview; James Nicholson interview; see also Deb Holston Selden interview re: Holston brothers.

42. List of potential signers, James L. Waits Papers, PTLA, box 1, folder 2; Harmon and Nona Tillman interview; *JMC*, 1962, 107; Tillman interview.

43. Kinnie Ford e-mail to author, March 8, 2010; Buford Dickinson, "Impressions of Mississippi," unpublished address given at Convocation at Claremont School of Theology, August 11, 1964, Dunnam PP; Tillman interview; *JMC*, 1964, 103; 1965, 106.

44. Lowry interview.

45. Lowry interview.

46. *JMC*, 1966, 97; Lowry interview.

47. *MCJ*, 1969, 93; Lowry interview.

48. The full story represented by this brief summary is beyond the scope of this book—see Murray, *Methodists and the Crucible of Race*, chs. 7–9, and Branch, "Born of Conviction," chs. 8–10.

49. Charles Nicholson interview; Rayford Woodrick interview; *JMC*, 1965, 105; *GM*, 1964, 290; Woodrick interview; Woodrick e-mail to author, August 8, 2014.

50. Re: freedom-of-choice plans as massive resistance strategy and the difficulties they caused for black families, see Bolton, *The Hardest Deal of All*, chs. 5–6; Lovett Weems e-mail to author, August 30, 2013; Woodrick interview; Woodrick e-mail to author, August 8, 2014.

51. Woodrick interview.

52. Woodrick interview; *JMC*, 1966, 111; *GM*, 1968, 428; re: Yazoo City school desegregation, see Morris, *Yazoo*.

53. Clay interview. A black Methodist minister in Brandon said something similar to James Conner in 1963—Betty Conner Currey interview; Clay interview.

54. Dittmer, *Local People*, 181; Victoria J. Gray to Dear Sir (Bertist Rouse), Ashmore Papers, box 1, folder 4; Mars, *Witness in Philadelphia*, 197, 219;

55. Clay interview; *GM*, 1966, 427; *Laurel Leader-Call*, July 29, 1966; Clay interview. For more on Bowers, see Marsh, *God's Long Summer*, ch. 2.

56. *GM*, 1967, 386; Jack Nelson, *Terror in the Night: The Klan's Campaign against the Jews* (New York: Simon and Schuster, 1993), 65–6; *Laurel Leader-Call*, November 15, 1967 and December 1, 1967; *Laurel Leader-Call*, March 20, 1968.

57. *MCJ*, 1973, 125–7. Concerning black conference fears of absorption and tokenism, see Branch, "Born of Conviction," 284, and Murray, *Methodists and the Crucible of Race*, 217–18.

58. *MCJ*, 1989, 66; 1979, 81, 168; 1982, 91. Other evidence of the long-term process of merger comes in *MCJ*, 1975, 88; 1977, 83–4, 171–2; 1978, 171.

CHAPTER 11

1. Author's transcript from Mississippi Conference video of the Elzy Award ceremony, June 9, 2013.

2. Deb Holston Selden e-mail to author, June 17, 2013.

3. After the 1970s mergers of the black and white conferences, Mississippi and North Mississippi merged in 1989 to form the new Mississippi Conference. Dora S. Washington to author, August 6, 2014; *MMA*, July 16, 2003.

4. Rush interview. Hardin presided over the Alabama-West Florida and the South Carolina Conferences from 1960 to 1964, and then only South Carolina from 1964 to 1972. For more on Hardin and the race issue in Alabama and South Carolina, see Bass, *Blessed Are the Peacemakers*, 66–7, 163, 205–7, and Collins, *When the Church Bell Rang Racist*, 77–8, 85–7, 98–100. Rush's statement was not completely true—the Florida Conference accepted signers Carter and Kellar.

5. Betty Conner Currey interview; *MCJ*, 1989, 189; Joe Way interview—Matheny later told Way about the conversation. *MMA*, March 28, 1984; McRae interview.

6. Charles Duke, "Born of the Spirit," January 20, 1963, enclosed with March 1963 letter, John and Margrit Garner Letters, MDAH; Bishop C. P. Minnick e-mail to author, August 4, 2006.

7. Bishop C. P. Minnick e-mail to author, August 4, 2006; *MCJ*, 1983, 81; Crespino, *In Search of Another Country*, 270–1; *JCL*, May 7, 1981.

8. Ed King, *White Church* manuscript, IV, 113 (handwritten addition); Galloway UMC worship bulletin, November 13, 2005; http://ecclesialrepentance.blogspot. com/2014/03/reflections-on-fiftieth-anniversary.html (accessed August 9, 2014) and Haynes, *The Last Segregated Hour.* Joe Purdy had died by 2014.

9. Re: white privilege, see Tim Wise, *White Like Me: Reflections on Race from a Privileged Son* (Brooklyn, NY: Soft Skull Press, 2005). Dietrich Bonhoeffer, *The Cost of Discipleship* (New York: Macmillan, 1963), ch. 1; Terrance Roberts, *Lessons from Little Rock* (Little Rock: Butler Center for Arkansas Studies, 2009), 174.

10. Charles Nicholson interview.

11. Rebecca Brent e-mail to author, August 6, 2014; Wilson Brent's story is told in Chapter 10. Jim Matheny, one of my best Mississippi friends, has said this to me more than once.

12. Fentress, "Ending 50 Years of Silence about Mississippi's Freedom Summer," *The Atlantic*, June 19, 2014, http://www.theatlantic.com/politics/archive/2014/06/ excavating-memories-of-the-freedom-summer-in-mississippi/373025/ (accessed July 24, 2014); Jim Matheny e-mail to author, August 3, 2013. Fentress also discusses "collective generational memory" and collective forgetting and remembering.

13. Chris Cumbest to Dr. O. Gerald Trigg, September 7, 2006, copy in author's possession; *PMPC*, January 17, 1963; Chris Cumbest to Trigg, September 7, 2006.

14. Chris Cumbest, "Growing the Beloved Community," Daily Lenten Devotional for the Mississippi Conference, February 26, 2010; Cumbest to Trigg, September 7, 2006.

15. Cumbest to Trigg, September 7, 2006; Chris and Sheila Cumbest interview.

16. Cumbest to Trigg, September 7, 2006; C. and S. Cumbest interview.

17. C. and S. Cumbest interview; Cumbest to Trigg, September 7, 2006; *MCJ*, 2007, 65.

18. C. and S. Cumbest interview; Cumbest to Trigg, September 7, 2006; Chris Cumbest Facebook post, June 9, 2013.

19. Selden, "One Family's Response to the Born of Conviction Statement."

20. Selden, "One Family's Response . . ."; Selden interview.

21. Selden, "One Family's Response . . ."; James Nicholson II interview.

22. James Nicholson II interview.

23. James Nicholson II interview; interviews with David Conner, Tommy Conner, Betty Conner Currey, and J. Syd Conner (known as John in his childhood);

J. Syd Conner, "The Brandon Winter," unpublished memoir, n.d. (c. 2000), J. Syd Conner PP.

24. David Conner interview; Betty Conner Currey e-mail to author, October 4, 2006; David Entrekin interview; Shelton interview; Dolores Carter interview—Wilton and Dolores Carter divorced in the 1970s.

25. Thais Brown Tonore, Becky Brown Chambers, and Virginia Brown Dungan interview.

26. Deb Holston Selden, Syd Conner, Kim Dunnam Reisman, Edwin Hall (born Nancy Powell Hall), and Miriam Berele (born Carole Toy Hall) each shared unpublished memoirs with me (the last two are by far the longest), while Jacquie Hall-Williams and Sandra Napier Dyess each shared an unpublished poem; J. Hall-Williams e-mail to author, January 22, 2009.

27. Edwin Hall, "Homecoming," section of unpublished memoir, Edwin Hall PP.

28. Kathryn Dickinson interview; *Born of Conviction* play produced by White Bird Productions and directed by Kara-Lynn Vaeni at the Irondale Center, Brooklyn, NY.

29. Dickinson, *Born of Conviction*, 2010; Herbert W. Beasley, "To the editor of the Mississippi Methodist Advocate and the preachers that expressed their feelings in the advocate [sic] in the article 'Born of Conviction,'" January 9, 1963, Ashmore Papers, box 1, folder 1. '

30. "DEAR SIR" and "The Kiss of Death," Nicholson PP, including envelope with postmark.

31. Dickinson, *Born of Conviction*.

32. Dickinson, *Born of Conviction*; Minus interview (though she goes by Jean, Ms. Minus's first name is Mary). Kathryn Dickinson's mother told her this story, but she has her father's character tell it in the play. In a May 31, 2011, Facebook post, she characterized her play as "about family exodus from Mississippi to CA."

33. Tonore, Chambers, and Dungan interview, quotations in that order; Dyess interview, 2009; Selden, "One Family's Response . . ."; Mark Trigg interview.

34. Shelton interview; Miriam Berele e-mail to author, November 24, 2009; John S. Hall interview.

35. David Conner interview. Children of signers who have pursued ordained ministry include David Conner, Kathryn Dickinson, Riley McRae, Buff Oliver, and Kim Dunnam Reisman. J. Syd Conner and Beth Conner Nicholson also attended seminary.

36. Selden interview; David Entrekin interview.

37. *Washington* (Iowa) *Evening Journal*, December 26, 2003.

38. *Washington* (Iowa) *Evening Journal*, December 26, 2003—the newspaper told the whole story in three parts plus a feature column—December 26, 29, and 30, 2003, and January 5, 2004; James Nicholson II interview.

39. http://msfume.webs.com/apps/blog/show/1863787-grace-the-bible-and-holiness-resisting-worldliness-; http://www.confessingumc.org/our-story/; http://

www.confessingumc.org/about/board-of-directors/ (all accessed August 11, 2014).

40. http://msfume.webs.com/apps/blog/show/1863787-grace-the-bible-and-holiness-resisting-worldliness- (accessed August 11, 2014)–the blog includes a report of Dunnam's speech by a clergyman.

41. Author's transcript from conference video of the service; author's notes from the service. Rob Gill, sitting next to me, made the comment. For a news story on the controversy the service caused, see *JCL*, June 25, 2009.

42. Tonkel interview, 2014; quote from Tonkel 2012 Charge Conference report posted on Facebook by Justin White on November 1, 2012.

43. UMC *Book of Discipline*, 2012, ¶161, F; ¶303.3; http://um-insight.net/blogs/ben-gosden/coming-clean-about-taboo-topics/ (accessed August 10, 2014). For Dunnam's perspective on the issue, see Preface and "The Creation/Covenant Design for Marriage and Sexuality," in Maxie D. Dunnam and H. Newton Malony, eds., *Staying the Course: Supporting the Church's Position on Homosexuality* (Nashville: Abingdon Press, 2003), 13–14, 104–14.

44. Dunnam interview, 2004; see Dunnam's Elzy Award remarks at the beginning of this chapter.

45. UMC *Book of Discipline*, 2012, ¶2702.1; http://unitedmethodistreporter.com/special-coverage-trial-rev-frank-schaefer/; *NYT*, July 12, 2014; http://unitedmethodistreporter.com/2013/12/19/frank-schaefer-loses-ministerial-credentials/; and http://www.calpacumc.org/bishop-carcano/bishop-carcanos-invitation-to-rev-frank-schaefer/ (all accessed August 10, 2014). Since 1963 the Southern California-Arizona Conference has changed names and also split into the Desert Southwest Conference (Arizona) and the California-Pacific Conference (Southern California and Hawaii).

46. http://wesleyanaccent.seedbed.com/2014/01/22/maxie-dunnam-in-honor-of-bishop-gerald-kennedy/ (accessed August 10, 2014; emphasis in original).

47. James L. Waits e-mail to Bishop Minerva Carcaño, March 5, 2014, copied to the author and to Maxie Dunnam; Inman Moore, "Reply to Maxie Dunnam," copy in author's possession. Moore claims that all twelve signers who attended the 2005 Born of Conviction reunion disagree with Dunnam on homosexuality. Dunnam e-mail to author, March 10, 2014. For a summary of the UMC struggle, see Amy Frykholm, "A Time to Split? Covenant and Schism in the UMC," *Christian Century*, April 16, 2014, 22–5.

48. E. Brooks Holifield, *God's Ambassadors: A History of the Christian Clergy in America* (Grand Rapids, MI: Eerdmans, 2007), 9.

49. Keith Tonkel blog post, June 11, 2013, http://wellschurch.org/blogs/keiths-blog (accessed September 2, 2014). The final quote is adapted from Robert Frost's "Stopping by Woods on a Snowy Evening."

50. *DMC*, 1960, 580 (¶1921).

51. David Entrekin interview; I John 4:18; see also Tonkel blog post, December 3, 2013, http://wellschurch.org/blogs/keiths-blog (accessed September 2, 2014).

52. Roberts, *Lessons from Little Rock*, 174.

53. Martin died in 2012 at the hands of George Zimmerman in Sanford, Florida, and Scott was killed in 2015 by police officer Michael Slager in North Charleston, South Carolina.

54. *MCJ*, 1973, 125; Dora Washington to author, August 6, 2014.

55. *MCJ*, 2007, 61; Ludrick Cameron interview.

56. Dora Washington to author, August 6, 2014; Religion and Race report, 2004 Mississippi Conference Pre-Conference Workbook, 77–9.

Bibliography

MEC, MECS, METHODIST CHURCH, AND UNITED METHODIST
CHURCH JOURNALS AND OTHER VOLUMES

Part of the Born of Conviction story is told through the records of Methodist/United Methodist Annual Conferences, and the number of different annual conference journals cited in the notes testifies to the diaspora of nineteen of the twenty-eight Born of Conviction signers. In addition, other church volumes cited include the following:

Discipline of The Methodist Church, 1940–64 (*DMC*), published quadrennially
Discipline of The United Methodist Church, 1968–present (*DUMC*), published
　　quadrennially
General Minutes of The Methodist Church or *The United Methodist Church* (*GM*),
　　published annually
Journal of the General Conference, published quadrennially

Newspapers and Newsletters

Arkansas Democrat
Atlanta Daily World
Atlanta Journal-Constitution
Baltimore Afro-American
The Baptist Record (Mississippi Baptist Convention)
Baton Rouge Morning Advocate
Biloxi-Gulfport *Sun Herald*
Birmingham World
Calhoun City (Mississippi) *Monitor-Herald*

Carthaginian (Leake County, Mississippi)

Chicago Sun-Times

Columbian-Progress (Marion County, Mississippi)

Dallas Morning News

Deer Creek Pilot (Rolling Fork, Mississippi)

Delta Democrat Times (*DDT*—Greenville, Mississippi)

East Valley Tribune (Mesa, Arizona, and other cities)

Hattiesburg American

Jackson *Clarion-Ledger (JCL)*

Jackson Daily News (JDN)

Jackson *State Times*

Laurel (Mississippi) *Leader-Call*

Lexington (Mississippi) *Advertiser*

MAMML Information Bulletin (Jackson, Mississippi)

McComb (Mississippi) *Enterprise-Journal (MEJ)*

Memphis *Commercial Appeal*

Meridian (Mississippi) *Star (MS)*

Mississippi Coast *Daily Herald (DH)*

Mississippi Methodist Advocate (MMA)

Mobile Press-Register

Nashville Tennessean

Neshoba Democrat

New Orleans *Times-Picayune*

New York Times (NYT)

Pasadena (California) *Star News*

Pascagoula/Moss Point (Mississippi) *Chronicle (PMPC)*

The Petal (Mississippi) *Paper*

Pittsburgh Courier

Purple and White (Millsaps College)

Richmond News-Leader

Richmond Times-Dispatch

Southern School News (Nashville)

Summit (Mississippi) *Sun*

Tupelo (Mississippi) *Daily Journal*

Wall Street Journal

Washington (Iowa) *Evening Journal*

INTERVIEWS (CONDUCTED BY AUTHOR; AUDIOTAPES,
SOUND FILES, AND NOTES IN HIS POSSESSION)

Barlow, Hubert, February 18, 2006 (telephone).

Berele, Miriam (nee Carole Toy Hall) and Jacqueline Hall-Williams, Abingdon,VA,
November 29, 2009.

Brown, D. Elton, Rod Entrekin, and John Ed Thomas, Hattiesburg, MS, July 10, 2003.

Brown, D. Elton and Juliette, Purvis, MS, June 6, 2009.

Cameron, Ludrick, Quitman, MS, October 4, 2014 (telephone).

Carder, Bishop Kenneth, Durham, NC, November 18, 2005.

Carter, Dolores, Ocean Springs, MS, June 25, 2009 (telephone).

Carter, Wilton C., Ridgefield, WA, June 7, 2004.

Clark, Bishop Roy C., Lake Junaluska, NC, August 7, 2003; July 12, 2007.

Clay, Jr., Henry C., Jackson, MS, July 30, 2004.

Collins, Patricia, Harlingen, TX, May 16, 2010 (telephone).

Conner, David Emory, Wheat Ridge, CO, June 10, 2004.

Conner, J. Syd, Hattiesburg, MS, July 10, 2003.

Conner, Tommy, Hattiesburg, MS, November 7, 2005.

Cumbest, Chris and Sheila, Abingdon, VA, June 30, 2013.

Cumbest, Lum, Elvis Cumbest, Ida Mae Cumbest, Halsey Cumbest, Chris Cumbest, George Sholl, and Brian Scott, Caswell Springs UMC, Jackson County, MS, July 21, 2010.

Currey, Betty Conner, and George T. Currey, Pensacola, FL, August 1, 2004.

Dickinson, Kathryn, Brooklyn, NY, June 20, 2007.

Dickson Family (Mary Myers Dickson, Marilyn Dickson Foxworth, and Mike Dickson), Columbia, MS, November 6, 2005.

Dickson, Steve, Canton, MS, February 12, 2013 (telephone).

Dunnam, Maxie D., Jackson, MS, July 28, 2004; June 12, 2009.

Dyess, Sandra Napier, Jackson, MS, June 8, 2009; June 8, 2012.

Entrekin, David, Madison, MS, June 7, 2009.

Entrekin, Rod, Hattiesburg, MS, August 2, 2011; see also Brown, Entrekin, and Thomas, 2003.

Entrekin, Rod and Virginia (Ginny), Hattiesburg, MS, July 21, 2007.

Furr, E. S., Tupelo, MS, January 27, 2006 (telephone).

Furr, Jerry and Marlene, Palm Desert, CA, June 3–4, 2004.

Gill, Clinton, Hattiesburg, MS, June 13, 2011.

Gill, Rob, Jackson, MS, June 13, 2006.

Hall, Edwin Powell, Fayetteville, NC, July 29, 2010.

Hall, John Storrs, Abingdon, VA, July 11, 2009.

Hall, Powell and Julia Hewitt, Hermitage, TN, September 20, 2003.

Harjes, Mabel Anne Ashmore, Lawrenceville, GA, July 22, 2006.

Harrison, James M., Meridian, MS, October 30, 2005.

Hillman, Jr., A. Byrd and Sara, Kosciusko, MS, July 29, 2004.

Jones, Bishop L. Bevel, Atlanta, GA, July 26, 2009.

Kellar, Ned, Merritt Island, FL, August 9, 2004.

King, R. Edwin, Jackson, MS, March 9, 2004.

Lee, Bishop Clay F., Byram, MS, August 15, 2003; June 5, 2014.

Lewis, Donald D., Hernando, MS, February 27, 2006.

Loflin, Jack M., Star, MS, March 10, 2004.

Lowry, William T. and Barbara, Lake Junaluska, NC, August 7, 2003.

Matheny, Emily Stafford, Meridian, MS, March 4, 2006.

Matheny, Jim, Grenada, MS, July 28, 2004.

McAtee, William, Lexington, KY, August 31, 2010 (telephone).

McConnell, Thelma Briggs, Sue Gunn Meacham, Peggy Aust Persons, Clyde Warren Jones, and Mamie Warren Cochran, Scooba, MS, October 31, 2005.

McCormick, James R., Big Canoe, GA, July 6, 2005.

McRae, Edward W. and Martina Riley, Simi Valley, CA, June 5, 2004.

Miller, Dean M. and Gloria H., Jackson, MS, February 28, 2006.

Minus, Mary E. (Jean) Clegg Dickinson, Young Harris, GA, August 28, 2004.

Mitchell, T. Jerry, Ridgeland, MS, July 30, 2007.

Moore, Jr., R. Inman, Pasadena, CA, June 4, 2004.

Napier, Denson, Jackson, MS, July 9, 2003.

Nicholson, Sr., Charles Warren, Lake Junaluska, NC, July 9, 2004.

Nicholson, James B., Washington, IA, June 12, 2004.

Nicholson II, James (Jimmy), Slidell, LA, June 3, 2009.

Oliver, Buff, Greenback, TN, October 5, 2006.

O'Neil, Jr., Arthur M., Lake Junaluska, NC, September 29, 2005.

Perrine, Marilyn, Jackson, MS, June 12, 2006.

Reiff, Lee H., Lake Junaluska, NC, March 9, 2007.

Roberts, Kenneth R., Jackson, MS, November 3, 2005.

Rush, James P. and Elizabeth P., Edisto Island, SC, July 22, 2004.

Selden, Deborah Holston, Branford, CT, June 18, 2007.

Shelton, Cathy Hall, Westover, AL, April 4, 2009.

Thomas, John Ed, see Brown, Entrekin, and Thomas, 2003.

Thomas, Margaret Ewing, Hattiesburg, MS, June 5, 2009.

Tillman, Jr., Harmon E. and Nona K., Winona, MS, July 29, 2004.

Tonkel, D. Keith, Jackson, MS, July 11, 2003; June 5, 2014.

Tonore, Thais Brown, Becky Brown Chambers, and Virginia Brown Dungan, Jackson, MS, June 9, 2009.

Trigg, Mark G., Atlanta, GA, July 19, 2009.

Trigg, O. Gerald and Rose Cunningham, Colorado Springs, CO, June 10, 2004.

Troutman, Jack S., Mesa, AZ, June 3, 2004.

Waits, James L., Atlanta, GA, July 21, 2003; September 27, 2005; May 11, 2009; and November 13, 2010 (telephone).

Walters, Summer L. and Betty Barfield, Franklin, IN, June 13, 2004.

Way, Joseph C., Jackson, MS, June 12, 2006.

Williamson, Jerry M., Jackson, MS, November 1, 2005.

Winstead, Jr., Henry G., Hattiesburg, MS, November 7, 2005.

Woodrick, James Rayford., Madison, MS, March 11, 2004.

ARCHIVAL COLLECTIONS

Archives, Pitts Theology Library, Emory University (PTLA):
  Smith, Bishop John Owen Papers, MSS 242
  Waits, James L. Papers, MSS 287
College Archives, Millsaps-Wilson Library, Millsaps College (MCA):
  Adams, John Quincy Papers, F16
      Oral History Interviews conducted by Gordon Henderson
          Clark, Roy C., Memphis, TN, August 2, 1965
  Faculty Meeting Minutes, Memos, and Reports, B1
  Goodbread, Ronald Papers, F7
  Lewis, T. W. Papers, F25
  Photograph Collection
  White, Milton C. Papers, F10
Department of Archives and Special Collections, J. D. Williams Library, University of Mississippi (UMDASC):
  Cunningham, W. J./Galloway Papers
  Satterfield, John C./American Bar Association Collection
  Silver, James Wesley Papers
General Commission on Archives and History, The United Methodist Church, Drew University
J. B. Cain Archives of Mississippi Methodism, Millsaps-Wilson Library, Millsaps College (JBCA):
  Ashmore (Dr. Sam E. and Ann Lewis) Papers, M100
  Bishop's Office Papers, M63 (BOP)
  Franklin (Bishop Marvin A.) Papers, M61
  Pendergrass (Bishop E. J.) Papers, M85
  Selah (Dr. William Bryan) Papers, M84
  Walters (Summer and Betty) Papers, M79
Library of Congress, Manuscript Division, Washington, D.C. (LoC):
  McCormick, Ken D. Publishing Case File, Author File: Delamotte, Roy [pseud. Gregory Wilson] *The Stained Glass Jungle*
McCain Library and Archives, University of Southern Mississippi (USMMLA):
  Campbell (Will D.) Papers, M341
  East (P. D.) Papers, M324
Mississippi Department of Archives and History, Jackson (MDAH):
  Garner (John and Margrit) Letters 1962–77, Z1725
  Microfilm Mississippi Newspaper Collection
  Records of the Mississippi State Sovereignty Commission (http://mdah.state.ms.us/arrec/digital_archives/sovcom/#basicfolder)
  Stevens, Ray E. "Galloway Church History, 1956–1995."

Private Papers Collections (author has copies of virtually all documents from these collections cited in notes):

Berele, Miriam

Brent, Wilson

Carter, Wilton

Clark, Bishop Roy C.

Conner, James S.

Conner, J. Syd

Deppe, Martin

Dunnam, Maxie D.

Entrekin, Rod

Gray, Jr., Duncan M.

Hall, Edwin P.

Hall, Powell

Kellar, Ned

King, R. Edwin

Matheny, Jim

Moore, R. Inman

Napier, Denson

Nicholson, James B.

Reiff, Lee H.

Reisman, Kim Dunnam

Rush, James P.

Trigg, O. Gerald

Troutman, Jack

Waits, James L.

Walters, Summer L.

Way, Joseph C.

Southeastern Jurisdiction Heritage Center and Archive, Lake Junaluska, NC

Special Collections Department, Mitchell Memorial Library, Mississippi State University (MSUSCD):

Cox, A. E. Papers, Acc. # 45

Humphrey, John David Papers, Acc. # 463

University of Southern Mississippi Center for Oral History and Cultural Heritage

Oral History Interviews conducted by Orley B. Caudill:

Lee, Clay F. Jackson, Mississippi, July 8, 1980

BOOKS, ARTICLES, DISSERTATIONS, PLAYS, DOCUMENTARIES, VIDEOS

Albright, Jr., William E. "Stained Glass Jungle or Modern Aldersgate?," *Christian Advocate* 7, no. 7 (March 28, 1963): 11–12.

Allen, L. Scott. "Mississippi Methodism Refreshed." *Central Christian Advocate* 138, no. 4 (February 15, 1963): 3.

Alvis, Jr., Joel L. *Religion and Race: Southern Presbyterians, 1946–1983.* Tuscaloosa: University of Alabama Press, 1994.

Bailey, Kenneth K. *Southern White Protestantism in the Twentieth Century.* New York: Harper and Row, 1964.

Barefield, Sam. Portion of "Report from the South." *Motive* 16, no. 5 (February 1956): 19.

Barrett, Russell H. *Integration at Ole Miss.* Chicago: Quadrangle Books, 1965.

Bartley, Numan V. *The Rise of Massive Resistance: Race and Politics in the South During the 1950s.* Baton Rouge: Louisiana State University Press, 1997 (originally published 1969).

Bartley, Numan V., and Hugh D. Graham. *Southern Politics and the Second Reconstruction.* Baltimore: Johns Hopkins University Press, 1975.

Bass, S. Jonathan. *Blessed Are the Peacemakers: Martin Luther King, Jr., Eight White Religious Leaders, and the "Letter from Birmingham Jail."* Baton Rouge: Louisiana State University Press, 2001.

Bauman, Mark K., and Berkley Kalin, eds. *The Quiet Voices: Southern Rabbis and Black Civil Rights, 1880s to 1990s.* Tuscaloosa: University of Alabama Press, 1997.

Blanchard, Eric D. "The National Council in Mississippi." *Christian Advocate* 8, no. 17 (August 13, 1964): 3.

Blue, Ellen. *St. Mark's and the Social Gospel: Methodist Woman and Civil Rights in New Orleans, 1895–1965.* Knoxville: University of Tennessee Press, 2011.

Bolton, Charles C. *The Hardest Deal of All: The Battle Over School Integration in Mississippi, 1870–1980.* Jackson: University Press of Mississippi, 2005.

Bonhoeffer, Dietrich. *The Cost of Discipleship.* New York: Macmillan, 1963.

Bonhoeffer, Dietrich. *No Rusty Swords: Letters, Lectures and Notes, 1928–1936.* Translated by Edwin H. Robertson and John Bowden. London: Collins; New York: Harper and Row, 1965.

Bowen, Boone M. *The Candler School of Theology ~ Sixty Years of Service.* Atlanta: Emory University, 1974.

Branch, Ellis Ray. "Born of Conviction: Racial Conflict and Change in Mississippi Methodism, 1945–1983." PhD diss., Mississippi State University, 1984.

Branch, Taylor. *Parting the Waters: America in the King Years, 1954–63.* New York: Touchstone, 1988.

Brock, Edwin L. "Methodism's Growing Cleavage." *Christian Century* 72, no. 34 (August 24, 1955): 971–2.

Burnett, Thomas Stevens. "Ministerial Roles and Institutional Restraints: The Mississippi Conference of the United Methodist Church." D.Min. Project, Claremont School of Theology, 1976.

Campbell, Clarice T. *Civil Rights Chronicle: Letters from the South.* Jackson: University Press of Mississippi, 1997.

Campbell, Clarice T., and Oscar Allan Rogers Jr. *Mississippi: The View from Tougaloo.* Jackson: University Press of Mississippi, 1979.

Campbell, Ernest Q., and Thomas F. Pettigrew. *Christians in Racial Crisis: A Study of Little Rock's Ministry.* Washington, DC: Public Affairs Press, 1959.

Campbell, Ernest Q., and Thomas F. Pettigrew. "Racial and Moral Crisis: The Role of Little Rock Ministers." *American Journal of Sociology* 64, no. 5 (March 1959): 509–16.

Campbell, Will D. *And Also With You: Duncan Gray and the American Dilemma.* Franklin, TN: Providence House Publishers, 1997.

Canzoneri, Robert. *"I Do So Politely": A Voice from the South.* Boston: Houghton Mifflin, 1965.

Carter III, Hodding. *The South Strikes Back.* Garden City, NY: Doubleday, 1959.

Cauthen, Kenneth. *I Don't Care What the Bible Says: An Interpretation of the South.* Macon, GA: Mercer University Press, 2003.

Chappell, David L. *A Stone of Hope: Prophetic Religion and the Death of Jim Crow.* Chapel Hill: University of North Carolina Press, 2003.

"The Church Considers the Supreme Court Decision." Pamphlet reprinted from *The Church News,* Episcopal Diocese of Mississippi, August 1954.

"The Church in Crisis" and "Call to Repentance." *Christianity Today* 7, no. 2 (October 26, 1962): 35–6.

Clemons, James T., and Kelly L. Farr, eds. *Crisis of Conscience: Arkansas Methodists and the Civil Rights Struggle.* Little Rock: Butler Center for Arkansas Studies, 2007.

Collins, Donald E. *When the Church Bell Rang Racist: The Methodist Church and the Civil Rights Movement in Alabama.* Macon, GA: Mercer University Press, 1998.

Cook, James Graham. *The Segregationists.* New York: Appleton-Century-Crofts, 1962.

Cousins, Ralph E., et al., eds. *South Carolinians Speak: A Moderate Approach to Race.* Dillon, SC: South Carolinians Speak, 1957.

Crespino, Joseph. *In Search of Another Country: Mississippi and the Conservative Counterrevolution.* Princeton, NJ: Princeton University Press, 2007.

Culver, Dwight W. *Negro Segregation in The Methodist Church.* New Haven, CT: Yale University Press, 1953.

Cunningham, David. "Shades of Anti-Civil Rights Violence: Reconsidering the Ku Klux Klan in Mississippi." In Ted Ownby, ed., *The Civil Rights Movement in Mississippi,* 180–203. Jackson: University Press of Mississippi, 2013.

Cunningham, W. J. *Agony at Galloway: One Church's Struggle with Social Change.* Jackson: University Press of Mississippi, 1980.

Dailey, Jane. "Sex, Segregation, and the Sacred after *Brown.*" *Journal of American History* 91, no. 1 (June 2004): 119–44.

Daniel, Bradford, ed. *Black, White and Gray: Twenty-One Points of View on the Race Question.* New York: Sheed and Ward, 1964.

Davies, David R. *The Press and Race: Mississippi Journalists Confront the Movement.* Jackson: University Press of Mississippi, 2001.

Davis, Jack E. *Race against Time: Culture and Separation in Natchez since 1930.* Baton Rouge: Louisiana State University Press, 2001.

Davis, Morris L. *The Methodist Unification: Christianity and the Politics of Race in the Jim Crow Era.* New York: New York University Press, 2008.

DeLaughter, Bobby. *Never Too Late: A Prosecutor's Story of Justice in the Medgar Evers Case.* New York: Scribner, 2001.

Dickinson, Kathryn. *Born of Conviction.* Unpublished play, 2010.

Dittmer, John. *Local People: The Struggle for Civil Rights in Mississippi.* Urbana: University of Illinois Press, 1994.

Dollard, John. *Caste and Class in a Southern Town.* Madison: University of Wisconsin Press, 1988 (originally published 1937).

Dorgan, Howard. "Response of the Main-line Southern White Protestant Pulpit to *Brown v. Board of Education,* 1954–1965." In Calvin M. Logue and Howard Dorgan, eds., *A New Diversity in Contemporary Southern Rhetoric,* 15–51. Baton Rouge: Louisiana State University Press, 1987.

Doyle, William. *An American Insurrection: The Battle of Oxford, Mississippi, 1962.* New York: Doubleday, 2001.

Dunnam, Maxie D. *Exodus (The Communicator's Commentary).* Waco, TX: Word, 1987.

Dunnam, Maxie D. "The Creation/Covenant Design for Marriage and Sexuality." In Maxie D. Dunnam and H. Newton Malony, eds., *Staying the Course: Supporting the Church's Position on Homosexuality,* 104–114. Nashville, TN: Abingdon Press, 2003.

Dupont, Carolyn. *Mississippi Praying: Southern White Evangelicals and the Civil Rights Movement, 1945–1975.* New York: New York University Press, 2013.

Dykeman, Wilma, and James Stokely. "Clinton, Tennessee: A Town on Trial." *New York Times Magazine,* October 26, 1958: 8, 61–5.

Eagles, Charles W. "Toward New Histories of the Civil Rights Era." *Journal of Southern History* 66, no. 4 (November 2000): 815–48.

Eagles, Charles W. "The Closing of Mississippi Society: Will Campbell, *The $64,000 Question,* and Religious Emphasis Week at the University of Mississippi." *Journal of Southern History* 67, no. 2 (May 2001): 331–72.

Eagles, Charles W. *The Price of Defiance: James Meredith and the Integration of Ole Miss.* Chapel Hill: University of North Carolina Press, 2009.

East, P. D. *The Magnolia Jungle: The Life, Times and Education of a Southern Editor.* New York: Simon and Schuster, 1960.

Egerton, John. *A Mind to Stay Here: Profiles from the South.* New York: Macmillan, 1970.

Eubanks, W. Ralph. *Ever Is a Long Time: A Journey into Mississippi's Dark Past.* New York: Basic Books, 2003.

Evers-Williams, Myrlie, and Manning Marable, eds. *The Autobiography of Medgar Evers: A Hero's Life Revealed through His Writings, Letters, and Speeches.* New York: Basic Civitas Books, 2005.

Fentress, Ellen Ann. "Ending 50 Years of Silence about Mississippi's Freedom Summer." *The Atlantic,* June 19, 2014. http://www.theatlantic.com/politics/archive/2014/06/excavating-memories-of-the-freedom-summer-in-mississippi/373025/.

Findlay, Jr., James F. *Church People in the Struggle: The National Council of Churches and the Black Freedom Movement, 1950–1970.* New York: Oxford University Press, 1993.

Flynt, Wayne. *Alabama Baptists: Southern Baptists in the Heart of Dixie.* Tuscaloosa: University of Alabama Press, 1998.

Frank, Thomas Edward. *Polity, Practice, and the Mission of The United Methodist Church.* Rev. ed. Nashville, TN: Abingdon Press, 2006.

Friedland, Michael B. *Lift Up Your Voice Like a Trumpet: White Clergy and the Civil Rights and Antiwar Movements, 1954–1973.* Chapel Hill: University of North Carolina Press, 1998.

Frykholm, Amy. "A Time to Split? Covenant and Schism in the UMC." *Christian Century* 131, no. 8 (April 16, 2014): 22–5.

Germany, J. Horace. *At Any Cost: The Story of a Life in Pursuit of Brotherhood.* Anderson, IN: Warner Press, 2001.

Gilligan, Carol. *In a Different Voice: Psychological Theory and Women's Development.* Cambridge, MA: Harvard University Press, 1982.

Gilmore, J. Herbert. *They Chose to Live: The Racial Agony of an American Church.* Grand Rapids, MI: Eerdmans, 1972.

Gipson, Charles Ray. "Preaching on Controversial Issues: A Study of Theory and Practice." Master's thesis, Perkins School of Theology, Southern Methodist University, 1968.

Graetz, Robert S. *A White Preacher's Memoir: The Montgomery Bus Boycott.* Montgomery, AL: Black Belt Press, 1998.

Graham, Stephen A. *Ordinary Man, Extraordinary Mission: The Life and Work of E. Stanley Jones.* Nashville, TN: Abingdon Press, 2005.

Galloway, Charles Betts. *Great Men and Movements: A Volume of Addresses.* Nashville, TN: Publishing House, Methodist Episcopal Church, South, 1914.

Hadden, Jeffrey K. *The Gathering Storm in the Churches.* New York: Doubleday, 1969.

Harmon, Nolan B. *The Organization of the Methodist Church: Historic Development and Present Working Structure.* 2nd ed. rev. Nashville, TN: The Methodist Publishing House, 1953 .

Harrell, Jr., David E. ed. *Varieties of Southern Evangelicalism*. Macon, GA: Mercer University Press, 1981.

Hartt, Julian N. "Dallas Ministers on Desegregation." *Christian Century* 75, no. 21 (May 21, 1958): 619–20.

Harvey, Paul. *Freedom's Coming: Religious Culture and the Shaping of the South from the Civil War through the Civil Rights Era*. Chapel Hill: University of North Carolina Press, 2005.

Haynes, Stephen R. *The Last Segregated Hour: The Memphis Kneel-ins and the Campaign for Southern Church Desegregation*. New York: Oxford University Press, 2012.

Heitzenrater, Richard P. *Wesley and the People Called Methodists*. Nashville, TN: Abingdon Press, 1995.

Heitzenrater, Richard P. "Connectionalism and Itinerancy: Wesleyan Principles and Practice." In Russell E. Richey, Dennis M. Campbell, and William B. Lawrence, eds., *Connectionalism: Ecclesiology, Mission, and Identity*, 23–38. Nashville, TN: Abingdon Press, 1997.

Hempton, David. *Methodism: Empire of the Spirit*. New Haven, CT: Yale University Press, 2005.

Hendrickson, Paul. *Sons of Mississippi: A Story of Race and Its Legacy*. New York: Vintage Books, 2003.

Hill, Samuel S. *Southern Churches in Crisis Revisited*. Tuscaloosa: University of Alabama Press, 1999 (originally New York: Henry Holt, 1966).

Hilton, Bruce. *The Delta Ministry*. London: Collier-Macmillan, 1969.

Holifield, E. Brooks. *God's Ambassadors: A History of the Christian Clergy in America*. Grand Rapids, MI: Eerdmans, 2007.

Houck, Davis W., and David E. Dixon, eds. *Rhetoric, Religion, and the Civil Rights Movement, 1954–1965*, Vol. 1. Waco, TX: Baylor University Press, 2006.

Houck, Davis W., and David E. Dixon, eds. *Rhetoric, Religion, and the Civil Rights Movement, 1954–1965*, Vol. 2. Waco, TX: Baylor University Press, 2014.

Huey, Gary. *Rebel with a Cause: P. D. East, Southern Liberalism and the Civil Rights Movement, 1953–1971*. Lanham, MD: Rowman and Littlefield, 1985.

Johnson, Mary Lynn. Portion of "Report from the South." *Motive* 16, no. 5 (February 1956): 20–1.

Jones, E. Stanley. *The Choice before Us*. New York: Abingdon Press, 1937.

Jones, John G. *A Complete History of Methodism as Connected with the Mississippi Conference of the Methodist Episcopal Church, South*, Vol. 1. Nashville, TN: Southern Methodist Publishing House, 1887.

Jones, L. Gregory, and Kevin Armstrong. *Resurrecting Excellence: Shaping Faithful Christian Ministry*. Grand Rapids, MI: William B. Eerdmans, 2006.

Katagiri, Yasuhiro. *The Mississippi State Sovereignty Commission: Civil Rights and States' Rights*. Jackson: University Press of Mississippi, 2001.

Kellar, Ned. *Sandersville*. Bloomington, IN: Xlibris, 2010.

Kelley, Dean M. *Why Conservative Churches Are Growing: A Study in Sociology of Religion.* New York: Harper and Row, 1972.

King, Ed. "Bacchanal at Woolworth's." In Susie Erenrich, ed., *Freedom Is a Constant Struggle: An Anthology of the Mississippi Civil Rights Movement,* 27–35. Montgomery, AL: Black Belt Press, 1999.

King, Ed. *The White Church in Mississippi.* Unpublished manuscript, n.d., Edwin King PP.

King, Jr., Martin Luther. *Why We Can't Wait.* New York: Harper and Row, 1964.

Knight, Walker. "Race Relations: Changing Patterns and Practices." In Nancy T. Ammerman, ed., *Southern Baptists Observed: Multiple Perspectives on a Changing Denomination,* 165–181. Knoxville: University of Tennessee Press, 1993.

Lampton, William. *The Complete Communicator: Change Your Communication—Change Your Life.* Franklin, TN: Hillsboro Press, 1999.

Leidholdt, Alexander. *Standing before the Shouting Mob: Lenoir Chambers and Virginia's Massive Resistance to Public-School Integration.* Tuscaloosa: University of Alabama Press, 1997.

Lindsey, J. Allen. *Methodism in the Mississippi Conference, 1920–1939.* Jackson: Hawkins Foundation, Commission on Archives and History, Mississippi Conference, 1980.

Lord, Walter. *The Past That Would Not Die.* New York: Harper and Row, 1965.

Lowe, Maria R., and J. Clint Morris. "Civil Rights Advocates in the Academy: White Pro-Integrationist Faculty at Millsaps College." *Journal of Mississippi History* 69, no. 2 (Summer 2007): 120–45.

Lowry, Bill. *The Antechamber of Heaven: A History of Lake Junaluska Assembly.* Franklin, TN: Providence House Publishers, 2010.

Lyon, Carter Dalton. "Lifting the Color Bar from the House of God: The 1963–1964 Church Visit Campaign to Challenge Segregated Sanctuaries in Jackson, Mississippi." PhD diss., University of Mississippi, 2010.

Lyon, Carter Dalton. "Easter in Jackson, Mississippi, 1964." *Methodist History* 49, no. 2 (January 2011): 99–115.

"The Man Who Dreams About a Library." *Together* 9, no. 6 (June 1965).

Manning, Gene. Portion of "Report from the South." *Motive* 16, no. 5 (February 1956): 20–1.

Mars, Florence. *Witness in Philadelphia.* Baton Rouge: Louisiana State University Press, 1977.

Marsh, Charles. *God's Long Summer: Stories of Faith and Civil Rights.* Princeton, NJ: Princeton University Press, 1997.

Marsh, Charles. *Strange Glory: A Life of Dietrich Bonhoeffer.* New York: Alfred A. Knopf, 2014.

Martin, Jr., Gordon A. *Count Them One by One: Black Mississippians Fighting for the Right to Vote.* Jackson: University Press of Mississippi, 2010.

Martinez, Elizabeth Sutherland, ed. *Letters from Mississippi*. Brookline, MA: Zephyr Press, 2002.

Mason, Gilbert R., M.D. *Beaches, Blood, and Ballots: A Black Doctor's Civil Rights Struggle*. Jackson: University Press of Mississippi, 2000.

Mathews, Donald G. *Slavery and Methodism: A Chapter in American Morality, 1780–1845*. Princeton, NJ: Princeton University Press, 1965.

Mathews, James K. "Easter in Jackson." *Christian Century* 81, no. 16 (April 15, 1964): 478–80.

Mays, Benjamin E. *Born to Rebel*. New York: Charles Scribner's Sons, 1971.

McAtee, William G. *Transformed: A White Pastor's Journey into Civil Rights and Beyond*. Jackson: University Press of Mississippi, 2011.

McGill, Ralph. "The Agony of the Southern Minister." *New York Times Magazine*, September 27, 1959: 16, 57–60.

McMillen, Neil R. *The Citizens' Council: Organized Resistance to the Second Reconstruction*. Urbana: University of Illinois Press, 1994 (originally published 1971).

McNeill, Robert B. *God Wills Us Free: The Ordeal of a Southern Minister*. New York: Hill and Wang, 1965.

Melton, J. Gordon. *A Will to Choose: The Origins of African American Methodism*. Lanham, MD: Rowman and Littlefield, 2007.

"Methodist Ministers Shatter Vacuum." *Christian Century* 80, no. 8 (February 20, 1963): 229–30.

Metz, Johann Baptist. *Faith in History and Society: Toward a Practical Fundamental Theology*. New York: Seabury Press, 1980.

Miller, Gene Ramsey. *A History of North Mississippi Methodism, 1820–1900*. Nashville, TN: Parthenon Press, 1966.

"Mississippi: Is This America? 1962–1964." *Eyes on the Prize*, Episode 5, Season 1. Directed by Orlando Bagwell. Blackside, Inc., 1987.

"Mississippi Methodists Lead in Attack on Segregation." *Presbyterian Outlook*, January 21, 1963: 3–4.

Mitchell, Joseph. *There Is an Election! Episcopal Elections in the Southeastern Jurisdiction of the United Methodist Church*. Troy, AL: Leader Press, 1980.

Morris, Willie. *Yazoo: The Integration of a Deep-Southern Town*. New York: Harper's Magazine Press, 1971.

Muelder, Walter G. *Methodism and Society in the Twentieth Century*. New York: Abingdon Press, 1961.

Murray, Peter C. *Methodists and the Crucible of Race, 1930–1975*. Columbia: University of Missouri Press, 2004.

Nelson, Jack. *Terror in the Night: The Klan's Campaign against the Jews*. New York: Simon and Schuster, 1993.

Newman, Mark. *Getting Right with God: Southern Baptists and Desegregation, 1945–1995*. Tuscaloosa: University of Alabama Press, 2001.

Nicholson, James. B. "A Trail through the Wilderness." *New South* 18, no. 3 (March 1963): 5–8.

Nicholson, James B. "Jesus Does Not Exclude—He Includes." *Bible Lessons for Adults* 21, no. 4 (June–August 1966): 6–8.

Niebuhr, Reinhold. *Moral Man and Immoral Society.* New York: Charles Scribner's Sons, 1932.

Nossiter, Adam. *Of Long Memory: Mississippi and the Murder of Medgar Evers.* Cambridge, MA: Da Capo Press, 2002 (originally published 1994).

Noble, Phil. *Beyond the Burning Bus: The Civil Rights Revolution in a Southern Town.* Foreword by William McClain. Montgomery: New South Books, 2003.

Norwood, Frederick A. *The Story of American Methodism.* Nashville, TN: Abingdon, 1974.

Orleck, Annelise. *Storming Caesar's Palace: How Black Mothers Fought Their Own War on Poverty.* Boston: Beacon Press, 2005.

Oswald, Roy M. *Crossing the Boundary between Seminary and Parish.* Washington, DC: Alban Institute, 1985.

Ownby, Ted, ed. *The Civil Rights Movement in Mississippi.* Jackson: University Press of Mississippi, 2013.

Payne, Charles M. *I've Got the Light of Freedom: The Organizing Tradition and the Mississippi Freedom Struggle.* Berkeley: University of California Press, 1995.

Percy, Walker. "Mississippi: The Fallen Paradise." In Patrick Samway, ed., *Signposts in a Strange Land,* 39–52. New York: Farrar, Straus, and Giroux, 1991.

Peters, William. *The Southern Temper.* Garden City, NY: Doubleday, 1958.

Purifoy, Lewis M. "The Southern Methodist Church and the Proslavery Argument." *Journal of Southern History* 32, no. 3 (August 1966): 325–41.

Reiff, Joseph T. "'Born of Conviction' Statement," *Mississippi Encyclopedia,* University Press of Mississippi, forthcoming.

Reiff, Joseph T. "Born of Conviction: White Methodist Witness to Mississippi's Closed Society." In L. Edward Phillips and Billy Vaughan, eds., *Courage to Bear Witness: Essays in Honor of Gene L. Davenport,* 124–142. Eugene, OR: Wipf and Stock, 2009.

Reiff, Joseph T. "Conflicting Convictions in White Mississippi Methodism." *Methodist History* XLIX, no. 3 (April 2011): 162–75.

Reiff, Joseph T. "Born of Conviction: White Mississippians Argue Civil Rights in 1963." In Ted Ownby, ed., *The Civil Rights Movement in Mississippi,* 157–179. Jackson, MS: University Press of Mississippi, 2013.

Reimers, David M. *White Protestantism and the Negro.* New York: Oxford University Press, 1965.

Richey, Russell E. *Early American Methodism.* Bloomington: Indiana University Press, 1991.

Richey, Russell E. *The Methodist Conference in America: A History.* Nashville, TN: Kingswood Books, 1996.

Richey, Russell E., Kenneth E. Rowe, and Jean Miller Schmidt. *The Methodist Experience in America: A History (Volume I)*. Nashville, TN: Abingdon Press, 2010.

Richey, Russell E., Kenneth E. Rowe, and Jean Miller Schmidt. *The Methodist Experience in America: A Sourcebook (Volume II)*. Nashville, TN: Abingdon Press, 2000.

Roberts, Terrance. *Lessons from Little Rock*. Little Rock: Butler Center for Arkansas Studies, 2009.

Roy, Ralph Lord. *Communism and the Churches*. New York: Harcourt, Brace and Company, 1960.

Rush, James P. "Secularized Christianity: Salvation by Faith or Works?" *Christian Advocate* 11, no. 6 (March 23, 1967): 7–8.

Salter, Jr., John R. *Jackson, Mississippi: An American Chronicle of Struggle and Schism*. Hicksville, NY: Exposition Press, 1979.

Sarratt, Reed. *The Ordeal of Desegregation: The First Decade*. New York: Harper and Row, 1966.

Sessions, Robert Paul. "Are Southern Ministers Failing the South?" *Saturday Evening Post* 234, no. 19 (May 13, 1961): 37, 82–8.

Sessums, Kevin. *Mississippi Sissy*. New York: St. Martin's Press, 2007.

Shattuck, Jr., Gardiner H. *Episcopalians and Race: Civil War to Civil Rights*. Lexington: University Press of Kentucky, 2000.

Silver, James W. *Mississippi: The Closed Society*. New Enlarged Edition. New York: Harcourt, Brace and World, 1966.

Slade, Peter. *Open Friendship in a Closed Society: Mission Mississippi and a Theology of Friendship*. New York: Oxford University Press, 2009.

Sledge, Robert Watson. *Hands on the Ark: The Struggle for Change in the Methodist Episcopal Church, South, 1914–1939*. Lake Junaluska, NC: Commission on Archives and History, The United Methodist Church, 1975.

Smith, Frank E. *Congressman from Mississippi*. New York: Pantheon Books, 1964.

Sokol, Jason. *There Goes My Everything: White Southerners in the Age of Civil Rights, 1945–1975*. New York: Alfred A. Knopf, 2006.

Southard, Samuel. "Are Southern Churches Silent?" *Christian Century* 80 (November 20, 1963): 1429–32.

Southard, Samuel. "The Southern 'Establishment.'" *Christian Century* 81, no. 53 (December 30, 1964): 1618–21.

"The Southern Churches and the Race Question." *Christianity and Crisis* 18, no. 3 (March 3, 1958): 17–28.

"Southern Ministers Speak Their Minds." *Pulpit Digest* 39 (December 1958): 13–17.

Sparks, Randy J. *Religion in Mississippi*. Jackson: University Press of Mississippi, 2001.

Strong, Douglas M. *They Walked in the Spirit: Personal Faith and Social Action in America*. Louisville, KY: Westminster John Knox Press, 1997.

Thomas, James S. *Methodism's Racial Dilemma: The Story of the Central Jurisdiction.* Nashville, TN: Abingdon Press, 1992.

Thompson, Tyler. "Another Pilgrimage to Jackson." *Christian Century* 81, no. 17 (April 22, 1964): 511–12.

Tonkel, D. Keith. *Finally the Dawn.* Kansas City, MO: E. L. Mendenhall, 1959.

Tonkel, D. Keith. *Heart Stuff.* Jackson, MS: Wells Press, 1995.

Tonkel, Keith. *God Stuff.* Jackson, MS: Wells Press, 2011.

Trillin, Calvin. *An Education in Georgia: Charlayne Hunter, Hamilton Holmes, and the Integration of the University of Georgia.* Athens, GA: University of Georgia Press, 1992.

Umoja, Akinyele Omawale. *We Will Shoot Back: Armed Resistance in the Mississippi Freedom Movement.* New York: New York University Press, 2013.

"Virginians Are Told Segregation Is Sin." *Christian Century* 75, no. 36 (September 3, 1958): 990.

Waddle, Ray. "Days of Thunder: The Lawson Affair." *Vanderbilt Magazine,* Fall 2002, 34–43.

Waits, Jim L. "Race Discussion Causes Crisis." *Concern* 1, no. 7 (March 28, 1958): 3, 8.

Waits, Jim L. "To Live in Controversy." *Concern* 5, no. 5 (March 1, 1963): 8–10.

Walters, Paul. "Video for Born of Conviction Reunion." 2005.

Waltz, Alan K. *The Mississippi Annual Conference, Southeastern Jurisdiction: A Survey of Selected Characteristics of Methodist Ministers, Lay Leaders, and Churches.* Philadelphia: Department of Research and Survey, Division of National Missions of the Board of Missions of the Board of Missions of the Methodist Church, 1963.

Weill, Susan. *In a Madhouse's Din: Civil Rights Coverage by Mississippi's Daily Press, 1948–1968.* Westport, CT: Praeger, 2002.

Whitfield, Stephen J. *A Death in the Delta: The Story of Emmett Till.* New York: Free Press, 1988.

Whitman, Ardis. "How the Civil Rights Struggle Challenges Our Churches." *Redbook* 125, no. 4 (August 1965): 55–57, 131–4, 141.

Wilkie, Curtis. *Dixie: A Personal Odyssey through Events That Shaped the Modern South.* New York: Touchstone, 2001.

Wilson, Gregory (pseud. for Roy C. Delamotte). *The Stained Glass Jungle.* Garden City, NY: Doubleday, 1962.

Wise, Tim. *White Like Me: Reflections on Race from a Privileged Son.* Brooklyn, NY: Soft Skull Press, 2005.

Wogaman, John Philip. "A Strategy for Racial Desegregation in The Methodist Church." PhD diss., Boston University, 1960.

Wroten, Joseph E. "Implications of the Violence at Oxford." *Concern* 4, no. 23 (December 15, 1962): 3–5.

Yates, Gayle Graham. *Mississippi Mind: A Personal Cultural History of an American State*. Knoxville: University of Tennessee Press, 1990.

Young, Andrew. *An Easy Burden: The Civil Rights Movement and the Transformation of America*. New York: HarperCollins, 1996.

Zellner, Bob, with Constance Curry. *The Wrong Side of Murder Creek: A White Southerner in the Freedom Movement*. Montgomery, AL: New South Books, 2008.

Index

(*BoC* = *Born of Conviction*)